Family Emergency Procedures

A guide to child protection and

CW01514539

NICOLA WYLD is a solicitor who has worked for the Children's Legal Centre and the Family Rights Group.

NANCY CARLTON is a solicitor and senior lecturer in law at the University of the West of England, Bristol.

Family Emergency Procedures
A guide to child protection and domestic violence

SECOND EDITION

Nicola Wyld
and
Nancy Carlton

LAG Legal Action Group
1998

This edition published in Great Britain 1998
by LAG Education and Service Trust Limited
242 Pentonville Road, London N1 9UN

First edition published 1993

British Library Cataloguing in Publication Data
A CIP catalogue record for this book is available from the British Library

ISBN 0 905099 68 0

Typeset by RefineCatch Ltd, Bungay, Suffolk
Printed in Great Britain by Bell & Bain Ltd, Glasgow

Preface

This book is a comprehensive account of the law and procedure relating to children and domestic violence in emergency situations. It contains a detailed discussion of the new law relating to domestic violence contained in the Family Law Act 1996, and the new revised procedures under that Act are summarised and explained in a way which is intended to aid busy practitioners. The relevant practice rules, forms and sections of the 1996 Act are annexed for handy reference.

Emergency work is disruptive and demanding. In order to do it well it is essential to be familiar with the appropriate law and practice, and we would suggest that initially you skim-read the book to become acquainted with its contents. The text has been organised by making reference to the sorts of issues that typically arise in an emergency, setting out the main legal provisions and giving detailed information about procedure and practical matters. Every attempt has been made to make each chapter complete without cross-referencing to other parts of the book. However, practitioners should become familiar with the terms discussed in Chapter 10 *Essential definitions*, which form part of the core of the new framework for domestic violence remedies.

It is important to remember that clients in emergency situations will usually be feeling worried and powerless. They may not always be clear in identifying what they want and a careful balance has to be established between allowing clients the time to formulate their instructions and instituting the appropriate legal proceedings as soon as possible. In dealing with the issues raised in this book, practitioners may also find themselves providing informal counselling support to their clients to deal with the distress and anger underlying their legal problems.

Emergencies sometimes raise new issues and ways of working with procedural rules. The authors would be pleased to hear from practitioners who have such experience for inclusion in the next edition.

The law in England and Wales is stated as at 1 January 1998.

Nicola Wyld
Nancy Carlton

February 1998

Contents

PART II: EMERGENCIES IN CARE OR ACCOMMODATION

PART III: CHILD ABDUCTION

PART IV: DOMESTIC VIOLENCE EMERGENCIES

x *Contents*

PART VI: MATERIALS

Table of cases

Table of statutes

Table of statutory instruments

Table of European legislation

Abbreviations

ACPC	area child protection committee
Allocation Order	Children Act (Allocation of Proceedings) Order 1991 SI No 1677
CA 1989	Children Act 1989
CAA 1984	Child Abduction Act 1984
CACA 1985	Child Abduction and Custody Act 1985
CCR	County Court Rules 1981 SI No1687
CSA	Child Support Agency
C(SA)R 1991	Children (Secure Accommodation) Regulations 1991 SI No 1505
EPO	emergency protection order
FD	Family Division
FLA	Family Law Act (followed by relevant year of Act)
FLR	Family Law Reports (Jordan Publishing)
FPC(MP)R 1991	Family Proceedings Courts (Matrimonial Proceedings etc) Rules 1991 SI No 1991
FPCR 1991	Family Proceedings Courts (Children Act 1989) Rules 1991 SI No 1395 (L17)
FPR 1991	Family Proceedings Rules 1991 SI No 1247 (L20)
GP	general practitioner
HMO	houses in multiple occupation
LCD	Lord Chancellor's Department
LEA	local education authority
LGO	Local Government Ombudsman
MHA 1983	Mental Health Act 1983
NHS	National Health Service
NI	national insurance
NSPCC	National Society for the Protection of Cruelty to Children
RSC	Rules of the Supreme Court 1965 SI No 1776

Part I

Emergency protection of children at risk

In this part:

Introduction to Part I

The primary responsibility for child protection lies with the local authority social services department whose duty under Children Act (CA) 1989 s47 requires it to make enquiries where there are suspicions that a child is, or may be, at risk of significant harm. As a result of these enquiries, the authority must decide whether it is necessary to take action to protect the child. This may range from the provision of services to support the family in caring for the child to the institution of legal proceedings for his/her protection.

This book is about emergencies. It therefore concentrates on the specific emergency measures which can be taken by the local authority, the NSPCC and the police. It also looks at steps that can be taken by concerned relatives or other individuals who have serious worries about the welfare and safety of a particular child.

However, it is important for practitioners to have an understanding of the context in which emergency action may be taken. There are clear duties in the CA 1989 requiring local authorities to support parents in caring for their children at home by the provision of family support services such as day care, advice and counselling, home help, support at a family centre, etc.[1] Support services also include the provision of accommodation where those caring for the child are prevented from doing so for whatever reason and duration of time.[2] Where children are looked after away from home there is a positive duty to place them with relatives, friends or other people significant to the child.[3]

Where children are looked after by the local authority, the Act stresses the importance of partnership in planning for the child's welfare with

---

1 CA 1989 s17.
2 Ibid, s20(1)(c).
3 Ibid, s23(6).

parents and older children. Common sense, borne out by research,[4] shows that it will be considerably easier for parents to work co-operatively with social services for the protection of their children where compulsory measures have not been taken.

Practitioners should be familiar with Department of Health guidance which is referred to where relevant in the text. It should be noted that this guidance is issued under Local Authority Social Services Act 1970 s7. This means that while it does not have statutory effect, local authorities should follow it unless there are local circumstances which justify departure from it.

It should be stressed that emergency measures apply to a minority of children involved with local authorities. Where this happens, advisers are likely to be acting for parents but possibly also other family members. Children should be represented by a solicitor from the Law Society Children Panel but for the sake of completeness reference is made in the text to the representation of children.

This is an area in which practitioners will be working in a responsive capacity to deal with an emergency order or the prospect of legal proceedings. However, it does not mean that there is not scope for looking creatively at alternatives to these outcomes. Inevitably, clients will be very upset, panicked and angry and a great deal of patience and support will be needed to get them through their ordeal.

4   *Child Protection: Messages from Research* Department of Health (HMSO, 1995).

CHAPTER 1

Emergency protection orders

The law

1.1 All references in this chapter are to the Children Act (CA) 1989, unless otherwise stated.

Grounds

1.2 Under CA 1989 s44(1) *any* person may apply for an emergency protection order (EPO) and the court may make the order only if it is satisfied that there is reasonable cause to believe that the child is likely to suffer significant harm if s/he is not removed to accommodation provided by the applicant or s/he does not remain in his/her present accommodation (such as a hospital).

1.3 An EPO may also be made where enquiries made under s47 are frustrated because access to the child has been unreasonably refused to a person authorised to seek access and the applicant has reasonable cause to believe that access to the child is required as a matter or urgency. Similar provisions apply to the frustration of enquiries made by the NSPCC.

1.4 The court must also apply the s1(1) welfare principle although it is not obliged to take into account the welfare checklist. The court must also consider whether or not the making of an order is better for the child.[1]

1.5 Significant harm is defined in s31(9) and (10) as ill-treatment including sexual abuse and non-physical ill-treatment. It also includes the impairment of physical or mental health, or physical, intellectual, emotional, social or behavioural development in comparison with that which could be reasonably be expected of a similar child.

---

1   CA 1989 s1(5).

Effect of order

1.6 An EPO lasts for a maximum of eight days. If the first day is a Sunday or public holiday, the order may end at noon the following day.[2] It may be extended for a further seven days if the court has reasonable cause to believe that the child is likely to suffer significant harm if the order is not extended.[3]

1.7 An EPO gives parental responsibility to the applicant, but this can be exercised only as is reasonably required to safeguard or promote the welfare of the child bearing in mind the duration of the order.[4]

Contact

1.8 There is a presumption that the child should be allowed reasonable contact with parents, people with parental responsibility, other carers or anyone with a s8 or s34 contact order.[5] Where this is not felt to be appropriate, or there is a dispute about the arrangements for contact, the court can make directions at the first or subsequent hearing.[6]

Power of removal

1.9 An EPO authorises removal or detention of a child but the power to remove should be exercised only in order to safeguard the child's welfare.[7] Decisions about removal of children remain in the hands of the applicant. This is most likely to be relevant in relation to the 'frustrated access' ground. Social workers may be assisted in making their decision by seeking a direction that they may be accompanied by a GP, nurse or health visitor.[8] The child should be returned, or allowed to be removed, where the applicant thinks that s/he is safe.[9] Intentional obstruction of someone exercising the power of removal is an offence.[10]

---

2 Ibid, s45(1).
3 Ibid, s45(5).
4 Ibid, s44(5)(b).
5 Ibid, s44(13).
6 Ibid, s44(6)(a).
7 Ibid, s44(5)(a).
8 Ibid, s45(12).
9 Ibid, s44(10).
10 Ibid, s44(15) and (16); a level 3 fine, presently £1,000.

Medical examinations

1.10 The court may make directions about medical or psychiatric examinations or other assessment of the child, and such directions may include a direction that no examination or assessment is to take place.[11] A child of sufficient understanding to make an informed decision may refuse to give consent even though a direction has been made.[12] However, in the case of *South Glamorgan CC v W and B*[13] concerning a 15-year-old girl subject to an interim care order, it was held that the High Court under its inherent jurisdiction had the right to override consent where powers under the CA 1989 had been exhausted and did not achieve the desired result. These principles are likely to apply equally to directions made under an EPO.

Entry and search

1.11 The court may direct that the child's whereabouts be disclosed to the applicant.[14] An EPO may also authorise the applicant to enter premises specified in the order and search for the child[15] and if there is reasonable cause to believe that there is another child in need of protection, to search for that other child.[16] Intentional obstruction of a person exercising the power of entry and search is an offence.[17]

1.12 Where an applicant has been prevented from exercising his/her powers under an EPO or is likely to be obstructed, a warrant may be issued to a police officer to assist in the entry and search, using reasonable force if necessary.[18] The court may order that a constable be accompanied by a GP, a nurse or by a health visitor.[19]

Discharge

1.13 There is no right of appeal against an EPO but there is a right to apply for an EPO to be discharged.[20] The child, parents, people with parental responsibility and other carers may apply to do so after

11 Ibid, s44(6) and (8).
12 Ibid, s44(7).
13 [1993] 1 FLR 575, FD.
14 CA 1989 s48(1).
15 Ibid, s48(3).
16 Ibid, s48(4).
17 Ibid, s48(7) and (8); a level 3 fine, presently £1,000.
18 Ibid, s48(11).
19 Ibid.
20 Ibid, s45(8) and (9).

72 hours giving one day's notice.[21] This does not apply if the original application was made on notice and the hearing was attended by the person who was given notice.[22] This has important implications for practice (see paras 1.54 to 1.73). Applications to vary or discharge a direction for contact or medical examination may be made at any time.

Transfer of responsibility for EPO

1.14 When an EPO is made in favour of a non-local authority applicant the local authority must decide whether or not to take over responsibility for it. This is based on a number of considerations including the wishes and feelings of the child, the circumstances that gave rise to the application, the likely effect on the child which may be caused by a transfer and the plans of the applicant.[23] Once a decision has been made the local authority must give notice of the date and time of transfer to the applicant, the court and all other parties, the effect of which is to make the transfer automatic.[24]

Exclusion requirement

1.15 The Family Law Act (FLA) 1996 has introduced a new provision which may be attached to an EPO or an interim care order so that an alleged abuser is required to leave the family home instead of the child.[25] Exclusion requirements include one or more of the following:

- that the 'relevant person' must leave all or part of the home where the child is living;
- that s/he must not enter that home;
- that s/he is excluded from a defined area in which the home is located.

Grounds

1.16 Where a court is satisfied that any of the grounds for the making of an EPO are made out and:

- there is reasonable cause to believe that if a person is excluded from

21 Family Proceeding Courts (Children Act 1989) Rules 1991 SI No 1395 (L17) Sch 2 and Family Proceedings Rules 1991 SI No 1247 (L20) Appendix 3.
22 CA 1989 s45(11).
23 Emergency Protection Orders (Transfer of Responsibilities) Regulations 1991 SI No 1414 reg 2.
24 Ibid, reg 3(2).
25 FLA 1996 Sch 6 para 3, inserting new CA 1989 s44A.

the family home the child will not be likely to suffer significant harm him/herself if not removed or that enquiries will cease to be frustrated; and

– that another person living in the family home (whether a parent or some other person) is able and willing to give the child the care s/he would expect of a reasonable parent and that this person consents to the inclusion of the exclusion requirement;

the court may include an exclusion requirement to an EPO.[26]

Duration

1.17 An exclusion requirement lasts for the duration of the EPO but may be ordered to take effect for a shorter period. It may be extended on an application to vary or discharge the EPO.[27] If the child is removed for a continuous period of more than 24 hours the exclusion requirement lapses.[28]

Power of arrest

1.18 The court may attach a power of arrest to an exclusion requirement and this may be for a shorter period than the exclusion requirement itself.[29] A constable may arrest without warrant where s/he has reasonable cause to believe that the requirement is being breached.[30] Any tier of court may deal with a breach.

Power of remand

1.19 The respondent must be brought before the court within 24 hours of arrest (excluding Christmas Day, Good Friday or any Sunday) and if the matter is not disposed of immediately the respondent may be remanded in custody or on bail.[31] A remand in custody should not normally exceed eight days. Where such a remand is for three days or shorter the respondent may be remanded to the police.[32] The normal provisions relating to bail apply but in addition a respondent may be ordered to comply with certain requirements specified by the court.[33]

1.20 The court may remand where it considers that it needs a medical

26 CA 1989 s44A(1) and (2).
27 Ibid, s44A(4) and (7).
28 Ibid, s44A(10).
29 Ibid, s44A(5) and (6).
30 Ibid, s44A(8).
31 Ibid, s44A(9), applying FLA 1996 s47(7).
32 Ibid and FLA 1996 Sch 5 paras 5 and 6.
33 Ibid, FLA 1996 s47(12).

report.[34] Where the respondent is in custody the court must not adjourn the case for more than three weeks.[35] Where the court considers that the respondent is suffering from mental illness or severe mental impairment it may make an order under Mental Health Act 1983 s35.[36]

Undertakings

1.21 The court may accept an undertaking instead of imposing an exclusion requirement but no power of arrest may attach to an undertaking. Breach of an undertaking may be enforced by normal means of committal in the High Court and county court.[37]

Discharge

1.22 A respondent may apply to discharge the exclusion requirement even though s/he may not be a party to the original EPO proceedings.[38]

The practice

Negotiations with the local authority before an EPO has been made

1.23 Where instructed before an application for EPO has been made there may be scope to persuade the local authority to adopt a different approach from court action and practitioners should always attempt to do so. Department of Health guidance stresses than an application for an EPO should not be regarded as a routine response to allegations of abuse, or as a routine first step to initiating care proceedings.[39] The philosophy of working in partnership with parents means that social workers should be more willing to enter into discussions with parents and their advisers about plans for the care of their children but practice still varies greatly around the country. Alternatives to an EPO may be achieved through the provision of family support, removal of an alleged abuser, placement of the child(ren) with relatives or friends or provision of accommodation.

34 Ibid, s48(1).
35 Ibid, s48(3).
36 Ibid, s48(4).
37 Ibid, s44B.
38 Ibid, s45(8A), as inserted by FLA 1996 Sch 6, para 4.
39 *Children Act 1989: Guidance and Regulations* (HMSO, 1991), Volume 1, Court Orders, para 4.30.

1.24 It may be possible to negotiate directly with the local authority. However, in virtually all cases where there are sufficiently serious child protection concerns to warrant the consideration of seeking an EPO the local authority will have called an initial child protection conference to consider what steps are necessary to protect the child. Where the solicitor has already been instructed it is essential that s/he attends the conference on the parents' behalf where the alternatives suggested above, and discussed in greater detail below, can be raised.

1.25 The following section sets out the child protection administrative framework within which solicitors can attempt to negotiate alternatives.

Child protection procedures

1.26 These are administrative procedures established by local Area Child Protection Committees (ACPC) which follow from the local authority duty under CA 1989 s47 to make enquiries where there are suspicions that a child may be at risk. Practitioners should be familiar with these local procedures as well as government guidance *Working Together* which covers the purpose and conduct of child protection conferences. *Working Together* is issued under Local Authority Social Services Act 1970 s7 which means that while not of statutory force it should be complied with unless local circumstances indicate exceptional reasons which may justify a variation.

Initial child protection conference

1.27 The purpose of the initial child protection conference is to bring together professionals from the agencies involved with child protection such as the local authority, education authority, health authority, the police, the probation service, etc, and family members to 'share and evaluate the information gathered during the investigation, to make decisions about the level of risk to the child(ren), to decide on the need for registration and to make plans for the future.'[40] The conference is not empowered to make decisions about the appropriateness of legal action but may make recommendations that the local authority takes proceedings.

1.28 *Partnership with parents and children. Working Together* emphasises the importance of professionals working in partnership with parents and other family members or carers.

40 *Working Together* Home Office, Department of Health, Department of Education and Science and Welsh Office (HMSO, 1991), para 6.5.

It cannot be emphasised too strongly that the involvement of children and adults in child protection conferences will not be effective unless they are fully involved from the outset in all stages of the child protection process, and unless from the time of referral there is as much openness and honesty as possible between families and professionals.[41]

1.29 Most ACPCs have policies about the participation of parents and older children in child protection conferences and practitioners should obtain local policy statements for further information. Some ACPCs allow parents to attend for the whole of the conference while others allow parents to attend for part only. Law Society guidance states that the attendance of parents should be encouraged, so far as possible, for the whole of the conference.[42]

1.30 Sometimes one or both parents may be excluded where there is conflict between them or allegations of violence against staff or each other. *Working Together* states that the exclusion of parents should be kept to a minimum and must be justified in accordance with specific criteria.[43]

1.31 *Attendance of solicitors/legal advisers.* Working Together acknowledges that parents may feel more confident if accompanied by a friend or supporter. That person may be a solicitor but it will be necessary for the conference chair to clarify the solicitor's role which may vary according to local circumstances. *Working Together* stresses that the 'conference is not a tribunal to decide whether abuse has taken place and legal representation is therefore not appropriate'.[44]

1.32 Wherever possible, solicitors should attend the conference with the parents. Legal aid under an existing emergency legal aid certificate will cover attendance but otherwise an extension to the green form can be obtained for this purpose. Law Society guidance recommends that where it is not possible for the solicitor to attend personally it is important that a representative of the firm is knowledgeable in child protection law and procedures and is fully informed of the circumstances of the case.[45]

1.33 Where it is not possible to arrange attendance, practitioners should make sure that the parents are as fully prepared for the conference as

41   Ibid, para 6.11.
42   The Law Society *Attendance of solicitors at child protection conferences* (June 1997).
43   *Working Together* (see n40), para 6.15.
44   Ibid, para 6.18.
45   Law Society guidance (n42), p 7.

possible. This may involve the preparation of a written statement and advice about the implications of giving information to the conference especially where there is a likelihood of court proceedings. Where other family members are willing and able to care for the child this should be made known to the conference.

1.34 *Children.* Law Society guidance recommends that the child's solicitor or representative of the firm should attend the conference either to accompany the child or to attend on the child's behalf where the child is too young or does not wish to attend.[46] This presupposes that a solicitor has been appointed in EPO proceedings and is unlikely to be relevant at an earlier stage.

Family support

1.35 Research findings from the Department of Health have shown that for many children in need of protection insufficient attention is given to the provision of supportive services for their families with the main emphasis on the administrative process of investigation and decision-making.[47] In appropriate circumstances, therefore, practitioners should focus on trying to obtain family support for parents to help them look after their children in safety.

1.36 CA 1989 s17 places local authorities under a duty to promote and safeguard the welfare of children in need and, where consistent with this, to promote the upbringing of such children in their families by providing a range and level of appropriate services. 'In need' is defined by s17(10) and certainly covers children (and their families) who are considered to be at risk. Specifically, local authorities are required to take all reasonable steps to prevent children suffering ill-treatment or neglect through the provision of services.[48] Services include advice, guidance and counselling, the provision of home helps, family centres to facilitate such services and daycare for under five year-olds and after-school and holiday facilities for those aged under eight.[49] In exceptional circumstances, cash payments may be made.[50] Practitioners should obtain a copy of the local authority's policy statement for further information about local provision.

46 Law Society guidance (n42), p 6.
47 *Child Protection: Messages from Research* Department of Health (HMSO, 1995).
48 CA 1989 Sch 2 para 4(1).
49 Ibid, Sch 2 paras 8 and 9 and s18.
50 Ibid, s17(6).

14 Family emergency procedures

Removal of alleged abuser

1.37 Department of Health guidance recognises the importance of an alleged abuser leaving home as an alternative to the child doing so: 'local authorities will always want to explore the possibility of providing services to and/or accommodation to an alleged abuser . . .'.[51] CA 1989 Sch 2 para 5 provides that local authorities may assist an alleged abuser to obtain alternative accommodation and this help may be by way of cash. Some local authorities have developed policies including the promotion of work with non-abusing parents, which may include provision of accommodation for mothers and children away from home. Again, practitioners should obtain policy documents about local practice. The FLA 1996 does not allow for a local authority to seek a free-standing exclusion order where an alleged abuser refuses to vacate the family home on a voluntary basis: an exclusion requirement is an integral part of an EPO.

1.38 Where the local authority is unwilling to seek an exclusion requirement, perhaps because it does not consider that the non-abusing parent is able to provide the child with proper care or to resist any attempted breach on the part of the alleged abuser, practitioners will have to consider advising their clients to seek an occupation order under the FLA 1996 (for further details see Chapter 12).

Accommodation elsewhere

1.39 Where there are relatives or friends willing to look after the child, practitioners should suggest that the child is placed with them as an alternative to being removed from the parents. This may be arranged by the local authority formally providing accommodation under CA 1989 s20. CA 1989 s23(6) provides that local authorities should make arrangements for children to be placed with relatives or friends unless inconsistent with the child's welfare. Relatives or friends will need to be approved as foster carers under the Foster Placement (Children) Regulations 1991.[52] Regulation 11(3) provides that immediate placements of up to six weeks may be made with relatives or friends, subject to certain formalities being met.

1.40 Placements may also be made on an informal basis and a number of local authorities proceed in this way. Practitioners should discuss this option carefully with the relatives or friends concerned since

---

51 *Children Act 1989: Guidance and Regulations* (HMSO, 1991), Volume 1, Court Orders, para 4.31.
52 SI No 910.

there are likely to be implications in terms of financial and social work support. There is no obligation to pay a fostering allowance and it is merely at the discretion of the local authority to make cash payments to children in need.[53] Although there is an obligation to provide services to children in need (see paras **1.35** and **1.36**) the degree of support offered is likely to be minimal if a child is placed informally.

1.41 Where there is no offer of support within the extended family, practitioners should nonetheless suggest that the child be accommodated under s20 as an alternative to an EPO. Parents are far more likely to feel able to co-operate with the local authority where the arrangements are by agreement. The provisions of the Arrangements for Placement (General) Regulations 1991 require parents and others with parental responsibility to be consulted and to agree with placement plans.[54] It will of course be essential that the parents give a firm commitment not to remove the child from accommodation irresponsibly.[55]

Role of legal adviser where notice of hearing has been given

1.42 Usually EPO applications are made ex parte, but notice may be given. Only one day's notice is required by the rules.[56] Since attendance at the hearing precludes any subsequent application to discharge the order practitioners must think very carefully about whether to represent their clients at this hearing. In all cases the balance between trying to prevent the child being removed from home and preserving the right to make an application to discharge will be a delicate one. Parents should never be advised to attend in person. Since it will be extremely difficult to prepare adequately in all but the most straightforward of cases or where the client is already well known to the solicitor, it is suggested that practitioners do not represent their clients at EPO hearings.

Negotiations after an EPO has been made

1.43 Once an EPO has been made, the major issue will be whether it is possible to negotiate acceptable changes about how the EPO is put

---

53 CA 1989 s17(6)–(9).
54 SI No 890 reg 3(4).
55 CA 1989 s20(8).
56 Family Proceedings Courts (Children Act 1989) Rules 1991 SI No 1395 (L17) Sch 2.

into effect without the need to make a court application to discharge the order.

Contact

1.44 Where the order is silent about contact or there is a direction as to reasonable contact, negotiations may need to be held about the arrangements for contact. Practitioners should remember that there is a presumption of contact to a wide range of people[57] and so there may be several different negotiations taking place. Department of Health guidance stresses that the local authority will need to explore fully the wishes and feelings of the child and that no child should be forced to have contact against his/her will.[58]

Return of child

1.45 The applicant is under a duty to return the child if it appears safe to do so, either to the person from whom s/he was removed or to a parent or other person with parental responsibility or to anyone else that the applicant (with the agreement of the court) considers appropriate.[59] This is likely to be of particular importance in the 'frustrated access' cases where an EPO has been obtained to facilitate access to the child. If all is well, or voluntary arrangements can be made with the parents, the child should be returned at once. It may also be possible to negotiate an alternative placement with relatives or friends if the child has been placed with foster carers.

Future plans

1.46 Where a child protection conference has already been held it is likely to have made recommendations for the child on the expiry of the EPO. Usually this will involve the initiation of care proceedings unless it has been possible to arrange for the child to be accommodated or placed with an extended family member informally.

1.47 Otherwise, where the local authority has obtained an EPO it is obliged to make enquiries under CA 1989 s47 to determine how to safeguard and promote the child's welfare. In particular it must decide whether to initiate care proceedings or to provide services under CA 1989 Part III. Practitioners should participate in the child protection process as described at paras **1.26** to **1.42**.

57 CA 1989 s44(13).
58 *Children Act 1989: Guidance and Regulations* (HMSO, 1991), Volume 1, Court Orders, para 4.62 and Volume 3, Family Placements, para 6.25.
59 CA 1989 s44(10) and (11).

CHECKLIST FOR INSTRUCTIONS

Parent/carer
Name
Address
Age
Marital status
Own children and any other children cared for
Occupation
Financial circumstances
Accommodation
Personal family history
Medical or psychiatric history (letters of authority)
Criminal convictions (if any)
Support from extended family or friends

Child
Name
Address
Age and date of birth
Childminder/nursery
School/college, involvement of educational welfare service
Health and medical history
Developmental history
Behavioural difficulties
Involvement of professionals (child guidance, psychiatric, psychologist)

Previous involvement of local authority (if any)
Length of local authority involvement
Previous family support/services offered
Relationship with social worker
Response to allegations made by local authority
Parents' perceptions of child's needs

Proposals
Placement with parents and plan for protection
Placement with relatives or friends
Provision of accommodation under CA 1989 s20
Contact arrangements and proposals for supervision if necessary
Medical directions
Exclusion requirement or application for occupation order

Legal aid

1.48 Non-means- and non-merits-tested legal aid is available to children, parents and others with parental responsibility. Other parties to the proceedings, and those applying to be joined as parties, must satisfy the means test but not the merits test.[60]

1.49 There is a distinction in the procedure to be followed depending on whether the application is for free legal aid or a means-tested application and whether or not the firm holds a franchise.

1.50 Applications for non-means- and non-merits-tested cases are made on Form CL5A. This is signed by the solicitor stating that the applicant is entitled to free legal aid and covers emergencies. The solicitor is immediately covered for all costs relating to EPO proceedings provided that the application form reaches the Legal Aid Board within three working days.

1.51 Applications in means-tested cases are made on Form CLA5 plus the appropriate means form and Form CLA3 (emergency applications). From 1 April 1997, the Legal Aid Board has required urgent emergency applications to be made by fax instead of by telephone as in the past.[61] Special fax forms FEA1 and FEA1a should be submitted to which the Legal Aid Board should respond by fax within 24 hours. The normal postal forms should be submitted within five working days. In emergencies where the work needs to be done within the next few hours and there is no time to access a fax machine, a telephone application can still be made.

1.52 In both circumstances, the certificate will come into effect from the start of the case by virtue of the deeming provisions in the Civil Legal Aid (General) Regulations 1989.[62] An emergency certificate automatically lapses after a period of six weeks although this may be extended. It is also limited to a costs ceiling of £1,500 in London and £1,200 outside London which includes disbursements and counsel's fees.

1.53 In franchised firms solicitors may issue their own emergency certificates for all types of case provided that they are satisfied that

---

60 Civil Legal Aid (General) (Amendment No 2) Regulations 1991 SI No 2036.
61 *Legal Aid Focus* No 17, March 1997.
62 SI No 339 reg 103(6).

the applicant has a good case, that s/he is financially eligible and that it is an emergency. Their costs are limited to £10,000.

The procedure

1.54 The procedure described here applies to all applications made in relation to any EPO proceedings. Usually practitioners will be required to act in relation to a discharge application but since it is possible for any person to seek an EPO it may occasionally be necessary for solicitors to take this action on behalf of their clients.

1.55 The procedural rules are similar in all three tiers of court and are governed by the Family Proceedings Courts (Children Act 1989) Rules 1991[63] (FPCR) and the Family Proceedings Rules 1991[64] (FPR). Rules about the allocation of court proceedings are contained in the Children Act (Allocation of Proceedings) Order 1991[65] (Allocation Order).

Which court?

1.56 All EPO proceedings start in the family proceedings court of the magistrates' court unless they arise out of a CA 1989 s37 investigation or there are other public law proceedings pending in another court, in which case they may commence in the court which directs the investigation or the court where the other proceedings are pending.[66] Unlike other public law proceedings, applications relating to EPOs may not be transferred to a county court or the High Court.[67]

Application

1.57 All proceedings must start by application.[68] The statutory forms can be found in FPCR 1991 Sch 1 and FPR 1991 as amended.

Notice

1.58 One day's notice of hearing is required for a discharge application

63 SI No 1395 (L17).
64 SI No 1247 (L20).
65 SI No 1677.
66 Allocation Order art 3.
67 Ibid, art 7 (2).
68 FPCR 1991 r4(1)(a) and FPR 1991 r4.4(1)(a).

and for all other EPO applications made on notice.[69] Where an application for an EPO is made ex parte it is necessary to file the application form at the time of the application, or if made over the telephone, within 24 hours of the application.[70]

Respondents

1.59 There are two categories of people who should be informed about the court proceedings: those who have automatic party status and those who are entitled to notice so that they can apply for leave to be made a party if they wish to do so.[71]

Party status

1.60 The following have automatic party status:

- the child and any person with parental responsibility (all proceedings);
- those with party status in the original proceedings (applications to discharge or vary);
- those caring for the child prior to the making of the order and any person whose contact is likely to be affected by the proposed application (variation of directions);
- any person against whom an exclusion requirement has been made (application to discharge or vary exclusion requirement or power of arrest).

Notice

1.61 Those entitled to notice are:

- any person caring for the child immediately before the proceedings (all proceedings);
- the local authority and any person believed by the applicant to be affected by the application (variation of directions).

Service

1.62 There is no requirement for personal service. Service may be by delivery at, or first class post to, the last known address of the person to be served.[72] Where solicitors are involved service may be by fax.

69 FPCR 1991 Sch 2 and FPR 1991 Appendix 3.
70 FPCR 1991 r4(4) and FPR 1991 r4.4.
71 FPCR 1991 Sch 2 and FPR 1991 Appendix 3.
72 FPCR 1991 r4(8) and FPR 1991 r4.4(8).

Service on children is carried out by the court where there is no solicitor or guardian ad litem. Ex parte applications and orders must be served within 48 hours of the hearing.[73]

Exclusion requirements

1.63 There must be personal service on the excluded person of an EPO with an exclusion requirement, together with any attached power of arrest.[74] Where there is a power of arrest, a copy of the order must be delivered to the police station in the area of the child's family home (or other station specified by the court) with a statement stating that the excluded person has been served or informed of the terms of the order.[75] Any variation or discharge of an exclusion requirement with a power of arrest should be sent to the original police station or a new one if the applicant has moved.[76] There is no requirement for personal service where an excluded person applies for variation of discharge.[77]

Representation of children

1.64 EPO proceedings are 'specified proceedings' for the purposes of CA 1989 s41 and so there is a presumption that a guardian ad litem will be appointed unless the court does not consider it necessary to protect the interests of the child. In many parts of the country, court duty schemes have been established.

1.65 The guardian ad litem is required to safeguard the interests of the child by reference to the welfare checklist. The guardian is also required to:

- appoint a solicitor for the child;
- advise the court of the child's wishes and feelings;
- advise the court about whether the child has sufficient understanding to withhold consent to medical and other examinations;
- deal with various procedural matters such as timetabling, court venue and party status.[78]

1.66 Solicitors for the child must act on the instructions of the

73 FPCR 1991 r4(4)(ii) and FPR 1991 r4.4(4)(ii).
74 FPR 1991 r4.24A(1), as amended by the Family Proceedings (Amendment No 3) Rules 1997 SI No 1893 (L29).
75 FPR 1991 r4.24A(3), as amended (see n74).
76 FPR 1991 r4.24A(4), as amended (see n74).
77 FPR 1991 r4.24A (5), as amended (see n74).
78 FPCR 1991 r11(1)–(5) and FPR 1991 r4.11(1)–(5).

guardian unless it appears that the child is capable of giving instructions. If these instructions conflict with those of the guardian, the child's instructions prevail and the guardian must represent him/herself independently.[79]

1.67 Court rules specifically deal with the child's attendance at court. There is a presumption that proceedings must take place in the absence of the child if the court considers that it is in the child's best interests, bearing in mind the nature of the evidence, and the child is represented by a guardian ad litem or solicitor. In considering a decision for the child to attend the hearing, the court must hear from the guardian, the solicitor and the child, where of sufficient understanding.[80] In *Re C (A Minor) (Care: Child's Wishes)*[81] the court reiterated the view that it was not normally desirable for children to attend court hearings.

Evidence

1.68 Written statements must be filed and served on all parties before the hearing or as directed by the court.[82] The rules do not specify how long before the hearing evidence should be filed and in an emergency it may not be possible to serve evidence much before the hearing itself. It should be remembered that the application form contains reasons for the application and so provides the gist of the case.

1.69 CA 1989 s47(7) provides that the court may take into account hearsay evidence in a report or in oral evidence which it considers relevant to the proceedings concerning any application connected with an EPO. The courts recognise the sensitivity of hearsay evidence and will still need to assess the weight and credibility of such evidence. In *Re W (Minors) (Wardship Evidence)*[83] the Court of Appeal said that in a case in which direct evidence could be produced hearsay evidence had to be regarded with grave caution, unless uncontroversial.

1.70 In addition to the evidence of their own clients, practitioners will need to consider the question of lay and professional witnesses. The court's leave must be obtained before seeking a medical, psychi-

---

79 FPCR 1991 rr11(3) and 12(1)(a) and FPR rr4.11(3) and 4.12(1)(a).
80 FPCR 1991 r16(2) and FPR 1991 r4.16(2).
81 [1993] 1 FLR 832.
82 FPCR 1991 r17 and FPR 1991 r4.17.
83 [1990] 1 FLR 203.

atric or other assessment of the child[84] and in practice there will be insufficient time to organise this for the purposes of an application to discharge an EPO. Where relevant, it may be possible to obtain a medical or psychiatric report on the parent but this is likely to be possible only where the professional is already involved in the case.

1.71 Practitioners should be aware of the complex issue regarding disclosure of unfavourable reports. In *Re L (A Minor) (Police Investigation: Privilege)*[85] the House of Lords distinguished between solicitor/client privilege and litigation privilege attaching to third party reports in children cases. In that case the court had given leave for a report which was unfavourable to the mother and the House of Lords held that it should be disclosed. The court did not answer the question of whether there is a duty on lawyers to give voluntary disclosure of reports obtained without the necessity of the court's leave. For further information about this subject, readers should refer to more detailed texts.

1.72 Professional witnesses usually require a witness summons to attend court. The FPR 1991 do not provide for the compulsory attendance of witnesses in non-matrimonial cases concerning children. Judges in the High Court have the power to order the attendance of potential witnesses. Procedure in the family proceedings court is governed by Magistrates' Courts Act 1980 s97(1) and by FPCR 1991 r33. These provide that a magistrate must issue a witness summons for the attendance of a witness or for the production of a document where there is evidence that the witness will not attend voluntarily. Professional witnesses usually accept service of the summons at court. Conduct money must be supplied to cover reasonable travel expenses.

Exclusion requirement

1.73 The court requires evidence of the consent of the 'non-abusing' parent to the exclusion requirement. Rules of court provide that this should be given in writing or orally at court although the latter is unlikely to be very common in relation to EPO applications.[86] Rules also specify that any written consent should include a statement that the person giving consent is able and willing to give to the child the

---

84 FPCR 1991 r18 and FPR 1991 r4.18.
85 [1996] 1 FLR 731.
86 FPR 1991 r4.24(1)(b), as amended by the Family Proceedings (Amendment No 3) Rules 1997 SI No 1893 (L29).

care which it would be reasonable to expect a parent to give him/her and understands that such consent could lead to the exclusion of the 'relevant person' from the home in which the child lives.[87]

---

87 FPR 1991 r4.24A, as amended by the Family Proceedings (Amendment No 3) Rules 1997 SI No 1893 (L29).

CHAPTER 2

Police protection

The law

2.1 The power of the police officers to protect children is known as police protection and does not require any application to court.

2.2 The Children Act (CA) 1989 provides that where a constable has reasonable cause to believe that a child would otherwise be likely to suffer significant harm, s/he may remove the child to suitable accommodation or take steps to prevent the child's removal from any hospital or other place in which s/he is accommodated.[1]

2.3 A senior police officer must make enquiries into the case, and on completion of his/her enquiries must release the child unless s/he considers that there is still reasonable cause for believing that the child would be likely to suffer significant harm.[2] Police protection lasts for a maximum period of 72 hours.[3] An application may be made by the police for an EPO on behalf of the local authority,[4] even though the authority may not know of or agree to the application. The duration of the EPO is inclusive of the period in police protection.[5] The child, parents and other carers must be informed of the steps that have been taken by the police, the reasons for them and what further steps may be taken.

2.4 The police do not acquire parental responsibility but may do what is reasonable to safeguard and promote the child's welfare. There is a presumption of contact with parents, those with parental

---

1 CA 1989 s46(1).
2 Ibid, s46(5).
3 Ibid, s46(6).
4 Ibid, s46(7).
5 Ibid, s45(3).

responsibility or other carers, and with any person who had a contact order in his/her favour.[6]

The practice

2.5 Since there are no legal remedies to challenge the exercise of police protection, the role of the practitioner will be as a negotiator on behalf of parents or children. Reference should be made to the practice in relation to EPOs (see paras **1.23** to **1.47**). It is important to find out whether the local authority are likely to become involved, whether a child protection case conference will be called, or whether there is likely to be an application for an EPO.

6 Ibid, s46(10).

CHAPTER 3

Section 8 orders

Introduction

3.1 The purpose of this chapter is to look at steps that can be taken by relatives or other concerned private individuals who may wish to take emergency action to protect a child or young person. They may be caring for a child whom a parent threatens to remove or consider that the local authority is failing to comply with its statutory duties. Alternatively, they may be approached by an older child or young person who is seeking protection from abuse, relief from family breakdown and/or has run away from home.

3.2 As a temporary measure such individuals may apply for an EPO since an application may be made by any person and there is no absolute requirement that the child should be placed with the local authority (see para 1.14). They may also apply for any CA 1989 s8 order although they will first have to satisfy the court that leave should be granted.

3.3 This chapter looks at the private law and how this can be used for the protection of children. All references in this chapter are to the Children Act (CA) 1989, unless otherwise stated.

The law

3.4 There are four s8 orders designed to provide practical and flexible solutions relating to the care of children:

– *Residence order.* This specifies with whom a child should live. It may contain directions about how this is to be put into effect or it may impose conditions.
– *Contact order.* This requires the person with whom the child lives to allow the child to visit, or stay or otherwise have contact with the person named in the order. 27

- *Prohibited steps order.* This is an order whereby no step (specified by the court) which could be taken by a parent in meeting his/her parental responsibility shall be taken by anyone without the leave of the court.
- *Specific issues order.* This is a directions order for the purpose of determining a specific question that has arisen or may arise in connection with any aspect of parental responsibility.

3.5 Section 8 orders may be made on application or by the court of its own motion under the CA 1989, or in any other specified family proceedings,[1] including matrimonial, magistrates' court domestic proceedings and proceedings under the Family Law Act (FLA) 1996.

Entitlement

3.6 Parents, guardians and others with a residence order in their favour may apply for any s8 order.[2] Step-parents, relatives or friends with whom the child has lived for three out of the past five years, and others with certain specified consents, may apply for a residence or contact order.[3]

Leave

3.7 Anyone may apply for a s8 order with the court's leave.[4] Leave is subject to a set of criteria set out in s10(9):

a) the nature of the proposed application;
b) the applicant's connection with the child;
c) any risk that the proposed application might cause harm to the child.

3.8 The position of foster carers is an exception to this rule. They may apply for leave only if they have the consent of the local authority, they are a relative of the child or the child has been living with them for three out of the previous five years.

3.9 In deciding whether to grant leave the court does not have to apply the welfare principle since the application itself does not relate

---

1   See CA 1989 s10(1).
2   Ibid, s10(4).
3   Ibid, s10(5).
4   Ibid, s10(2)(b).

to the child's upbringing.[5] In granting leave the court must decide whether the applicant has a good arguable case and not, as previously decided, whether it is reasonably likely to succeed.[6]

3.10 Children may apply for leave. They do not have to satisfy the above criteria but the court must be satisfied that they have sufficient understanding to make the proposed application.[7] The courts have considered the principles involved in establishing whether a child has sufficient understanding. In essence the court must balance the rights of the child to express a view with the need to protect the child's interests.[8] It must also take into account all the circumstances of the case in light of what has happened in the past as well as what is likely to happen in the future.[9] In practice, the courts are unlikely to grant applications by children under the age of 11 or 12.

Grounds

3.11 In deciding whether to make a s8 order, the court must give paramount consideration to the child's welfare by reference to the statutory checklist in s1(3):

- the ascertainable wishes and feelings of the child concerned (considered in the light of his/her age and understanding);
- his/her physical, emotional and educational needs;
- the likely effect on him/her of any change in his/her circumstances;
- his/her age, sex, background and any characteristics of his/hers which the court considers relevant;
- any harm which s/he has suffered or is at risk of suffering;
- how capable each of his/her parents, and any other person in relation to whom the court considers the question to be relevant, is of meeting his/her needs;
- the range of powers available to the court under the CA 1989.

3.12 In addition, the court must make no order unless it considers that it is better for the child than making no order at all.[10]

---

5   A v W (*Minors*) (*Leave to Apply*) [1992] 2 FLR 154.
6   Re M (*Care: Contact: Grandmother's Application*) (1995) Fam Law 540.
7   CA 1989 s10(9).
8   Re S (*A Minor*) (*Independent Representation*) [1993] 2 FLR 437.
9   Re H (*A Minor: Role of Official Solicitor*) [1993] 2 FLR 552.
10 CA 1989 s1(5).

The practice

Relatives or friends

3.13 How the matter is dealt with will depend on the circumstances of the case, the degree of risk to the child, the nature of the relationship between the person concerned and the parents, whether or not the local authority is already involved and what the relatives or friends are able to offer. Practitioners should tease out these issues at the outset.

3.14 Where the local authority is already involved and the child is not at immediate risk, practitioners should request an urgent meeting with the local authority to try to negotiate a solution. Although the local authority has no statutory duty to consult with relatives/ friends about children it is not looking after, Department of Health guidance[11] recommends that the CA 1989 s22 consultation duty should be extended to families where there is extensive social work input.

3.15 Whether or not there is any existing involvement with the child, the local authority should be reminded of its duty under CA 1989 s47 to carry out enquiries in relation to any child whom it has reasonable cause to suspect is suffering or is likely to suffer significant harm with a view to deciding whether it should take any action to safeguard or promote the child's welfare.

3.16 Where relatives are worried about the parents knowing of their involvement, they should always be reassured that any information provided to the local authority will be kept confidential unless they give consent to its disclosure or it can be given without identifying its source.[12]

3.17 If there is no ultimate resolution of the matter, relatives may wish to make a complaint under the statutory complaints procedure, but this cannot be used if the local authority has not assessed the child as being 'in need'.[13] Depending on the circumstances, an order for judicial review may be sought (see Chapter 6).

3.18 Relatives may not wish to involve the local authority at all. In some cases, it may be helpful to seek the involvement of a trusted third party as mediator in an attempt to discuss and resolve the issues. In other cases, legal action should be taken immediately.

11 *Children Act 1989: Guidance and Regulations* (HMSO, 1991) Volume 2, Family Support, Day Care and Educational Provision for Young Children, para 2.10.
12 Access to Personal Files (Social Services) Regulations 1989 SI No 206.
13 CA 1989 s26 (3).

Young people

3.19 The nature of legal assistance given to young people will depend on whether or not there are family members or friends who can offer support and/or a home. In such circumstances an application should be made for leave to seek a residence order either by the adult concerned or by the young person. Where the adult is likely to be outside the limits for legal aid and cannot afford to pay privately, the application should be made by the young person. In *Re SC (A Minor)*[14] the court refuted the suggestion that adults and not children should be responsible for making the application for leave although the Legal Aid Board is now unlikely to grant legal aid to do so.[15]

3.20 Where there are no relatives or friends, practitioners must endeavour to persuade the local authority to comply with its statutory duties to provide accommodation or to take care proceedings. A local authority must provide accommodation to a young person aged 16 or 17 where s/he is in need and where the authority considers that his/her welfare is otherwise likely to be prejudiced.[16] Parents and others with parental responsibility do not have the right to discharge such young people from accommodation.[17] In *Re T (Accommodation by Local Authority)*[18] the court held that it was inappropriate to seek a specific issues order requiring a local authority to provide accommodation: this was a matter that should be dealt with by way of judicial review.

3.21 Local authorities do not have an obligation to accommodate those under the age of 16 who refer themselves since their parents have the right at any time to discharge them. In these circumstances, practitioners should try to persuade the authority to start care proceedings immediately and, depending on the degree of urgency, seek an EPO. There is no legal provision compelling the local authority to do so, and thus the only remedy may be an urgent application for judicial review (see Chapter 6).

Legal aid

3.22 Means- and merits-tested legal aid applies to all private law applications. Forms CLA5 plus CLA4A/CLA4B and Form CLA3

14 [1994] 1 FLR 96.
15 See *Legal Aid Focus* No 19, May 1997, para 5.4.2(b) and (c).
16 CA 1989 s20(3).
17 Ibid, s20(11).
18 [1995] 1 FLR 159.

CHECKLIST FOR INSTRUCTIONS

Adult
Name
Address
Age
Occupation
Financial position
Medical or psychiatric history
Criminal convictions
Relationship with child's parents/carers
Relationship with child

Child/young person
Name
Address
Date of birth/age
School/college, any problems
Medical or psychiatric history
Behavioural/emotional difficulties
Involvement with police
Local authority involvement

Parents/carers
Name
Address
Occupation
Financial circumstances
Other children
Medical or psychiatric history
Criminal convictions
Difficulties in caring for child/ren
Local authority involvement

Nature of concerns
Duration of problem
Evidence to support concerns
Discussions with family

Proposals for change
Local authority involvement
Involvement of mediator

(emergency legal aid) should be completed. From 1 April 1997, the Legal Aid Board has required urgent emergency applications to be made by fax instead of by telephone as in the past.[19] Special fax application forms FEA1 and FEA1a should be submitted to which the Legal Aid Board will respond within 24 hours by fax. The normal postal forms should be submitted within five working days. In emergencies necessitating work within the next few hours and there is no time to access a fax machine, a telephone application can still be made.

3.23 In both circumstances, the certificate will come into effect from the start of the case by virtue of the deeming provisions in the Civil Legal Aid (General) Regulations 1989.[20] An emergency certificate automatically lapses after a period of six weeks although it may be extended. It is also limited to a costs ceiling of £1,500 in London and £1,200 outside London which includes disbursements and counsel's fees.

3.24 In franchised firms solicitors may issue their own emergency certificates for all types of case provided that they are satisfied that the applicant has a good case, that s/he is financially eligible and that it is an emergency. Their costs are limited up to £10,000.

3.25 Legal aid applications for children and young people must be signed by a next friend or guardian ad litem. Where the solicitor has assessed the young person as competent to give instructions the solicitor may sign the form personally.[21] In all cases, the financial circumstances of the child are assessed for the purposes of the means test[22] and Form CLA4F should be completed.

3.26 The legal aid form requires applicants to give the reason(s) why they wish to start proceedings in a court other than the magistrates' court. Practitioners should, therefore, construct their arguments carefully in support of an application to the higher courts.

The procedure

3.27 The following describes the procedure to be followed in relation to any s8 proceedings. The procedural rules are similar in all three

---

19 *Legal Aid Focus* No 17, March 1997.
20 SI No 339 reg 103(6).
21 Civil Legal Aid (General) (Amendment) Regulations 1992 SI No 590.
22 Civil Legal Aid (Assessment of Resources) (Amendment) Regulations 1990 SI No 484.

tiers of court and are governed by the Family Proceedings Courts (Children Act 1989) Rules 1991[23] (FPCR) and the Family Proceedings Rules 1991[24] (FPR). Rules about the allocation of court proceedings are contained in the Children Act (Allocation of Proceedings) Order 1991[25] (Allocation Order).

Which court?

3.28 There is no legal prohibition on where cases may start, and cases may, therefore, be commenced in the family proceedings court of the magistrates' court, in the county court or the High Court (but see remarks on legal aid above). At county court level there are 94 family hearing centres where private law cases may be heard, and 54 are also care centres which hear both private and public law cases. Applications in the county court must be started in the divorce county court but, if that court is not a family hearing centre and there is an opposed s8 application, the case must be transferred to a family hearing centre for trial.[26]

Application

3.29 All proceedings must start by way of a formal application.[27] The statutory forms can be found in FPCR 1991 Sch 1 and FPR 1991 Appendix 1 (as amended). The relevant form is Form C1. Detailed information is required, including the order sought and any directions, reasons for the application and plans for the future care of the child including residence and contact. It is no longer necessary to complete one application for each child.[28]

Leave

3.30 The person seeking leave must complete Form C2 together with a draft of the application.[29] The request may be granted without a hearing, or a date may be fixed for a hearing on the issues. The rules do not specify a notice period and it may, therefore, take some time to

23 SI No 1395 (L17).
24 SI No 1247 (L20).
25 SI No 1677.
26 Allocation Order arts 15 and 16.
27 FPCR 1991 r4(1)(a) and FPR 1991 r4.4(1)(a).
28 FPCR 1991 r4(1A)(b) and FPR 1991 r4.4(1A)(b).
29 FPCR 1991 r3 and FPR 1991 r4.3.

obtain leave unless it is dealt with ex parte. In an emergency practitioners should make the application for leave at the same time as the substantive application.

3.31 Children seeking leave must apply to the High Court.[30] The courts have said that it is not necessary but usually appropriate for parents or others with parental responsibility to be given notice of the leave application.[31] Court rules[32] state that a child need not apply by a next friend where a solicitor accepts instructions from the child whom s/he has assessed as competent to give instructions and the court endorses the solicitor's assessment[33] or where the child has sought the court's leave to proceed without a next friend. The request for leave should be made in writing setting out the reasons, or an oral request can be made at any stage of the substantive hearing.

Notice

3.32 Twenty-one days' notice of hearing is required for all applications made on notice.[34] Applications for all s8 orders may be made ex parte.[35] In *Re B (A Minor) (Residence Order)*[36] the court held that ex parte applications for residence orders should be granted only occasionally, where exceptional circumstances warrant it. The application form should be filed with the court at the time of the application or, if made over the telephone, within 24 hours of the application.

Respondents

3.33 There are two categories of person who should be informed about the court proceedings:

a) those who have automatic party status; and
b) those who are entitled to notice so that they can apply for leave to be made parties if they so wish.[37]

---

30 *Practice Direction (Fam.D.) (Children Act 1989: Applications by Children: Leave)* [1993] 1 FLR 668.
31 *Re S (A Minor) (Independent Representation)* [1993] 2 FLR 437, CA.
32 FPR 1991 r9.2A.
33 *Re CT (A Minor) (Wardship Representation)* [1993] 2 FLR 278.
34 FPCR 1991 Sch 2 and FPR 1991 Appendix 3.
35 FPCR 1991 r4(4) and FPR 1991 r4.4, as amended by Family Proceedings Courts (Miscellaneous Amendment) Rules 1992 SI No 2068 and Family Proceedings (Amendment No 2) Rules 1992 SI No 2067.
36 [1992] 2 FLR 1, CA.
37 FPCR 1991 Sch 2 and FPR 1991 Appendix 3.

Party status

3.34 Those who have automatic party status are:

- any person believed to have parental responsibility;
- in applications to vary or discharge an order, those with party status in the original proceedings;
- where the child is subject to a care order, every person believed to have had parental responsibility before the making of that order.

Notice

3.35 Those who are entitled to notice are:

- any person named in a court order with respect to the same child unless not considered to be relevant to the application;
- any person believed to be a party to pending proceedings with respect to the same child unless not considered to be relevant to the application;
- any person with whom the child has lived for at least three previous years.

Service

3.36 There is no requirement for personal service, and service may be by delivery at, or by first class post to, the residence or last known residence of the person to be served.[38] Where solicitors are involved, service may be effected by fax. Where there is no solicitor or guardian ad litem, service of documents for children will be carried out by the court. Where an order is made ex parte, the application must be served within 48 hours of making the order.[39]

Representation of children

3.37 Since children are not conferred automatic party status in s8 proceedings, their views will usually be represented to the court via the court welfare officer. National standards for family court welfare officers require them to ascertain the wishes and feelings of the child and report these to the court.[40]

3.38 Children may sometimes be made parties by the court. This is

---

38 FPCR 1991 r8(1) and FPR 1991 r4.8(1).
39 FPCR 1991 r4(4)(ii) and FPR 1991 r4.4(4)(ii).
40 National Standards for Probation Service Family Court Welfare Work (Home Office 1994) paras 4.17 to 4.18.

usually where there is some child protection element to the case, where the parents are intractably opposed, where there is complex expert evidence or where older children have strong views about the future. Section 8 proceedings are not 'specified proceedings' for the purposes of s41, and the model of representation of children by solicitor and guardian ad litem does not apply. Court rules[41] provide that children must be represented by a guardian ad litem (or next friend if they have initiated the application)[42] in the High Court and county court. There are no rules about separate representation of children in the family proceedings court. The guardian may be the Official Solicitor or a 'proper person' and the courts have requested that the Official Solicitor should be asked first before appointing another guardian ad litem.[43] There is no definition of 'proper person' and the courts have appointed court welfare officers or children panel solicitors to carry out this task.

3.39 Court rules[44] state that a child may be separately legally represented where a solicitor accepts instructions from the child whom s/he has assessed as competent to give instructions and the court endorses the solicitor's assessment[45] or where the child has sought the court's leave to participate independently. The court must grant this request where it considers that the child has sufficient understanding.

Evidence

3.40 Written statements must be filed and served on all parties before the hearing or as directed by the court.[46] In an emergency it may not be possible to serve evidence much before the hearing itself. There is prohibition on the filing of evidence in s8 proceedings until such time as directed by the court. It is suggested that statements should be prepared in the normal way and the court's leave should be obtained at the hearing to file and serve this evidence.

3.41 The Children (Admissibility of Hearsay Evidence) Order 1993[47] provides that hearsay evidence is admissible in all three tiers of court. However, the courts recognise the sensitivity of hearsay evidence and

---

41 FPR 1991 Part IX.
42 FPR 1991 r9.2A.
43 *L v L (Children: Separate Representation)* [1994] 1 FLR 890.
44 FPR 1991 r9.2A.
45 *Re CT (A Minor) (Wardship Representation)* [1993] 2 FLR 278.
46 FPCR 1991 r17 and FPR r4.17.
47 SI No 621.

will still need to assess the weight and credibility of such evidence. In *Re W (Minors) (Wardship evidence)*[48] the Court of Appeal said that in a case in which direct evidence could be produced hearsay evidence had to be regarded with grave caution, unless uncontroversial.

3.42 In addition to the evidence of their own clients, practitioners will need to consider the question of lay and professional witnesses. The court's leave must be obtained before seeking a medical, psychiatric or other assessment of the child[49] and in practice there is unlikely to be sufficient time to organise this for the purposes of an emergency application.

3.43 Professional witnesses usually require a witness summons to attend court. The FPR 1991 do not provide for the compulsory attendance of witnesses in non-matrimonial cases concerning children. Judges in the High Court have the power to order the attendance of potential witnesses. Procedure in the family proceedings court is governed by Magistrates' Courts Act 1980 s97(1) and FPCR 1991 r33. These provide that a magistrate must issue a witness summons for the attendance of a witness or for the production of a document where there is evidence that the witness will not voluntarily attend. Professional witnesses usually accept service of the summons at court. Conduct money must be supplied to cover reasonable travel expenses.

---

48 [1990] 1 FLR 203.
49 FPCR 1991 r18 and FPR 1991 r4.18.

Part II

Emergencies in care or accommodation

In this part:

Introduction to Part II

With good social work practice, unplanned events should not usually arise while children are looked after by a local authority. However, there are circumstances where genuine emergencies may arise or social work practice leaves something to be desired. The following are examples of the types of emergencies that could arise while a child is looked after by a local authority:

- A young child, aged two, has been living with short-term foster carers since she was four weeks old. Adoption is planned and the foster carers have been told that she will be removed by the end of the week.
- A 15-year-old girl is pregnant. She and the local authority want her to have a termination. Her mother does not.
- An 11-year-old boy living in a children's home has been forcibly sedated for control purposes.
- Two children, sexually abused by their father, have been having contact with their paternal grandmother. This has suddenly stopped. They wish to continue seeing her.
- An eight-year-old child has been provided with accommodation for the past three years. Her mother suddenly announces that she wishes her to return home to the mother's new partner and baby. The child is attached to her foster carers and does not wish to leave.

Decision-making

Local authorities have similar duties towards all children they look after whether the child is accommodated on a voluntary basis or is subject to a care order. The local authority has a duty to promote and safeguard the welfare of the child and in doing so it must give due consideration to the wishes and feelings of the child (considered in light of his/her age and understanding), the parents, people with

41

parental responsibility, and others who the local authority considers to be significant to the child. It must also give due consideration to the religious persuasion, racial origin, cultural and linguistic background of the child.[1]

The Children Act (CA) 1989 has also constructed a detailed framework of planning for all children looked after by the local authority.[2] Plans for accommodated children must be agreed in writing with a parent or other person with parental responsibility.[3] Department of Health guidance stresses the importance of working in partnership wherever possible with parents and with older children.[4] As part of the process of greater openness and accountability the CA 1989 provides for a representations and complaints procedure against any decision made under CA 1989 Part III (family support and local authority welfare duties to children).

Legal challenge

The availability of legal remedies depends on the nature of the issue and the legal status of the child.

The main distinction between accommodated children and children in care is that a parent retains parental responsibility of an accommodated child and has the legal right to remove the child at any time (although from the child's perspective a planned removal is always preferrable). In theory, therefore, there should be less opportunity for disagreement between parents and the local authority but this is not always so. The parent's retention of parental responsibility also gives rise to the right to seek a relevant CA 1989 s8 order in relation to any significant disagreement with the local authority about the way in which it is exercising its duties towards the child. Other people may seek leave as appropriate.

As a general rule, decisions made in relation to a child in care cannot be challenged or reviewed by the court unless they relate to contact.[5] The High Court may be able to exercise its discretion in judicial

1   CA 1989 s22(4) and (5).
2   Arrangements for Placement of Children (General) Regulations 1991 SI No 890 and Review of Children's Cases Regulations 1991 SI No 895.
3   Arrangements for Placement of Children Regulations 1991 SI No 890 reg 3(4).
4   *Children Act 1989: Guidance and Regulations* (HMSO, 1991), Volume 3, Family Placements, para 2.10.
5   CA 1989 s34.

review if the grounds are satisfied (see Chapter 6). Otherwise, non-judicial approaches will need to be made, which inevitably take too long in emergencies.

Decisions in relation to secure accommodation are constrained by the provisions of CA 1989 s25 and the relevant regulations.

CHAPTER 4

Contact between children and parents

4.1 All references in this chapter are to the Children Act (CA) 1989, unless otherwise stated.

The law

4.2 There is a presumption under the CA 1989 that contact with parents, extended family members and other significant people is in the best interests of children who are being looked after by the local authority. This reflects research findings that for the majority of children their welfare is enhanced by continuing some form of contact with their parents and extended family members.[1] Practitioners should be familiar with Department of Health guidance about contact.[2]

Promotion of contact

4.3 Local authorities have a duty to endeavour to promote contact between children and their parents, others with parental responsibility, relatives, friends or other people connected with the child,[3] unless this would be contrary to the child's best interests. This duty applies equally to children in accommodation or subject to a care order. Local authorities also have a discretion to provide expenses for travelling, subsistence, or other matters either to the child or to any of the people above where it appears that the visits could not otherwise happen without undue financial hardship.[4]

---

1 Fratter J, Rowe J, Sapsford D and Thoburn J, *Permanent Family Placement: a decade of experience* (BAAF, 1991); Sellick C and Thoburn J, *What Works in Family Placement* (Barnados, 1996).
2 *Children Act 1989: Guidance and Regulations* (HMSO, 1991), Volume 3, Family Placements, Chapter 6.
3 CA 1989 Sch 2 para 15(1).
4 Ibid, para 16.

4.4 CA 1989 s34 provides that the local authority must allow children in care reasonable contact with their parents, guardians and those with a residence order or an order for care and control under the inherent jurisdiction.[5]

Temination of contact

4.5 In general, a local authority must not refuse children in care contact with their parents, etc, without the court's authority. Sometimes at the final care hearing the court may make an order terminating contact after a certain time, eg, when the child has been placed for adoption.

4.6 However, there is provision for the local authority to stop contact where it is satisfied that it is necessary to promote the child's welfare, the decision is made as a matter of urgency and the termination lasts for no longer than seven days.[6] Contact with Children Regulations 1991[7] reg 2 requires the local authority to give notification of this decision, with reasons, and to give information about available remedies, to parents, guardians, those with a residence order or order for care and control under the inherent jurisdiction, and to the child, if of sufficient understanding, and to any other person whose wishes and feelings the authority consider to be relevant.

4.7 There is no statutory provision prohibiting termination of contact with children who are accommodated. Nor is there any provision in relation to children in care who have contact with people who do not come within those specified under s34.

Court orders

Section 34 applications
4.8 Parents, guardians, those with residence orders or orders for care and control may apply for contact with the child. Other people may seek the court's leave to do so.[8] There are no statutory criteria for leave applications. Children themselves may apply for contact with any specific person.[9] They may also apply for contact to be refused.[10]

5   Ibid, s34(1).
6   Ibid, s34(6).
7   SI No 891.
8   CA 1989, s34(3).
9   Ibid, s34(2).
10 Ibid, s34(4).

Orders for contact may contain conditions such as supervision.[11] Thus, there are clear remedies to challenge an emergency refusal of contact although there may be difficulties in obtaining a hearing date within the seven-day period.

Section 8 applications

4.9 A s8 application for contact may be made where there is any dispute about contact arrangements with an accommodated child. This may include an order for no contact. Parents, guardians, those with a residence order, step-parents, relatives or friends with whom the child has lived for three out of the past five years, and others with certain specified consents may apply for a contact order as of right.[12]

4.10 Any other person may apply for the court's leave. In deciding whether to grant leave, the court must consider the following criteria:[13]

a) the nature of the proposed application;
b) the applicant's connection with the child;
c) any risk that the proposed application might cause harm to the child;
d) the local authority's plans for the child's future and the wishes and feelings of the child's parents.

4.11 In deciding whether to grant leave the court does not have to apply the welfare principle since the application itself does not directly relate to the child's upbringing.[14] In *A v W (Minors) (Leave to Apply)*[15] the Court of Appeal ruled that any departure from the local authority's plans was likely to disrupt the child to the extent that s/he would be harmed because the local authority was vested with the duty to safeguard and promote the child's welfare.

4.12 In granting leave, the court must decide whether the applicant has a good arguable case and not, as previously thought, whether it is reasonably likely to succeed.[16] It is difficult to obtain leave where the interests of the applicant are identical to those of one of the parties.[17]

4.13 Children may apply for leave. They do not have to fulfil the above criteria but the court must be satisfied they have sufficient

---

11 Ibid, s34(7).
12 Ibid, s10(5).
13 Ibid, s10(9).
14 *A v W (Minors) (Leave To Apply)* [1992] 2 FLR 154.
15 Ibid.
16 *Re M (Care: Contact: Grandmother's Application)* (1995) Fam Law 540.
17 *Re M (Minors) (Representation)* (1992) *Times*, 19 November, CA.

understanding to make the proposed application.[18] Applications must be made to the High Court.

4.14 Foster carers may not apply for leave unless they have the consent of the authority, they are relatives of the child or the child has lived with them for three of the past five years.[19]

The practice: local authority negotiations

4.15 There is usually little that can be achieved by way of negotiation if contact has been terminated under the emergency provisions since it is a matter of judgment about whether or not the child is at risk. It may be possible to suggest that contact should be supervised, if this is not already the case, or to negotiate a suspension of the decision to terminate contact pending an application to court, but this will depend on the cirumstances and the percieved degree of risk to the child.

4.16 Where contact between a child in care and his/her parent, etc, has been stopped without court sanction or receipt of notice of the emergency provisions, practitioners should invite the local authority to reinstate contact immediately or make an urgent application to court. They may also wish to consider an application for judicial review (see paras 6.6 to 6.18)

4.17 In other circumstances where contact has been stopped or substantially altered, practitioners should seek clarification in writing of the local authority's concerns for the child's welfare in the context of the previous contact arrangements. Such information may give some opportunity for realistic negotiations to take place.

4.18 The benefit of contact to the child with each individual concerned should always be assessed independently of whether or not there is contact with the parents. The most common circumstances are where contact has been refused as a result of parental abuse and yet there are positive and caring relationships with grandparents or other family members. The local authority should be reminded of Department of Health guidance, which stresses that 'contact, however occasional, may continue to have a value for the child when there is no question of returning to his family'.[20] This principle applies to

---

18 CA 1989 s10(8).
19 Ibid, s9(3).
20 *Children Act 1989: Guidance and Regulations* (HMSO, 1991), Volume 3, Family Placements, para 6.9.

CHECKLIST FOR INSTRUCTIONS

Adult applicant
Name
Address and telephone number
Date of birth
Occupation (if any) and financial circumstances
Family composition
Medical or psychiatric problems (letters of authority where necessary)
Criminal convictions
Relationship to child in question
Quality of relationship with parents (where relevant)
Reasons for child living away from home, details of agreement with local authority or care order where appropriate

Parent(s)
Same information as above

Child
Same information as above and, in addition:

– Reasons for wanting contact
– Reasons for not wanting contact
– Evidence to support behavioural or psychological effect on child of visits

Previous contact
Frequency of visits
Reasons for missed visits (where relevant)
Quality of relationship with child
Activities on visit, etc
Benefit to child of contact with siblings

Proposals for contact
Where visits are to take place and how time to be spent
Accommodation and sleeping arrangements (where staying contact proposed)
Attitude of parents/relatives to foster carers/adoptive parents. Is supervision necessary and, if so, by whom?
Financial implications, whether assistance required

children placed not only with long-term foster carers but also with adoptive parents.

4.19 Practitioners may be consulted by children or young people who do not wish to have contact with their parents or other relatives. Department of Health guidance states that social workers, with the assistance of trusted adults, should try to understand the source of those feelings but that ultimately 'a child should not be forced to persist unwillingly or unhappily with seeing a parent or other person'.[21]

Legal aid

4.20 Unlike legal aid for other public law applications, full means- and merits-tested legal aid is required for all parties' applications for contact under s34. Legal aid is, therefore, the same for both s34 and s8 applications. However, recent guidance from the Legal Aid Board states that applications for contact to a child in care will be limited in the first instance to the solicitor's report on the issues and prospects of success and will not cover issuing proceedings and, if extended, will be limited to all steps short of the final hearing.[22] It may, therefore, not be possible to obtain emergency legal aid for s34 applications.

4.21 Form CLA5 plus CLA4A/CLA4B and Form CLA3 (emergency legal aid) should be completed. From 1 April 1997, the Legal Aid Board has required urgent emergency applications to be made by fax instead of by telephone as in the past. Special fax forms FEA1 and FEA1a should be submitted to which the Legal Aid Board will respond within 24 hours. The normal postal forms should be submitted within five working days. In emergencies where the work needs to be done within the next few hours and there is no time to access a fax machine, a telephone application can still be made.

4.22 In both circumstances, the certificate will come into effect from the start of the case by virtue of the deeming provisions in the Civil Legal Aid (General) Regulations 1989.[23] An emergency certificate automatically lapses after a period of six weeks although it may be extended. It is also limited to a cost ceiling of £1,500 in London and £1,200 outside London which includes disbursements and counsel's fees.

21   Ibid, para 6.25.
22   *Legal Aid Focus* No 19, May 1997, para 5.4.5.
23   SI No 339 reg 103(6).

4.23 In franchised firms solicitors may issue their own emergency certificates for all types of case provided that they are satisfied that the applicant has a good case, that s/he is financially eligible and that it is an emergency. Their costs are limited to £10,000.

4.24 Legal aid applications for children and young people must be signed by a next friend or guardian ad litem. Where the solicitor has assessed the young person as competent to give instructions the solicitor may sign the form personally.[24] In all cases, the financial circumstances of the child are assessed for the purposes of the means test[25] and Form CLA4F should be completed.

4.25 The legal aid form requires applicants to give the reason(s) why they wish to start proceedings in a court other than the magistrates' court. Practitioners should, therefore, construct their arguments carefully in support of an application to the higher courts.[26]

The procedure

4.26 The following describes the procedure to be followed in relation to an application for a s34 or s8 contact order. The procedural rules are similar for both kinds of proceedings and in all three tiers of court. They are governed by the Family Proceedings Courts (Children Act 1989) Rules 1991[27] (FPCR) and the Family Proceedings Rules 1991[28] (FPR). Rules about the allocation of court proceedings are contained in the Children Act (Allocation of Proceedings) Order 1991[29] (Allocation Order).

Which court?

Section 34

4.27 All contact applications start in the family proceedings court of the magistrates' court unless there are other public law proceedings pending in another court, in which case they may commence in that other court.[30]

---

24 Civil Legal Aid (General) (Amendment) Regulations 1992 SI No 590.
25 Civil Legal Aid (Assessment of Resources) (Amendment) Regulations 1990 SI No 484.
26 See also *Legal Aid Focus* No 19, May 1997, paras 5.4.11 to 5.4.18.
27 SI No 1395 (L17).
28 SI No 1247 (L20).
29 SI No 1677.
30 Allocation Order art 3.

4.28 Proceedings may be transferred laterally from one court to another, or vertically up from the magistrates' court to the county court, from the county court to High Court, or down.

4.29 On application by a party or on the court's initiative, a case may be transferred from the magistrates' court to the county court where the magistrates' court considers it in the interests of the child, having regard to the principle in s1(2) (delay being prejudicial to the interests of the child) and:

a) whether the proceedings are exceptionally grave, important or complex;
b) whether it would be appropriate for those proceedings to be heard with other private law proceedings which are pending in another court; and
c) whether the transfer is likely to accelerate the determination of the proceedings.[31]

4.30 Cases may be transferred from the county court to the High Court where, having regard to the principle in s1(2), the court considers that the proceedings are appropriate for determination in the High Court and it is in the interests of the child.[32]

4.31 Where a magistrates' court refuses to transfer a case, any party to the proceedings may apply to the appropriate care centre,[33] which may transfer the case applying the same principles set out in Allocation Order art 7. It may decide to transfer the case to the High Court if it considers that the proceedings are appropriate for determination in the High Court and this is in the interests of the child.[34]

Section 8

4.32 There is no legal prohibition on where cases may start, and cases may therefore be commenced in the family proceedings court of the magistrates' court, in the county court or in the High Court (but see note on legal aid above). At county court level there are 94 family hearing centres where private law cases may be heard, and 54 are also care centres which hear both private and public law cases. Applications in the county court must be started in the divorce county court but, if that court is not a family hearing centre and there is an

31 Ibid, art 7(1).
32 Ibid, art 12.
33 FPCR 1991 Sch 2 column ii and FPR 1991 Appendix 3.
34 Allocation Order art 9.

opposed s8 application, the case must be transferred to a family hearing centre for trial.[35]

Application

4.33 All proceedings must start by way of application.[36] The statutory forms can be found in FPCR 1991 Sch 1 and FPR 1991 Appendix 1. The relevant forms for s34 applications are general form C1 with supplement form C15. Detailed information is required in each form, including the reasons for the application and details about the contact sought. The form for a s8 application is Form C1, where information is required about the order sought and any directions, and reasons for the application.

Leave

4.34 The person seeking leave must complete Form C2 together with a draft of the application.[37] The request may be granted without a hearing, or a date may be fixed for a hearing on the issues. The rules do not specify a notice period and it may, therefore, take some time to obtain leave unless it is dealt with ex parte. In an emergency practitioners should make their application for leave at the same time as their substantive application.

4.35 Children seeking leave must apply to the High Court.[38] The courts have said that it is not necessary but usually appropriate for parents or others with parental responsibility to be given notice of the leave application.[39] Court rules[40] state that a child need not apply by a next friend where a solicitor accepts instructions from the child whom s/he has assessed as competent to give instructions and the court endorses the solicitor's assessment[41] or where the child has sought the court's leave to proceed without a next friend. The request for leave should be made in writing setting out the reasons, or an oral request can be made at any stage of the substantive hearing.

35 Ibid, arts 15 and 16.
36 FPCR 1991 r4(1)(a) and FPR 1991 r4.4(1)(a).
37 FPCR 1991 r3 and FPR r4.3.
38 *Practice Direction (Fam. D.) (Children Act 1989: Applications by Children: Leave)* [1993] 1 FLR 668.
39 Re S *(A Minor) (Independent Representation)* [1993] 2 FLR 437, CA.
40 FPR 1991 r9.2A.
41 *Re CT (A Minor) (Wardship Representation)* [1993] 2 FLR 278.

Notice

Section 34 applications

4.36 Three days' notice of hearing is required for all applications.[42] There is provision for abridgement of service[43] but given the short notice period it is unlikely that it would be granted in most cases.

Section 8 applications

4.37 Twenty-one days' notice of hearing is required for all applications made on notice.[44] Contact applications can be made ex parte where appropriate.[45]

Respondents

4.38 There are two categories of people who should be informed about the court proceedings:

a) those who have automatic party status, and
b) those who are entitled to notice so that they can apply for leave to be made parties if they so wish.[46]

Section 34

4.39 Those who have automatic party status are:

– the child and any person with parental responsibility;
– every person whom the local authority believes had parental responsibility before the making of the care order;
– the person whose contact with the child is the subject of the application.

4.40 Any person who is caring for the child immediately before the proceedings is entitled to notice.

Section 8

4.41 Any person believed to have parental responsibility has automatic party status.

4.42 Those who are entitled to notice are:

– any person named in a court order with respect to the same child unless not considered to be relevant to the application;

42 FPCR 1991 Sch 2 and FPR 1991 Appendix 3.
43 FPCR 1991 r8(8) and FPR 1991 r4.8(8).
44 FPCR 1991 Sch 2 and FPR 1991 Appendix 3.
45 FPCR 1991 r4(4) (as amended by the Family Proceedings Courts (Miscellaneous Amendment) Rules 1992 SI No 2068) and FPR 1991 r4.4(4) (as amended by Family Proceedings (Amendment No 2) Rules 1992 SI No 2067.
46 FPCR 1991 Sch 2 and FPR 1991 Appendix 3.

- any person believed to be a party to pending proceedings with respect to the same child unless not considered to be relevant to the application;
- any person with whom the child has lived for at least three previous years.

Service

4.43   There is no requirement for personal service, and service may be by delivery at, or by first class post to, the residence or last known residence of the person to be served.[47] Where solicitors are involved, service may be effected by fax. Where there is no solicitor or guardian ad litem, service of documents by children will be carried out by the court.

Representation of children

Section 34 proceedings

4.44   Contact proceedings are 'specified proceedings' for the purposes of CA 1989 s41, and there is a presumption that a guardian ad litem will be appointed unless the court does not consider it necessary to protect the interests of the child. The guardian ad litem is required to safeguard the interests of the child by reference to the welfare checklist. The guardian is also required to:

- appoint a solicitor for the child;
- advise the court of the child's wishes and feelings;
- advise the court about whether the child has sufficient understanding to withhold consent to medical and other examinations;
- deal with various procedural matters such as timetabling, court venue and party status.[48]

4.45   Solicitors for the child must act on the instructions of the guardian unless it appears that the child is capable of giving instructions. If these instructions conflict with the guardian's, the child's instructions prevail and the guardian must represent him/herself independently.[49]

4.46   Court rules specifically deal with the child's attendance at court. There is a presumption that proceedings must take place in the

47 FPCR 1991 r4(8) and FPR 1991 r4.4(8).
48 FPCR r11(1) to (5) and FPR r4.11(1) to (5).
49 FPCR 1991 rr11(3) and 12(1)(a) and FPR rr4.11(3) and 4.12(1)(a).

absence of the child if the court considers that it is in the child's best interests, bearing in mind the nature of the evidence, and the child is represented by a guardian ad litem or solicitor. In considering a decision for the child to attend the hearing, the court must hear from the guardian, the solicitor and the child where of sufficient understanding.[50] In *Re C (A Minor) (Care: Child's Wishes)*[51] the court reiterated the view that it was not normally desirable for children to attend court hearings.

Section 8 proceedings

4.47 Since children are not conferred automatic party status in s8 proceedings, their views will usually be represented to the court via the court welfare officer. National standards for family court welfare officers requires them to ascertain the wishes and feelings of the child and report these to the court.[52]

4.48 Children may sometimes be made parties by the court. This is usually where there is some child protection element to the case, where the parents are intractably opposed, where there is complex expert evidence or where older children have strong views about the future. Section 8 proceedings are not 'specified proceedings' for the purposes of CA 1989 s41, and the model of representation of children by solicitor and guardian ad litem does not apply. Court rules[53] provide that children must be represented by a guardian ad litem (or next friend if they have initiated the application)[54] in the High Court and county court. There are no rules about separate representation of children in the family proceedings court. The guardian may be the Official Solicitor or a 'proper person' and the courts have requested that the Official Solicitor should be asked first before appointing another guardian ad litem.[55] There is no definition of 'proper person' and the courts have appointed court welfare officers or children panel solicitors to carry out this task.

4.49 Court rules[56] state that a child may be separately legally represented where a solicitor accepts instructions from the child whom s/he

50 FPCR r16(2) and FPR r4.16(2).
51 [1993] 1 FLR 832.
52 National Standards for Probation Service Family Court Welfare Work (Home Office 1994) paras 4.17–4.18.
53 FPR 1991 Part IX.
54 FPR 1991 r9.2A.
55 *L v L (Children: Separate Representation)* [1994] 1 FLR 890.
56 FPR 1991 r9.2A.

has assessed as competent to give instructions and the court endorses the solicitor's assessment[57] or where the child has sought the court's leave to participate independently. The court must grant this request where it considers that the child has sufficient understanding.

Evidence

4.50 Written statements must be filed and served on all parties before the hearing or as directed by the court.[58] In an emergency it may not be possible to serve evidence much before the hearing itself. There is a prohibition on the filing of evidence in s8 proceedings until such time as directed by the court.[59] In relation to an application for contact, the court's leave should be obtained at the time of seeking abridgement of service.

4.51 The Children (Admissibility of Hearsay Evidence) Order 1993[60] provides that hearsay evidence is admissible in all three tiers of court. The courts recognise the sensitivity of hearsay evidence and will still need to assess the weight and credibility of such evidence. In *Re W (Minors) (Wardship: Evidence)*[61] the Court of Appeal said that in a case in which direct evidence could be produced hearsay evidence had to be regarded with grave caution, unless uncontroversial.

4.52 Solicitors for parents or any other person seeking contact will need to consider the question of lay and expert witnesses. Evidence of the quality of relationship between the child and person in question will be very important, and psychiatric evidence may be crucial. The court's leave must first be obtained before a medical, psychiatric or other assessment is carried out for the purposes of expert evidence.[62] Where relevant, it may be possible to obtain a medical or psychiatric report on the parent but this is likely to be possible only where the professional is already involved with the case.

4.53 Practitioners should be aware of the complex issue regarding disclosure of unfavourable reports. In *Re L (A Minor) (Police Investigation: Privilege)*[63] the House of Lords distinguished between

---

57 *Re CT (A Minor) (Wardship Representation)* [1993] 2 FLR 278.
58 FPCR 1991 r17 and FPR r4.17.
59 FPCR 1991 r17(5) and FPR 1991 r4.17(5).
60 SI No 621.
61 [1990] 1 FLR 203.
62 FPCR 1991 r18 and FPR 1991 r4.18.
63 [1996] 1 FLR 731.

solicitor/client privilege and litigation privilege attaching to third party reports in children cases. In that case the court had given leave for a report which was unfavourable to the mother and the House of Lords held that it should be disclosed. The court did not answer the question of whether there is a duty on lawyers to give voluntary disclosure of reports obtained without the requirement of obtaining the court's leave. For further information about this subject, readers should refer to more detailed texts.

4.54 Professional witnesses usually require a witness summons to attend court. The FPR 1991 do not provide for the compulsory attendance of witnesses in non-matrimonial cases concerning children. Judges in the High Court have the power to order the attendance of potential witnesses. Procedure in the family proceedings court is governed by Magistrates' Courts Act 1980 s97(1) and FPCR 1991 r33. These provide that a magistrate must issue a witness summons for the attendance of a witness or for the production of a document where there is evidence that the witness will not voluntarily attend. Professional witnesses usually accept service of the summons at court. Conduct money must be supplied to cover reasonable travel expenses.

Directions and interim orders

4.55 The rules provide for directions to be made in all proceedings, determining timetabling, court allocation and other procedural matters.[64] These are likely to be made at the first hearing, at which time the substantive hearing will be adjourned.

Section 34 application

4.56 There is no specific provision for the making of an interim s34 contact order, and some courts are making final contact orders at the first hearing. In *West Glamorgan County Council v P (No 1)*[65] it was held that the court had the power to make temporary orders. In *Re B (A Minor) (Care Order: Review)*,[66] the court held that since there is no power for the court to review a final contact order it should make an order for interim contact with a provision for a final hearing.

---

64 FPCR 1991 r14 and FPR 1991 r4.14.
65 [1992] 2 FLR 369.
66 [1993] 1 FLR 421.

Section 8 application

4.57 CA 1989 s11(7)(c) provides that a s8 order may be made to have effect for a specified period. Thus an interim contact order may be made in these terms at the first hearing.

CHAPTER 5

Secure accommodation

5.1 All references in this chapter are to the Children Act (CA) 1989, unless otherwise stated.

The law

5.2 Local authorities have the power to place young people in secure accommodation for a total of 72 hours out of any period of 28 consecutive days following which they must make an application to the court for authorisation of that placement to continue.[1] The maximum period for such an authorisation is three months upon the local authority's first application to the court[2] and thereafter for up to six months.[3] No young person under the age of 13 should be placed in a secure unit (see below) without proper authorisation from the Secretary of State.[4]

5.3 Practitioners should note that a court order provides authorisation for a local authority to place a young person in secure accommodation. It does not direct the authority to do so. During the period of the order the young person may be transferred to open accommodation which does not restrict liberty. The local authority must transfer a young person when the criteria justifying the placement (see below) cease to apply. Practitioners should be alert to the role of judicial review in circumstances when children are not transferred and where a local authority has not made a court application at the correct time.

5.4 The Children (Secure Accommodation) Regulations 1991[5]

1 Children (Secure Accommodation) Regulations 1991 SI No 1505 reg 10.
2 Ibid, reg 11.
3 Ibid, reg 12.
4 Ibid, reg 4.
5 SI No 1505.

(C(SA)R) state that the following bodies may also seek secure accommodation orders: private residential care, nursing and mental nursing homes and health and education authorities are now permitted to place young people in secure accommodation and to make court applications.[6] Voluntary homes and private children's homes are forbidden to restrict liberty.[7] In practice, it is likely that court applications will be made only by local authorities, private mental hospitals and NHS psychiatric units.

Preventive duty

5.5 The CA 1989 imposes a duty on local authorities to take reasonable steps designed to reduce the need for children in their area to be placed in secure accommodation.[8] Local authorities should have developed alternative facilities and services, met by themselves or in co-operation with other agencies. Department of Health guidance states that the use of secure accommodation must:

> ... be a 'last resort' in the sense that all else must first have been comprehensively considered and rejected – never because no other placement was available at the relevant time, because of inadequacies in staffing, because the child is simply being a nuisance or runs away from his accommodation and is not likely to suffer significant harm in doing so, and never as a form of punishment.[9]

Grounds

5.6 CA 1989 s25(1) specifies the grounds for placement in secure accommodation:

> ... a child who is being looked after by a local authority may not be placed, and, if placed, may not be kept, in accommodation provided for the purpose of restricting liberty ('secure accommodation') unless it appears–
> (a) that
>   (i) he has a history of absconding and is likely to abscond from any other description of accommodation; and
>   (ii) if he absconds, he is likely to suffer significant harm; or

---

6   C(SA)R 1991 reg 7.
7   Ibid, reg 18.
8   CA 1989 Sch 2 para 7.
9   *Children Act 1989: Guidance and Regulations* (HMSO, 1991), Volume 4, Residential Care, para 8.5.

(b) that if he is kept in any other description of accommodation he is likely to injure himself or other persons.

5.7 'Harm' is defined in s31 as ill-treatment (which includes sexual abuse and forms of ill-treatment which are not physical), or the impairment of health or development (physical, intellectual, emotional, social or behavioural).

5.8 Where the court is satisfied that the criteria are met it must make an order: the welfare principle and 'no order' principle of the CA 1989 do not apply.[10]

Secure accommodation

5.9 This is defined in the legislation as accommodation provided for the purpose of restricting liberty, but there is no definition of what this means: it is a matter left to the court. A hospital maternity ward has been held to be secure accommodation since it wished to restrict the mother's discharge. By contrast, the courts have held that detention in an adolescent unit does not constitute restriction of liberty since that is not its primary purpose.[11]

5.10 Accommodation may be in one of the following:

- secure unit in local authority community home approved by the Secretary of State for Health;[12]
- youth treatment centre – St Charles in Brentwood, Essex and Glenthorne in Birmingham;
- NHS or NHS trust;
- independent schools of over 50 boarders;
- maintained boarding schools;
- private residential homes;
- private nursing and mental nursing homes.

Children looked after

5.11 The provisions of CA 1989 s25 apply to all children looked after by local authorities, including those in care or accommodation, subject to an EPO or police protection. They also apply to children accommodated by local education authorities, health authorities, in residential care or nursing or mental nursing homes.

10 *Re M (Secure Accommodation Order)* (1995) Fam Law 108.
11 *A Metropolitan Borough Council v DB* [1997] 1 FLR 767; *Re C (Detention: Medical Treatment)* [1997] 2 FLR 2.
12 C(SA)R 1991 reg 3.

5.12 Children subject to Mental Health Act 1983 provisions, and those sentenced under Children and Young Persons Act 1933 s53, may have their liberty restricted without the application of s25.[13] Young people aged between 16 and 21 provided with accommodation in a community home may not have their liberty restricted nor may children subject to a child assessment order.[14]

5.13 Children detained by the police under Police and Criminal Evidence Act 1984 s38(6), and certain children remanded to care under Children and Young Persons Act 1969 s23, are subject to modified s25 criteria so that they may not be placed in or kept in secure accommodation:

> ... unless it appears that any accommodation other than that provided for the purpose of restricting liberty is inappropriate because –
> (a) the child is likely to abscond from other accommodation, or
> (b) the child is likely to injure himself or other people if he is kept in any such other accommodation.[15]

The practice

Local authority negotiations

5.14 Department of Health guidance stresses that local authorities should consider a placement in secure accommodation as part of the overall plan for the child, and they should comply with their s22 duties to consult with the young person as they would in any other case.[16] Practitioners should, therefore, ensure that the local authority has complied with this process by supporting their young clients in meetings, etc. It is also vital to explore alternatives with the local authority before the court application, reminding it of its duty to prevent the use of secure accommodation under Sch 2 para 7. Practitioners representing parents should approach the local authority in a similar manner.

Legal aid

5.15 Non-means- and non-merits-tested legal aid is available to children only.[17] The application is made on Form CLA5A. This is signed

13 Ibid, reg 5(1).
14 Ibid, reg 5(2).
15 Ibid, reg 6.
16 *Children Act 1989: Guidance and Regulations* (HMSO, 1991), Volume 3, Family Placements, para 8.7.
17 Civil Legal Aid (General) (Amendment No 2) Regulations 1991 SI No 2036.

CHECKLIST FOR INSTRUCTIONS

Child/young person
Full name and address
Date of birth
School/college
Out of school activities
Health
Behavioural/emotional difficulties
Name and address of GP/hospital doctor(s)
Name and address of psychiatrist/psychologist/child guidance

Looked after history
Length of time in accommodation or care
Reason for entry into accommodation or care
Number of placements
Nature of placements
Present placement
Relationship with members of staff
Relationship with other children/young people

Criteria
Frequency of absconding
Where does young person abscond to and for what lengths of time
Reasons for absconding
Exposure to risk: criminal, sexual, financial, self-harm
Young person's awareness of risks

Alternative placements
Views about alternatives and whether or not they have been tried before

by the solicitor certifying that the client is entitled to free legal aid. The solicitor is covered immediately for all costs relating to the proceedings provided that the form reaches the Legal Aid Board within three working days.

5.16 Parents will have to apply for means- and merits-tested legal aid in the normal way by completing Form CLA5, plus the forms CLA4A/

CLA4B and Form CLA3 (emergency legal aid). Recent guidance from the Legal Aid Board requires urgent emergency applications to be made by fax instead of by telephone as in the past.[18] Special fax forms FEA1 and FEA1a should be submitted to which the Legal Aid Board will respond within 24 hours. The normal postal forms should be submitted within five working days. The certificate will come into effect from the start of the case by virtue of the deeming provisions in the Civil Legal Aid (General) Regulations 1989.[19] An emergency certificate automatically lapses after a period of six weeks although it may be extended. It is also limited to a costs ceiling of £1,500 in London and £1,200 outside London which includes disbursements and counsel's fees.

5.17 In franchised firms solicitors may issue their own emergency certificates for all types of case provided that they are satisfied that the applicant has a good case, that s/he is financially eligible and that it is an emergency. Their costs are limited to up to £10,000.

The procedure

5.18 The same procedural rules apply whether an application is brought by the local authority or one of the other bodies authorised by regulations. The rules are similar in all three tiers of court and are governed by the Family Proceedings Courts (Children Act 1989) Rules 1991[20] (FPCR) and the Family Proceedings Rules 1991[21] (FPR). Rules about the allocation of court proceedings are contained in the Children Act (Allocation of Proceedings) Order 1991[22] (Allocation Order).

Which court?

5.19 All secure accommodation proceedings start in the family proceedings court of the magistrates' court, unless they arise out of a s37 investigation or there are other public law proceedings pending in another court, when they may commence in the court which directs the investigation or the court where the other proceedings are pending.[23]

18 See *Legal Aid Focus* No 17, March 1997.
19 SI No 339 reg 103(6).
20 SI No 1395 (L17).
21 SI No 1247 (L20).
22 SI No 1677.
23 Allocation Order art 3.

5.20 Proceedings may be transferred laterally from one court to another, or vertically up from the magistrates' court to the county court, from the county court to High Court, or down.

5.21 On application by a party or on the court's initiative, a case may be transferred from the magistrates' court to the county court where the magistrates' court considers it in the interests of the child, having regard to the principle in s1(2) (delay being prejudicial to the interests of the child) and:

a) whether the proceedings are exceptionally grave, important or complex;
b) whether it would be appropriate for those proceedings to be heard with other private law proceedings which are pending in another court; and
c) whether the transfer is likely to accelerate the determination of the proceedings.[24]

5.22 Cases may be transferred from the county court to the High Court where, having regard to the principle in s1(2), the court considers that the proceedings are appropriate for determination in the High Court and it is in the interests of the child.[25]

5.23 Where a magistrates' court refuses to transfer a case, any party to the proceedings may apply to the appropriate care centre,[26] which may transfer the case applying the same principles set out in Allocation Order art 7. It may decide to transfer the case to the High Court if it considers that the proceedings are appropriate for determination in the High Court and this is in the interests of the child.[27]

Application

5.24 All proceedings must start by way of application.[28] The statutory forms can be found in FPCR 1991 Sch 1 and FPR 1991 Appendix 1. The relevant forms are Form C1 plus supplemental Form C20. Each form requires detailed information including grounds, reasons for the application and directions sought, where appropriate.

---

24 Ibid, art 7(1).
25 Ibid, art 12.
26 FPCR 1991 Sch 2 column ii and FPR 1991 Appendix 3.
27 Ibid, art 9.
28 FPCR 1991 r4(1)(a) and FPR 1991 r4.4(1)(a).

Notice

5.25 One day's notice of hearing is required for all applications made on notice.[29]

Respondents

5.26 There are two categories of person who should be informed about the court proceedings:

a) those who have automatic party status, and
b) those who are entitled to notice so that they can apply for leave to be made parties if they so wish.[30]

5.27 Those who have automatic party status are:

– the child and any person with parental responsibility;
– where the child is in care, every person whom the local authority believes had parental responsibility before the making of the care order.

5.28 Any person who is caring for the child immediately before the proceedings is entitled to notice.

Service

5.29 There is no requirement for personal service, and service may be by delivery at, or by first class post to, the residence or last known residence of the person to be served.[31] Where solicitors are involved, service may be effected by fax. Where there is no solicitor or guardian ad litem, service of documents by children will be carried out by the court.

Representation of children

5.30 Secure accommodation proceedings are 'specified proceedings' for the purposes of CA 1989 s41. There is a presumption that guardians ad litem will be appointed unless the court does not consider it necessary to protect the interests of the child.

5.31 The guardian ad litem is required to safeguard the interests of

29 FPCR 1991 Sch 2 and FPR 1991 Appendix 3.
30 FPCR 1991 Sch 2 and FPR 1991 Appendix 3.
31 FPCR 1991 r4(8) and FPR 1991 r4.4(8).

the child by reference to the welfare checklist. The guardian is also required to:

- appoint a solicitor for the child;
- advise the court of the child's wishes and feelings;
- advise the court about whether the child has sufficient understanding to withhold consent to medical and other examinations;
- deal with various procedural matters such as timetabling, court venue and party status.[32]

Young people's views

5.32 Young people must be legally represented in s25 proceedings unless they refuse, or fail to apply for legal aid.[33] Where there is no solicitor, a guardian ad litem must appoint a solicitor and instruct that solicitor unless it appears to the solicitor that the young person is capable of giving instructions. If these conflict with those of the guardian, the young person's instructions prevail and the guardian must represent him/herself separately.[34] Where the young person is not instructing his/her solicitor directly, the guardian will represent the only opportunity for the child's wishes and feelings to be conveyed to the court.

Young person's attendance at court

5.33 The rules state that the proceedings must take place in the absence of the child if the court considers it is in the child's interests and s/he is represented by a guardian ad litem or solicitor. In considering this decision the court must hear representations from the guardian, solicitor and any child of sufficient understanding.[35] In *Re W (A Minor) (Secure Accommodation Order: Attendance at Court)*[36] the court said that where a child is unruly it can refuse the child's attendance in court. Solicitors should be prepared to make representations for young people in most circumstances since these are proceedings concerning the deprivation of the young person's liberty.

Alternative placements

5.34 The role of the guardian is very significant in advising the court

32 FPCR 1991 r11(1) to (5) and FPR 1991 r4.11(1) to (5).
33 CA 1989 s25(6).
34 FPCR 1991 rr11 and 12 and FPR 1991 rr4.11 and 4.12.
35 FPCR 1991 r16(2) and FPR 1991 r4.16(2).
36 [1994] 2 FLR 1092.

of alternatives to the making of a secure accommodation order and, in particular, alternatives to a locked placement. The guardian will have the expertise and the time to explore why alternative placements are not feasible and to seek out successful examples of open accommodation. S/he will also need seriously to consider the question of obtaining a second medical or psychiatric opinion, since most secure accommodation applications are made for treatment reasons and the local authority is likely to rely upon psychiatric evidence from the consultant to the secure unit. The court's leave must be obtained for such an examination for the purposes of expert evidence.[37]

Evidence

5.35 Written statements must be filed and served on all parties before the hearing or as directed by the court.[38] The statement should contain the evidence that will be given at court. The rules do not specify how long before the hearing and in an emergency it may not be possible to serve evidence much before the hearing itself. It should be remembered that the application form contains the reasons for the application itself.

5.36 The Children (Admissibility of Hearsay Evidence) Order 1993[39] applies to secure accommodation proceedings even though they are not defined in the CA 1989 as family proceedings.[40] This Order provides that hearsay evidence is admissible in all three tiers of court. The courts recognise the sensitivity of hearsay evidence and will still need to assess the weight and credibility of such evidence. In *Re W (Minors) (Wardship Evidence)*[41] the Court of Appeal said that in a case in which direct evidence could be produced hearsay evidence had to be regarded with grave caution, unless uncontroversial.

5.37 In addition to the evidence of their own client, practitioners will need to consider the question of lay and professional witnesses. Psychiatric evidence is usually required by the court to determine self-harm and threats to others[42] and practitioners may wish to obtain an

---

37 FPCR 1991 r18 and FPR 1991 r4.18.
38 FPCR 1991 r17 and FPR 1991 r4.17.
39 SI No 621.
40 See *R v Oxfordshire CC (Secure Accommodation Order)* [1992] 1 FLR 648, which held that secure accommodation proceedings must be treated as family proceedings.
41 [1990] 1 FLR 203.
42 *R v Oxfordshire CC (Secure Accommodation Order)* (above).

independent report. The court's leave must be obtained before doing so.[43] It may be necessary to agree the identity of any independent psychiatrist or other expert witness, since the court is unlikely to agree to the young person being examined more than once. Practitioners should advise their young clients aged 16 and 17 and those of 'sufficient understanding and intelligence' that the court may be able to override their refusal to give consent to a psychiatric assessment.[44]

5.38 Practitioners should be aware of the complex issue regarding disclosure of unfavourable reports. In *Re L (Police Investigation: Privilege)*[45] the House of Lords distinguished between solicitor/client privilege and litigation privilege attaching to third party reports in children cases. In that case the court had given leave for a report which was unfavourable to the mother and the House of Lords held that it should be disclosed. The court did not answer the question of whether there is a duty on lawyers to give voluntary disclosure of reports for which the court's leave has not been required. For further information about this subject, readers should refer to more detailed texts.

5.39 Professional witnesses usually require a witness summons to attend court. The FPR do not provide for the compulsory attendance of witnesses in non-matrimonial cases concerning children. Judges in the High Court have the power to order the attendance of potential witnesses. Procedure in the family proceedings court is governed by Magistrates' Courts Act 1980 s97(1) and by FPCR 1991 r33. These provide that a magistrate must issue a witness summons for the attendance of a witness or for the production of a document where there is evidence that the witness will not voluntarily attend. Professional witnesses usually accept service of the summons at court. Conduct money must be supplied to cover reasonable travel.

Directions and interim orders

5.40 The rules provide for directions to be made in all proceedings, determining timetabling, court allocation and other procedural matters.[46] These are likely to be made at the first hearing, at which time

---

43 FPCR 1991 r18 and FPR1991 r4.18.
44 See *Re R (A Minor) (Wardship: Medical Treatment)* [1992] 1 FLR 190 and *Re W* [1993] 1 FLR 1.
45 [1996] 1 FLR 731.
46 FPCR 1991 r14 and FPR 1991 r4.14.

the substantive hearing will be adjourned. The court may order an interim secure order for the period of the adjournment. Legal representatives should note that the criteria do not have to be satisfied on the making of an interim order, nor is there any time limit to its duration.[47]

47   CA 1989 s25(5).

CHAPTER 6

Non-judicial remedies and judicial review

6.1 All references in this chapter are to the Children Act (CA) 1989, unless otherwise stated.

Non-judicial remedies

6.2 As indicated throughout this part of the book, practitioners should always try to negotiate with the local authority for resolution of any dispute. The philosophy of working in partnership with parents and older children has led to a positive change in practice in local authorities, although this does vary between authorities. Where this approach fails and there is no legal remedy available, practitioners should consider invoking non-judicial measures, such as the statutory complaints procedure,[1] the default power of the Secretary of State,[2] complaint to the Local Government Ombudsman or political pressure through the involvement of a local councillor or an MP. With the exception of political pressure, none of these approaches can deal satisfactorily with an emergency since they take too long. Nevertheless, they are often worth pursuing in order to deal with matters of principle.

Complaints procedure

6.3 CA 1989 s26(3) provides that every local authority should establish a representations and complaints procedure about the discharge of any of its functions under CA 1989 Part III (covering duties in relation to children in need and looked after children). The procedure may be used by children in need or being looked after by the authority, parents (or others with parental responsibility), foster carers and

---

1 CA 1989 s26.
2 Ibid, s84.

any other person whom the local authority considers has a sufficient interest in the child's welfare. Minimal procedural requirements are set out in the Representation Procedure (Children) Regulations 1991.[3] These include strict time limits (often breached and not quick enough to deal with an emergency) and the involvement of an independent person at both stages of the process. Local authorities are obliged to publish their own procedures which practitioners should obtain for further information. The local authority must have due regard to any findings made but is not obliged to take any action as a consequence.

Section 84 default power of Secretary of State

6.4 CA 1989 s84 provides that if the Secretary of State is satisfied that the local authority has failed, without reasonable excuse, to comply with any of its duties under the Act, s/he may make a declaration to this effect containing directions for implementation. Any direction may be enforced by judicial review on application by the Secretary of State.

Local Government Ombudsman

6.5 The Local Government Ombudsman (LGO) deals with complaints about local authority maladministration resulting in injustice. It will not usually deal with matters that have not previously been through the local authority internal complaints procedures and hence is a time-consuming process.

Judicial review

6.6 Judicial review is the means whereby the High Court exercises its supervisory jurisdiction to review the legality of actions and decisions of administrative bodies. It is a remedy to examine how decisions are made: it is not an appeal on the merits of the case. It is not an emergency remedy, although it is possible to obtain early hearing dates in emergencies and to obtain injunctions.

---

3   SI No 894.

Grounds

Illegality

6.7 This ground covers an error of law or abuse of power, such as a failure to comply with the requirements of a statute or failure to exercise a discretion.

Irrationality

6.8 This forms the basis of the *Wednesbury* principles, ie, that the authority has taken into account irrelevant matters or has refused to take into account matters which it ought to take into account or has reached a conclusion so unreasonable that no authority could have come to it.[4] Case examples include the failure of a local authority to inform a guardian ad litem of its plans and listen to his views;[5] the decision of a local authority to disregard the views expressed by the magistrates' court;[6] and the decision of a local authority to close a children's home without first consulting the children living there.[7]

Impropriety

6.9 This constitutes acting in breach of the rules of natural justice. Case examples include the refusal of a local authority to continue with a rehabilitation plan of a child to his father because of unsubstantiated allegations against him;[8] where a local authority placed a child for adoption before care proceedings were concluded;[9] and where a local authority removed a person's name from the list of approved foster carers without giving that person an opportunity to answer allegations against him.[10]

Practice

6.10 Where the court quashes the decision it usually directs the authority to reconsider the matter in the appropriate manner. Sometimes it may remit the matter with a direction to reconsider the decision and reach a conclusion in accordance with the findings of the

---

4   *Associated Provincial Picture Houses Ltd v Wednesbury Corporation* [1948] 1 KB 223, CA.
5   *R v North Yorkshire CC, ex p M* [1989] 1 FLR 203.
6   *R v Waltham Forest LB ex p G* [1989] 2 FLR 138.
7   *R v Solihull MBC ex p C* [1984] FLR 363.
8   *R v Bedfordshire CC ex p C* [1987] 1 FLR 239.
9   *R v North Yorkshire CC ex p M* [1989] 1 FLR 203.
10 *R v Wandsworth LBC ex p P* (1989) 19 Fam Law 185.

court. Thus judicial review is not usually satisfactory in children's cases since, in the interests of the child, a decision is required on the merits of the case. Prior to the CA 1989, it was suggested that the judge who had given leave for judicial review proceedings should make a recommendation that wardship proceedings be instituted, although this was not binding on the local authority.[11] Now that local authorities are severely restricted in seeking leave to invoke the inherent jurisdiction this case can no longer be good law, although the court could recommend that the local authority apply for leave to seek an appropriate s8 order.

Legal aid

6.11 A civil legal aid application on Form CLA1, with the appropriate means form, plus an emergency legal aid certificate on Form CLA3, should be completed. Recent guidance from the Legal Aid Board requires urgent emergency applications to be made by fax instead of by telephone as in the past. Special fax forms FEA1 and FEA1a must be submitted to which the Legal Aid Board will respond in 24 hours. The normal postal forms should be submitted within five working days. In emergencies requiring the work to be done within the next few hours and there is no time to access a fax machine, a telephone application can still be made. The certificate will come into effect from the start of the case by virtue of the deeming provisions in the Civil Legal Aid (General) Regulations 1989.[12] An emergency certificate automatically lapses after a period of six weeks although it may be extended and is limited to costs of £1,500 in London and £1,200 outside London which include disbursements and counsel's fees.

6.12 In franchised firms solicitors may issue their own emergency certificates for all types of case provided that they are satisfied that the applicant has a good case, that s/he is financially eligible and that it is an emergency. Their costs are limited to £10,000.

6.13 Practitioners should be aware that the Legal Aid Board usually imposes a limitation to a legal aid certificate to obtaining counsel's opinion. This can cause delay in an emergency and can be avoided by suggesting to the Legal Aid Board that the limitation should be expressed to be for the purposes of obtaining leave and any interlocu-

11 *R v Newham LBC ex p McL* [1988] 1 FLR 416.
12 SI No 339 reg 103(6).

tory application. Such a proposal will need to be supported by a carefully prepared application setting out the arguments why an application for leave is likely to be successful.

Procedure

6.14 All applications for judicial review are made to the Queen's Bench Division of the High Court (although a request can be made for the matter to be heard by a Family Division judge). Procedure is governed by RSC Ord 53. No application for judicial review can be made without first obtaining the leave of the court.[13] The procedure described below relates to the initial application for leave and for an injunction. The substantive application is unlikely to be dealt with for some months and therefore falls outside the scope of this book.

Application

6.15 The application for leave must be made ex parte by filing in the Crown Office a notice on Form 86A. In an emergency it is possible to make this application outside London but the Crown Office should be consulted for guidance. The notice should include the relief sought and grounds, whether or not a hearing is required and a request that if leave is granted, the matter should be heard by a Family Division judge.[14] The notice should be accompanied by an affidavit in support citing all relevant facts and making full and frank disclosure.

Grant of leave

6.16 In emergencies there is an advantage in asking for an oral hearing since it usually means that the matter is dealt with more quickly. There is no right of appeal if leave is refused. A renewed application can be made but only if there has been no previous oral hearing. A notice of renewal on Form 86B must be lodged with the Crown Office.

Injunctions

6.17 An application for an injunction should be made at the same time as the application for leave. The affidavit in support of the application for leave should also contain all the relevant facts in support of the injunction. In order to obtain a hearing at the earliest possible opportunity, the Crown Office should be contacted by telephone,

13 Supreme Court Act 1981 s31(3) and RSC Ord 53 r3(1).
14 *R v Dover Magistrates' Court ex p Kidner* [1983] 1 All ER 475.

informed of the nature of the application and asked for a judge. It may be possible for an application to be made on oral evidence on the undertaking of the practitioner to file the papers within 24 hours.

6.18 *R v Kensington and Chelsea LBC ex p Hammell*[15] considered the principles involved in granting injunctions. An injunction can only be made where the court has granted leave (both applications can be made at the same time). In deciding whether to grant an injunction ex parte the judge should consider whether the urgency or other circumstances of the case warrant it. If not, the matter should be adjourned for a hearing on notice. In order to avoid two hearings, the applicant should give notice of any ex parte application to allow the respondent(s) to attend. A mandatory injunction should only be granted where a strong prima facie case is made out.

15 [1989] 1 All ER 1202.

Part III

Child abduction

In this part:

Introduction to Part III

The unilateral removal of children by one parent without the consent of the other parent (or settled carer) is an extremely distressing experience for children and parents alike. Frequently abductions occur because the separated parent feels excluded from the child's life and this is usually coupled with hostility and anger towards the carer. In some cases children are abducted because the separated parent has genuine concerns about the child's welfare and a lack of confidence in the legal system to deal with the issues appropriately. Whatever the motivation for abduction it represents a traumatic and possibly violent experience for a child resulting in sudden disturbance, removal from a settled home, familiar surroundings, school and friends and also from contact with the parent or settled carer.

Child abductions abroad are ever-increasing because of greater numbers of relationships between partners of different nationalities and easier and cheaper travel facilities. Government sources have estimated that there were over 208 Convention abductions in 1996 and unofficially those working in the field estimate that the numbers are more likely to be nearer to 1,000. Unless the child is removed to a country covered by one of two international conventions, wronged parents have no legal remedy in this country to secure his or her return. Their only option is to travel to the foreign country to institute proceedings in that jurisdiction. Not only is this time-consuming and expensive, but also, because of its own legal provisions, the foreign court may make decisions in favour of abducting parents.

There are three statutes relating to international child abduction and child abduction which occurs between countries within the UK. The Child Abduction Act (CAA) 1984 creates a criminal offence of taking children out of the UK without consent. The Child Abduction and Custody Act (CACA) 1985 gives effect to the Hague Convention on the Civil Aspects of International Child Abduction and the

79

European Convention on the Recognition and Enforcement of Decisions concerning Custody of Children. Lastly, the Family Law Act (FLA) 1986 introduced a system of registration and enforcement of decisions within the UK.

CHAPTER 7

Threat of abduction

7.1 All references in this chapter are to the Children Act (CA) 1989, unless otherwise stated.

Practical steps

7.2 The most effective way of combating abduction is to limit the opportunities for it to occur, although in practice this may be very difficult. Where possible, the resident parent or another trusted adult should be with the child at all possible times and older children should be given clear instructions what to do in the event of an attempted abduction. The school, childminder or nursery should be instructed in writing not to hand over the child to the feared abductor or to any other person not authorised by the carer and a photograph or good description should be supplied. However, it should be remembered that where there is no court order, people with parental responsibility have a right to take the child. In these circumstances, a prohibited steps order or an injunction should be sought.

Contact

7.3 Settling arrangements for appropriate contact are also vital. Parents separated from their children often feel uninvolved and resentful, which may lead them to act irresponsibly. The philosophy of shared parental responsibility is intended to enable non-carers to take a continuing interest and responsibility for their children, but it will undoubtedly take time for attitudes to change. Carers should try to find a balance between facilitating the involvement of the separated parent and protecting the child against unwarranted removal.

7.4 Where there is a real fear of abduction, contact should be stopped or arrangements made for supervision. Where an order for contact already exists, the carer should return to court for a variation of that order. It is very difficult to obtain orders stopping contact altogether, and the court is therefore more likely to make an order for supervised contact. Supervision is best done by a mutual friend or relative if possible. Alternatively, supervision may take place at a contact centre where contact can take place in a neutral setting with supervision on site. Where there is a family assistance order supervision may be provided by the court welfare officer but this cannot continue beyond the six-month life of the order and is likely to be much shorter.

Passports

7.5 It is very important to keep the child's passport in a safe place such as a safe or bank. It is also important to keep equally safe other documents which could enable the potential abductor to obtain a passport such as birth certificates or NHS cards, and photographs.

7.6 The Passport Agency will usually issue a passport to a child with the consent of either parent or a person acting in loco parentis. The mother's consent is required in relation to a non-marital child where the father does not have parental responsibility. Parents can ask the Passport Agency not to issue a passport for the child where any court in the UK has made one of the following orders:

- a prohibited steps order;
- an order confirming that the child's removal from the jurisdiction is contrary to the wishes of the court;
- a residence order to the objector;
- an order for custody, care and control under the Guardianship of Minors Act 1973, or in wardship and/or in addition an order upholding the objector's objections to the child having a passport or leaving the country;
- an order specifying that the objector's consent to the removal of the child from the jurisdiction is necessary.

7.7 A mother of a non-marital child may lodge an objection without a court order. The Passport Agency has no power to request the surrender of a passport where it has accepted an objection in relation to a passport which has already been issued to the child. It will note the name of the child for 12 months so that it can act on the objection if a further application for a passport is made.[1]

---

1 See 'Family Law Brief' [1994] Fam Law 651.

7.8 Before 1996 this procedure did not apply to the issue of a British visitor's passport. However, this type of passport now no longer exists.

7.9 Where a child has dual nationality, an abductor may try to obtain a non-British passport. There is unlikely to be any formal procedure for objection to the issue of a passport but it is worthwhile contacting the appropriate embassy or consulate, who may be prepared to take action voluntarily. The US Embassy and Canadian High Commission have systems in place and forms are available for completion.

Birth certificates

7.10 Where the child is a ward or the court has made a specific direction under CA 1989 s8, the Family Records Centre at the General Register Office in London will put a notation against a child's birth certificate so that solicitors acting for carers/parents will be informed should an attempt be made to obtain a duplicate. This information will also be passed on to the local registrar of births, marriages and deaths.[2]

Civil proceedings

7.11 Whether precautionary legal action can be taken depends on the availability of evidence to substantiate the fear of abduction. An underlying sense of disquiet is unlikely to be sufficient, but if there is a real fear that the child may be removed, legal action should be taken immediately. The court is unlikely to deal with such an application ex parte unless there is very strong evidence that the child is likely to be removed, or threats of violence or actual violence have been directed at the carer.

7.12 The following orders may be obtained:

a) prohibited steps order;
b) injunction under the inherent jurisdiction;
c) injunction in connection with an application for a residence order;
d) requirement of a financial bond or security in a case where leave is being given temporarily to remove the child from the jurisdiction (see para **7.27**).

7.13 The nature of the overall relief required will determine the type

---

2   Marriages and General Branch, Office of Population Censuses and Surveys.

of legal proceedings taken. In straightforward cases, a prohibited steps order will be sufficient. However, in many cases threats of abduction are coupled with violence, or threats of violence, against the resident parent and it is therefore necessary to seek protection for that parent as well as the child.

7.14 A prohibited steps order does not provide protection from violence for adults since it is an order that relates only to the exercise of parental responsibility. It is therefore necessary to seek a separate non-molestation order under the Family Law Act (FLA) 1996. Non-molestation and occupation orders are defined by both the CA 1989 and the FLA 1996 as family proceedings and so applications can be heard concurrently with an application for a s8 order. However, it is time-consuming in an emergency to have to prepare two separate sets of proceedings which are still governed by different rules of procedure and evidence.

7.15 Under the pre-CA 1989 law it was possible to obtain injunctive relief for an adult in proceedings for the protection of children. This principle has now been extended to CA 1989 proceedings. In *M v M (Residence Order: Ancillary Injunction)*[3] the court held that the inherent jurisdictions of the High Court and the county court to make ancillary injunctions for protection from violence extends to applications for residence orders without the need for separate proceedings to be issued.

Prohibited steps order

7.16 This is an order which provides that no step which could be taken by a parent in meeting parental responsibility for a child, and which is of a kind specified in the order, shall be taken by any person without the consent of the court. An application may be made:

- under the CA 1989 in its own right, or in conjunction with an application for a residence order;
- in new or existing divorce proceedings;
- in any other specified family proceedings,[4] such as an application for a non-molestation order or occupation order under the FLA 1996.

7.17 Parents, guardians and others with a residence order in their

3   (1994) Fam Law 440.
4   See CA 1989 s10(1).

favour may apply for any s8 order.[5] Any other person may apply for a prohibited steps order with the court's leave.[6] Leave is subject to a set of criteria set out in s10(9):

- the nature of the proposed application;
- the applicant's connection with the child;
- any risk that the proposed application might cause harm to the child.

7.18 In deciding whether to grant leave the court does not have to apply the welfare principle since the application itself does not relate to the child's upbringing.[7] In granting leave the court must decide whether the applicant has a good arguable case and not, as previously ruled, whether it is reasonably likely to succeed.[8] It has also been held that this does not necessarily preclude consideration of the child's welfare.[9]

7.19 In considering the substantive application, the child's welfare is the court's paramount consideration looked at in light of the welfare checklist in s1(3):

a) the ascertainable wishes and feelings of the child concerned (considered in light of his/her age and understanding);
b) his/her physical, emotional and educational needs;
c) the likely effect on him/her of any change in his/her circumstances;
d) his/her age, sex, background and any characteristics of his/hers which the court considers relevant;
e) any harm which s/he has suffered or is at risk of suffering;
f) how capable each of his/her parents, and any other person in relation to whom the court considers the question to be relevant, is of meeting his/her needs;
g) the range of powers available to the court under the CA 1989 in the proceedings in question.

7.20 The court must not make an order unless it is satisfied that doing so is better for the child than not making an order.[10] In cases of threatened abduction there can be no argument against making an order.

---

5   Ibid, s10(4).
6   Ibid, s10(2)(b).
7   *A v W (Minors) (Leave to Apply)* [1992] 2 FLR 154.
8   *Re M (Care: Contact: Grandmother's Application)* (1995) Fam Law 540.
9   *Re A (Section 8: Grandmother's Application)* [1995] 2 FLR 153.
10 CA 1989 s1(5).

Application for a residence order and an injunction

7.21 A residence order is an order settling the arrangements regarding the person with whom a child is to live. It may contain conditions and directions as to its implementation,[11] and it could be directed that the non-resident parent should not remove the child from the resident parent or should return the child if so removed. An application may be made in any family proceedings (see above). Parents, guardians and others with a residence order in their favour may apply for any s8 order.[12] Step-parents, relatives or friends with whom the child has lived for three out of the past five years, and others with certain specified consents, may also apply for a residence order.[13] Any other person may apply for an order with the court's leave.[14] The criteria for leave and the approach taken by the courts to such applications are set out above.

7.22 Rules of court allow for ex parte applications to be made.[15] In *Re G (Minors) (Ex Parte Interim Residence Order)*,[16] the Court of Appeal held that it is only in child abduction cases that an ex parte order is justified.

7.23 In *M v M (Residence Order: Ancillary Injunction)*[17] the court held that in proceedings for a residence order in the High Court or in the county court the court can grant an ancillary injunction in respect of an infringement of the exercise of parental responsibility or any other right in relation to the child.

Injunction in wardship or the inherent jurisdiction

7.24 The role of wardship has been substantially diminished with the implementation of the CA 1989. In most cases, it is unlikely that legal aid will be granted to take these proceedings. Wardship proceedings have been used where the fullest protection is needed, such as in relation to abduction to Middle Eastern countries. There is also a strong argument for wardship proceedings where the Child

11 Ibid, s11.
12 Ibid, s10(4).
13 Ibid, s10(5).
14 Ibid, s10(2)(b).
15 FPCR 1991 r4(4), as amended by Family Proceedings Courts (Miscellaneous Amendment) Rules 1992 SI No 2068 and FPR 1991 r4.4(4), as amended by Family Proceedings (Amendment No 2) Rules 1992 SI No 2067.
16 [1993] 1 FLR 910, CA.
17 (1994) Fam Law 440.

Abduction Act (CAA) 1984 does not apply because the child concerned is aged over 16, or there is no legal relationship between the child and carer (since leave to apply for a s8 order would have to be obtained), and there is a real fear of an immediate abduction abroad. The issue of a sealed copy of an originating summons serves as evidence for the institution of port alert procedures (see paras 7.36 to 7.39).

Removal from the jurisdiction

7.25 If it is feared that the child may be taken out of the country, an order should be obtained prohibiting removal from the jurisdiction. This prohibition is automatic in wardship and in relation to a residence order. Where appropriate, an order should also be obtained under the FLA 1986 s37 requiring the surrender of any UK passport issued to the child or containing particulars of the child. In such cases the court will usually notify the Passport Agency to prevent a replacement passport being issued.[18] The court has no jurisdiction to order the surrender of a foreign passport.

7.26 Solicitors may undertake to hold passports on behalf of their clients. If they undertake not to allow the passport to come into the possession of the passport holder, they owe a duty to the other parent to take reasonable care to keep the passport in their possession and to inform the other parent if for any reason it ceases to be in their possession.[19] See also the guidance issued by the Law Society: *Confidentiality and Privilege: Child abuse and abduction.*[20]

Requiring a surety or bond

7.27 It is possible to require a person to enter into a bond for a sum of money, to be forfeited on non-compliance with an order of the court. It is probably not possible for the court to make such an order without the agreement of the parent against whom it is sought, and so its usefulness may be limited. However, it could be used when a parent proposes to take the child out of jurisdiction in order to encourage that parent to return the child. If the child is not returned the bond is forfeited, and the carer could use the money to finance proceedings in the foreign country for the return of the child. This

18 *Practice Direction (Minor: Passport)* [1983] 2 All ER 253.
19 *Al-Kandari v J R Brown and Co* [1988] 1 All ER 833, CA.
20 The Law Society's Family Law Committee's Guidance for Solicitors Working with Guardians ad Litem, Annex C.

could be particularly helpful to those carers who have no residence order or who have a joint residence order with the parent proposing the trip. The parent taking the child abroad should agree to lodge the bond with the court.[21]

Criminal proceedings

7.28 CAA 1984 s1, as amended, provides that it is an offence for a person connected with a child under the age of 16 to take or send him/her out of the UK without the appropriate consent. A person is connected with the child if s/he is:

- a parent of the child;
- an unmarried father, where there are reasonable grounds for believing that he is the father;
- a guardian;
- a person in whose favour there is a residence order;
- a person who has a sole or joint custody order or an order for care and control.

7.29 'Appropriate consent' means the consent of the following:

- the child's mother;
- the child's father if he has parental responsibility;
- any person in whose favour a residence or custody order is in force;
- leave of the court.

7.30 No offence is committed by a person with a residence order in his/her favour and where the trip is for less than a month.[22] In addition, there are three defences against this offence:

a) where the alleged abductor believes that the person has consented or would consent if s/he was aware of all the circumstances;
b) where the alleged abductor has taken all reasonable steps to communicate with the other person but has been unable to do so;
c) where the person whose consent is required has unreasonably refused to consent. This defence does not apply where there is a residence order, a custody order or an order prohibiting removal made by the court in favour of the person refusing consent. This defence is likely to be used in disputes between divorced parents where there is no court order.

7.31 Both offences are arrestable but, significantly, there is no

21 *Re H (Minors) (Wardship: Surety)* [1991] 1 FLR 40.
22 CAA 1984 s1(4A).

requirement that the child be returned to the person from whom s/he was removed.

7.32 The issue of attempt is clearly relevant, given the limited circumstances in which an offence under s1 can be committed. Home Office Circular No 75/1984 gives guidance to chief police officers in relation to enforcement. It acknowledges that police intervention at the stage of attempt will offer a particularly effective means of enforcement. An arrest can be made at this stage only if the test of reasonable suspicion is met and:

> . . . whether that test is met may often depend among other things on the nature of the information which the officer contemplating the arrest has received beforehand. Whether or not arrest should be resorted to will depend on the urgency of the situation (eg if a suspect is about to embark) and will have regard to the highly charged emotions of the case.

7.33 Although the consent of the DPP is required to bring a prosecution, it is not envisaged that this should be obtained before an arrest or before charges are made.

7.34 In view of the sensitive nature of child abduction within the family, the circular advises:

> . . . so far as is possible it will be important in such circumstances for those who receive the complaint to make what enquiries are practicable to satisfy themselves that the complaint is "bona fide" before any action is initiated.

7.35 It is therefore extremely important that clear and detailed information is given to the police.

Port alert procedures

7.36 The purpose of port alert procedures is to alert immigration officers at all ports and airports to the possibility of a child being taken out of the country unlawfully. Requests for port alerts should be made to the police.[23] Port alert procedures can be invoked if the child is aged under 16 and there is reason to believe that an offence has been committed under the CAA 1984, or if an order has been made in wardship, s8, matrimonial, custody or custodianship proceedings containing a restriction on removal from the jurisdiction. Note that FLA 1996 s35 provides for orders restricting removal from the jurisdiction to Scotland and Northern Ireland.

23 *Practice Direction* [1986] 1 All ER 983; Home Office Circular No 21/1986.

7.37 The police will send out an 'All Ports' message on the Police National Computer. There will be local arrangements at ports between the police and the immigration service, and the child's name will be placed on an immigration 'stop list' held by immigration officers at points of exit. It will be placed on the stop list only where danger of removal is 'real and imminent'. 'Imminent' means within 48 hours and 'real' that the port stop is not being used as an insurance policy. The police are likely to want to know whether threats of removal have been made, whether the person has unsupervised contact and, if so, whether the child is with that person and whether the child has previously been returned on time.

7.38 The child will remain on the list for four weeks unless a further port alert application is made. Immigration officers do not have legal powers to detain or hold the child but they will notify the police, who do. In view of the numbers of children travelling abroad and the limitation on the immigration officer's powers to detain, this is by no means a foolproof system.

7.39 Practitioners should contact the duty detective inspector at the local police station on behalf of their client. The police must be satisfied that an offence has been attempted under the CAA 1984, or be shown evidence of court orders. In cases of extreme urgency, a sealed copy of an originating summons in wardship will suffice. They will also need as much of the following information as possible:

a) *child*: names, sex, date of birth, description, nationality, passport number (if known);
b) *person likely to remove*: names, age, description, nationality, passport number (if known), relationship to child and whether the child is likely to assist him/her;
c) *person applying for port alert*: names, relationship to child, nationality, telephone number, solicitor's name and telephone number, if appropriate;
d) *likely destination, time of travel and port of embarkation*;
e) *grounds for port alert*; and
f) *details of person to whom the child should be returned if intercepted.*

Legal aid

7.40 Means- and merits-tested legal aid applies to all s8 and wardship proceedings. Legal aid Forms CLA5 or CLA2A (in matrimonial or non-CA 1989 family proceedings), plus the appropriate means

CHECKLIST FOR INSTRUCTIONS

Wronged parent
Full name
Address and telephone number
Date of birth
Occupation (if any) and financial circumstances
Family composition
Medical or psychiatric problems (NB authority for report if necessary)
Criminal convictions (if any)
Relationship with abductor:
  Married/co-habiting/single: dates and length of relationship
Court proceedings in UK and abroad (if any): court names and dates

History of relationship
Events leading up to abduction
Children (see under abductor below)
Details of abductor (see below)
Abductor's relationship with children (see below) .
Threat of removal from jurisdiction? (see below)

Abductor
As for wronged parent (above) plus:
Other known addresses
NI number or name and address of present and previous employers
NHS number and name and address of GP
Passport number
Whether has travelled abroad and on what dates
Photograph or good description
Names and addresses of relatives and friends and other places frequented
Other known children, their addresses and involvement with him

Children
For each:
Full name
Address
Date of birth
Name and address of nursery/school, etc
Name and address of clinic and health visitor
Name and address of GP
Name and address of hospital (if any) with hospital number
Letter of authority
Name and address of social worker (if any) plus length of and reason for involvement
Photograph or good description

Abductor's relationship with child(ren)
Violence or other abuse to child
Quality of relationship with child
Childcare experience
Availability of relatives/friends for assistance

Future contact
Child's wishes and feelings
Arrangements, if any
Supervision by whom?

Threatened removal from jurisdiction
Abductor's country of origin and citizenship
Is child on abductor's passport?
When and why was threat of abduction made?
Have threats been made before?
Previous removal of child and in what circumstances
Friends or relatives in country of origin or elsewhere
Frequency of visits (if any) to country of origin or elsewhere, with dates
Resignation from employment and/or sale of property?
Property in country of origin or elsewhere

form, and Form CLA3 (emergency legal aid) must be completed. Recent guidance from the Legal Aid Board requires urgent emergency applications to be made by fax instead of the telephone as in the past. A fax application takes three hours to process although it can be expedited. In emergencies arising within the three-hour period a telephone application can still be made. The certificate will come into effect from the start of the case by virtue of the deeming provisions in the Civil Legal Aid (General) Regulations 1989.[24] An emergency certificate automatically lapses after a period of six weeks although it may be extended. It is also limited to a costs ceiling of £1,500 in London and £1,200 outside London which includes disbursements and counsel's fees.

7.41 The legal aid application requires applicants to give the reason(s) why they wish to start proceedings in a court other than the magistrates' court. Practitioners should therefore carefully assemble their arguments in support of an application in the higher courts (see below).[25]

7.42 In franchised firms solicitors may issue their own emergency certificates for all types of case provided that they are satisfied that the applicant has a good case, that s/he is financially eligible and that it is an emergency.

The procedure

Section 8 proceedings

7.43 The following describes the procedure to be followed in relation to any s8 proceedings. The procedural rules are similar in all three tiers of court and are governed by the Family Proceedings Courts Rules 1991[26] (FPCR) and the Family Proceedings Rules 1991[27] (FPR). Rules about the allocation of court proceedings are contained in the Children Act (Allocation of Proceedings) Order 1991[28] (Allocation Order).

Which court?

7.44 There is no legal prohibition on where cases may start, and cases may therefore be commenced in the family proceedings court of the

24 SI No 339 reg 103(6).
25 See also *Legal Aid Focus* No 19, May 1997, para 5.4.18.
26 SI No 1395 (L17).
27 SI No 1247 (L20).
28 SI No 1677.

magistrates' court, in the county court or in the High Court. However, legal aid forms state that cases should be tried in the family proceedings court unless a case can be made out for hearing at county court or High Court level. For enforcement purposes (see paras **8.4** to **8.19**) it will be necessary for all but the most straightforward cases to be heard in the county court and, in many cases, in the High Court.

7.45 At county court level there are 94 family hearing centres where private law cases may be heard, and 54 are also care centres which hear both private and public law cases. Applications in the county court must be started in the divorce county court but, if that court is not a family hearing centre and there is an opposed s8 application, the case must be transferred to a family hearing centre for trial.[29]

Application

7.46 All proceedings must start by way of application.[30] The statutory forms can be found in FPCR 1991 Sch 2 and FPR 1991 Appendix 3. The relevant form is Form C1 (general application). Detailed information is required, including the order sought and any directions, reasons for the application and plans for the future care of the child, including residence and contact.

Leave

7.47 The person seeking leave must complete Form C2 together with a draft of the application.[31] The request may be granted without a hearing, or a date may be fixed for a hearing on the issues. The rules do not specify a notice period and it may therefore take some time to obtain leave unless it is dealt with ex parte. Practitioners should make an application for leave with their substantive application in readiness so that this can be dealt with immediately thereafter if leave is granted.

Respondents

7.48 There are two categories of person who should be informed about the court proceedings:

a) those who have automatic party status; and
b) those who are entitled to notice so that they can apply for leave to be made parties if they so wish.[32]

29 Allocation Order art 16.
30 FPCR 1991 r4(1)(a) and FPR 1991 r4.4(1)(a).
31 FPCR 1991 r3(1) and FPR 1991 r4.3(1).
32 FPCR 1991 Sch 2 and FPR 1991 Appendix 3.

7.49 Those who have automatic party status are:

- any person believed to have parental responsibility;
- in applications to vary or discharge an order, those with party status in the original proceedings.

7.50 Those who are entitled to notice are:
- any person named in a court order with respect to the same child, unless not considered to be relevant to the application;
- any person believed to be a party to pending proceedings with respect to the same child, unless not considered to be relevant to the application;
- any person with whom the child has lived for at least three previous years.

Evidence

7.51 The rules state that written evidence is required in all proceedings. Signed statements containing the substance of the oral evidence which will be given must be filed and served on the parties, as directed by the court or before the hearing.[33] This together with the application form should be filed with the court at the time of the application or, if this is made over the telephone, within 24 hours of the application. However, there is a prohibition on the filing of evidence in s8 proceedings until such time as directed by the court.[34] This clearly poses a difficulty in ex parte applications. Statements should be prepared in the normal way and the court's leave obtained at the hearing of the application to file and serve the evidence.

Service

7.52 Ex parte orders should be served within 48 hours.[35] They should always be served personally; if this is not done problems may arise over enforcement.[36] In addition, the application itself must be served within 48 hours after the making of the order.[37]

Application for an injunction in wardship

7.53 See paras **8.34** to **8.38**.

---

33 FPCR 1991 r17 and FPR 1991 r4.17.
34 FPCR 1991 r17(5) and FPR 1991 r4.17(5).
35 FPCR 1991 r21 and FPR 1991 r4.21.
36 FPCR 1991 r4(8) and FPR 1991 r4.4(8).
37 FPCR 1991 r4(4)(ii) and FPR 1991 r4.4(4)(ii).

CHAPTER 8

Abduction within the United Kingdom

Abduction within England and Wales

Practical steps

8.1 Where the parent/carer is the mother of a non-marital child without parental responsibility to the father or has a residence order or custody order or is divorced with no order, then in law the parent has the right to collect the child from the parent who has abducted the child. It may be possible to persuade the police to attend at the address on the basis that a breach of the peace is likely to occur. In practice legal proceedings are almost always necessary.

Civil private law proceedings

8.2 Applications should be made for a residence order,[1] a specific issues order seeking the return of the child, and a prohibited steps order restraining future removal and, where appropriate, restraining removal from the jurisdiction. As an alternative, depending on the circumstances, applications may be made for injunctions in wardship, in the inherent jurisdiction or in connection with an application for a residence order. For further details see paras 7.11 to 7.27.

8.3 The key issue in these cases is enforcement. This is a complex issue determined by a number of factors: the likely response of the abductor to knowledge of the proceedings, whether the child's whereabouts are known or unknown, and also the tier of court in which the proceedings have been commenced (see paras **8.26** to **8.30**).

Enforcement

8.4 *Enforcement of residence orders.* Where a parent, or any other

---

1 These applications may now be made ex parte (see p 86).

person, is in breach of arrangements settled by a residence order, then provided that the order has been served it may be enforced under Magistrates' Courts Act 1980 s63(3) as if it were an order to him/her to produce the child. This provision empowers the court to fine the parent £50 each day s/he is in default or £2,000, or commit him/her to prison for a maximum of two months.

8.5 *Committal.*   In family cases committal should be a remedy of very last resort.[2] Its usefulness is in any event less appropriate in abduction cases, since the object is to secure the return of the child which can be sought by other means such as a seek and find order, a s34 order or by sequestration.

8.6 *Disclosure of whereabouts.*   By its inherent jurisdiction in wardship, the High Court may order any person whom it believes has relevant information about the child's whereabouts to disclose it to the court. Family Law Act (FLA) 1986 s33 gives statutory effect to this provision, extending its remit to all Part I orders (see paras **8.47** to **8.51**) and all three tiers of court. The court may order the information to be given to the applicant's solicitor or to the police. The court has the power to require the solicitor for an abducting parent to disclose his/her address and it has been held that the child's welfare overrides solicitor-client privilege.[3]

8.7 *Disclosure by government departments.*   There are formal arrangements with government departments, such as the Department of Health, the Department of Social Security, the Passport Agency and the Ministry of Defence, for disclosing addresses when tracing children whose whereabouts are unknown. This now covers all Part I orders under FLA 1986 although the 1989 Practice Direction has not been amended.[4] A court application for a court order should be made to the appropriate department. The following information about the abductor will be required:

a) full names and date of birth;
b) last known address and other known addresses;
c) names and addresses of all known relatives;
d) national insurance number;

2   *Ansah v Ansah* [1977] 2 WLR 760.
3   *Re B (Abduction: Disclosure)* [1995] 1 FLR 774.
4   *Practice Direction (Disclosure of Addresses by Government Departments)* [1989]
    1 All ER 765.

e) NHS number or name and address of GP;
f) passport number;
g) occupation;
h) whether s/he has travelled abroad and on what dates.

8.8 The court does not have the power to require the Child Support Agency (CSA) to disclose information but under a CA 1989 s8 application the court may request the CSA to disclose to the child the address of the father.[5]

8.9 It may be possible to obtain an order against an employer for disclosure of the abductor's national insurance number in order to use these tracing provisions. It may also be possible to obtain court orders against credit card companies and banks for tracing information.

8.10 It is now possible to obain orders from the court authorising British Telecom and other telecommunications companies to monitor telephone calls over their systems. Practitioners should first contact British Telecom's Network Special Investigations Unit[6] for advice about the type of facility that can be offered without a material interference to the abductor's service.[7]

8.11 *Publicity.* Where there is no idea of the child's whereabouts, publicity in the press and/or media may be the only means of locating the child. However, the decision to invoke publicity will be a tactical one determined by the circumstances of the case and the personality and behaviour of the abductor.

8.12 Administration of Justice Act 1960 s12, as amended, prohibits the publication of information relating to proceedings before any court sitting in private where the proceedings are brought under the inherent jurisdiction of the High Court or the CA 1989. However, publication of a court order is permitted.[8] Thus, it is lawful to give basic information about the child if no reference is made to the court proceedings or this is limited to disclosure about the order made. Where there is any doubt, the court's leave should be sought. It is always necessary to obtain the court's leave in relation to wards of court.

5   *Re C (A Minor: Child Support Agency: Disclosure)* [1995] 1 FLR 201.
6   British Telecom, PP721, Proctor House, 100–10 High Holborn, London WC1B 6LD, tel 0171 728 8311, fax 0171 728 8302.
7   For further information, see Christopher Atkinson and Michael Nicholls, *Tracing and recording telephone calls* [1996] Fam Law 104.
8   Administration of Justice Act 1960 s12(2).

8.13 *Seek and find orders.* An order to seek and find the child can be obtained only in wardship or proceedings under the inherent jurisdiction of the High Court. This empowers the Tipstaff to receive the child into his/her custody and bring him/her before the court, or to deliver the child to the person named in the order. A seek and find order is usually backed up with a bench warrant which gives the Tipstaff the authority to arrest the abductor in the event of non-compliance with the order.

8.14 There is a close relationship between the Tipstaff and the police, and in practice it is the police who are responsible for executing seek and find orders, but only under the authority of the Tipstaff. The police have the power of entry and search, provided there is reasonable suspicion that the child is present, and the child may be removed by force.

8.15 *Search and recovery orders.* FLA 1986 s34 applies to all Part I orders (these are mainly CA 1989 s8 orders but see also para 8.47) and to all three tiers of court. FLA 1986 s34(1) provides that, when a person is required by a Part I order, or by an order for the enforcement of a Part I order, to give up a child to another person and the court is satisfied that the child has not been given up the court may authorise an officer of the court (bailiff in the county court, Tipstaff in the High Court) or a constable to take charge of the child and hand him/her to the carer. FLA 1986 s34(2) provides that in discharging this authority the officer may enter and search premises where the child is believed to be and use such force as may be necessary.

8.16 A residence order may contain a direction that the child be returned.[9] Otherwise it does not constitute an order requiring the child to be given up unless an application is made under CA 1989 s14 for its enforcement. In such circumstances it is necessary to prove service.[10] It is unclear whether it is necessary to do so in other cases but it would be prudent if possible.

8.17 The requirement to give up a child may also apply to breach of a contact order. For the court to be satisfied that the child has not been given up the terms of the requirement must be clear. It may be difficult for a parent to prove that informal arrangements made following an order for reasonable contact have been breached unless s/he can show that the period of withholding the child has become unreasonable in the circumstances of that case.

---

9   *Re B (A Minor) (Residence Order: Ex Parte)* [1992] 2 FLR 1.
10 See CA 1989 s14(2).

8.18 It is unclear how far the police may be willing to assist in implementing a FLA 1986 s34 order, and this therefore gives rise to concern about applications in the family proceedings court. In *R v Chief Constable of Cheshire ex p K*[11] the Court of Appeal held that a police force is entitled as a matter of policy to decline to intervene to enforce custody orders. That case did not concern a FLA 1986 s34 order although it was discussed. It is difficult to see how the police can decline to act given the statutory requirement of s34.

8.19 *Sequestration.* Sequestration is a High Court remedy for breach of a High Court order, by which sequestrators are authorised to hold the contemnor's property until such time as the order is complied with. It is a very useful remedy where the abductor has financial means, particularly in relation to threatened abduction abroad, since it may impede the plans of an abductor with assets in this country. It is also possible for the court to allow the applicant/wronged parent to take the monies which are subject to the sequestration and use them to commence proceedings in the country where the child has been taken. The sequestrators can raise money against the security of the property by way of rents, or a loan to fund the overseas litigation. It has also been held that there is a power to sell the property.[12]

Civil public law proceedings

8.20 It has been suggested that the emergency protection order (EPO) procedure could be a useful and an appropriate remedy in certain child abduction cases. It is open for *any person* to make an application for an EPO and the court may make an order if, but only if, it is satisfied that there is reasonable cause to believe that the child is likely to suffer significant harm if s/he is not removed to accommodation provided by or on behalf of the applicant.[13] Further, civil legal aid application Form CLA5 does not preclude applicants, as distinct from respondents, from seeking legal aid for this purpose.

8.21 An EPO 'operates as a direction to any person who is in a position to do so to comply with any request to produce the child to the applicant'.[14] There are additional provisions giving applicants the right to enter and search premises[15] and, where that person has been

11 [1990] 1 FLR 70.
12 *Mir v Mir* (1992) 22 Fam Law 378.
13 CA 1989 s44(1)(a).
14 Ibid, s44(4)(a).
15 Ibid, s48(3).

refused entry to the premises or access to the child, to apply for a warrant empowering a police officer to assist the applicant, using reasonable force if necessary.[16] For further details about EPOs, see Chapter 1.

8.22 It may be argued that it is generally not appropriate to use the public law to deal with child abduction. Any application would have to be limited to those cases where there was some evidence that the child was at risk of significant harm (and while this may be a factor in some child abduction cases, the greater risk is that the abductor will move on from detection). The enforcement remedies in CA 1989 s48(3) and (9), although initially attractive, are virtually identical to those provided by FLA 1986 s34 (see para **8.43**). Magistrates are also likely to be very wary of using this procedure to deal with child abduction cases.

8.23 However, where it is not possible to represent a client, or arrange alternative representation, it may be appropriate to advise him/her of this procedure if the grounds are satisfied so that s/he may make an application in person. The procedure for all CA 1989 applications is more straightforward, whereas applications under the FLA 1986 are by summons and affidavit. An additional attraction is the fact that it is an offence intentionally to obstruct any person exercising the powers under an EPO.[17] It is possible that a police officer might accompany the parent to enforce the EPO, without a warrant, but this is unlikely.

Criminal proceedings

8.24 The Child Abduction Act (CAA) 1984 (see paras 7.28 to 7.35) does not apply to abductions within the UK. However, there is a common-law offence of kidnapping which was considered by the House of Lords in 1984 in *R v D*.[18] The court held that the offence may be committed by a parent against his/her own child aged under 18 if the child is taken by force or fraud without lawful excuse and without the child's consent. In the case of an older child, it would be a matter of fact for the jury to decide whether the child had sufficient understanding and intelligence to give a valid consent. Lord Brandon considered the relationship between the civil and criminal law and said that it

---

16 Ibid, s48(9).
17 Liable to a fine not exceeding level 3 on the standard scale; see CA 1989 ss44(15) and 48(7).
18 [1984] AC 778.

was desirable as a matter of policy that such parents be dealt with by civil proceedings rather than by a criminal prosecution, save in exceptional cases 'where the conduct of the parent concerned is so bad that an ordinary, right-thinking person would immediately and without hesitation regard it as criminal in nature'. The consent of the Director of Public Prosecutions is required in most cases before a prosecution may be brought.[19]

8.25   Where the abduction falls within the offences of the CAA 1984, it is wrong also to bring charges of kidnapping.[20]

The practice

Which proceedings?

8.26 In the past, wardship proceedings were considered to be the most effective means of retrieving abducted children. The need for wardship diminished with the introduction of the FLA 1986, which gave the county court and magistrates' court equivalent powers to the High Court in relation to the disclosure of the whereabouts of abducted children and their search and return (see paras **8.13** to **8.18**). Further, in 1989 a Practice Direction[21] in relation to the location of missing children, by means of disclosure of addresses by Government departments, extended its remit from orders in wardship to all custody orders. Procedural arrangements introduced by the CA 1989 have extended the system of duty judges dealing with urgent business out of court hours, from the High Court to the county court.

8.27 The provisions of the CA 1989 have further eroded the need to use wardship proceedings, and there appear to be only limited circumstances in which wardship can be justified. Where an abducted child is over the age of 16 or there is no legal relationship with the carer, and there is a very serious risk of the child being immediately removed from the jurisdiction, it may be necessary to act more swiftly than is possible by making an court application before a duty judge. A sealed copy of an originating summons in wardship is sufficient for the purposes of the police to set in motion a port alert warning. It is unclear whether the power of the High Court in wardship (or under its inherent jurisdiction) to make a bench warrant to secure the arrest

---

19   CAA 1984 s5.
20   *R v G* (1990) *Times* 9 November.
21   *Practice Direction* (*Disclosures of Addresses by Government Departments*) [1989] 1 All ER 765.

of an abductor in the event of non-compliance with a seek and find order extends to other High Court family proceedings, or whether such proceedings are strictly limited by the provisions of the FLA 1986.

8.28 Nonetheless, there continue to be advantages in using the High Court. First, from their experience in wardship, Family Division judges are more familiar with the issues raised by child abduction cases. Secondly, in obtaining orders for the return of children, there are advantages in using the Tipstaff (see para **8.14**). S/he has a long-standing relationship with the police in locating abducted children and enforcing seek and find orders. Since FLA 1986 s34 orders for the search and return of the child (see paras **8.41** and **8.42**) are rarely used, county court bailiffs are less likely to be familiar with their operation. Furthermore, because of their usual functions in enforcing debts and other property matters, they are unlikely to exercise the sensitivity and awareness needed in child abduction work. In the magistrates' courts FLA 1986 s34 orders are enforced by the police, but this only *authorises* them to hand over the child and they may decline to do so if satisfied that the child is adequately cared for (see para **8.44**). Last but not least, the remedy of sequestration is only available in the High Court. This is becoming increasingly useful in relation to abductors with assets, and may be vital in preventing a removal abroad.

Urgent business scheme

8.29 The High Court and county court have their own urgent business schemes, whereby urgent applications may be made outside normal working hours. In the past each High Court and county court circuit had its own urgent business officer who was responsible for arranging its own listing. On receiving an enquiry, the urgent business officer would determine the level of judge, ie, High Court or circuit judge, and would then allocate the case. This system is presently being updated to provide a national centralised service. Practitioners should make enquiries of the Civil and Business Branch of the Court Service Agency for further details.[22]

8.30 There is an urgent business scheme for private law applications at the Inner London family proceedings court. This is likely to be the case around the country, but there may be variations and enquiries should be made of the local clerk.

---

22 South Side, 105 Victoria Street, London SW1E 6QT, tel 0171 210 1686.

Checklist for instructions

8.31 See p 91.

Legal aid

8.32 See para 7.40. Note also should be taken of recent Legal Aid Board guidance which states that legal aid is unlikely to be granted in relation to FLA 1986 ss33 and 34 proceedings where there are threats of international child abduction and where a port alert can be put in place by the police and where the child has already been removed from the jurisdiction unless an order would be likely to lead to the return of the child.[23] Legal aid is likely to be granted where no other remedy is appropriate such as involving the police or social services.

The procedure

Application for CA 1989 s8 order

8.33 See para 7.43.

Injunction in wardship or the inherent jurisdiction

8.34 *Application.*   Wardship proceedings are governed by the Family Proceedings Rules 1991[24] (FPR) Part V, and also by the Rules of the Supreme Court (RSC). Proceedings under the inherent jurisdiction should also follow these rules.

8.35 The proceedings are started by originating summons, which contains information about the parties (and their interest in the child), a statement of claim, the child's date of birth and his/her whereabouts (or that the plaintiff is unaware of the child's whereabouts).[25] The following documents should be filed with the court:

– originating summons, plus copy;
– notice of first appointment, plus copy;
– certificate as to other pleadings;
– fee; and
– birth certificate (may be filed at first appointment).

8.36 An application for an injunction should be by summons supported by affidavit.[26]

23 *Legal Aid Focus* No 19, May 1997 paras 5.3.2.2.3 and 5.3.2.4.
24 SI No 1247 (L20).
25 FPR 1991 rr5.6 and 5.7.
26 RSC Ord 29 r1.

8.37 *Notice.* The summons should be served personally[27] giving two days' notice.[28] In very urgent ex parte cases, applications may be made on oral evidence only[29] and an injunction may be granted before the issue of proceedings on the advocate's undertaking to do so thereafter.[30]

8.38 *Service.* An injunction should be served by personal service.[31] Thought should be given as to how to effect service and whether the additional protection of the court is required through a seek and find order. The Tipstaff/police will not serve the injunction when enforcing a seek and find order, and so if there is any question of committal proceedings the order must be served. Where it has not been possible to effect personal service, an application for substituted service can be made, supported by an affidavit of attempts.[32]

Enforcement

Disclosure of whereabouts

8.39 In the High Court and county court the application should be made by summons to a judge in the court that made the original order. Depending on the circumstances, an ex parte application may be made. The order should be endorsed with a penal notice so that in the event of non-compliance it may enforced by means of committal proceedings.

8.40 In a magistrates' court the penalty for failure to obey the order is a fine of up to £2,000 or a committal to prison for up to two months.[33] This penalty must be clearly marked as part of the order.

Seek and find orders

8.41 An application should be made by summons supported by affidavit (this need not be a separate affidavit from the one supporting the injunction summons). This application is made at the time of the substantive application. In very grave emergencies the court may dispense with these formalities.

---

27 Ibid, Ord 65 r1.
28 Ibid, Ord 32 r3.
29 Ibid, Ord 29 r1(3).
30 *Re N (Infants) (No 2)* [1967] Ch 512; RSC Ord 29 r1(3).
31 RSC Ord 65 r1.
32 Ibid, Ord 45 r47.
33 Magistrates' Courts Act 1980 s63(3).

8.42 Implementation of a seek and find order is a delicate matter and it is vital that practitioners keep in touch with the Tipstaff's department to provide up-to-date information, find out what progress has been made and suggest ways in which the order might best be enforced. Practitioners should also be aware that the police are not empowered to make enquiries of individuals about the child's whereabouts (other than through the normal Police National Computer procedure), and so where a child's whereabouts are unknown, it may be appropriate to instruct an enquiry agent whose investigations can be conducted in parallel with the Tipstaff.

Section 34 orders
8.43 In the High Court and county court the application should be made to a judge, supported by affidavit where possible. An ex parte application may be made in an emergency.

8.44 As with seek and find orders, implementation of FLA 1986 s34 orders is a delicate matter and close contact should be kept with the relevant officer. Where there is a possibility of the abductor returning the child voluntarily on receipt of such an order, it is possible that the order may be phrased as an 'unless' order, ie, that unless the child is delivered by a certain date and time the officer is authorised to search for and recover him/her. Such an approach is likely to cause less resentment on the part of the abducting parent, and so may offer better protection for the child in the future.

Magistrates' courts procedure
8.45 A summons should be issued, alleging the breach and requiring an appearance to show cause why an order requiring the payment of money, or a committal to prison, should not be made.

Sequestration
8.46 Procedure is governed by RSC Ords 45 and 46. The abductor must have been served with the order (unless an order was made dispensing with service) and in time for him/her to comply. Leave to issue a writ of sequestration must be made on notice of motion before a judge, although the court may dispense with service or order substituted service. The application must be supported by affidavit, which should include proof of service and state the facts of disobedience. The application and affidavit must be served personally. The matter may be heard in chambers at the discretion of the judge.

Abduction to Scotland and Northern Ireland

Family Law Act 1986

8.47 FLA 1986 s25 provides that a Part I order made in any part of the UK concerning a child aged under 16 can be recognised in any other part of the UK. This applies to any Part I order made after 4 April 1988. In England and Wales, a Part I order covers:

– a CA 1989 s8 order;
– orders for care and control, contact or relating to education under the inherent jurisdiction;
– any pre-CA 1989 custody order.

8.48 So as to avoid the possibility of more than one court within the UK deciding custody and the problems of conflicting judgments, the FLA 1986 created a statutory code for assuming jurisdiction. Except for matrimonial proceedings, the basic principle is that the court can make a Part I order only if, on the date of application, the child is either habitually resident in England and Wales or present in England and Wales and not habitually resident in any other part of the UK.[34] For a child who is a ward of court, there is an alternative condition: an order can be made if the ward is present in England and Wales and the High Court considers that immediate exercise of its powers is necessary for the child's protection. Advisers should consult the Act for further guidance on these complex provisions.

8.49 Under FLA 1986 s27, any person who has rights conferred by a Part I order may apply to the court which made the order, for its registration in another part of the UK. The appropriate court for registration in England Wales and Northern Ireland is the High Court and in Scotland, the Court of Session. Where a Part I order has been registered, the court in which it is registered has the same powers of enforcement as if it had itself made the order.[35]

8.50 Practitioners should note that registration itself is not sufficient for enforcement purposes; it is also necessary to submit a specific application for enforcement. The court may not refuse to register or enforce an order.

8.51 However, it may stay the proceedings on the application of any person with an interest in the matter who satisfies the court that s/he

---

34 FLA 1986 s3.
35 Ibid, s29(1).

has taken or intends to take other proceedings in the UK or elsewhere as a result of which the order may cease to have effect or have a different effect. The stay may be removed if there has been unreasonable delay in taking these proceedings or those proceedings have been concluded and have no effect on the registered order.[36] This provision seems to contemplate proceedings being taken elsewhere by someone who may not be a party, for example: a non-resident father abducts the child to Scotland; the mother applies for registration and enforcement; the grandparents then apply for leave to apply for a residence order in the original proceedings on the ground that the mother does not look after the child properly.

Legal aid

8.52 An amendment to the legal aid certificate will be required to register an order under the FLA 1986. This can be dealt with by fax, or over the telephone in an acute emergency. However, it will be necessary to apply for a legal aid certificate in Scotland or Northern Ireland in order to enforce the order.

Procedure

8.53 Court rules describe the procedure for registration[37] in the High Court and county court.

8.54 The applicant should file with the court which made the order:

a) a certified copy of the order;
b) a copy of any order which may have varied any of the terms;
c) the affidavit of the applicant plus copy stating:
   (i) name and address of applicant and interest under the order;
   (ii) name and date of birth of child, his/her whereabouts or suspected whereabouts and name of person with whom s/he is alleged to be;
   (iii) name and address of any other person known to have an interest under the order and whether this has been served on him/her;
   (iv) where the order is to be registered;
   (v) whether the order is in force;
   (vi) whether and, if so, where the order is already registered;

---

36 Ibid, s30.
37 FPR 1991 Part VII rr7.7–7.15 and 10.6.

(vii) details of any order affecting the child in the jurisdiction where it is to be registered.

8.55 The copy documents are sent to the High Court or Court of Session.

8.56 The FLA 1986 provides for interim directions to be given at any time to secure the welfare of the child or to prevent changes in circumstances relevant to the application. This clearly contemplates the possibility of the abducting parent attempting to frustrate the operation of the Act by removing the child again, and possibly out of that jurisdiction. An ex parte application is therefore likely to be made in which restraining orders may be sought, together with a seek and find order (see paras **8.41** and **8.42**).

CHAPTER 9

International child abduction

9.1 Practitioners may be asked to act for parents whose children have been abducted and for those who have abducted their children and brought them to this country or have failed to return them following a period of agreed contact. These children may be British or overseas nationals.

9.2 International child abduction is a complex area which requires a high level of expertise. The Lord Chancellor's Department Child Abduction Unit is responsible for a designated panel of experienced solicitors which it instructs to take action under the Child Abduction and Custody Act (CACA) 1985 for parents whose children have been abducted to the UK. Any solicitor may act for such parents in relation to non-convention cases (although there is usually little that can be done) or for abductors, although practitioners should consider whether there is sufficient support and expertise within the firm before taking on such cases.

Convention countries

9.3 The CACA 1985 implements two international conventions on child abduction which were signed in 1980: the Hague Convention on the Civil Aspects of International Child Abduction and the European Convention on Recognition and Enforcement of Decisions concerning Custody of Children. The purpose of each Convention is to secure the summary return of children to their country of habitual residence and to ensure that international disputes over access are dealt with in the country of original jurisdiction. Both conventions actively discourage the courts from looking at the merits of the case except in particular circumstances and unlike all other legislation dealing with the upbringing of children, the child's welfare is not paramount.

9.4 The CACA 1985 covers the whole of the UK and Isle of Man.[1] The administrative body which initially deals with applications under each convention is known as the central authority. In the UK the Lord Chancellor's Department (LCD) deals with all incoming applications and with outgoing applications for England, Wales and Northern Ireland. The Scottish Office is responsible for outgoing applications from Scotland.

9.5 The duties of the central authority are broadly similar under both conventions.[2] It must discover the whereabouts of the child, prevent further harm to the child or prejudice to interested parties by taking provisional measures, secure the voluntary return of the child (omitted under the European Convention) or to bring about an amicable resolution of issues, exchange information relating to the social background of the child, bring judicial or administrative proceedings to secure the return of the child or to make arrangements for access and to provide legal aid. The European Convention also provides that where enforcement is refused and the wronged parent wishes to bring custody proceedings in the overseas state, the central authority has a discretion to secure legal representation to institute legal proceedings.[3]

9.6 The English courts have developed a considerable body of case-law about many features of the conventions but these cases are not binding on foreign courts. However, parties to the Hague Convention have the opportunity to discuss issues arising from the operation of the Hague Convention through a Special Commission that meets regularly.

9.7 The following is a brief account of the main articles of the Convention. For further information practitioners should refer to more detailed texts and the case-law. Where approached by an innocent parent an immediate referral should be made to the Child Abduction Unit of the LCD which will arrange for contact with the relevant central authority.

Hague Convention

Contracting states

9.8 Those countries which have ratified the Hague Convention

1   Child Abduction and Custody Act 1985 (Isle of Man) Order 1994 SI No 2799.
2   Hague Convention art 7 and European Convention art 5.
3   Art 5(4).

(known as the 'contracting states'), with dates of ratification in brackets, are: Argentina (1.6.91), Australia (1.1.87), Austria (1.10.88), the Bahamas (1.1.94), Belize (1.10.89), Bosnia-Herzegovina (7.4.92), Canada (1.8.86), Chile (1.5.94), Columbia (1.3.96), Croatia (1.12.91), Cyprus (1.2.95), Denmark (1.7.91), Ecuador (1.6.92), Finland (1.8.94), France (1.9.86), Germany (1.12.90), Greece (1.6.93), Honduras (1.3.94), Hungary (1.10.91), Iceland (1.11.96), Irish Republic (1.10.91), Israel (1.9.86), Italy (1.5.95), Luxembourg (1.1.87), Macedonia (1.12.91), Mauritius (1.6.93), Mexico (1.10.91), Monaco (1.2.93), the Netherlands (1.1.90), New Zealand (1.10.91), Norway (1.4.89), Panama (1.12.91), Poland (1.11.92), Portugal (1.8.86), Roumania (1.2.93), Slovenia (1.6.94), St Kitts and Nevis (1.8.94), Spain (1.9.87), Sweden (1.6.89), Switzerland (1.8.86), the USA (1.7.88), Venezuela (1.1.97), Yugoslavia (27.2.92) and Zimbabwe (1.7.95).[4]

Main purpose

9.9 The Convention covers any child under the age of 16 and states that:[5]

> The removal or retention of a child is to be considered wrongful where–
> (a) it is in breach of rights of custody attributed to a person, an institution or any other body, either jointly or alone, under the law of the State in which the child was habitually resident immediately before the removal or retention; and
> (b) at the time of removal or retention those rights were actually exercised . . . Or would have been . . . but for the removal . . . .
> The rights of custody . . . may arise in particular by operation of law or by reason of a judicial or administrative decision or by reason of an agreement having legal effect under the law of that State.

9.10 A number of English cases have explored the meaning of 'rights of custody', 'habitual residence' and 'wrongful removal'.

9.11 *Rights of custody.* This is defined in art 5 and includes rights relating to the actual care of the child and, in particular, the right to determine the child's place of residence. Possession of a court order is not a requirement under this Convention. In addition to those holding court orders, married parents, divorced parents, unmarried mothers and unmarried fathers with parental responsibility agreements are eligible to invoke the Convention immediately.

---

4 Child Abduction and Custody (Parties to Conventions) Order 1986 SI No 1159, as amended by SI 1996 No 2874.
5 Art 3.

9.12 *Habitual residence.* The phrase is to be given its ordinary, everyday meaning[6] and is a question of fact to be decided by reference to all the circumstances of the particular case.[7] It is easier to renounce habitual residence than it is to acquire a new one which requires an appreciable period of time and a settled intention.[8] The habitual residence of a child follows that of the person(s) who has parental responsibility. When parents separate, the child's habitual residence follows that of the parent with whom s/he lives providing that there is legal authority for this to take place such as by agreement or order of the court.[9]

9.13 *Wrongful removal.* Removal is from the jurisdiction of the courts of habitual residence. 'Retention' is retention outside that jurisdiction, for example, after an agreed period of absence. They are mutually exclusive events and occur only on or after the date of ratification of the Convention by the relevant contracting state.[10] Art 15 states that the wronged parent may be requested to obtain a decision from the country of habitual residence, stating that the removal was wrongful within the meaning of the Convention. This is achieved by the High Court in England or the Court of Session in Scotland.[11]

Duty to return

9.14 The judicial or administrative authority (usually the court but may be some other decision-making forum) must order the return of the child if the application is made within 12 months. The only exception to this rule is if one of the provisions in art 13 applies (see below). If the application is made after 12 months, the authority must order return unless it can be shown that the child is now settled in his/her new environment.[12]

Exceptions to immediate return

9.15 Article 13 states that the judicial or administrative authority is not bound to order the return of the child in any one of the following circumstances:

6   *C v S (A Minor: Abduction: Illegitimate Child)* [1990] 2 All ER 961.
7   *V v B (A Minor) (Abduction)* [1991] 1 FLR 266.
8   *C v S (A Minor: Abduction: Illegitimate Child)* [1990] 2 All ER 961.
9   *Re O (A Minor) (Child Abduction: Habitual Residence)* [1995] 2 FLR 594.
10 *Re H (Minors) (Abduction: Custody Rights)* [1991] 3 All ER 230.
11 CACA 1985 s8.
12 Art 12.

a) the wronged parent consented to the removal or subsequently acquiesced in the removal or retention;
b) there is grave risk that his/her return would expose the child to physical or psychological harm or otherwise place the child in an intolerable situation; or
c) the child objects to being returned and has attained an age and degree of maturity at which it is appropriate to take account of his/her views.

9.16 There is a large body of English case-law examining the meaning of art 13(b) and (c). The child's welfare is not paramount and on the whole these provisions have been interpreted restrictively. The court has said that these articles are 'merely a discretionary release from an otherwise absolute obligation to return the child if the removal from his country of residence is . . . wrongful'.[13]

Grave risk

9.17 The risk of physical or psychological harm must be weighty, substantial and not trivial.[14] Intolerable situation must bear similarity in seriousness to grave risk of harm.[15] In one case the court did not accept that an allegation of sexual abuse was sufficient to justify an order for no return or in another that the child would be in an intolerable situation where a mother had no immigration status, would be unable to support herself and, therefore, would not be able to exercise any possession rights as defined by a Texan court.[16] However, in another case the court accepted that the child would be exposed to physical and psychological harm as a result of the father's violence towards the child and intimidation and harassment of the mother which affected the child.[17]

9.18 In many cases the English courts accept undertakings by the applicant in order to alleviate the evidence or risk. In *Re M (Minors) (Abduction: Undertakings)*[18] the Court of Appeal said that undertakings should have an effect until the court of habitual residence can hear the case and the English court must be careful not to usurp the function of that court and must not be too detailed so that their

---

13 *Re G (A Minor: Abduction)* [1989] 2 FLR 475.
14 *Re A (A Minor) (Abduction)* [1988] 1 FLR 365.
15 *Re N (Minors) (Abduction)* [1991] 1 FLR 413.
16 *N v N (Abduction: Article 13 Defence)* [1995] 1 FLR 104 and *Re K (Abduction: Psychological Harm)* [1995] 2 FLR 550.
17 *Re F (A Minor) (Abduction: Custody Rights Abroad)* [1995] 2 FLR 31.
18 [1994] 1 FLR 1021.

implementation gets bogged down in a series of protracted hearings and investigations. It should be remembered that undertakings made in this country are not binding on foreign courts.

The child's objections

9.19 It is up to the trial judge to determine the child's wishes and his/her degree of maturity in relation to a permanent return to the country of habitual residence.[19] The child's views about seeing the other parent, for example, for contact, are not relevant. In the past a rather artificial distinction was made between the child's objections to returning to the country of habitual residence and his/her feelings about the parent living in that country: the court is now entitled to take into account the child's objections to returning to the person.[20] It is incumbent on the defendant to raise this defence at the outset since the court is not obliged as a matter of course to ascertain the child's wishes and feelings. The court can then decide how to investigate.[21] The courts are more likely to allow this defence in relation to older children but orders refusing return have been made in relation to children aged seven and eight.

Proceedings in the foreign country

9.20 Articles 16 and 17 deal with the situation where the wronged parent has already travelled to the contracting state and instituted custody proceedings in that jurisdiction. Article 16 provides that such proceedings must not be decided until it has been determined that the child is not to be returned under the Convention or unless an application under the Convention has not been lodged within a reasonable time. Article 17 states that the fact that a custody decision has been made is not a ground for refusing to return the child, but the judicial or administrative authority may take account of the reasons for that decision in applying the Convention. Therefore, a custody decision in favour of the abductor would constitute a ground for refusal only if the facts came within the scope of art 13.

Access

9.21 Rights of access are defined in art 5(b) as including the right to take a child for a limited period of time to a place other than the child's habitual residence. The central authorities are bound by the obligations of co-operation set out in art 7 to 'promote the peaceful

---

19 *S v S (Child Abduction: Child's Views)* [1992] 2 FLR 492.
20 *Re M (A Minor) (Child Abduction)* [1994] 1 FLR 390.
21 Ibid.

enjoyment of access rights and the fulfilment of any conditions to which the exercise of those rights may be subject'. However, there is no obligation on the judicial authorities to make any orders concerning access. Applicants should therefore apply for a CA 1989 s8 order for contact.[22] In *Re T (Minors) (Hague Convention: Access)*[23] the court held that the only obligation on the central authority was to find English solicitors for the applicant who could make an application under the CA 1989.

European Convention

Contracting states

9.22 The following countries have ratified the European Convention (with dates of ratification in brackets): Austria (1.8.86), Belgium (1.8.86), Cyprus (1.10.86), Denmark (1.8.91), Finland (1.8.94), France (1.8.86), Germany (1.2.91), Greece (1.7.93), Iceland (1.11.96), Ireland (1.10.91), Italy (1.6.95), Liechtenstein (1.8.97), Luxembourg (1.8.86), the Netherlands (1.9.90), Norway (1.5.89), Portugal (1.8.86), Spain (1.9.87), Sweden (1.7.89) and Switzerland (1.8.86).[24]

9.23 The European Convention applies to children under the age of 16 and provides for the recognition or enforcement of 'decisions relating to custody' when there is an improper removal across international frontiers. 'Improper removal' includes a failure to return following a period of access or at the end of any other temporary stay, and a removal which is subsequently declared unlawful. There must be a decision relating to custody (not merely a right to custody), which can be made before or after the removal.[25] Thus, a court order is an essential prerequisite for the provisions of this Convention to be invoked. Art 7 provides that a custody decision which is enforceable in the state of origin must be recognised and made enforceable in every other contracting state.

Grounds for refusing recognition

9.24 Art 9 provides that recognition may be refused if there have been certain procedural defects relating to the original decision. Art 10 provides substantive grounds for refusal in the following circumstances:

22 *Re G (A Minor) (Enforcement of Access Abroad)* (1993) Fam Law 216.
23 [1993] 2 FLR 617.
24 Child Abduction and Custody (Parties to Conventions) Order 1986 SI No 1159, as amended by SI 1997 No 1747.
25 Art 12.

a) the effects of the decision are manifestly incompatible with the fundamental principles of the law relating to the family and children in the state addressed. It must be remembered that the purpose of the CACA 1985 is to secure the enforcement of orders made abroad and this provision is not intended as an opportunity to review the merits of the case;

b) change in circumstances, including the passage of time but not a mere change of residence, means that the original decision is manifestly no longer in accordance with the welfare of the child. Before reaching any decisions on this ground, the court must ascertain the child's views, unless this is impractical because of his/her age and understanding.[26] The fact that the court must consider the welfare of the child permits a far wider investigation than under art 13 of the Hague Convention. The passage of time is recognised as a relevant consideration and under this Convention there is no time limitation in bringing the application. Thus, if evidence is adduced from a number of witnesses of the child having settled in the state addressed, the application may be refused. However, access to the wronged parent will be a crucial matter for the court to consider in making its decision. In *Re F (Minors) (Custody: Foreign Order)*[27] the court ruled that a delay of 21 months before the institution of legal proceedings in the lives of young children could not be ignored and recognition was accordingly refused. This should be contrasted with *Re L (A Minor: Abduction)*[28] where the court held that in relation to a seven-year-old who had lived with her father for 16 months, the length of time was an important factor, but if the court were to determine the case in accordance with the paramountcy principle it would have ordered the child to return to her mother. Thus, the original decision could not be said to be manifestly incompatible with the child's welfare;[29]

c) the child has no relationship with the state of origin or had dual nationality but is living in the state addressed; or

d) the decision is incompatible with an earlier decision made in the state addressed. The earlier proceedings must have been begun before the request for recognition and the refusal to return the child must be in accordance with his/her welfare. Again, this suggests that a wider investigation will take place, in which the

---

26 Art 15(1).
27 [1990] 3 WLR 1272.
28 [1990] 1 FLR 387, FD.
29 See also *Re G (A Minor) (Child Abduction: Enforcement)* [1990] 2 FLR 325, FD.

evidence and judgment of the substantive proceedings may be put before the court. In *Re M (Child Abduction) (European Convention)*[30] enforcement of an Irish custody order was refused since the enforcement proceedings were begun after an ex parte interim residence order was made and the court considered it was in the interests of the children to remain in this country where they had been for 18 months pending the decision about their long term future.

Access

9.25   Article 11 provides that decisions on rights of access must be recognised and enforced unless art 9 or art 10 applies. However, the article also states that the court may attach conditions to the order to facilitate access, taking into account particularly undertakings given by the parents. Although English access orders are very difficult to enforce, the practical effect of this is likely to be similar to Hague Convention cases.

Procedure under both conventions

Acting for wronged parent

9.26   When a child has been abducted abroad, an immediate application should be made to the LCD. In accordance with Hague Convention art 8 and European Convention art 13, the LCD will require completion of a questionnaire (see Part V) and the supply of documentation to give the following information which is then forwarded on to the relevant central authority:

- name, address, telephone number and date and place of birth of applicant;
- applicant's nationality and passport number;
- applicant's relationship to child;
- applicant's solicitor;
- name and date and place of birth of child;
- child's nationality and passport number;
- child's country of habitual residence and length of residence;
- description of child (photograph if possible);
- similar details of mother and/or father;
- date and place of marriage;
- whereabouts of child (if whereabouts unknown, names and

30 [1994] 1 FLR 367.

addresses of other persons who may be able to supply information);
- details of other persons in the country to which the child could have been taken who may be able to supply information as to whereabouts;
- date, place and circumstances of removal from UK;
- abductor's name, last known address and date and place of birth;
- abductor's nationality and passport number;
- abductor's relationship to child;
- description of abductor (photograph if possible);
- details of custody or access orders in England and Wales;
- details of custody or access orders outside England and Wales;
- court proceedings now taking place in England and Wales;
- court proceedings now taking place outside England and Wales;
- evidence of exercise of parental rights;
- other relevant matters, eg, whether the child is thought to be at risk; and
- arrangements for the return of the child.

Legal aid

9.27 Both conventions state that there is no charge to overseas applicants. However, in respect of Hague Convention applications made abroad, this is subject to the legal aid provisions of the relevant overseas country. Applications in Australia, Belgium, Cyprus, France and Spain are dealt with directly by the state. In Canada, Germany and Ireland there is automatic entitlement to legal aid if eligible in the UK. The major problem relates to applications in the USA where there is no legal aid system. In California applications are dealt with by the district attorney but in all other states the central authority tries to negotiate with lawyers in private practice for a reduction in fee.

9.28 Non-means- and non-merits-tested legal aid is available to those making an application under the CACA 1985 provided that they have a letter of instruction from the LCD's Child Abduction Unit to their solicitor.

9.29 Means- and merits-tested legal aid is available to those defending an action under the CACA 1985 and will be granted where it is shown that this is justified in all the circumstances of the case (given that there will have been a breach of custody rights in favour of another party).[31]

31 See *Legal Aid Focus* No 19, May 1997, para 5.3.1.2.

Time factors

9.30 Overseas applications may take some considerable time depending on the circumstances of the case and whether or not the child can be traced. The average length of time is between five to six months. Children may be returned within a month from New Zealand, the Netherlands, Ireland and the Scandinavian countries.

Procedure

9.31 Procedure is governed by Family Proceedings Rules 1991 Part VI. Applications are made in the High Court to a judge in chambers. The following people are defendants to a CACA 1985 application:

- the person alleged to have brought the child into the UK;
- any person with the whom the child is alleged to be;
- any parent or guardian in the UK, if not otherwise a party;
- a person who has a custody order, if not otherwise a party;
- any other person who appears to the court to have a sufficient interest in the welfare of the child.

9.32 Defendants should return an acknowledgement of service within seven days. Evidence is by affidavit.[32] The rules state that a defendant may submit an affidavit and that this should be served on the plaintiff within seven days of service of the originating summons.[33] Since there is no right to give oral evidence, it is very important for defendants to file an affidavit including a short statement of any defence.[34] The court has the discretion to hear oral evidence[35] but it should be admitted sparingly so as not to undermine the main purpose of the conventions that the matters should be speedily resolved.[36]

9.33 The rules make no provision for children to be joined as parties but in exceptional circumstances there is power to do so.[37] Usually any enquiry about the child's views is made by the court welfare officer.[38]

9.34 The court may order any person whom it thinks has relevant

32 FPR 1991 r6.7.
33 FPR 1991 r6.7(2).
34 *Re W (Abduction: Procedure)* [1995] 1 FLR 878.
35 *Re E (A Minor) (Abduction)* [1989] 1 FLR 135.
36 *Re F (A Minor) (Child Abduction)* [1992] 1 FLR 548.
37 *Re M (A Minor) (Child's Objections)* [1994] 2 FLR 126.
38 *Re M (A Minor) (Child Abduction)* [1994] 1 FLR 390.

information about the child's whereabouts to disclose it.[39] It can require a solicitor to disclose his/her client's whereabouts.[40]

9.35 The court may make interim orders under both conventions to secure the welfare of the child or to prevent changes in his/her circumstances.[41] An ex parte application inevitably will be made under the appropriate convention including seek and find orders.

9.36 The court may order the abducting parent to pay the applicant's legal costs and other costs including those incurred in locating the child and travel expenses. In *V v B (A Minor) (Abduction)*[42] it was established that the courts should normally make an order that the abducting parent should pay the costs of returning the child and where it does so this payment should not be regarded as money recoverable by the applicant and not, therefore, subject to the legal aid statutory charge.

Non-convention countries

Children taken abroad

9.37 Civil court proceedings cannot be brought in England and Wales for the return of children taken abroad since no order made by the English courts can be enforced in a country outside this jurisdiction. The Consular Department of the Foreign and Commonwealth Office is usually willing to give practical (but not legal) advice with the help of consular posts in the country where the child has been taken.[43] The help they can offer may include providing lists of local lawyers who speak English; asking the local authorities for help in tracing the child; trying to obtain welfare reports and asking the local court to handle the case as quickly as possible. International Social Services[44] may be able to put the person in touch with social services agencies abroad, who might assist in obtaining a welfare report in that country. Parents may find it helpful to read the booklet on child abduction, produced by the LCD and the Foreign and Commonwealth Office, which clearly identifies what can and cannot be done by the government on their behalf. Practitioners should also be aware

39 CACA 1985 s24A.
40 *Re B (Abduction: Disclosure)* [1995] 1 FLR 774.
41 CACA 1985 ss5 and 19.
42 [1991] 1 FLR 266.
43 *Practice Direction (Child: Removal from Jurisdiction)* [1984] 3 All ER 640.
44 39 Brixton Rd, London SW9 6DD, tel 0171 735 8941.

of the organisation 'Reunite',[45] which provides advice, practical assistance and counselling. Parents whose children have been abducted are in great need of support, and Reunite has been a lifeline to many parents in this situation.

9.38 This situation does not necessarily preclude applications being made in this country even though for enforcement purposes it is necessary to start proceedings in the country where the child has been taken. Court orders obtained in this country may be useful in locating the whereabouts of the child or putting indirect pressure on the abductor to return the child. The following remedies could be considered:

– an application for disclosure of the child's whereabouts in wardship or under FLA 1986 s33 where there are relatives or friends in the country;
– an application for a specific issues order for the return of the child. In *Re D (A Minor)*[46] the Court of Appeal held that it had jurisdiction to make such an order even though the abducting parent was out of the jurisdiction, since it would help the wronged parent in foreign proceedings for the return of the child;
– an application for a sequestration order where the abductor has assets in this country. This may bring pressure to bear to return the child;
– applications for CA 1989 s8 orders or injunctions in wardship where the parent remains in this country but has arranged for the child to be abducted by another person on his/her behalf.

9.39 It is a criminal offence under the CAA 1984 to take or send a child abroad without the appropriate consent (see para 7.28). If the Director of Public Prosecutions gives consent to a prosecution and the abductor has taken the child abroad, extradition proceedings may be started against the abductor. This may facilitate the voluntary return of the child, but there is no legal requirement that the child be returned to this country. See Part V: Precedents, Extradition Treaties for list of countries with which England and Wales has extradition treaties.

Children brought to England and Wales

9.40 Wardship proceedings can be issued in relation to any child who

45 The National Council for Abducted Children, PO Box 4, London WC1V 9XY, tel 0171 404 8356.
46 [1992] 1 All ER 892.

is physically present or ordinarily resident in England and Wales and this includes children who are foreign nationals. There is no automatic presumption that an order will be made against the abducting parent for the return of the child although this is increasingly likely to be the case. The approach of the courts to these cases has changed since the implementation of the CACA 1985 and is best summarised in *Re M (Abduction: Non-Convention Country)*.[47] The Court of Appeal held that prima facie the English court should not make decisions relating to the child's custody but should order the return of the child since decisions relating to the child's welfare were best decided by the courts of the country in which the child had been habitually residence. An order for return should be made only if the English court was satisfied that the foreign court would apply principles about the child's welfare acceptable to the English court, that there were no contra-indications such as those under art 13 of the Hague Convention and that there was no risk of persecution or discrimination. This approach has been applied not only to member states of the EU but also to Malta and Dubai. However, in *Re P (Abduction: Non-Convention Country)*[48] a differently constituted Court of Appeal said that the court's sole consideration in non-convention cases is the child's welfare.

Legal aid

9.41 Subject to means, legal aid is available to persons resident outside the jurisdiction. The financial Form L1(a) must be signed before a magistrate (for applicants from the Commonwealth or Eire) or a consular officer. It is also necessary for evidence in writing from an employer or other responsible person verifying means.

Procedure

9.42 In light of the similarity of approach to that taken in convention cases it is probably worthwhile referring a wronged parent to the LCD's Child Abduction Unit panel of solicitors. The same principles apply to defending abducting parents as set out above in relation to convention applications.

---

47 [1995] 1 FLR 89.
48 [1997] 1 FLR 780.

Part IV

Domestic violence emergencies

In this part:

Introduction to Part IV

The need for reform

Experienced practitioners in family law will be familiar with the difficulties encountered in using the various domestic violence remedies available before the implementation of the Family Law Act (FLA) 1996. The remedies were provided by a number of different pieces of legislation and the inherent jurisdiction of the courts to grant injunctions. In order to decide which remedies were available, it was necessary to try to fit clients into one of the categories of applicants, depending on whether the parties were or were not married, how long they had been separated, whether the children had been harmed, etc. If contemplating proceedings in the magistrates' court, one also had to assess the level of harm sustained and ascertain whether it amounted to violence or threats of violence. Lord Scarman commented in *Richards v Richards*[1] that the law in this area was 'a hotchpot of enactments of limited scope . . . The sooner the range, scope and effect of these powers are rationalised into a coherent and comprehensive body of statute law, the better.'

The courts' powers varied considerably, depending on the jurisdiction. In some, but not all, proceedings it was possible to obtain powers of arrest, or occupation rents, or exclusion zones around the matrimonial home. Within an order, powers of arrest could be attached only to certain terms and not to others. Problems of jurisdiction arose where the parties were divorced and no longer living together, or where former cohabitants had been separated for a few months. Some statutes gave criteria for the exercise of the courts' discretion; others did not, and the courts set their own criteria through case-law.

---

1 [1984] AC 174.

The process of change

The need for revision of the law in this area was recognised by the House of Lords in 1984 in the *Richards* case,[2] but it was not until 1989 that the Law Commission published its consultation paper on domestic violence remedies, *Domestic Violence and Occupation of the Family Home.*[3] In 1992 the Law Commission published its Report under the same title[4] which contained a draft bill. The bill was designed to deal with:

> . . . two distinct but inseparable problems: providing protection for one member of a family against molestation or violence by another and regulating the occupation of the family home where the relationship has broken down whether temporarily or permanently.[5]

In fact, the categories of applicants in the bill went further than just family members and included members of the same household, who need not be members of the same family.

The process of legislative enactment moved exceedingly slowly, and it was not until February 1995 that the then government published the Family Homes and Domestic Violence Bill, which incorporated almost all of the recommendations made by the Law Commission. (For example, the Law Commission's recommendation that the police should have the power to pursue civil remedies on behalf of an aggrieved party, as they have in Australia[6] was not included. The bill was withdrawn in November of the same year after a vocal campaign against it was launched by the media and certain members of parliament, despite it having attracted all-party support and having completed the legislative process, apart from receiving the Royal Assent.

The government had been considering changes to the divorce procedure during this period, and was about to publish its reforms in the Family Law Bill. It was a convenient vehicle on which to tack the proposals for domestic violence remedies. The 1995 bill was amended superficially to deal with the complaints about 'family values', and it was included in the Family Law Bill 1996. After further amendments, it became Family Law Act 1996 Part IV and received Royal Assent in July 1996. Part IV was implemented on 1 October 1997.

2   Ibid.
3   Working paper no 113 (HMSO).
4   Report no 207 (HMSO).
5   Ibid, para 1.1.
6   Ibid, paras 5.18–5.23.

Outline of the new legislation

The aims of the Law Commission were to:[7]

- remove the gaps, anomalies and inconsistencies in the existing remedies, with a view to synthesising them, so far as possible, into a clear,
  simple and comprehensive code . . .
- not reduce the level of protection which is available at present [and
  maybe to improve it] . . .
- avoid exacerbating hostilities between the adults involved, so far as
  this is compatible with providing proper and effective protection both
  for adults and for children . . .

It would appear that the Law Commission has been largely successful
in achieving its aims. The FLA 1996 provides a unified code with a
set of remedies which are consistently available in all courts with
jurisdiction to hear family cases. (The restriction on magistrates'
powers which prevents them from dealing with proprietary interests
has been maintained, however.) The law and practice regarding
domestic violence will be the same, regardless of where proceedings
are commenced. Statutory guidelines are given for the exercise of
discretion, which should reduce the possibility of inconsistencies.

The courts have power to make non-molestation orders and occupation orders. 'Molestation' is not defined, and the nature of the
order is the same as that which existed under the Domestic Violence
and Matrimonial Proceedings Act 1976 and in case-law. Occupation
orders replace ouster injunctions and exclusion orders and they
can declare, suspend, restrict, terminate and regulate rights of
occupation.

The FLA 1996 recognises that domestic violence can occur in a
wide variety of situations and accordingly vastly expands the categories of potential applicants. This should reduce the necessity of the
courts having to rely on their inherent jurisdiction to make injunctions, although this power continues unchanged. It should also reduce
the number of applications that have to be made in tort proceedings,
which provide an inferior form of protection to that afforded by the
FLA 1996.

The law governing powers of arrest has been expanded, and has
become mandatory in some cases. The circumstances in which it will
be appropriate to seek an ex parte order have been relaxed, as well,
which will probably lead to an increase in such orders. The High

---

7   Ibid, para 1.2.

Court and county courts have been given the power to issue warrants for arrest, which will no doubt replace committal proceedings in practice, and to remand respondents on bail or in custody and to order medical reports.

In order to produce a unified code, the Domestic Violence and Matrimonial Proceedings Act 1976 has been repealed in its entirety; Domestic Proceedings and Magistrates' Courts Act 1978 ss16–18 have been repealed; the Children Act 1989 has been amended; and the Matrimonial Homes Act 1983 has been repealed, although the FLA 1996 substantially re-enacts matrimonial home rights.

Applications in tort and under the Protection from Harassment Act 1997

Although the categories of potential applicants under the FLA 1996 ('associated persons') is very wide, there are nonetheless some people who will fall outside the scope of the Act. They will have to seek injunctive relief in tort proceedings. A new tort of harassment has been created by the Protection from Harassment Act 1997, however, which should improve the protection available outside the range of FLA 1996 orders.

The Protection from Harassment Act 1997 creates two new criminal offences, in addition to the tort of harassment. It blurs the boundaries between civil and criminal law by giving magistrates the power to make the equivalent of injunctions, called 'restraining orders'. It also makes it a criminal offence to breach an injunction obtained under the Act in the civil courts. Consequently, the police will have the power to prosecute for breach of a civil court order.

CHAPTER 10

Essential definitions

Introduction

10.1 The FLA 1996 creates two remedies in cases of domestic violence: non-molestation orders and occupation orders. It also sets out criteria for the orders, which vary depending on the parties' relationship to each other and their occupational status. Non-molestation orders are similar to those which were previously available in divorce proceedings or under the Domestic Violence and Matrimonial Proceedings Act 1976. The courts' power to declare rights of occupation and to regulate the occupation of the former family home has been developed from previous law. The categories of people who can apply for either non-molestation orders or occupation orders has been vastly expanded from previous law; they are included in a class of people called 'associated persons' in the Act.

10.2 This chapter will discuss the definitions of basic terms used in the Act. It will be helpful to become familiar with these terms, which will no doubt become part of shorthand language associated with domestic violence remedies.

Associated persons

10.3 The remedies for domestic violence available under FLA 1996 Part IV are only available to 'associated persons' and any relevant children. The definition is therefore fundamental to all applications made under the Act. It implies that there is some family or other domestic relationship between the parties. The list of associated persons is contained in FLA 1996 s62(3), and is set out at para **10.4**. Fuller discussions of the categories in the list are set out at paras **10.5** to **10.31**.

10.4 FLA 1996 s62(3) provides that a person is associated with another if:

a) they are *spouses* or *former spouses*;
b) they are *cohabitants* or *former cohabitants*;
c) they live or have lived *in the same household*, otherwise than merely by reason of one of them being the other's employee, tenant, lodger or boarder;
d) they are *relatives*;
e) they have *agreed to marry each other*, even if that agreement has been terminated;
f) the applicant is a *parent* of a given child or has/has had *parental responsibility* for a given child, and the respondent is a parent of the same child or has/has had parental responsibility for the same child;
g) they are *parties to the same family proceedings*.

Spouses and former spouses

10.5 The Act does not require either spouses or former spouses to be living in the same household with the respondent. All that is necessary is to show that the parties are or have been married.

Cohabitants and former cohabitants

10.6 'Cohabitants' are defined as a man and a woman who, although not married to each other, are living together as husband and wife.[1] The definition clearly excludes gay and lesbian couples, but the phrase 'living together as husband and wife' is not defined. The following case-law with regards to state benefits may be considered if cohabitation is disputed.

10.7 In *Crake v Supplementary Benefits Commission*,[2] it was held that in order to establish that a man and a woman were 'living together as husband and wife' for the purposes of the Supplementary Benefits Act 1976, it was not sufficient merely to show that they were living in the same household. The manner in which they were living together in the same household must be ascertained. If there was an explanation as to why they were living in the same household other than as husband and wife, eg, as patient and carer, then their incomes could not be aggregated for the purposes of the 1976 Act. The nature of the parties' relationship had to be taken into account. Lord Woolf listed a number of factors which could be considered as 'signposts' of

1   FLA 1996 s62(1).
2   [1982] 1 All ER 498.

cohabitation: whether the parties are the members of the same household; the stability of their relationship; whether financial support is provided by one to the other; whether they have a sexual relationship; whether they have had children; whether they have acknowledged the nature of their relationship publicly.

10.8 In *Re J (Income Support: Cohabitation)*,[3] the Social Security Commissioner found that in determining whether the relationship which existed between people amounted to 'living together as husband and wife', the paramount factor was the relationship between the parties. One could not resolve the issue by reference to specific criteria; all of the relevant factors of the case must be considered. 'Signposts of a husband/wife relationship' included matters such as whether the couple were financially supportive of each other or had publicly declared themselves to be husband and wife. Whether there was a sexual relationship was an important factor. If no sexual relationship had ever existed, there must be strong alternative grounds for suggesting that the couple are living together as husband and wife. Although all of these factors were relevant, no single one of them could be considered to be conclusive evidence of cohabitation.

10.9 The FLA 1996 does not require cohabitants or former cohabitants to show that they are living in the same household at the time of application. In any case, the court has held that cohabitation in the sense of living together as husband and wife can continue, even though the parties may be forced to live apart due to given circumstances.[4]

Household

10.10 The FLA 1996 acknowledges that close, family-like relationships can exist between people who are not members of the same family. Although the word 'household' is not defined in the Act, there has been judicial consideration of its meaning, and it was discussed in the Law Commission Report.[5] The Law Commission intended for the definition to cover gay and lesbian couples or close friends living together for long periods of time. The Report states:[6]

---

3   [1995] 1 FLR 660.
4   *Santos v Santos* [1972] Fam 247.
5   Law Commission Report no 207, *Domestic Violence and Occupation of the Family Home* (HMSO, 1992) paras 3.19–3.22.
6   Ibid, para 3.21.

This is intended to include people who live in the same household, other than on a purely commercial basis . . . The phrase 'living in the same household' may be expected to retain the usual meaning which it has acquired in matrimonial proceedings. Thus, it is possible for people to live in different households, although they are actually living in the same house. The crucial test is the degree of community life which goes on. If the parties shut themselves up in separate rooms and cease to have anything to do with each other, they live in separate households. But if they share domestic chores and shopping, eat meals together or share the same living room, they are living in the same household, however strained their relations may be.

10.11 With regard to 'the usual meaning which it has acquired in matrimonial proceedings', Cretney and Masson[7] have examined the meaning of living in a household with regards to being able to prove that the parties have separated for the purposes of divorce proceedings. They state that, when considering whether the parties still have any sort of community of life, two practical tests are applied, as follows:

The practical test applied in cases where the parties are still living under the same roof is usually whether one party continues to provide matrimonial services for the other, and whether there is any sharing of domestic life. Thus if a husband shuts himself up in one or two rooms of the house and ceases to have anything to do with the wife, there will be a sufficient separation of households [*Hopes v Hopes* [1949] 2 All ER 920]. If, on the other hand, although there is an estrangement (and even a refusal to have intercourse [*Weatherley v Weatherley* [1947] AC 268]) the parties still share the same living room, eat at the same table and sit by the same fire [*J L Barton* (1970) 86 LQR 348, 350] (or perhaps watch television together), they are not to be regarded as living apart. They are still living in the same household . . .

10.12 The Law Commission Report, quoted above, follows exactly the test set out in *Mouncer v Mouncer*.[8] In that case, the relationship between the husband and wife had broken down, and they were attempting to live separate lives. They slept in separate bedrooms, did not have sexual intercourse, and generally had little to do with each other. However, the husband remained in the home because he wanted to continue to help look after the two children. The couple ate their meals together, sometimes with the children, and sometimes without them. They shared the house-cleaning, but the wife did not clean the husband's clothing. Wrangham J concluded on the facts that

7   *Principles of Family Law* (Sweet & Maxwell, 5th edn, 1990) p124.
8   [1972] 1 WLR 321.

the couple may have been living separate lives, but they were nevertheless living in the same household. He confirmed previous case-law regarding couples living apart, even though they lived in the same dwelling.[9]

10.13 In *Fuller v Fuller*,[10] the wife had left her husband to go and live with P 'as husband and wife'. The husband later had a heart attack and could no longer live on his own. On release from hospital he went to live as a lodger with his wife and P. Although he shared meals with his wife and P, he paid her for his room and board. The court held that during the period when the husband lived with his wife and P, he was living in a separate household from them.

10.14 The definition of 'associated persons' specifically excludes those people who are sharing accommodation through a contractual relationship, either as employer/employee, or landlord/tenant or landlord/licensee (including boarders and lodgers). This would exclude, for example, students or anyone else who rents a spare room or a live-in nanny.[11]

10.15 The Law Commission Report[12] points out that the definitions that the Law Commission devised creates an anomaly in the case of friends sharing accommodation. For example, if a number of friends are all joint tenants or joint owners of a house or flat, they would probably come within the jurisdiction of the FLA 1996. However, if only one of them is a tenant or owner and shares the accommodation with friends, they would not come within the jurisdiction of the Act because their relationship would be that of landlord and tenant/licensee. The Law Commission stated that 'the legal relationship of landlord and tenant is quite unlike that of equal household sharers', and they felt that the distinction should be preserved.

10.16 People who share essential living accommodation (living rooms, kitchens or bathrooms) with their landlord, whether as tenants or licensees, are in the precarious position of being 'excluded tenants or licensees' and have very little protection from eviction. This would apply to situations where an owner-occupier or a sole tenant shares a house or flat with friends. The friends will be living with a resident landlord, in effect, and as such will come within the

---

9 *Hopes v Hopes* [1948] 2 All ER 920, CA; *Jackson v Jackson* [1949] P 19; *Smith v Smith* [1939] 4 All ER 533; *Wilkes v Wilkes* [1943] 1 All ER 433.
10 [1973] 2 WLR 730.
11 Law Commission (n5) para 3.21.
12 Ibid, para 3.22.

'excluded category' under the Protection from Eviction Act 1977 s3A. They may be evicted by the landlord without the necessity of a court order. Their legal remedies if they are victims of violence lie in the law of tort and are considered in Chapter 16.

10.17 Where the occupiers are on an equal footing with regard to occupational status, then it will be necessary to show that they are members of the same household. Evidence may be required to show that the parties have some sort of communal existence in the form of sharing the cooking, shopping, cleaning, etc. Keeping a kitty for food and other outgoings would point to the existence of a household. The Law Commission states that the essential test 'is the degree of community life which goes on'.[13]

10.18 Whereas *Mouncer v Mouncer*[14] considered the meaning of 'household' in the context of family law, there have nevertheless been other cases which considered its meaning in the context of housing law. Whether or not a dwelling is occupied by a single household or by a multiple household is an important factor with regard to the regulation of houses in multiple occupation (HMOs) under the Housing Acts 1985 and 1996. The term 'multiple occupation' is defined under Housing Act 1985 s345 as 'a house which is occupied by persons who do not form a single household'. The Act does not define the word 'household', however, and it has been left to the courts to consider the definition.

10.19 In *Simmon v Pizzey*,[15] the House of Lords had to determine whether the 75 occupants of a women's refuge were living together as a single household. They had been issued with overcrowding directions, which could only be used for regulating HMOs. On behalf of the respondents it was argued that the occupants formed a single household because they organised themselves communally. They shared a kitty for food and ate together on a rota basis. The women and children slept in dormitories, and there was voluntary movement between rooms from day to day. Cooking was done on a rota basis, and the daily chores were sorted out in meetings of the whole group.

10.20 Lord Hailsham,[16] however, found that there could not be a single household made up of all of the occupants for three reasons:

13 Ibid, para 3.21.
14 [1972] 1 WLR 321.
15 [1977] 2 All ER 432.
16 Ibid, at p442a.

a) the number of occupants was too great to come within the meaning of what would ordinarily and reasonably constitute a
household;
b) the population of the refuge fluctuated on a daily or weekly basis;
and
c) a temporary place of refuge for people who arrive fortuitously
could never form itself into a single household.

10.21 In *Hackney LBC v Ezedinma*,[17] one of the issues was whether the
premises were used by single individuals each forming a single household, or whether the occupants had formed themselves into three
households. The premises consisted of a house with basement,
ground, first and second floors. The rooms were let to students on
individual tenancies. There were three kitchens in the building. The
occupants of the basement and ground floor shared the use of one
kitchen, and there were kitchens on the first and second floors which
were used by the respective occupants of those floors. The local
authority argued that the occupants were all single households. The
respondents argued that the occupants had formed themselves into
three households on the basis of which kitchen they used. The
Divisional Court found that whether single or multiple households
existed was a question of fact and degree, and the magistrates would
have been entitled to take either view. Their decision that there were
three households was not unreasonable in the circumstances of the
case.

10.22 Because what constitutes a household will be a question of fact
and degree in every case, it is foreseeable that whether the parties are
'associated persons' by virtue of FLA 1996 s62(3)(c) could lead to
difficulties if the application is contested on the basis that the parties
were not living in the same household. It is clear from the case-law
cited above that the lack of sexual intercourse between the occupants
is not a relevant factor, although the fact that the parties are sexually
intimate might help to prove an intention to live together as a single
unit. What is important is the equal occupational status of the parties
and the extent to which they live together communally.

Relatives

10.23 This category includes the immediate blood relatives of the
applicant and of her spouse/former spouse or cohabitant/former

17 [1981] 3 All ER 438.

cohabitant, plus their relatives by affinity. FLA 1996 s63(1) lists the categories of people who, by virtue of their relationship to the applicant or to the applicant's spouse/former spouse or the applicant's cohabitant/former cohabitant, will be 'associated persons':

- father;
- mother;
- stepfather;
- stepmother;
- son;
- daughter;
- stepson;
- stepdaughter;
- grandfather;
- grandmother;
- grandson;
- granddaughter;
- brother;
- sister;
- half-brother;
- half-sister;
- stepbrother;
- stepsister;
- uncle;
- aunt;
- nephew;
- niece; and
- the spouse/former spouse or cohabitant/former cohabitant of any of the above people.

Engaged and formerly engaged couples

10.24 Couples who have agreed to marry but who have never lived together as cohabitants or as members of the same household will be able to use the FLA 1996, provided they can produce some evidence of the agreement to marry.[18] The evidence must be in one of three forms:

- written evidence;[19] or

18 FLA 1996 s44.
19 FLA 1996 s44(1).

- the gift of an engagement ring in contemplation of the parties' marriage;[20] or
- a ceremony entered into by the parties in the presence of one or more other persons assembled for the purpose of witnessing the ceremony.[21]

10.25 Written evidence could be in the form of a letter from one party to the other which mentions wedding plans, or a newspaper announcement, or a wedding list, or invitations, etc. An affidavit in reply in which the respondent admits the engagement would also meet the requirement of written evidence.

10.26 If no written evidence is available, the existence of the agreement might be proven by the fact that one party gave the other an engagement ring. It would appear that it is proof of the gift of the ring which is required, not the production of the ring itself. One assumes that oral or affidavit evidence that a ring was given, but has since been lost or returned or sold or otherwise disposed of, would satisfy the terms of the FLA 1996. The ring must have been given in contemplation of marriage, however. Any other sort of gift will not suffice.

10.27 The third way of proving the existence of an agreement to marry is if the parties entered into an engagement ceremony which was witnessed. This is most likely to take place because of the religious beliefs of the parties. A simple party to celebrate the couple's engagement will not qualify under this heading, although a written invitation to such a party might produce the required written evidence of the agreement.

10.28 It will be up to the court in each case to decide whether the evidence presented meets the requirements of the FLA 1996 as proof of an agreement by the parties to marry. If the court decides that there is insufficient evidence under this heading, and the parties do not come under any of the other categories, the application may not proceed. It is unclear what would happen if the court found that the applicant had insufficient evidence of the existence of an agreement to marry, but the respondent admitted it orally. The easiest solution would be to get the respondent to sign a statement to that effect, if he were willing to do so.

---

20 FLA 1996 s44(2)(a).
21 FLA 1996 s44(2)(b).

Parents and those with parental responsibility

10.29 Everyone who is either a parent or who has or has had parental responsibility for a given child are 'associated persons'.[22] In FLA 1996 s63 'parental responsibility' is defined as having the same meaning as it has under the Children Act 1989. This could mean that people might be associated persons who are not related to each other and who have never lived together or in the same household, for example, where parental responsibility extended to a responsible adult other than the parents. Although local authorities are capable of being given parental responsibility for a child, they cannot be an 'associated person' for the purposes of the FLA 1996.[23]

10.30 Where a child has been adopted or freed for adoption, the natural parent or grandparent of the child will be associated with any person who has become the adoptive parent, or who has applied for an adoption order, or with whom the child has at any time been placed for adoption.[24]

Parties to the same family proceedings

10.31 'Family proceedings' are defined[25] as being proceedings taken under:

- the inherent jurisdiction of the High Court in relation to children (wardship);
- FLA 1996 Part II (divorce and separation);
- FLA 1996 Part IV (family homes and domestic violence);
- the Matrimonial Causes Act 1973;
- the Adoption Act 1976;
- the Domestic Proceedings and Magistrates' Courts Act 1978;
- Matrimonial and Family Proceedings Act 1984 Part III;
- Children Act 1989 Parts I, II and IV;
- Human Fertilisation and Embryology Act 1990 s30.

Relevant child

10.32 The FLA 1996 sometimes makes reference to 'any relevant child'. When considering whether and what type of order to make,

22 FLA 1996 s62(4).
23 FLA 1996 s62(6).
24 FLA 1996 s62(5).
25 FLA 1996 s63(1) and (2).

the court must have regard to the interests of any relevant child. The definition is contained in FLA 1996 s62(2) as follows:

(a) any child who is living with or might reasonably be expected to live with either party to the proceedings;
(b) any child in relation to whom an order under the Adoption Act 1976 or the Children Act 1989 is in question in the proceedings; and
(c) any other child whose interests the court considers relevant.

10.33 This is a very broadly defined term and might include any children in regular contact with the parties, even if they do not live or intend to live with them.

Persons entitled

10.34 The criteria for applications for the various types of occupation orders vary depending on whether either or both parties are 'persons entitled' to occupy the dwelling-house concerned. Those who are entitled to occupy are in a stronger position in the long term than those who are not entitled, although the latter may still be able to obtain temporary relief through an occupation order.

10.35 FLA 1996 s33(1) sets out requirements regarding the legal rights to occupy and the nature of the dwelling house which must be met in order to become an entitled applicant. A 'person entitled' is defined as someone who:[26]

(i) is entitled to occupy a dwelling-house by virtue of a beneficial estate or interest or contract or by virtue of any enactment giving him the right to remain in occupation, or
(ii) has matrimonial home rights in relation to a dwelling-house . . .

10.36 There is an additional requirement that the dwelling-house concerned:[27]

(i) is or at any time has been the home of the person entitled and of another person with whom he is associated, or
(ii) was at any time intended by the person entitled and any such other person to be their home . . .

10.37 Taking the latter definition first, it is clear that the home which is the subject of the occupation order must either have been somewhere where the parties lived together, or it must be somewhere where the parties intended to live together. Thus, the FLA 1996 will apply to

26 FLA 1996 s33(1)(a).
27 FLA 1996 s33(1)(b).

situations where, for example, a couple were living in temporary accommodation while the home they had bought was being renovated.[28] This is an extension of the court's jurisdiction, which previously only related to current or former homes of the parties.

10.38 The former definition relates to the occupational status of the parties. A person is 'entitled' if s/he has:

- sole or joint ownership;
- a sole or joint tenancy;
- a contractual licence;
- a beneficial interest;
- matrimonial home rights;
- a right to occupy by virtue of some enactment.

10.39 Entitled applicants can apply for occupation orders if the respondent comes within any of the categories of 'associated persons'. Non-entitled applicants can only apply for occupation orders if the respondent is his/her cohabitant, former cohabitant, or former spouse. If the parties are still married, the applicant will by definition be an entitled person, if not through a joint legal interest or a beneficial interest in the property, then by virtue of his/her matrimonial home rights.

Matrimonial home rights

10.40 Matrimonial home rights first came into being under the Matrimonial Homes Act 1967 and were re-enacted under the Matrimonial Homes Act 1983. They gave a non-entitled spouse statutory occupation rights in respect of the family home, which could be registered as a charge on the property. Thus, a wife's right of occupation could be protected against a subsequent purchaser's or mortgagee's claim, or against her husband's refusal to let her live in the home. There were other provisions which further protected the unentitled spouse by equating his/her occupation of the home with that of the entitled spouse; this required landlords and mortgagors to accept payments by the unentitled spouse as though they were made by the tenant or mortgagor. An unentitled spouse's occupation of the family home was treated as though it were occupation by the entitled spouse, thereby protecting the occupation rights of those who were deserted or who separated.

28 Law Commission (n5) para 4.4.

10.41 FLA 1996 s30 leaves all of those statutory provisions intact with regard to spouses. The Act goes even further, however, and extends them to non-entitled cohabitants, former cohabitants, and former spouses who have occupation orders made in their favour, so long as the orders remain in force.[29] The orders in favour of non-entitled occupants are limited to six months' duration in the first instance, but this will enable them to remain in the home while applying for property adjustment or transfer of tenancy orders, should they wish to do so. However, they will not be able to register their rights of occupation as a land charge, and thus will not be protected against third party rights, unless the court is willing to grant an injunction forbidding the other party to sell or mortgage the property for the duration of the occupation order.

10.42 The matrimonial homes rights set out in FLA 1996 s30 are as follows:

- if in occupation, a right not to be evicted or excluded from the home or any part of it by the other spouse except under a court order;[30]
- if not in occupation, a right to enter and occupy the home, with the leave of the court;[31]
- a right to pay the rent, mortgage, or other outgoings on the property as though it were the applicant making those payments;[32]
- the unentitled person's occupation will be treated as though the entitled person remained in occupation, thus preserving tenancies under the Rent (Agriculture) Act 1976, the Rent Act 1977, the Housing Act 1985 and the Housing Act 1988;[33]
- if the person entitled to occupy the home is so entitled because he is a beneficiary under a trust, the trustees must treat the unentitled person as though she were the beneficiary;[34]
- if married, the right to register matrimonial home rights as a land charge or as a notice under the Land Registration Act 1925.[35]

10.43 The above rights only apply to dwelling-houses that are, or were, or were intended to be the family home of the parties. It appears, therefore, that if the parties are living in rented property

29 FLA 1996 ss35 and 36.
30 FLA 1996 s30(2)(a).
31 FLA 1996 s30(2)(b).
32 FLA 1996 s30(3).
33 FLA 1996 s30(4).
34 FLA 1996 s30(6).
35 FLA 1996 s31.

whilst renovating a property they have bought with the intention of making it their home after the work is complete, matrimonial home rights would apply to both properties.

10.44 'Dwelling-house' is defined in FLA 1996 s63 as including:

> ... any building or part of a building which is occupied as a dwelling [and] any caravan, house-boat or structure which is occupied as a dwelling, ... and any yard, garden, garage or outhouse belonging to it and occupied with it ...

10.45 If the rights arise because the parties are still married, they will end when the spouse dies or when the marriage is otherwise terminated. It is possible, however, to apply to the court, before the marriage ends, for an order extending the matrimonial home rights beyond the date of termination.[36] Matrimonial home rights also only continue so long as the other party remains entitled to occupation, unless they have been registered at the Land Registry. If rights have been registered, the court has the power to order that they be removed from the Register.

10.46 In addition to enabling a non-entitled party to re-enter or to remain in occupation of the former home of the parties, matrimonial home rights also ensure that security of tenure will remain as good as it would be if the entitled party continued to occupy the home. For example, if the tenancy is a secure or an assured tenancy under the Housing Acts 1985 or 1988, security of tenure is lost if the tenant does not remain in occupation. Therefore, if the tenant moved out leaving the unentitled party in occupation, the tenancy would cease to be either secure or assured if it were not for the fact that she has matrimonial home rights. Her landlord will have to treat her as though she were the tenant, accept her payments of rent, and notify her of any legal proceedings involving the property. The same applies to mortgagors if the property is privately owned.

Transfer of tenancy orders

10.47 FLA 1996 Sch 7 gives the court the power to transfer protected and statutory tenancies under the Rent Act 1977, secure tenancies under the Housing Act 1985, assured tenancies under the Housing Act 1988, and statutory tenancies under the Rent (Agriculture) Act 1976 from one party to the other, or from joint names into the name

36 FLA 1996 s33(5).

of one of the parties. These powers were previously used only in ancillary relief proceedings, but they have now been extended to cohabitants and former cohabitants. The court also has power to order the transferee to pay compensation to the transferor for his loss of rights, or to order one party or both parties to remain jointly and severally liable to perform the obligations of the original tenancy. When deciding whether to apply for an occupation order, consideration should also be given to making an application for a transfer of tenancy order.

Balance of harm test

10.48   The Law Commission considered various tests which have been applied when making ouster orders in family proceedings, and consulted widely on which test was appropriate. They looked at the test applied under the Matrimonial Homes Act 1983; the interpretation of that test in *Richards v Richards*[37] and the trend since then towards requiring proof of the respondent's misbehaviour before making an ouster order; the 'balance of hardship' test applied in *Bassett v Bassett*;[38] and the paramountcy of the children's welfare rule which is applied under the Children Act 1989.

10.49   The two tests suggested by the Law Commission[39] were a compromise. It thought that the court should have a *power* to make an occupation order after considering the parties' respective financial and housing needs and resources, and the likely effect of the order on the health, safety and well-being of the parties and any relevant child. The court would be under a *duty* to make an order, however, if, by *not* making an order, the applicant and any relevant child will suffer significant harm which is greater than any significant harm the respondent and any relevant child will suffer if an order *is* made, which is a balance of harm test. The Law Commission thus improved the old balance of hardship test by the imposition of a duty on the court to make an order where there is a likelihood of significant harm.

10.50   This part of the Family Homes and Domestic Violence Bill 1995 was quite controversial and received considerable media attention. As a result, the criteria for discretionary and mandatory orders were expanded to include consideration of the parties' conduct.

37   [1984] AC 174.
38   [1975] Fam 76 at p87.
39   Law Commission (n5) para 4.34.

Consequently, when the Family Law Bill was drafted, it included a requirement that the likely harm suffered has to be attributed to the conduct of the respondent, and it added a requirement to consider the conduct of parties when deciding whether to make an order.

10.51 Before exercising its discretion to make an occupation order, the court must take into account the factors set out in FLA 1996 s33(6), as follows:

> In deciding whether to exercise its powers . . . and (if so) in what manner, the court shall have regard to all the circumstances including –
> (a) the housing needs and housing resources of each of the parties and of any relevant child;
> (b) the financial resources of each of the parties;
> (c) the likely effect of any order, or of any decision by the court not to exercise its powers . . ., on the health, safety or well-being of the parties and of any relevant child; and
> (d) the conduct of the parties in relation to each other and otherwise.

10.52 FLA 1996 s33(7) contains the balance of harm test, which states as follows:

> If it appears to the court that the applicant or any relevant child is likely to suffer significant harm attributable to conduct of the respondent if an order under this section . . . is not made, the court shall make the order unless it appears to it that –
> (a) the respondent or any relevant child is likely to suffer significant harm if the order is made; and
> (b) the harm likely to be suffered by the respondent or child in that event is as great as, or greater than, the harm attributable to conduct of the respondent which is likely to be suffered by the applicant or child if the order is not made.

10.53 The Act thus gives the court the discretion to make an occupation order after weighing up the consequences on the parties if such an order is made. However, the making of an occupation order becomes mandatory if the court considers that the balance of harm test in s33(7) favours the applicant and any relevant child.

10.54 The Law Commission explained its reasoning for devising these criteria as follows:[40]

> In cases where the question of significant harm does not arise, the court would have power to make an order taking into account the [four] factors set out [in FLA 1996 s33(6) quoted] above; but, in cases where there is a likelihood of significant harm, this power becomes a duty and the court

---

40 Ibid, para 4.34.

must make an order after balancing the degree of harm likely to be suffered by both parties and any children concerned. This approach would still work in the case of cross applications, where the court would firstly consider who would suffer the greatest risk of harm if the order were not made. In the event of the balance of harm being equal, the court would retain power to make an order, but would have no duty to do so, and so would still be able to reach the right result.

10.55 The Law Commission Report went on to discuss the meaning of 'harm':[41]

> Harm has a narrower meaning than hardship. It is defined [in the draft bill] as 'ill-treatment or impairment of physical or mental health'. In relation to children, the term will attract the definition used in section 31 of the Children Act 1989 [which includes ill-treatment or the impairment of health or development].

10.56 The Report then illustrated how the court would exercise its judgment in balancing the needs of the parties:[42]

> It is likely that a respondent threatened with ouster on account of his violence would be able to establish a degree of hardship (perhaps in terms of difficulty in finding or unsuitability of alternative accommodation or problems in getting to work). But he is unlikely to suffer significant harm, where his wife and children who are being subjected to his violence or abuse may very easily suffer harm if he remains in the house. In this way the court will be treating violence or other forms of abuse as deserving immediate relief, and will be directed to make an order where a risk of significant harm exists.

Significant harm

10.57 FLA 1996 s63 states that the word 'harm':

(a) in relation to a person who has reached the age of eighteen years, means ill-treatment or the impairment of health; and

(b) in relation to a child, means ill-treatment or the impairment of health or development.

It goes on to define 'health' as including physical or mental health. 'Development' means physical, intellectual, emotional, social or behavioural development. 'Ill-treatment' includes forms of ill-treatment which are not physical. In relation to a child, ill-treatment includes sexual abuse.

41 Ibid.
42 Ibid.

10.58 The word 'significant' is not defined in the Act. One encounters the phrase 'significant harm' in the Children Act 1989, however. The guidance to that Act uses the dictionary meaning of the word 'significant', as that which is 'considerable, noteworthy or important'.[43] That definition was confirmed in the case of *Humberside CC v B*.[44]

43 *The Children Act 1989: Guidance and Regulations* (HMSO, 1991), Volume 1, Court Orders, para 3.19.
44 [1993] 1 FLR 257.

CHAPTER 11

Non-molestation orders (FLA 1996 s42)

Introduction

11.1 Prior to the implementation of the FLA 1996, non-molestation injunctions were available in divorce proceedings or under the Domestic Violence and Matrimonial Proceedings Act 1976 to spouses or cohabitants. Personal protection orders were available to spouses, but not to cohabitants, under the Domestic Proceedings and Magistrates' Courts Act 1978 to protect the applicant from violence or threats of violence only. The protection afforded by proceedings in the magistrates' courts was thus much narrower than that given by non-molestation injunctions obtained in the county or High Courts.

11.2 One of the purposes of the FLA 1996 was to address this anomaly and to give all of these courts the same jurisdiction with regard to domestic violence remedies. The approach adopted by the FLA 1996 is similar to that taken in the 1976 Act, but the categories of potential applicants have been vastly expanded.

Definition of 'non-molestation order'

11.3 FLA s42(1) defines a 'non-molestation order' as:

> ... an order containing either or both of the following provisions –
> (a) provision prohibiting a person ('the respondent') from molesting another person who is associated with the respondent;
> (b) provision prohibiting the respondent from molesting a relevant child.

11.4 The order may be expressed so as to refer to molestation generally, or to specific acts of molestation, or both.[1]

---

1 FLA 1996 s42(6).

11.5 As recommended by the Law Commission,[2] the FLA 1996 does not contain a definition of the word 'molestation'. During consultation prior to the publication of its report, the Law Commission had found no evidence that the lack of a statutory definition had caused any problems in practice. Some concern had been expressed that a statutory definition would become too restrictive with regard to the types of behaviour it covered. It was felt that the courts had, appropriately, been interpreting the word in its broadest sense.

What amounts to 'molestation'?

11.6 The Law Commission Report[3] summarised the case-law regarding what amounts to 'molestation' as follows:

> Molestation is an umbrella term which covers a wide range of behaviour. ... Molestation includes, but is wider than violence [*Davis v Johnson* [1978] 1 All ER 841]. It encompasses any form of serious pestering or harassment [*Vaughan v Vaughan* [1973] 1 WLR 1159] and applies to any conduct which could properly be regarded as such a degree of harassment as to call for the intervention of the court [*Johnson v Walton* [1990] 1 FLR 350].

11.7 The Report[4] gives a good description of what may be termed 'domestic violence':

> Domestic violence can take many forms. The term 'violence' itself is often used in two senses. In its narrower meaning it describes the use of threat of physical force against a victim in the form of an assault or battery. But in the context of the family, there is also a wider meaning which extends to abuse beyond the more typical instances of physical assaults to include any form of physical, sexual or psychological molestation or harassment which has a serious detrimental effect upon the health and well-being of the victim, albeit that there is no 'violence' involved in the sense of physical force.

11.8 It then goes on to list examples of acts which have been held to amount to harassment or molestation:

- persistent pestering and intimidation through shouting, denigration, threats or argument;
- nuisance telephone calls;

2   Law Commission Report no 207, *Domestic Violence and Occupation of the Family Home* (HMSO, 1992) para 3.1.
3   Ibid.
4   Ibid, para 2.3.

- damaging property;
- following the applicant about and repeatedly calling at his/her home or place of work;
- installing a mistress into the matrimonial home with a wife and three children;
- filling car locks with superglue;
- writing anonymous letters;
- pressing one's face against a window while brandishing papers.

11.9 The most important factor in all of these actions is the effect of the respondent's behaviour on the victim. Some acts will be intrinsically threatening or damaging, but even seemingly innocuous actions become threatening when repeated over and over or when carried out in the context of previous violence. Psychological or sexual harassment can cause longer lasting damage than physical injury. Detailed instructions are required to establish a pattern of behaviour on the part of the respondent and the effect it has on the applicant and any children.

Who may apply?

11.10 The applicant and respondent must be 'associated persons' (see paras **10.3** to **10.31** for a full discussion of this term). The categories of associated persons are so wide that most forms of relationships will be covered. However, those that fall through the net include the following:

- employer/employee, eg, au pairs or nannies or housekeepers;
- landlord/tenant;
- landlord/lodger or boarder;
- current or former boyfriends and girlfriends who have never cohabited or lived in the same household or been engaged and who do not have parental responsibility for the same child.

11.11 Those people who are not associated persons will have to rely on other remedies, such as proceedings in tort or under the Protection from Harassment Act 1997 (see Chapter 16).

When may an order be made?

11.12 Where the respondent is associated (see paras **10.3** to **10.31**) with the applicant, orders can be made:[5]

5   FLA 1996 s42(2).

- on application in any family proceedings (see para **10.31**);
- on application under the FLA 1996 without other family proceedings being instituted;
- in any family proceedings in which the respondent is a party, the court may make an order of its own motion, without the necessity of an application from any of the parties, when it considers that an order should be made for the benefit of any of the parties or any relevant child.

11.13 The FLA 1996 thus gives the court the power to act immediately when it perceives a need to protect the parties or children. It can make an order on its own motion, for example, in proceedings under the Children Act 1989. It could also act on a verbal request from one of the parties if it became apparent during the course of family proceedings that an order would be of benefit. Non-molestation orders should be considered in particular when the court has made an EPO under Children Act 1989 s44 which includes a Children Act 1989 s44A order excluding the abuser from the home (see paras **1.15** to **1.22**).

11.14 When the parties are associated because they are engaged to marry, substantial proof of the engagement is required, as set out in FLA 1996 s44 (see paras **10.24** to **10.28** for a fuller discussion). Where the agreement has been terminated, no application for a non-molestation order can be made after three years have elapsed since the parties ended the engagement. The three-year period is calculated beginning with the day on which the engagement is broken. This could lead to evidential problems where it is disputed that the parties are associated because of a broken engagement. Not many people end their engagements in writing, and if they do, they are unlikely to keep copies of the letter. Given that non-molestation orders do not infringe personal rights, the courts will probably be willing to accept affidavit evidence about the date of termination, although proof about the existence of the engagement must be strictly followed as set out in FLA 1996 s44.

Criteria for making an order

11.15 When deciding whether to make an order, and if so, in what manner to make it, the court must have regard to:[6]

---

6 FLA 1996 s42(5).

... all the circumstances including the need to secure the health, safety and well-being –
(a) of the applicant, or [where the court makes an order without there being any written application], the person for whose benefit the order would be made; and
(b) of any relevant child.

'Health' means physical or mental health.[7]

Time-limits and duration of an order

11.16 There are no time-limits within which an application must be made, except in the case of engaged couples (see paras **10.24** to **10.28**). Clearly, the longer the lapse of time since the last incidence of harassment, the less likely it is that the court will accept that an order is necessary. But the difficulties which were previously encountered when trying to obtain injunctions post-decree absolute or under the Domestic Violence and Matrimonial Proceedings Act 1976 when couples had not been living together for more than six months have been removed by the FLA 1996. The list of associated persons includes people who have been married or who have at some time cohabited with the respondent.

11.17 The order may be made for a specified period or 'until further order'.[8] If the order is made in other family proceedings, rather than as separate proceedings under the FLA 1996, then it will cease to have effect if those proceedings are withdrawn or dismissed.[9]

11.18 Under the pre-FLA 1996 law, the court usually inserted a date when the order came to an end (usually in six months' time), and there was a space on the court form (N16) which gave that date. It may be that the courts will continue to make orders for a defined period, given the previous practice.[10]

---

7   FLA 1996 s63.
8   FLA 1996 s42(7).
9   FLA 1996 s42(8).
10 R Bird *Domestic Violence – the new law* (Jordans, 1996).

CHAPTER 12

Occupation orders

Introduction

12.1 One of the Law Commission's objectives in reforming the law on domestic violence was to remove the confusion that had arisen between the different types of court orders dealing with occupation of the home: ouster orders, occupation orders and exclusion orders.[1] It therefore called for one type of order, called an 'occupation order', which could have a variety of possible terms. The FLA 1996 has created five different kinds of occupation orders, which vary depending on the parties' relationship to each other and whether or not one or both of them is entitled to occupy the property. They are found in FLA 1996 ss33, 35, 36, 37 and 38 of the Act, and will no doubt come to be known generally by their section numbers.

12.2 In its Report the Law Commission distinguished between 'declaratory orders' which declare, confer or extend occupation rights, and 'regulatory orders' which control the exercise of existing rights.[2]

12.3 Declaratory orders are those which:[3]

(a) declare pre-existing occupation rights in the home;
(b) extend statutory occupation rights beyond the termination of the marriage on divorce or death;
(c) grant occupation rights in the home to non-entitled occupants.

12.4 Regulatory orders are those which:[4]

(a) require one party to leave the home;

1 Law Commission Report no 207, *Domestic Violence and Occupation of the Family Home* (HMSO, 1992) para 4.1.
2 Ibid.
3 Ibid, para 4.2.

4 Ibid.

(b) suspend occupation rights and/or prohibit one party from entering or re-entering the home, or part of the home;

(c) require one party to allow the other to enter and/or remain in the home;

(d) regulate the occupation of the home by either or both of the parties;

(e) terminate occupation rights; and/or

(f) exclude one party from a defined area in the vicinity of the home.

12.5 The court is given power to make orders which contain some of the above terms, but the power varies depending on under which section the order is being made. For each type of order, the applicant and respondent must be associated with one another (see paras **10.3** to **10.31**). The court has the widest range of powers under FLA 1996 s33, for example, which is available to applicants who are already legally entitled to occupy the home. Where the applicant is not otherwise entitled to occupy the home in her own right, she may only apply for an order against her spouse/former spouse or cohabitant/ former cohabitant, and the court's powers are restricted to some of the regulatory powers. Remember that occupation orders can be made in respect of existing or former family homes, but also in respect of a home in which the parties intended to live together, even if they never did so (see paras **10.34** to **10.39** for a fuller discussion).

12.6 Each of the possible orders will be discussed below and referred to by their section numbers. The type of applicant and the criteria for obtaining an order varies with each order. When the court makes an order under s33, s35 or s36 it has power under s40 to add ancillary terms to deal with issues arising out of occupation, such as payment of outgoings, etc. For definitions of crucial expressions such as 'associated persons', 'entitled persons', etc, please refer to Chapter 10 for a fuller discussion.

12.7 It should be noted that if the court decided that it had no power to make an order under one section, it could make an order under another section if the criteria for the latter order are met. For example, if the applicant applies for a FLA 1996 s33 order as an entitled applicant, and the court found that she was not an entitled person, it may nevertheless make an order under one of the other sections, which can be used by non-entitled applicants against their spouses/former spouses or cohabitants/former cohabitants.

Section 33 orders: entitled applicant

Who can be parties?

12.8 See also Chapter 10 for a full discussion of the meaning of terms used in this section.

12.9 The parties must each come within the 'associated persons' category. The applicant must be a 'person entitled', but it does not matter whether the respondent is entitled to occupy or not. A person entitled[5] is one who has:

- sole or joint ownership;
- a sole or joint tenancy;
- a contractual licence;
- a beneficial interest;
- matrimonial home rights;
- a right to occupy by virtue of some enactment.

12.10 In most cases it will be easy to establish that the applicant is an entitled person by virtue of being a sole or joint owner, or a sole or joint tenant, of the home. If the applicant is married to the respondent, she will be a person entitled by virtue of her matrimonial home rights. Occupational status is not always easy to determine, however. Whether a person occupies a property as a tenant or licensee can involve complex questions of housing law. Similarly, whether a person has a beneficial interest in a property may not be clearly established other than by taking court proceedings to obtain a declaration of a constructive trust.

12.11 The situations to which special regard should be paid are those where, for example, a woman has moved into a property of which her cohabitant or relative is the owner or tenant. If, for example, an elderly woman goes to live with her son in his home (whether he is a tenant or an owner-occupier), she may have a contractual licence if she pays an agreed amount for her board and lodging. On the other hand, she may only be a bare licensee if there was no agreement about the terms on which she would be staying in her son's home. It would be unusual for a cohabitant to have a contractual licence with her partner. Bare licensees are by definition non-entitled persons.

12.12 Another example where the applicant's status as an entitled person may not be obvious is where she has obtained a beneficial

---

5   FLA 1996 s33(1).

interest in the property through her contribution to the purchase price or mortgage repayments, but she is not the legal owner or mortgagor. Unless a deed of trust has been drawn up to evidence her beneficial ownership, she will have to apply to the court for a declaration of an implied, resulting or constructive trust.[6]

12.13 If the occupational status of the applicant is not clear, it would nevertheless be possible to apply for an order under FLA 1996 s33 and ask the court to make a declaration of her status. However, cases involving the declaration of a trust are generally quite involved and are more likely to be contested. If the applicant and respondent are cohabitants or former cohabitants, it would nevertheless be possible to apply for an occupation order under FLA 1996 s36 (non-entitled cohabitants). If the parties have never lived together as husband and wife, then the only way to obtain an occupation order under the FLA 1996 will be to establish first that the applicant is an entitled person.

12.14 If the parties are associated because they are or were engaged, an application for a FLA 1996 s33 order can only be brought within three years of the termination of the engagement (see paras **10.24** to **10.28**).[7]

What are the possible terms of the order?

12.15 FLA 1996 s33(4) gives the court the power to declare that the applicant is an entitled person and to specify her occupational status, as discussed above. If her status as an entitled person is contested, this would need to be resolved first, before the court considers whether to make an order and what terms to include.

12.16 The possible terms for regulating the occupation of the home are as follows:[8]

(a) enforce the applicant's entitlement to remain in occupation as against the other person ('the respondent');

(b) require the respondent to permit the applicant to enter and remain in the dwelling-house or part of the dwelling-house;

(c) regulate the occupation of the dwelling-house by either or both parties;

(d) if the respondent is entitled . . . , prohibit, suspend or restrict the exercise by him of his right to occupy the dwelling-house;

---

6 See Cretney and Masson *Principles of Family Law* (Sweet and Maxwell, 6th edn, 1997) pp126–148 for a discussion of implied trusts.

7 FLA 1996 s33(2).

8 FLA 1996 s33(3).

(e) if the respondent has matrimonial home rights in relation to the dwelling-house and the applicant is the other spouse, restrict or terminate those rights;

(f) require the respondent to leave the dwelling-house or part of the dwelling-house; or

(g) exclude the respondent from a defined area in which the dwelling-house is included.

12.17 It is also possible for the court to include a term that the applicant's matrimonial home rights in the dwelling-house will not be brought to an end by the death of the other spouse or by the termination (otherwise than by death) of the marriage.[9]

12.18 Each of these terms will be discussed more fully below.

(a) Enforce entitlement to remain in occupation

12.19 This term would be required where, for example, the respondent has threatened to make the applicant move out, or to throw her out, or where there is a genuine fear that she will be forced out of the home for some reason. Note that the court can only enforce her entitlement to remain in occupation *as against the respondent*. Thus, this term will not protect her against an order for possession obtained by a landlord or mortgagor.

(b) Permit the applicant to enter and remain in all or part of the dwelling-house

12.20 Where the applicant has been excluded by the respondent or has fled the home, the respondent may be ordered to permit her to move back in. This term envisages the possibility of ordering the parties to share all of the home or to occupy different parts of it. For example, if there is enough room, the respondent could be ordered to stay in one of the bedrooms and not to use the living room, etc.

(c) Regulate the occupation of the dwelling-house

12.21 This term appears to overlap with (b) above, but could be used to draw up a quite detailed order about which rooms could be used by whom and at what times. Such orders rarely work well in practice and should be avoided if possible, particularly in cases of serious molestation or violence.

(d) Prohibit, suspend or restrict respondent's exercise of his right to occupy

12.22 If the respondent is entitled to occupy the property in his own

9   FLA 1996 s33(5).

right, for example, as joint owner or joint tenant, the court can make an order which overrides his rights under property law to occupy the home. The order could prohibit him from living in the home entirely and indefinitely, or suspend his right to occupy for a given period or pending the making of another order, or restrict his right to occupy to certain parts of the property or to certain times.

(e) Restrict or terminate respondent's matrimonial home rights

12.23 Matrimonial home rights are set out in FLA 1996 s30 and discussed above, at paras 10.40 to 10.46. In essence they give a person the right to occupy the matrimonial home if the spouse is the sole owner or sole tenant. Thus, where a woman owned or rented the matrimonial home in her sole name, she could apply for her husband's right to occupy under FLA 1996 s30 to be restricted to part of the house or to be withdrawn entirely, thereby excluding him from the property. This would not deny him the right to apply for a property adjustment order, however.

(f) Require respondent to leave all or part of the dwelling-house

12.24 This term encompasses what used to be called an 'ouster order'. It overlaps with the above terms where the respondent is entitled to occupy, but can also be used where the respondent is a non-entitled person.

12.25 There are instances when it might be more beneficial for the applicant to use property law to eject an abuser than to apply for an occupation order. One such case is if the applicant is entitled to occupy because she is the owner-occupier or the tenant of the dwelling-house, and the respondent lives with her as a member of the household, or because he is a relative, or for any other reason apart from marriage or cohabitation. For example, let us suppose than an adult son lives with his mother, who is the sole owner or tenant of the family home. In property law terms he will be her licensee, and she will be his resident landlord. As such he comes within the category of people who are excluded from the protection given under the Protection from Eviction Act 1977, which otherwise requires a landlord to obtain a court order for possession before evicting a tenant or licensee. She will only need to give him reasonable or contractual (if a contract exists) notice, after which he becomes a trespasser. The notice need not be in writing. What is 'reasonable' depends on the circumstances. In cases of violence, it could be argued that no notice need be given. She may then make him leave without the necessity of obtaining a possession order, eg, change the locks and not allow him back in. Although such action may be fraught with physical difficulties, she would be within her rights to exclude him without the necessity of taking any legal proceedings. He would not be entitled to apply for an occupation order under the FLA 1996, nor would he be able to sue for wrongful eviction. This is worth remembering where the applicant might have difficulty in paying for an injunction or in obtaining legal aid.

(g) Exclude the respondent from a defined area around the home

12.26 This power is similar to that set out in the Domestic Violence and Matrimonial Proceedings Act 1976, and previous case-law under that Act will still be relevant. In the past the courts were reluctant to exercise their power to exclude the respondent from an area, given the possibilities for accidentally contravening the order. If the courts follow their previous practice, the applicant will have to demonstrate that such an order is necessary for her protection, for example, to keep the respondent from loitering outside her home and following her or harassing her from a distance.

(h) Extend the applicant's matrimonial home rights beyond the end of the marriage

12.27 If the applicant is entitled to occupy only by virtue of her matrimonial home rights, she could be left in a precarious position should her husband die or the marriage be dissolved without a property adjustment order having been made. The Act therefore gives the court the power to extend those rights beyond the date of the termination of the marriage. An application for an order in these terms should be made in every case where the applicant's spouse is the sole owner or tenant of the family home.

12.28 The court may make an order extending matrimonial home rights where it considers that in all of the circumstances it is just and reasonable to do so.[10]

What factors must the court take into account before making an order?

12.29 The court has a *power* to make an occupation order in some circumstances and a *duty* to make an order in other, more serious, circumstances, where it appears that significant harm may occur if an

10   FLA 1996 s33(8).

order is not made. The criteria applied in each case differ. When making a discretionary order, the court must consider the factors set out immediately below. The court must apply a balance of harm test in order to ascertain whether an occupation order is mandatory. See also paras **10.47** to **10.57**. If an order is made, the court has the power under s40 to include terms relating to ancillary issues (see paras **12.97** to **12.101**).

Criteria for discretionary orders

12.30 When deciding whether to make an occupation order and, if so, which of the terms shown in (*a*) to (*h*) above to include in the order, the court must take into account all of the circumstances of the case, including:[11]

a) the housing needs and housing resources of each of the parties and of any relevant child;
b) the financial resources of each of the parties;
c) the likely effect of any order, or of any decision by the court not to make an order, on the health, safety or well-being of the parties and of any relevant child; and
d) the conduct of the parties in relation to each other and otherwise.

'Health' is defined as physical and mental health. See paras **10.32** and **10.33** for the definition of 'any relevant child'.

12.31 This list of factors gives the court a very wide discretion. None of the four criteria is given more weight than the others by the FLA 1996. It will be for the judge to decide in each case how an order, or the lack of an order, will affect the parties and any children. The addition of the fourth factor, conduct, permits the judge to make a value judgment about the behaviour of the parties.

Criteria for mandatory orders

12.32 If, when hearing an application, the judge considers that the applicant or a child is likely to suffer 'significant harm' if an order is not made, then s/he should take into account the factors set out in FLA 1996 s33(7). The harm likely to be caused must be attributable to the respondent's conduct. The FLA 1996 does not state whether the harm has to be a direct result of the respondent's behaviour, or whether it can be the indirect result. How the courts will interpret 'attributable' remains to be seen.

12.33 The balance of harm test set out in s33(7) is as follows:

11 FLA 1996 s33(6).

If it appears to the court that the applicant or any relevant child is likely
to suffer significant harm attributable to conduct of the respondent if an
order . . . is not made, the court shall make the order unless it appears to
it that –
  (a) the respondent or any relevant child is likely to suffer significant
      harm if the order is made; and
  (b) the harm likely to be suffered by the respondent or child in that event
      is as great as, or greater than, the harm attributable to conduct of the
      respondent which is likely to be suffered by the applicant or child if
      the order is not made.

12.34 How will these tests work in practice? First of all, they dis-
tinguish between 'hardship' and 'harm'. FLA 1996 s63 states that the
word 'harm':

  (a) in relation to a person who has reached the age of eighteen years,
      means ill-treatment or the impairment of health; and
  (b) in relation to a child, means ill-treatment or the impairment of
      health or development . . .

12.35 It goes on to define 'health' as including physical or mental
health. 'Development' means physical, intellectual, emotional, social
or behavioural development. 'Ill-treatment' includes forms of ill-
treatment which are not physical. In relation to a child, ill-treatment
includes sexual abuse. Where the question of whether the harm suffered by a child is significant turns on the question of his/her health or
development, then a comparison must be drawn with the health or
development which could reasonably be expected of a similar child.[12]

12.36 The word 'significant' is not defined in the Act. One encounters
the phrase 'significant harm' in the Children Act 1989, however. The
guidance to that Act uses the dictionary meaning of the word 'significant', as that which is 'considerable, noteworthy or important'.[13] That
definition was confirmed in the case of *Humberside CC v B*.[14]

12.37 In relation to adult applicants, one must show that, unless an
order is made, the respondent is likely to carry on ill-treating the
applicant in some significant way; or one must show that the applicant's physical or mental health is likely to be impaired as a result of
the respondent's behaviour if an order is not made. This will be easier
to prove if the applicant is still living with or in the same household as
the respondent, and in such cases an occupation order will be manda-

12 FLA 1996 s63(3).
13 *The Children Act 1989: Guidance and Regulations* (HMSO, 1991), Volume 1,
    Court Orders, para 3.19.
14 [1993] 1 FLR 257.

tory. If she has moved to a place of safety which is available to her for a long time, then she may not necessarily be likely to suffer significant harm if an order is not made, although she may suffer greater hardship. In the latter instance, an occupation order would be discretionary rather than mandatory.

12.38 Where an order will affect a relevant child, the definition of 'harm' is expanded to include the child's development. Therefore, one must show that the child will be ill-treated, or that his/her physical or mental health or his/her development will suffer as a result of the respondent's behaviour if an order is not made. Where the child is still living in the respondent's home at the time of the application, and the respondent is abusing or ill-treating the child in some way, then an order will be mandatory. Similarly, if the child's mental health or development is being badly affected by observing the respondent's conduct towards the applicant, then the court may consider that s/he is likely to suffer significant harm if the respondent remains in the home. If the child has been removed to a place of safety, then it may be that his/her development is likely to be impaired by the move, which was caused by the respondent's conduct. In such a case it is arguable that the harm is attributable to the respondent's conduct, but it will depend on what type of accommodation is available and how being moved out of the family home has affected the child.

12.39 When preparing an application for an occupation order, consideration should always be given to whether and how 'significant harm' can be shown to be a likely effect if an order is not made. Medical evidence may be required, and photographs of injuries may be helpful.

What is the maximum duration of an order?

12.40 Occupation orders under FLA 1996 s33 can be made for a specified period, until the occurrence of a specified event, or until further order.[15] Given that the applicant must be entitled to occupy the premises in order to obtain a s33 order, the court may be willing to make an order which continues 'until further order'. This could effectively mean that the order would continue indefinitely, if no other proceedings were brought. However, an occupation order can never be a final order in the same sense as a property adjustment order is final. Ouster orders were commonly limited to three or six months'

---

15 FLA 1996 s33(10).

duration, and it may be that the courts will continue to impose time limits on occupation orders.

Section 35 orders: non-entitled former spouse

Who can be parties?

12.41 An application for an occupation order under this section can only be made by a non-entitled former spouse. The respondent will be her former husband who is entitled to occupy the home as legal or beneficial owner, tenant, licensee, or under any enactment giving him a right to occupy.[16]

12.42 Applications can thus be made for occupation orders after decree absolute in situations where the former husband is solely entitled to occupy the dwelling-house that was or was intended to become the matrimonial home of the parties.[17] Applications by people who are still married should be made under FLA 1996 s33, because they will be entitled to occupy by virtue of their matrimonial home rights.

12.43 If the applicant has an equitable interest in the home because, for example, she contributed to the purchase price or to the repayment of the mortgage, she may nevertheless apply for an occupation order under this section[18] as though she were non-entitled, without such an application being viewed as an admission that she is not entitled. This provision will enable women in this situation to obtain an occupation order pending the outcome of any application for a declaration of trust or other applications regarding the property.

What terms must be included in the order?

12.44 Set out below are the mandatory terms which must be included in every order, depending on whether the applicant is in or out of occupation. There are also discretionary terms which may be included to regulate the occupation of the home by the respondent. Guidelines are given in the FLA 1996 in respect of both mandatory and discretionary terms. The court also has power to include terms relating to ancillary matters under s40 (see paras **12.97** to **12.101**).

---

16 FLA 1996 s35(1).
17 FLA 1996 s35(1)(c) and (2).
18 FLA 1996 s35(11).

12.45 The decision-making process for FLA 1996 s35 orders can be seen as having two stages. The court must first decide whether a s35 order should be made, following the guidelines for mandatory terms. If it decides an order should be made, it must then consider which, if any, of the discretionary terms should be included, following the guidelines for discretionary terms and applying the balance of harm test.

Mandatory terms where applicant is in occupation

12.46 If the applicant is still in occupation at the time the application is made and at the hearing, then the order must contain terms:[19]

(a) giving the applicant the right not to be evicted or excluded from the dwelling-house or any part of it by the respondent for the period specified in the order; and

(b) prohibiting the respondent from evicting or excluding the applicant during that period.

12.47 These terms are self-explanatory and protect the applicant from being excluded from the dwelling-house by her former husband. It will obviously not protect her occupation as against third parties, such as mortgagees or landlords, who obtain possession orders. The right to remain in occupation will only continue for the duration of the order, which is discussed below.

Mandatory terms where applicant is not in occupation

12.48 If the applicant is no longer in occupation, then the order must contain terms:[20]

(a) giving the applicant the right to enter into and occupy the dwelling-house for the period specified in the order; and

(b) requiring the respondent to permit the exercise of that right.

12.49 If the applicant has been thrown out of the dwelling by her former spouse, or if she has had to leave for her own protection, then the order must contain terms which give her a right to occupy and which require the respondent to permit her to live there. Again, these terms only give the applicant rights as against the respondent. If the dwelling were, for example, owned by her former spouse and his father, there would appear to be no protection for her if the former father-in-law will not co-operate.

19 FLA 1996 s35(3).
20 FLA 1996 s35(4).

What factors must be taken into account when deciding whether to make a s35 order?[21]

Criteria for mandatory terms

12.50 If an order is made under FLA 1996 s35, it will have to include one or other set of mandatory terms discussed in paras **12.44** to **12.49** above. When deciding whether to make a s35 order, the court must take into account all of the circumstances of the case, including:[22]

(a) the housing needs and housing resources of each of the parties and of any relevant child;

(b) the financial resources of each of the parties;

(c) the likely effect of any order, or any decision by the court not [to make an order], on the health, safety or well-being of the parties and of any relevant child;

(d) the conduct of the parties in relation to each other and otherwise;

(e) the length of time that has elapsed since the parties ceased to live together;

(f) the length of time that has elapsed since the marriage was dissolved or annulled; and

(g) the existence of any pending proceedings between the parties –

　(i) for an order under section 23A or 24 of the Matrimonial Causes Act 1973 (property adjustment orders in connection with divorce proceedings etc.);

　(ii) for an order under paragraph 1(2)(d) or (e) of Schedule 1 to the Children Act 1989 (orders for financial relief against parents); or

　(iii) relating to the legal or beneficial ownership of the dwelling-house.

The factors set out in FLA 1996 s35(6)(a) to (d) are also found in FLA 1996 s33 and are discussed in paras **12.30** and **12.31**.

12.51 FLA 1996 s35(6)(e) and (f) require the court to take into account how much time has passed since the parties stopped living together and/or since the marriage ended. The FLA 1996 therefore recognises that problems between couples can extend beyond the time they stop living together and even after the marriage has been dissolved. It will presumably become harder to obtain a s35 order as time passes. It would be prudent, if possible, to avoid having an applicant in this position, because the orders have limited duration; the better alternative is to apply to extend her matrimonial home rights before decree absolute.

12.52 The court must also take into account the existence of other

21　FLA 1996 s35(6) and (7).
22　FLA 1996 s35(6).

proceedings relating to property and finances either in ancillary relief proceedings, under the Children Act 1989, or in proceedings in equity for a declaration of trust. Such proceedings could adjust occupation rights between the parties permanently or for a long period of time. It is suggested that an applicant who is involved in such proceedings would be in a stronger position than one who has accepted that her former husband ultimately has the sole legal and beneficial interests in the property.

What discretionary terms may be included in the order?

Discretionary terms where applicant is or is not in occupation

12.53   Having decided to make an order, the court must include mandatory terms either protecting the applicant's occupation or permitting her to re-enter and occupy the former matrimonial home. It may then include any of the following terms, which will affect the respondent's occupation of the dwelling:[23]

(a) regulate the occupation of the dwelling-house by either or both of the parties;
(b) prohibit, suspend or restrict the exercise by the respondent of his right to occupy the dwelling-house;
(c) require the respondent to leave the dwelling-house or part of the dwelling-house; or
(d) exclude the respondent from a defined area in which the dwelling-house is included.

These are some of the same terms which can be included in s33 orders. See paras **12.15** to **12.28** for discussion of these terms.

What factors must be taken into account when deciding whether to include discretionary terms?

Criteria for discretionary terms

12.54   In deciding whether to include one or some of the discretionary terms, which deal with the respondent's occupation of the dwelling-house, the court must take into account the factors listed in FLA 1996 s35(6)(a) to (e)[24] (see para **12.50**), and also apply the balance of harm test (see paras **12.32** to **12.39**).

12.55   Therefore, when deciding what kind of order to make, the

23 FLA 1996 s35(5).
24 FLA 1996 s35(7).

court must first decide whether the non-entitled former spouse can make a case for occupying the former matrimonial home, and then decide whether the respondent should be excluded or have his right of occupation restricted in some way. The latter order will not automatically follow if the applicant is allowed to live in the home, *unless* there is a danger of the applicant or a relevant child suffering significant harm attributable to the respondent's conduct. If the court considers that the applicant or child is likely to suffer significant harm, then one of the regulatory terms must be included in the order, unless the respondent can show why such an order should not be made.

12.56 In other words, where there appears to be a likelihood of significant harm to the applicant or a child, the court will be under a *duty* to include one or more of the otherwise discretionary terms,[25] unless the respondent can show that he and any relevant child would suffer greater harm if an order is made.

12.57 Consequently, having convinced the court that she should be allowed to live in the former matrimonial home, the applicant will then have to show that it will not be safe or healthy for her and the child(ren) to live there with the respondent. If she can convince the court that she or the child is likely to suffer significant harm, the onus then shifts to the respondent to show that he will suffer equal or greater harm if an order is made. If he is unable to do so, the court must make an order excluding him or restricting his occupation in some way.

What is the maximum duration of a s35 order?

12.58 The order must be limited initially to a period not exceeding six months, but it can be extended one or more times for periods of up to six months each time.[26]

12.59 Orders cannot be made after the death of either of the former spouses, and they end automatically on the death of either of them.[27]

Effect of a s35 order on security of tenure

12.60 The FLA 1996 states that where a s35 order is made, the occupation by the applicant shall count as occupation by the respondent. Consequently, security of tenure will not be lost in rented properties

25 FLA 1996 s35(8).
26 FLA 1996 s35(10).
27 FLA 1996 s35(9).

by the non-occupation of the respondent tenant. If the dwelling is privately owned, the applicant will be entitled to make mortgage payments, which the mortgagee must treat as having come from the respondent. The same applies to payment of any other liabilities or outgoings relating to the dwelling.

Section 36 orders: non-entitled cohabitant or former cohabitant

12.61 The terms of an order under FLA 1996 s36 are exactly the same as those set out in s35 for former spouses. The difference between the two orders is in the list of factors which the court must take into account before making an order. FLA 1996 s36 orders are more limited in duration, as well. The FLA 1996 thus requires the court to take into account that fact that, although the parties may have lived together as husband and wife – perhaps for years – they never actually got married. How the courts will make this distinction in practice remains to be seen.

Who may be the parties?

12.62 An application under FLA 1996 s36 can only be made by a cohabitant or former cohabitant who is not entitled to occupy the home. The respondent must be an entitled person.[28] See paras 10.6 to 10.9 and 10.34 to 10.39 for a full discussion of the meaning of the terms 'cohabitant' and 'entitled person'.

12.63 If the applicant has an equitable interest in the property or in the proceeds of sale of the property, she may nevertheless apply for an occupation order under s36,[29] without it being taken as an admission in other proceedings that she does not have an equitable interest. This will enable women who need to take proceedings for a declaration of trust to obtain an occupation order pending the hearing of other applications relating to the ownership of the home.

What are the possible terms of the order?

Mandatory terms when applicant is or is not in occupation (s36(3) and (4))

12.64 As previously explained, these terms are exactly the same

28 FLA 1996 s36(1) and (2).
29 FLA 1996 s36(11).

as the mandatory terms under FLA 1996 s35 (see paras **12.44** to **12.49**). If an order is made, the court has power under s40 to include terms relating to ancillary issues (see paras **12.97** to **12.101**).

What factors must be taken into account when deciding whether to make a s36 order (s36(6) and (7))?

12.65 The criteria for making an order under s36 are similar to those for a s35 order, but with additional factors reflecting the difference in the nature of the parties' relationship.

Criteria for mandatory terms

12.66 If an order is made under FLA 1996 s36, it will have to include one or other set of mandatory terms discussed in paras **12.44** to **12.49**. When deciding whether to make such an order, the court must take into account all of the circumstances of the case, including:[30]

(a) the housing needs and housing resources of each of the parties and of any relevant child;

(b) the financial resources of each of the parties;

(c) the likely effect of any order, or any decision by the court not [to make an order], on the health, safety or well-being of the parties and of any relevant child;

(d) the conduct of the parties in relation to each other and otherwise;

(e) the nature of the parties' relationship;

(f) the length of time during which they have lived together as husband and wife;

(g) whether there are or have been any children who are children of both parties or for whom both parties have or have had parental responsibility;

(h) the length of time that has elapsed since the parties ceased to live together; and

(i) the existence of any pending proceedings between the parties –
   (i) for an order under paragraph 1(2)(d) or (e) of Schedule 1 to the Children Act 1989 (orders for financial relief against parents); or
   (ii) relating to the legal or beneficial ownership of the dwelling-house.

12.67 FLA 1996 s41(2) adds another factor in relation to cohabitants or former cohabitants:

Where the court is required to consider the nature of the parties' relationship, it is to have regard to the fact that they have not given each other the commitment involved in marriage.

12.68 The factors set out in s36(6)(a) to (d) above are exactly the

30   FLA 1996 s36(6).

same as those under ss33 and 35, discussed at paras **12.30, 12.31** and **12.50**.

12.69 The factors in s36(6)(e) to (h) ensure that the court will take into account the nature of the parties' relationship to each other. FLA 1996 s41 makes explicit the requirement to differentiate between married and unmarried couples. Presumably the court would treat an applicant who has lived with the respondent for only a few weeks differently to one who has lived with someone for years.

12.70 The Law Commission concluded that distinctions ought to be made according to life-style when considering occupation orders, and that line of thinking underlies the whole Act. It is presumed, therefore, that an applicant whose relationship resembles that of a 'normal' married couple will receive a more sympathetic response than, say, the applicant whose life-style is more towards the 'double income, no kids' independent way of living.

12.71 Even where a couple's relationship resembles that of a married couple in every respect except that of a formal ceremony, FLA 1996 s41 ensures that they will be treated differently to married couples. When taking instructions, one should obtain as much information as possible about the parties' relationship and the level of commitment which existed, as these factors will be important.

12.72 Finally, the court must take into account whether there are any proceedings which have financial or property adjustment implications for the parties. For example, a non-entitled woman with children may be permitted to stay in the dwelling-house with the children as long as it is required as the family home.

What discretionary terms may be included in a s36 order?

Discretionary terms (s36(5))

12.73 Again, these terms replicate those found in FLA 1996 s35 (see para **12.53** and also paras **12.15** to **12.28**).

What factors must the court take into account when deciding whether to include discretionary terms?

Criteria for discretionary terms

12.74 In deciding whether to include any of the regulatory (discretionary) terms in an occupation order, which will affect the respondent's right to occupy the dwelling (see paras **12.15** to **12.28** and para **12.53**), the court must take into account all of the circumstances of the case, including the factors set out in (a) to (d) in para **12.66**.[31] In addition, the court must consider questions which are similar to the balance of harm test, as follows:[32]

> (a) whether the applicant or any relevant child is likely to suffer significant harm attributable to conduct of the respondent if [one of the discretionary terms] is not included in the order; and
> (b) whether the harm likely to be suffered by the respondent or child if the [discretionary term] is included is as great as or greater than the harm attributable to conduct of the respondent which is likely to be suffered by the applicant or child if the [term] is not included.

12.75 In other words, the court must consider the level of hardship and the likely harm which the parties might suffer in every case, when deciding whether or not to include any terms which will restrict the respondent's right of occupation or exclude him from the property. Unlike orders under FLA 1996 s33 or s35, the court will *not* be under a duty to exclude the respondent, even if it considers that the applicant or a relevant child is at risk of suffering greater harm than the respondent is likely to suffer. The balance of harm is merely one of the factors to which the court must give consideration; it is not an overriding factor. Thus the regulatory terms will always be discretionary where an application is made by a non-entitled cohabitant.

What is the maximum duration of a s36 order?

12.76 The court must initially limit the duration of the order for a specified period not exceeding six months. It may be extended one further time for a period not exceeding six months.[33] This is another way in which the FLA 1996 discriminates between applicants who are or have been married and those who are single.

12.77 FLA 1996 s36 orders cannot be made after the death of either of the parties, and end automatically if either party dies.

Effect of a s36 order on security of tenure

12.78 The FLA 1996 states that where a s36 order is made, the occupation by the applicant shall count as occupation by the respondent

31 FLA 1996 s36(7).
32 FLA 1996 s36(8).
33 FLA 1996 s36(10).

(s36(13)). Consequently, security of tenure will not be lost in rented properties by the non-occupation of the respondent tenant. If the dwelling is privately owned, the applicant will be entitled to make mortgage payments, which the mortgagee must treat as having come from the respondent. The same applies to payment of any other liabilities or outgoings relating to the dwelling.

Section 37 orders: neither spouse/former spouse entitled to occupy

Who may be parties?

12.79 An order can only be made under this section if:[34]

a) the parties are or have been married to each other;
b) both are still in occupation of the matrimonial or former matrimonial home; and
c) neither of them is entitled to remain in occupation by virtue of having legal or equitable ownership, a tenancy, a contractual licence, or through any enactment giving a right of occupation.

12.80 From the above requirements, it can be seen that applications under this section will be rare. Because neither of the parties can be 'entitled persons', it effectively means that an order can only be made in situations where both the parties are in occupation as squatters or bare licensees, or are in occupation after the date given by a court order for possession of the premises. People occupying in the first and third set of circumstances are hardly likely to apply for an occupation order. Indeed, since squatters are trespassers, it seems odd that parliament should give the courts the power to regulate how they occupy premises in which they have no right to live. The Law Commission thought that squatters ought to be able to obtain an occupation order, however, and this is what has been enacted. An application might be more likely where a couple are living with friends or relatives as bare licensees (without the formality of a contractual licence).

What are the possible terms of the order?

12.81 All of the possible terms of a FLA 1996 s37 order are discretionary, but the court will be under a duty to make an order

---

34 FLA 1996 s37(1).

including one or more of these terms if the applicant or a child is likely to suffer significant harm. They are as follows:[35]

(a) require the respondent to permit the applicant to enter and remain in the dwelling-house or part of the dwelling-house;
(b) regulate the occupation of the dwelling-house by either or both of the spouses [or former spouses];
(c) require the respondent to leave the dwelling-house or part of the dwelling-house; or
(d) exclude the respondent from a defined area in which the dwelling-house is included.

The words in brackets in sub-paragraph (b) above are not in the FLA 1996 itself. This would appear to be an oversight on the part of the draughtsmen, since the section is meant to be available for use by former spouses.

12.82 These terms are some of the terms possible under FLA 1996 s33 and are discussed more fully at paras **12.15** to **12.28**.

12.83 The Law Commission was being very thorough by including this section in its draft bill, but it is difficult to envisage its use. For example, people who are living as bare licensees with someone who is the owner or tenant of the premises will be excluded licensees under the Protection from Eviction Act 1977 s3A. The owner or tenant may eject a bare licensee by giving reasonable notice, which need not be in writing, and without the necessity of obtaining a court order for possession. In cases of domestic violence, one possible remedy would be for the owner/tenant to tell the perpetrator to move out, and then to change the locks once he has left. The protection of a non-molestation order may still be needed in some circumstances, but eviction by a resident landlord would save any argument about whether the respondent had a right to remain in occupation.

12.84 Note that this section only regulates occupation as between the parties. If the perpetrator of the violence is the owner/tenant with whom the couple are living, then an occupation order in favour of the victim will not be possible under FLA 1996, although she could obtain a non-molestation order if the perpetrator is an associated person (see paras **10.3** to **10.31**).

---

35 FLA 1996 s37(3).

What factors must be taken into account when making a s37 order (s37(4))?

12.85 As stated previously, all of the possible terms under this section are discretionary, but the court will be under a duty to make an order in certain circumstances.

Criteria for discretionary terms

12.86 The factors which the court must take into account are exactly the same as those set out in FLA 1996 s33(6), as follows:

(a) the housing needs and housing resources of each of the parties and of any relevant child;
(b) the financial resources of each of the parties;
(c) the likely effect of any order, or of any decision by the court not to [make an order], on the health, safety or well-being of the parties and of any relevant child; and
(d) the conduct of the parties in relation to each other and otherwise.

'Health' is defined as physical and mental health. See paras **10.32** and **10.33** for the definition of 'any relevant child'.

Criteria for mandatory orders

12.87 If, when hearing an application, the judge considers that the applicant or a child is likely to suffer 'significant harm' if an order is not made, then s/he should take into account the factors set out in FLA 1996 s33(7). The harm likely to be caused must be attributable to the respondent's conduct. The Act does not state whether the harm has to be a direct result of the respondent's behaviour, or whether it can be the indirect result. How the courts will interpret 'attributable' remains to be seen.

12.88 The balance of harm test set out in s33(7) is as follows:

If it appears to the court that the applicant or any relevant child is likely to suffer significant harm attributable to conduct of the respondent if an order . . . is not made, the court shall make the order unless it appears to it that –
(a) the respondent or any relevant child is likely to suffer significant harm if the order is made; and
(b) the harm likely to be suffered by the respondent or child in that event is as great as, or greater than, the harm attributable to conduct of the respondent which is likely to be suffered by the applicant or child if the order is not made.

See paras **10.48** to **10.58** for a full discussion of the balance of harm test.

What is the maximum duration of a s37 order?

12.89 An order under this section must be limited initially to a period not exceeding six months, and may be extended on one or more occasions for a further specified period not exceeding six months.[36]

Section 38 orders: neither cohabitant/former cohabitant entitled to occupy

12.90 The terms of orders under this section are exactly the same as those under FLA 1996 s37, but the factors which the court must take into account differ to reflect the difference in status between couples who have never been married and those who have.

Who may be the parties?

12.91 An order can only be made under this section if:[37]

a) the parties are or have been cohabitants;
b) both are still in occupation of the home in which they live or have lived together as husband and wife; and
c) neither of them is entitled to remain in occupation by virtue of having legal or equitable ownership, a tenancy, a contractual licence, or through any enactment giving a right of occupation.

See paras **12.79** and **12.80** for a discussion of these requirements, which are the same as those for FLA 1996 s37 orders, except that the parties' marital status differs.

What are the possible terms of the order?

12.92 All of the possible terms of a FLA 1996 s38 order are discretionary. They are as follows:[38]

(a) require the respondent to permit the applicant to enter and remain in the dwelling-house or part of the dwelling-house;

36　FLA 1996 s37(5).
37　FLA 1996 s38(1).
38　FLA 1996 s38(3).

(b) regulate the occupation of the dwelling-house by either or both of the parties;

(c) require the respondent to leave the dwelling-house or part of the dwelling-house; or

(d) exclude the respondent from a defined area in which the dwelling-house is included.

See paras **12.81** to **12.84** for a discussion of the meaning of these terms.

What factors must be taken into account when making a s38 order (s38(4))?

12.93 The guidance for making a FLA 1996 s38 order is similar to that for a s36 order, but not exactly the same. An order under s38 will not be interfering with any property rights of the respondent (he will by definition have none), and consequently the nature of the parties' relationship is not really taken into account.

12.94 All of the terms for a s38 order are discretionary and the court will never be under a duty to make an order, even if it considers that the applicant or a child will be likely to suffer significant harm unless an order is made. Before making an order the court must take into account all of the circumstances of the case including:[39]

(a) the housing needs and housing resources of each of the parties and of any relevant child;

(b) the financial resources of each of the parties;

(c) the likely effect of any order, or of any decision by the court not [to make an order], on the health, safety or well-being of the parties and of any relevant child;

(d) the conduct of the parties in relation to each other and otherwise; and

(e) the questions mentioned in subsection (5).

The questions contained in subsection (5) are:

(a) whether the applicant or any relevant child is likely to suffer significant harm attributable to the conduct of the respondent if [one of the discretionary terms] is not included in the order; and

(b) whether the harm likely to be suffered by the respondent or child if the [discretionary term] is included is as great as or greater than the harm attributable to conduct of the respondent which is likely to be suffered by the applicant or child if the [term] is not included.

12.95 In other words, the court must consider the level of hardship

39 FLA 1996 s38(4) and (5).

and the likely harm which the parties might suffer in every case, when deciding whether or not to make an order and which terms to include in it. Unlike orders under FLA 1996 s33 or s35, the court will *not* be under a duty to exclude the respondent, even if it considers that the applicant or a relevant child is at risk of suffering greater harm than the respondent is likely to suffer. The balance of harm is merely one of the factors to which the court must give consideration; it is not an overriding factor. As under FLA 1996 s36, the regulatory terms will always be discretionary where an application is made by a non-entitled cohabitant.

What is the maximum duration of a s38 order?

12.96 The court must initially limit the duration of the order for a specified period not exceeding six months. It may be extended one further time for a period not exceeding six months.[40]

Section 40 orders: ancillary terms for s33, s35 or s36 orders

12.97 The Law Commission intended for occupation orders to be similar in nature to orders under the Matrimonial Homes Act 1983. Consequently, the FLA 1996 empowers the courts to deal with issues arising out of the occupation of premises, such as payment of the rent or mortgage instalments, protection of furnishings, repairs, etc. These ancillary terms can only be attached to orders under s33, s35 or s36, which are used when one of the parties is entitled to occupy.

What ancillary terms may be imposed?

12.98 Under FLA 1996 s40(1) the court, either when making an occupation order under s33, s35 or s36, or at any time thereafter, may:

   (a) impose on either party obligations as to –
      (i) the repair and maintenance of the dwelling-house; or
      (ii) the discharge of rent, mortgage payments or other outgoings affecting the dwelling-house;
   (b) order a party occupying the dwelling-house or any part of it (including [an entitled] party . . .) to make periodical payments to the other party in respect of the accommodation, if the other party would (but for the order) be entitled to occupy the dwelling-house [as an entitled person] . . . ;

40 FLA 1996 s38(6).

(c) grant either party possession or use of furniture or other contents of the dwelling-house;

(d) order either party to take reasonable care of any furniture or other contents of the dwelling-house;

(e) order either party to take reasonable steps to keep the dwelling-house and any furniture or other contents secure.

12.99 The court thus has the power to order either or both parties to help maintain the property and furnishings, regardless of whether they are in occupation or have been excluded from the home. Term (b) above means that where the parties are jointly entitled to occupy, or where the respondent is solely entitled to occupy, the applicant may be ordered to pay an 'occupation rent' to the excluded respondent. Terms (c) to (e) give the court the power to distribute the furniture and other chattels between the parties, regardless of who remains in occupation. These terms may cause problems where the furniture is not jointly owned or where ownership is disputed, and careful instructions should be taken.

What factors must the court take into account?

12.100 In deciding whether to attach any of the above terms to an FLA 1996 s33, s35 or s36 order, and if so, which terms to use, the court must take into account all of the circumstances of the case including:[41]

(a) the financial needs and financial resources of the parties; and

(b) the financial obligations which they have, or are likely to have in the foreseeable future, including financial obligations to each other and to any relevant child.

What is maximum duration of a s40 order?

12.101 An FLA 1996 s40 order will come to an end automatically when the substantive occupation order under s33, s35 or s36 to which it relates comes to an end.[42]

---

41 FLA 1996 s40(2).
42 FLA 1996 s40(3).

CHAPTER 13

Ex parte orders (FLA 1996 s45) and undertakings (FLA 1996 s46)

Introduction

13.1 Prior to the implementation of the FLA 1996, the courts' powers to make ex parte orders varied. The magistrates' court had no power to make ex parte exclusion orders under the Domestic Proceedings and Magistrates' Courts Act 1978, but could make expedited personal protection orders. In the county court and High Court ex parte non-molestation and ouster injunctions could be made, but it was practice only very rarely to grant the latter order. This anomaly was corrected under the FLA 1996, and courts now have equal powers.

13.2 Although essential to the administration of justice, ex parte orders, by their nature, offend the rules of natural justice by not giving one of the parties the opportunity to attend the hearing and answer the allegations made against him. They should only be granted, therefore, when the case is sufficiently grave and urgent to justify immediate intervention. The types of cases in which it might be justifiable to make an ex parte order are those in which there is an urgent need for protection, where a violent response is expected to the issue of other proceedings, or where the respondent is deliberately evading service. (Note, however, that ex parte orders do not become effective until the respondent is served with a copy.)

Jurisdiction and guidelines

13.3 The court may make ex parte non-molestation and occupation orders 'in any case where it considers that it is just and convenient to do so'.[1]

1 FLA 1996 s45(1).

13.4 Having given the courts a very wide discretion to make ex parte orders, however, the FLA 1996 then goes on to set out the following guidelines which should be used in reaching a decision:[2]

> . . . the court shall have regard to all the circumstances including –
>
> (a) any risk of significant harm to the applicant or a relevant child, attributable to conduct of the respondent, if the order is not made immediately;
>
> (b) whether it is likely that the applicant will be deterred or prevented from pursuing the application if an order is not made immediately; and
>
> (c) whether there is reason to believe that the respondent is aware of the proceedings but is deliberately evading service and that the applicant or relevant child will be seriously prejudiced by the delay involved –
>
>   (i) where the court is a magistrates' court, in effecting service of proceedings; or
>
>   (ii) in any other case, in effecting substituted service.

13.5 The meaning of the phrase 'significant harm' is examined in the discussion about the balance of harm test, found in paras **10.48** to **10.58**. The Law Commission Report[3] explained that this guideline would cover:

> . . . cases in which there is evidence that the respondent has been violent towards or threatened violence to the applicant or a child, and there is a genuine risk that the violence will be repeated or the threat carried out unless an immediate order is made.

However, the definition of 'harm' given in FLA 1996 s63 is a slightly wider definition than just acts or threats of violence; it includes 'ill-treatment or the impairment of [physical or mental] health'.

13.6 The guideline in FLA 1996 s45(2)(b) above covers situations where the respondent is likely to react violently when he is served with the proceedings. This would include cases where, although the remedy sought in the application may not in itself be urgent, the applicant needs the court's immediate protection in order to be able to take proceedings without fear of the respondent's reaction to them.

13.7 If the respondent is evading service of an application for a non-molestation or occupation order, then the applicant or a child may be at risk until a hearing on notice can take place. There may be a further delay if an application for substituted service has to be made

---

2 FLA 1996 s45(2).
3 Law Commission Report no 207, *Domestic Violence and Occupation of the Family Home* (HMSO, 1992) para 5.8.

in the county or High Court, and magistrates' courts do not even have the power to make orders for substituted service. The guideline in FLA 1996 s45(2)(c) suggests that it would be appropriate for the court to make an ex parte order in such cases. However, it should be borne in mind that ex parte orders are not effective until they are served on the respondent.

When appropriate

13.8 Although it is not stated explicitly in the FLA 1996, the Law Commission Report suggests that ex parte occupation orders, particularly those that exclude the respondent, should be made only rarely[4] and quotes the dicta of Ormrod LJ in *Ansah v Ansah*[5] to the effect that:

> ... the court should only act ex parte in an emergency when the interests of justice or the protection of the applicant or a child clearly demand immediate intervention ... Such cases should be extremely rare.

In practice it will be easier to obtain an ex parte non-molestation order than an ex parte occupation order, but the Act specifically empowers the court to make both types of order.

13.9 The practice rules require the applicant for an ex parte order to state the reasons for not giving notice in her sworn statement supporting the application.

Duration

13.10 Ex parte orders should only be made for a short duration. The court must give the respondent the opportunity to attend a full hearing 'as soon as just and convenient' to do so.[6] Consequently, when making an ex parte order, the court must also fix a return date for the inter partes hearing.

13.11 Occupation orders will normally be made for a limited period of time, which is calculated by reference to the date on which the first order is made. If an ex parte order has been made initially, time will start to run from the date of the ex parte order.[7]

---

4   Ibid, paras 5.5 and 5.6.
5   [1977] Fam 138.
6   FLA 1996 s45(3).
7   FLA 1996 s45(4).

Powers of arrest

13.12 The court has an unfettered discretion as to whether to attach a power of arrest. It is never placed under a duty to attach a power of arrest, as may be the case in applications on notice (see paras **14.7** to **14.19**).

13.13 FLA 1996 s47(3) states that:

> . . . the court may attach a power of arrest to one or more provisions of the [ex parte] order if it appears to it –
> (a) that the respondent has used or threatened violence against the applicant or a relevant child; and
> (b) that there is a risk of significant harm to the applicant or child, attributable to conduct of the respondent, if the power of arrest is not attached to those provisions immediately.

13.14 Where a court attaches a power of arrest to any provisions of an ex parte order, it may provide that the power of arrest is to have effect for a shorter period than the other provisions of the order.[8]

Undertakings (FLA 1996 s46)

13.15 An undertaking is a promise given to the court by a party to the proceedings. The court under the FLA 1996 has power to accept an undertaking in cases where it has the power to make a non-molestation or an occupation order.[9]

13.16 Under the old law, an undertaking could be accepted by the court without having to make a finding of fact. Therefore, a party was able to give an undertaking without admitting any of the allegations made against him/her. Undertakings were widely used as a means of compromising injunction proceedings, as they were seen as a means of reaching a solution without the respondent losing too much face, and often avoided the need for a contested hearing. This has changed under the FLA 1996, as will be seen below.

13.17 No power of arrest can be attached to an undertaking,[10] so that it affords less protection than an order with a power of arrest. However, the courts are now under a duty not to accept undertakings in cases where they would have attached a power of arrest to an order,

---

8   FLA 1996 s45(4).
9   FLA 1996 s46(1).
10   FLA 1996 s46(2).

had an order been made.[11] In other words, they now have first to make a finding of fact as to whether the grounds exist for attachment of a power of arrest, ie, whether violence has been used or threatened. If a power of arrest should be made, then the court cannot accept an undertaking (see paras **14.7** to **14.19** for a fuller discussion of powers of arrest).

13.18 Note that the courts have become used to routinely accepting undertakings. Practitioners should be prepared to argue the need for a power of arrest and be on guard against the acceptance of an undertaking in such cases.

13.19 Breach of an undertaking is a contempt of court and is punishable in the same way as breaches of court orders.[12] Therefore, even if an undertaking is accepted, the standard procedure for enforcement will be by warrant for arrest (see paras **14.21** to **14.25**).

13.20 If the terms of the undertaking given exceed the rights of the other party to the protection of the court (for example, an undertaking not to molest given in proceedings for assault and battery), it is nevertheless binding on the person giving the undertaking. An undertaking remains in force in accordance with the terms and time-limits set out in it, unless and until it is varied or discharged by the court.[13]

---

11 FLA 1996 s46(3).
12 FLA 1996 s46(4); see *Roberts v Roberts* [1990] 2 FLR 111, CA; *Hussain v Hussain* [1986] 1 All ER 961, CA.
13 *Johnson v Walton* [1990] 1 FLR 350.

CHAPTER 14

Enforcement

Introduction: changes under the FLA 1996

14.1 Because injunctions are civil remedies, the police would not normally become involved in their enforcement. When a power of arrest is attached to a civil court order, however, it gives the police power to arrest the respondent if he breaches the relevant term of the injunction.[1] Since 1976 the civil courts have been able to attach powers of arrest to certain domestic violence injunctions where the parties were living together as husband and wife and the applicant had suffered actual bodily harm.[2]

14.2 However, powers of arrest are not generally available in all cases where injunctions are made. It should be noted that the courts could not, and still cannot, attach a power of arrest to an injunction made in tort proceedings.[3] The categories of potential applicants under the FLA are so wide that the need to use tort proceedings in cases of domestic violence will no doubt be considerably reduced.

14.3 The courts' jurisdiction to deal with breaches of orders previously varied, depending on whether the order was made in the civil courts or magistrates' courts, and the type of proceedings being used. The FLA 1996 has expanded the courts' options for dealing with

---

1 The police nevertheless have the power to take criminal proceedings against perpetrators of domestic violence whenever a crime is committed, which they sometimes choose not to use in 'domestic situations'.
2 Domestic Violence and Matrimonial Proceedings Act 1976 s2. The distinction between the civil and criminal jurisdictions in law has become increasingly blurred in recent legislation, which has crossed those boundaries by increasing the use of powers of arrest in civil injunctions (the Housing Act 1996) and by giving magistrates the power to make the equivalent of injunctions (the Protection from Harassment Act 1997).
3 If an order made under the Protection from Harassment Act 1997 is breached, an application may be made for a warrant of arrest.

breaches of injunctions, and has standardised the powers held by all of the courts who might hear applications for committal in proceedings brought under that Act.

14.4 The recommendation from the Law Commission[4] was:

> . . . that where there has been violence or threatened violence the court should be required to attach a power of arrest . . . unless in all the circumstances the applicant or child will be adequately protected without such a power.

14.5 Thus, although the attachment of a power of arrest will not be automatic in FLA 1996 proceedings, nevertheless the presumption is now weighted more in favour of powers of arrest being attached in serious cases. The courts will have to consider whether to attach a power of arrest in every case where violence has occurred or has been threatened. The requirement that the applicant must have suffered actual bodily harm has been dropped. The requirement that the parties have been living together as husband and wife has also been dropped.

14.6 The courts have been given power to issue warrants for arrest where there has been a breach of an order to which no power of arrest was attached. By FLA 1996 s46(4), an undertaking is enforceable as if it were an order of the court, which means that a warrant can also be issued for breach of an undertaking. The civil courts have been given power to remand the respondent in custody or on bail, which brings them in line with the previously existing powers of magistrates' courts.

Powers of arrest

14.7 When a power of arrest is attached to provisions of either a non-molestation order or an occupation order, a police constable 'may arrest without warrant a person whom he has reasonable cause for suspecting to be in breach of any such provision'.[5] If an arrest is made, the respondent must be brought before the court who made the original order. The police must produce the respondent to the court within 24 hours of the time of the arrest (excluding Christmas Day, Good Friday and any Sundays).[6]

---

4   Law Commission Report no 207, *Domestic Violence and Occupation of the Family Home* (HMSO, 1992) para 5.13.
5   FLA 1996 s47(6).
6   FLA 1996 s47(7).

14.8 *Note* that there is no requirement that the parties have been living together as husband and wife for a power of arrest to be attached. Consequently, a power of arrest can be attached even where the parties are not directly related, so long as they are 'associated persons' and there has been at least a threat of violence.

14.9 The duties and powers of the courts in respect of attaching a power of arrest vary, depending on whether the relevant order is made inter partes or ex parte.

Inter partes hearings

14.10 FLA 1996 s47(2) provides that, if the court makes a non-molestation order or an occupation order, and

> . . . it appears to the court that the respondent has used or threatened violence against the applicant or a relevant child, it shall attach a power of arrest to one or more provisions of the order unless satisfied that in all the circumstances of the case the applicant or child will be adequately protected without such a power of arrest.

14.11 Having made a decision to make a non-molestation order or an occupation order, the court will now have to make a finding of fact as to whether the respondent has used or threatened violence. If such a finding is made, the court must attach a power of arrest to one or more terms of the order *unless* there is some evidence that the applicant or relevant child will be adequately protected without it. Note that the power of arrest can be attached selectively to certain provisions of the order.

14.12 This is a change in the approach previously followed in domestic violence cases. Prior to the passage of the FLA 1996, powers of arrest were entirely discretionary and were only available when the applicant had suffered violence and sustained actual bodily harm. Now the courts are obliged to attach powers of arrest unless they are convinced that a power of arrest is not needed. Thus, they will be obliged to attach powers of arrest even in cases where violence has been threatened but no injuries sustained.

14.13 This follows the view taken by the Law Commission that women and children should not have to wait to be injured before they can obtain effective protection.[7] Its Report goes on to say[8] that:

7   Law Commission Report (n3), para 5.13.
8   Ibid, para 5.15.

[t]he use of powers of arrest should be confined to serious cases where it is necessary to give extra weight to an order to drive home to the respondent the need to keep within its terms. Powers of arrest can be counter-productive and may exacerbate tensions unless they are reserved for cases in which they are shown to be necessary to prevent future injury.

14.14 The FLA 1996 does not define the term 'one or more of the provisions' to which the power must be attached. Nor is there any guidance about that point or about how long ago the threat or violence could have occurred in order to justify the attachment of a power of arrest. The Law Commission commented[9] that 'the particular breach which will give rise to the operation of the power of arrest should be clearly specified'.

Ex parte hearings

14.15 Whereas the courts are under a duty to attach a power of arrest to orders made at inter partes hearings in certain cases, they only have a power to make an attachment to ex parte orders. Whether or not to attach a power of arrest to an ex parte order will always be at the court's discretion.

14.16 FLA 1996 s47(3) provides that:

... the court may attach a power of arrest to one or more provisions of the [ex parte] order if it appears to it –
(a) that the respondent has used or threatened violence against the applicant or a relevant child; and
(b) that there is a risk of significant harm to the applicant or child, attributable to conduct of the respondent, if the power of arrest is not attached to those provisions immediately.

14.17 Thus the courts must consider the question of whether 'significant harm' is a possibility should a power of arrest not be attached (see paras **10.48** to **10.58** for a discussion of this phrase). Even then, they will still have a discretion as to whether or not a power of arrest should be attached. In the past, powers of arrest were infrequently attached to ex parte orders, and it may be that the judicial stance on this point will remain the same. The FLA 1996 reflects the Law Commission's view[10] that a more stringent approach should be taken when the respondent has not had the opportunity to state his case.

9   Ibid, para 5.14.
10 Ibid.

Duration of powers of arrest

14.18 The courts may decide that a power of arrest should be attached for a shorter period than the full duration of the order.[11] In the past, powers of arrest were generally specified to last for three months, even if the substantive order was made for six months.[12] It is possible that the practice will continue.

14.19 By FLA 1996 s47(5), a power of arrest may be extended by the court on one or more occasions, when there is an application to vary or discharge the relevant order.

Undertakings

14.20 The court cannot attach a power of arrest to an undertaking.[13] The FLA 1996 states specifically that the court shall not accept an undertaking in any case which merits the attachment of a power of arrest.[14] In other words, the court must first consider the duty set out above to attach a power of arrest. If it considers that a power of arrest is appropriate and necessary, then it cannot accept an undertaking from the respondent. However, if an undertaking is broken, the court has the power to issue a warrant for the respondent's arrest.[15]

Warrants for arrest

14.21 Prior to the FLA 1996, magistrates' courts had the power to issue warrants for arrest in domestic violence cases. The Act extends that power to the High Court and county courts. FLA 1996 s47(8) states:

> If the court has made a relevant order but –
> (a) has not attached a power of arrest . . . to any provisions of the order, or
> (b) has attached that power only to certain provisions of the order,
> then, if at any time the applicant considers that the respondent has failed to comply with the order, he may apply to the relevant judicial authority for the issue of a warrant for the arrest of the respondent.

14.22 Note that the respondent need only have 'failed to comply with

11 FLA 1996 s47(4).
12 *Practice Note* [1981] 1 All ER 224.
13 FLA 1996 s46(2).
14 FLA 1996 s46(3).
15 FLA 1996 s46(4).

the order'. The FLA 1996 does not state that the respondent needs to have threatened or used violence before a warrant could be issued. One assumes that a warrant could be issued in circumstances which, prior to the implementation of the FLA 1996, would have led to an application for committal. It follows, therefore, that an application for a warrant can be made where a term of an order has been breached but which is not covered by a power of arrest. A warrant should not be applied for if the breach relates to a term of the order to which a power of arrest has been attached.

14.23   The Law Commission Report[16] gives the impression that warrants should be used more extensively than applications for committal, given that the police are more experienced than bailiffs or the Tipstaff in handling domestic violence issues. It is anticipated that in cases in which no power of arrest was attached to the order or where the time limit placed on a power of arrest has expired, the normal means for dealing with breaches of injunctions will be by application for a warrant.

14.24   The application for a warrant is made ex parte and must be made on oath (either by affidavit in the civil courts or in person in the magistrates' courts). The warrant can only be issued if the court has reasonable grounds for believing that the respondent has failed to comply with the order.[17] The application should be made to the same level of court which made the original order. For example, if a county court judge made the original order, a district judge could hear the application for the issue of a warrant. The court has a discretion as to whether to issue a warrant, even if satisfied that there has been a breach of the order.

14.25   The FLA 1996 states that undertakings are enforceable under the Act in the same way as orders are enforced;[18] it follows, therefore, that breaches of undertakings can also be dealt with by applications for warrants, even though powers of arrest cannot be attached to undertakings.

Arrest

14.26   Whether an arrest is made pursuant to a power of arrest or a warrant for arrest, the police must produce the respondent in the

16   See n3, para 5.15.
17   FLA 1996 s47(9).
18   FLA 1996 s46(4).

court within 24 hours, beginning at the time of the arrest,[19] but excluding Christmas Day, Good Friday, and any Sunday. Consequently, if an arrest is made on a Saturday, the respondent must be produced the following Monday, regardless of any statutory holidays other than Christmas Day. The relevant court will be a court at the same level as that which made the original order. If the order was made in the county court, district judges now have jurisdiction to punish any breaches.[20]

14.27   When a power of arrest is attached to relevant provisions in an order, Form FL406 must be completed, setting out only those terms of the order to which the power of arrest applies. A copy of Form FL406 must then be delivered to the officer for the time being in charge of the applicant's local police station and any other station which the court directs. The form must be accompanied by a statement, usually made by the applicant's solicitor, that the respondent has been served with the order or has been informed of its contents either by being present in court or by telephone or otherwise.

Remands

14.28   FLA 1996 s47(10) extends to the High Court and county courts the power to remand the respondent, which is governed by FLA 1996 Sch 5. The magistrates' courts already have such a power, which is contained in Magistrates' Courts Act 1980 ss128 and 129, and the power given to the civil courts corresponds to that of the magistrates.

Remands in custody or on bail

14.29   The court may remand the respondent in custody for a period up to but not exceeding eight clear days.[21] Where the period of remand does not exceed three clear days, the court may remand him to the custody of a constable.[22]

14.30   Alternatively, the court can remand the respondent on bail on his own recognisance (with or without sureties) to appear before the court at the end of his remand period or at every subsequent hearing.[23]

---

19   FLA 1996 s47(7).
20   Allocation to Judiciary Directions 1997 s58.
21   FLA 1996 Sch 5 para 2(1)(a) and (5).
22   Ibid, para 2(6).
23   Ibid, para 2(1)(b)(i).

It could also remand the respondent on bail by fixing the amount of the recognisances with a view to their being taken subsequently, and in the meantime committing the respondent in custody.[24]

14.31 Applications for bail made by a person arrested either under a power of arrest or a warrant may be made orally or in writing.

14.32 Written applications must contain the following information:

a) the full name of the person making the application (the respondent);
b) the address where he is detained at the time of the application;
c) the address where he would reside if he were to be granted bail;
d) the amount of the recognisance in which he would agree to be bound;
e) the grounds on which the application is made; and
f) where a previous application was refused, full particulars of any change in circumstances which has occurred since that refusal.

14.33 A written application must be signed either by the person making the application (the respondent) or by someone authorised by him to do so. Where the person making the application is a minor or is incapable of acting, the application must be signed by a guardian ad litem. A copy of the bail application must be served on the other party (the applicant in the substantive proceedings).

14.34 If the respondent is remanded on bail, the court may remand him for a period longer than eight days, so long as both the applicant and respondent give their consent.[25]

14.35 Whenever the respondent is granted bail (either under the FLA 1996 or the Magistrates' Courts Act 1980), the court may require him to comply with bail conditions which it deems necessary to ensure that he does not interfere with witnesses or otherwise obstruct the course of justice.[26]

Remands for medical examination and report

14.36 The courts have power to remand respondents on bail or in custody for the purpose of enabling a medical examination to take place and a report to be made.[27] If the respondent is remanded on bail,

24 Ibid, para 2(1)(b)(ii).
25 Ibid, para 2(5)(a).
26 FLA 1996 s47(12).
27 FLA 1996 s48(1).

the case cannot be adjourned for longer than four weeks at a time.[28] If the respondent is remanded in custody, the period of adjournment must not be for more than three weeks at a time.[29] In either case, the respondent can be remanded for the full period of the adjournment.[30]

14.37 The courts have the power, where the respondent has been arrested either under a power of arrest or under a warrant, to make an order under the Mental Health Act 1983 s35. This enables the court to remand for a report on the respondent's mental condition, where there is reason to suspect that he is suffering from mental illness or severe mental impairment.[31]

Further remands

14.38 When the respondent has been remanded but is unable to attend at court on the date due for his appearance because of illness or an accident, the court may remand him for a further period in his absence.[32] Furthermore, the court can be remanded for a further period by enlarging his recognisance and those of any sureties for him to a later time. The court can also enlarge his recognisances in his absence, which acts as a further remand.[33]

Committal

The committal hearing

14.39 The procedure for the hearing itself is the same regardless of the means used to get the respondent to court. Committal hearings take place in open court, except in certain limited types of proceedings, eg, proceedings relating to children.

14.40 The burden of proof is the same as in criminal proceedings, ie, beyond reasonable doubt.[34] It is necessary to prove that the respondent deliberately did something and that his action was in breach of the order or undertaking. It is not necessary to prove that the respondent was being contumacious of the court. If someone is incapable of

28 FLA 1996 s48(2).
29 FLA 1996 s48(3).
30 FLA 1996 Sch 5 para 2(5)(b).
31 FLA 1996 s48(4).
32 FLA 1996 Sch 5 para 3(1).
33 Ibid, Sch 5 para 3(2) and (3).
34 *Re Bramblevale Ltd* [1970] Ch 128, CA; *Dean v Dean* [1987] 1 FLR 517, CA.

understanding what he is doing within the terms of the *M'Naghten* rules, he cannot be guilty of contempt.[35] The respondent must be given the opportunity to cross-examine on any allegations which he does not accept.[36]

14.41 The court will require proof that the order was served on the respondent (unless the hearing relates to a breach of an undertaking). This is normally presented in the form of an affidavit of service. If service is disputed, then the person who effected service will have to attend the committal hearing and give evidence.

Possible punishments in the county court and the High Court

14.42 On a finding of contempt, the county court and the High Court have power to sentence the respondent to be committed to prison for up to two years and to impose a fine, or both.[37] There is no limit to the amount of the fine which the court can impose. Where the contemnor is aged at least 17 but under 21, the court can order him to be detained under Criminal Justice Act 1982 s9. If the contemnor is aged under 17, there is no power at all to detain him (and it is questionable whether an injunction should be granted against someone that age).[38]

14.43 The court, if considering an immediate committal, must take into account the effect of the sentence on the children of the family, and on the financial position of the respondent.[39] In *Ansah v Ansah*[40] the court stated that committal orders should be used only as a last resort, particularly in family cases; the real purpose of the court is usually to secure future compliance rather than to punish the disobedience. Before imposing an immediate sentence, the court should consider whether it should be suspended.[41] If committing the respondent to prison, the court must specify the length of the sentence; it cannot make an order for an indefinite period of time.

14.44 A sentence of imprisonment may be suspended for a period of time or on terms and conditions specified by the court. If a further breach occurs, the court has a discretion as to whether to implement

35 *Wookey v Wookey* [1991] 2 FLR 319, CA.
36 *Smith v Smith* [1988] 1 FLR 179, CA.
37 County Courts (Penalties for Contempt) Act 1983 s14.
38 See *Re S (A Minor)* [1991] 2 FLR 319, CA.
39 *Goff v Goff* [1989] 1 FLR 436, CA.
40 [1977] 2 All ER 638, CA.
41 *McIntosh v McIntosh* [1990] FCR 351, CA.

the sentence.[42] The court may also impose consecutive sentences in respect of separate contempts.[43]

14.45 When considering sentence, the judge should also consider what is to happen to the original order, whether it should be continued or varied. If the hearing is for a breach of an undertaking, consideration should be given to upgrading the undertaking to an order. A power of arrest could be attached at this stage.

14.46 The court also has the option of adjourning the proceedings without considering what penalty should be imposed, while imposing conditions with which the respondent must comply. If the respondent fails to comply with the conditions, the court can restore consideration of the penalty, but has discretion as to the punishment. It need not necessarily impose a prison sentence, and may substitute a fine instead, depending on the seriousness of the breach.[44]

Possible punishments in the magistrates' court

14.47 Under Magistrates' Courts Act 1980 s63, where someone disobeys a magistrates' court order to do anything other than pay money or abstain from doing anything, the court may fine him up to £5,000 or impose a daily fine of £50 for every day during which he is in default. The court may alternatively commit him to prison for up to two months. The magistrates' courts now have power under the FLA 1996 to make suspended committal orders for breaches of occupation orders or non-molestation orders.

42 *Re W (B) (An Infant)* [1969] 2 Ch 50, CA.
43 *Lee v Walker* [1985] 1 All ER 781, CA.
44 *Re W (B) (An Infant)* [1969] 2 Ch 50, CA.

CHAPTER 15

Transfer of tenancies (FLA 1996 Sch 7)

Introduction

15.1 Occupation orders are by their nature short-term, pragmatic responses to situations which require some regulation of occupation of the family home. Usually the questions surrounding property rights will have to be resolved between the parties at a later stage. If the parties are married, this will normally be done through ancillary relief proceedings under the Matrimonial Causes Act 1973.

15.2 If the parties are not married but living in property they jointly own, an application will have to be made under the Trusts of Land and Appointment of Trustees Act 1996. If the parties are not married and live in a property solely owned by one of them, the means of resolving disputes over the property are much more complicated. The party who is not the legal owner of the property may be able to establish that s/he has a beneficial interest through having contributed directly or indirectly to the purchase of the home; s/he will have to commence proceedings for a declaration of a constructive trust in order to resolve any disputes over ownership. Making an application for an occupation order as a non-entitled applicant will not have a detrimental effect on a subsequent or pending application to establish a beneficial interest.[1]

15.3 Until the passage of the FLA 1996, there was no means available to cohabitants to apply to the court to resolve disputes about the transfer of tenancies, either from joint names into one name, or from one person to the other (except where applications could be made under the Children Act 1989 for the benefit of children). The FLA 1996 has extended rights relating to the transfer of tenancies which were previously only enjoyed by married persons to cohabitants, former cohabitants, and former spouses.

1   FLA 1996 s36(11).

15.4 The Matrimonial Homes Act 1983 has been abolished by the FLA 1996, which now confers on spouses and former spouses the rights which they had under the 1983 Act, as well as extending those rights to cohabitants.

15.5 When a cohabitant applies for an occupation order, she should also consider making an application for a transfer of tenancy. If such an application is made at the same time as the application is made for an occupation order, it may lead to the latter application being defended and thus delayed. Practitioners should therefore think tactically about the timing of applications.

15.6 Note that magistrates have no power to make orders affecting property rights, so such applications will have to be made in the county court.

Tenancies which can be transferred

15.7 FLA 1996 Sch 7 para 1 lists the tenancies which can be transferred as:

– a protected tenancy or statutory tenancy under the Rent Act 1977;
– a statutory tenancy under the Rent (Agriculture) Act 1976;
– a secure tenancy under the Housing Act 1985;
– an assured tenancy or assured agricultural occupancy under Housing Act 1988 Part I.

15.8 Note that assured shorthold tenancies and long leases are excluded from this provision. However, the term 'tenancy' includes sub-tenancies.

15.9 Orders for the transfer of tenancies can only be made in respect of dwellings in which the parties, whether married or unmarried, lived as husband and wife.

Applicants

Spouses and former spouses

15.10 Applications for transfer can be made in cases where the spouses and former spouses are joint tenants, or where the tenancy is in the name of only one of them. Former spouses who have remarried lose their right to make such applications.

15.11 The courts may hear applications under the FLA 1996 for transfers of tenancies at any time when they have power to make property adjustment orders under Matrimonial Causes Act 1973 s23A (divorce or separation) or s24 (nullity). This does *not* mean, however, that an application has to be made under the Matrimonial Causes Act 1973. It simply means that no application under the FLA 1996 can be made until after a statement of marital breakdown has been filed in the case of divorce/separation, or after the grant of a decree in nullity proceedings. Orders cannot take effect until after the grant of a decree absolute.

15.12 The court only has power under the FLA 1996 to transfer relevant tenancies. Applications relating to other types of property will have to be made under the Matrimonial Causes Act 1973.

Cohabitants and former cohabitants

15.13 Applications for transfer can be made in cases where the cohabitants or former cohabitants are joint tenants, or where the tenancy is in the sole name of one of them. Note the inference that a cohabitant may still apply for a transfer after s/he has stopped cohabiting. S/he may also apply even after marrying someone else. The only provision is that the application must relate to the home where s/he lived as husband and wife with the respondent.

15.14 There is no restriction on the time within which a former cohabitant must make an application, though the court must take account of the length of separation when deciding whether to make an order.

15.15 See paras **10.6** to **10.9** for the definition of 'cohabitant'.

Factors which the court must take into account

15.16 In deciding whether to order the transfer of a tenancy between spouses/former spouses or cohabitants/former cohabitants, and if so, in what manner, the court must have regard to all of the circumstances of the case, including:

- the circumstances in which the tenancy was granted to either or both of the parties, or, as the case requires, the circumstances in which either or both of them became a tenant;
- the housing needs and housing resources of each of the parties and of any relevant child;

- the financial resources of each of the parties;
- the likely effect of any order, or of any decision by the court not to exercise its powers, on the health, safety or well-being of the parties and of any relevant child;
- the suitability of the parties as tenants.

15.17 If the parties are cohabitants or former cohabitants, the court must also take into account the following:

- the nature of the parties' relationship;
- the length of time during which they lived together as husband and wife;
- whether there are or have been any children of both parties or for whom both parties have or have had parental responsibility;
- the length of time that has elapsed since the parties ceased to live together.

15.18 Note that the court is not directed to consider the 'greater harm' test when making transfer orders, nor is it directed to consider the conduct of the parties, as it must do when making occupation orders.

15.19 Landlords are entitled to be notified of any applications for transfer and to have their views taken into consideration. The court may nevertheless make an order for transfer over the objections of a landlord.

15.20 The effect of the above factors is to give the court a wide discretion to make whatever orders it considers to be just in all of the circumstances.

Orders that may be made (Sch 7 Part II)

15.21 Note that applications for property adjustment orders in divorce/separation proceedings cannot be made until after the filing of the statement of marital breakdown. Orders cannot be worded to take effect before the making of a divorce/separation order, except in exceptional circumstances and where the court is satisfied that it would be just and reasonable for the order to become effective prior to the divorce order. Orders cannot be made after the grant of a divorce order unless the application was made prior to the divorce order. In nullity cases, orders cannot be worded to take effect until after the grant of a decree absolute.

15.22 There is no special provision as to when an order can be made if the parties are cohabitants or former cohabitants.

Protected tenancies (Rent Act 1977), secure tenancies (Housing Act 1985), assured tenancies (Housing Act 1988) and assured agricultural occupancies (Housing Act 1988)

15.23 If a spouse/cohabitant or former spouse/cohabitant has one of the above tenancies, the court may order that as from a specified date the tenancy will be transferred to and vested in the other party. The tenancy which is transferred is that which the transferor was entitled to immediately before the date of transfer. The transfer of tenancy includes the transfer of all of the rights and privileges attached to it. All of the covenants, obligations, liabilities and incumbrances to which the tenancy is subject are transferred at the same time, and the transferee will be liable for any obligations falling due after the date of transfer. If the transferor became liable under the terms of the tenancy before the date of transfer, s/he will remain personally liable. Where the transferor is an assignee of the tenancy, his/her liability under any express or implied covenant of indemnity will be transferred at the same time.

15.24 Transfers of secure and assured tenancies under these provisions will not count as a succession under the respective Acts. However, if the transferor is a successor, the transferee will be deemed to be a successor.

15.25 Where a transfer of an assured agricultural occupancy is made, the occupation of the dwelling by the transferee will meet the requirements of the agricultural worker condition under the Housing Act 1988.

15.26 All of the above tenancies are transferred by the order itself, without the need for any further documentation. New tenancy agreements do not, therefore, need to be issued to protect the transferee's right of occupation.

Statutory tenancies under the Rent Act 1977

15.27 Statutory tenancies under the Rent Act 1977 (1977 Act) are personal rights to occupy. The FLA 1996 empowers the court to order that the statutory tenant is to cease to be entitled to occupy the dwelling, and that the other party is to be deemed to be the tenant or sole tenant under the statutory tenancy. The succession rights under the 1977 Act will take effect as though the transferee were in exactly the same position as the transferor was, ie, if s/he were a successor, the transferee will be treated as a successor.

Statutory tenancies under the Rent (Agriculture) Act 1976

15.28 Where one of the parties is a statutory tenant under the 1976 Act, the court can order that s/he is to cease to be entitled to occupy the dwelling-house and that the other party is to be deemed to be the tenant or the sole tenant under the statutory tenancy. Again, if the transferor was a successor, the transferee will be deemed to be in the same position as the transferor.

Compensation (Sch 7 Part III)

15.29 When the court makes an order for transfer of a tenancy, it may order that the transferee pays compensation to the transferor. It may direct that payment of the whole or part of the compensation:

- be deferred until a specified date; or
- be deferred until the occurrence of a specified event; or
- be paid in instalments.

15.30 Note the court's powers to order immediate payment of a certain amount and defer payment of the rest or order the rest to be paid in instalments. When an order for compensation has been made, either party may request such a deferment or payment in instalments if the court does not do so in the first instance. Where the court has already ordered that payment of the whole or part of the sum be deferred or made in instalments, either party may request a variation of those arrangements at any time before the date by which compensation has been ordered to be paid in full.

15.31 The factors which the court must take into account when deciding whether and in what matter to order payment of compensation are as follows:

- the financial loss that would otherwise be suffered by the transferor as a result of the order;
- the financial needs and financial resources of the parties;
- the financial obligations which the parties have, or are likely to have in the foreseeable future, including financial obligations to each other and to any relevant child.

15.32 The court must not order deferred payments or payment by instalments unless it appears that to order immediate payment would cause the transferor greater financial hardship than the transferee would suffer if payment were delayed or made by instalments.

Dealing with liabilities and obligations which have arisen before the date of transfer

15.33 If the court orders a transfer of a tenancy, it may direct that both parties are to be jointly and severally liable to discharge or perform any or all of the liabilities and obligations in respect of the dwelling which:

- at the date of the order have fallen due to be discharged or performed by only one of them; or
- would fall due to be discharged between the date of the order and the date it is to take effect.

15.34 If the court makes such an order, it can direct that one party is liable to indemnify the other in whole or in part against any payment made or expenses incurred by the other in discharging or performing any such liability or obligation.

15.35 The most common form of such liabilities will be rent arrears. This provision will permit the court to resolve the issue about who is to be responsible for repayment of the arrears.

CHAPTER 16

Protection from Harassment Act 1997 and other claims in tort

Introduction

16.1 Practitioners should be aware of the provisions of the Protection from Harassment Act (PFHA) 1997, as the kind of behaviour it is meant to address is similar to that dealt with by the FLA 1996. The main purpose of the PFHA 1997 was to provide civil and criminal remedies to victims of 'stalking'; it was drafted in response to public concern arising from some well-publicised cases in which women were subjected to distressing obsessive behaviour. It may be useful not only to victims of domestic violence, but also to victims of other sorts of harassment such as racial harassment or neighbour nuisance.

16.2 The PFHA 1997 is an unusual blend of the traditional criminal and civil jurisdictions. It gives the criminal courts the power to make 'restraining orders' similar to injunctions. It also creates a statutory tort of harassment, and victims can not only apply for injunctions to prevent further harassment, but also ask for damages. If an injunction is breached, the plaintiff can ask for a warrant for arrest, as in the FLA 1996. Breach of an injunction is also made a criminal offence, however, and practitioners will have to consider whether it is more advantageous to the client to try to bring about a criminal prosecution, or to apply for committal.

16.3 It remains to be seen how effective a remedy the PFHA 1997 will provide in practice, and whether the police will readily take action in domestic violence cases if remedies exist in the civil jurisdiction. Given the constraints involved in obtaining legal aid, the PFHA 1997 may be helpful to women who are unable to afford legal proceedings and to those women who fall outside the definition of 'associated persons'.

16.4 In addition to the tort of harassment, other claims in tort may be useful to people who are unable to use the FLA 1996 because they do not meet the 'associated persons' definition. This chapter will briefly consider other causes of action which may be used. It should be noted that no powers of arrest can be attached to injunctions in tort, and enforcement will require an application for committal, unless the injunction is obtained under the PFHA 1997.

Protection from Harassment Act 1997

Prohibition of harassment

16.5 PFHA 1997 s1 prohibits harassment, which is the basis of both the criminal offences and the civil remedies. It states:

> (1) A person must not pursue a course of conduct –
> (a) which amounts to harassment of another, and
> (b) which he knows or ought to know amounts to harassment of the other.
>
> (2) For the purposes of this section, the person whose course of conduct is in question ought to know that it amounts to harassment of another if a reasonable person in possession of the same information would think the course of conduct amounted to harassment of the other.

16.6 'Harassment' is not defined, but it includes alarming or causing a person distress.[1] Examples of types of behaviour which the courts have said amount to harassment are found in paras. **11.8** and **11.9**.

16.7 'Course of conduct' is conduct on at least two occasions,[2] and includes speech.[3] The length of time between the two occasions is not specified, and may lead to problems of interpretation in future.

16.8 PFHA 1997 s1(2) provides an objective test for the course of conduct, the test of the reasonable person. The defendant will not be able to argue that he did not realise that he was causing distress.

Defences to criminal and civil proceedings

16.9 PFHA 1997 s1(3) sets out statutory defences, which could be used

---

1   PFHA 1997 s7(2).
2   PFHA 1997 s7(3).
3   PFHA 1997 s7(4).

in either civil or criminal proceedings. It includes conduct pursued:

- when preventing or detecting crime;
- under any enactment or rule of law;
- if the course of conduct is reasonable.

Consequently, people such as police officers, bailiffs, process-servers, private investigators, etc, will have a defence in addition to the objective test.

16.10 PFHA 1997 s12 creates other defences for conduct which relates to national security, the economic well-being of the UK, or the prevention or detection of serious crime, which was done on behalf of the Crown. The certificate of the Home Secretary will be conclusive in this regard.

Criminal offences

16.11 The PFHA 1997 creates two criminal offences: criminal harassment and putting a person in fear of violence.

Criminal harassment (s2)

16.12 Criminal harassment is an arrestable offence committed by 'a person who pursues a course of conduct in breach of s1' (see para 16.5). It is a summary offence, punishable by up to six months' imprisonment and/or a fine not exceeding level 5.

Putting people in fear of violence (s4)

16.13 The offence created by PFHA 1997 s4 overlaps with that of criminal harassment, but a person found not guilty of a s4 offence may nevertheless be convicted of criminal harassment under PFHA 1997 s2.[4] PFHA 1997 s4(1) states:

> A person whose course of conduct causes another to fear on at least two occasions that violence [as opposed to less serious forms of harassment] will be used against him is guilty of an offence if he knows or ought to know that his course of conduct will cause the other so to fear on each of those occasions.

16.14 This offence is triable either way. It is punishable on conviction on indictment by up to five years' imprisonment and/or an unlimited fine. On summary conviction, it is punishable by up to six months' imprisonment and/or a fine not exceeding the statutory maximum.

4   PFHA 1997 s4(5).

16.15 PFHA 1997 s7(2) provides the same reasonableness test as that given for harassment. Consequently the defendant will not be able to argue his lack of intention to cause fear of violence.

Restraining orders (s5)

16.16 The Act deals only with offences which have been committed and affords no protection where harassment may be reasonably expected, but has not yet occurred. The criminal courts have been given the power to prevent future harassment, however, by making restraining orders when sentencing defendants. This will eliminate the need for the victim to institute proceedings for an injunction, once the defendant has been convicted. The restraining order may be worded to have effect for a specified period or until further order.

16.17 The prosecutor, defendant, or any other person mentioned in the order (the victim, presumably) may apply to the court which made the order for it to be varied or discharged.[5]

16.18 PFHA 1997 s5(5) makes it an offence to breach a restraining order without reasonable excuse, which is triable either way. It is punishable on conviction on indictment by up to five years' imprisonment and/or a fine, and on summary conviction by up to six months' imprisonment and/or a fine.

Civil remedies

Injunctions and damages (s3)

16.19 The civil remedies provided by the Act relate only to ss1 and 2; they do not include s4 relating to putting people in fear of violence, although one might argue that causing a person to fear violence is a form of harassment; see paras 11.8 and 11.9). The tortious cause of action is set out in s3:

> (1) An actual or apprehended breach of s1 may be the subject of a claim in civil proceedings by the person who is the victim of the course of conduct in question.
> (2) On such a claim, damages may be awarded for (among other things) any anxiety caused by the harassment and any financial loss resulting from the harassment.

16.20 Although the right to apply for an injunction is not specifically referred to, the general law relating to interlocutory and final injunctions will apply. The remedy will be available where one act of

---

1 PFHA 1997 s5(4).

harassment has taken place and there is a reasonable fear that there will be more acts of harassment in future.

16.21 PFHA 1997 s3(2) permits general and special damages to be claimed. Special damages could be quite substantial if the victim has had to give up working or change her accommodation, etc. General damages currently awarded for anxiety are around £500 to £600. The limitation period for a personal injury claim under this Act has been extended from three years to six years.

16.22 This remedy could be used in addition to other causes of action, such as assault and battery, trespass to land, trespass to goods, etc.

Enforcement through the civil courts

16.23 Warrants for arrest can be applied for where an injunction has been obtained, and the defendant has breached it.[6] Applications can be made either on notice or ex parte. The application for a warrant must be supported by either affidavit or oral evidence, showing that there are reasonable grounds for believing that the defendant has breached the injunction. Where an injunction has been made in a county court, the application may be heard by either a district judge or a judge in *any* county court.[7] Where a warrant has been issued, the procedure will be similar to that under the FLA 1996.

16.24 Applications for committal can also be used as means of enforcement, but no doubt warrant for arrest will prove to be the most popular means of enforcement. Committal proceedings are an alternative to criminal proceedings for a breach of an injunction; if the defendant has been prosecuted for the breach, he may not also be punished for contempt of court.[8]

Enforcement through criminal proceedings

16.25 As with breaches of restraining orders, breaches of injunctions made in the High Court or county courts can be a criminal offence. PFHA 1997 s3(6) provides that where an injunction has been made prohibiting the defendant from pursuing any course of conduct which amounts to harassment, and he breaches the injunction without reasonable excuse, he will be guilty of an offence.

6   PFHA 1997 s3(3).
7   PFHA 1997 s3(4).
8   PFHA 1997 s3(7).

16.26 The criminal breach of an injunction is triable either way. If a conviction on indictment is obtained, it is punishable by up to five years' imprisonment and/or an unlimited fine. Summary offences are punishable by up to six months' imprisonment and/or a fine. The defendant cannot be prosecuted for breach of an injunction if he has been punished for contempt of court in committal proceedings.[9]

Other torts

The courts' jurisdiction

16.27 Injunctions may be granted in tort proceedings to prohibit the repetition of a tort which has already been committed. An injunction can also be made to prevent a tort which is likely to be committed, where there is a real possibility that the plaintiff will suffer damage unless an injunction is granted, and the intervention of the court is warranted.[10]

16.28 The courts' powers are not limited to restraining tortious or unlawful behaviour. Injunctions against other behaviour may be made if they are reasonably regarded as necessary to protect the plaintiff's legitimate interests. For example, orders which create exclusion zones may be made in tort proceedings, but they should not be imposed without very good reason.[11]

Causes of action

16.29 The torts which are most likely to be of use in domestic violence cases are assault and battery, trespass to land, trespass to goods, nuisance, and harassment (see above).

16.30 Battery is the deliberate or negligent direct, unwanted physical contact with the plaintiff, except for the ordinary and acceptable physical contact one experiences every day.[12] An assault is any act which puts another person in immediate and reasonable fear of a battery. It must be a threatening act; words alone cannot amount to an assault.[13] It is not necessary to prove any damage or physical harm has been sustained or was intended.

9   PFHA 1997 s3(8).
10   *Khorasandjian v Bush* [1993] 3 All ER 669.
11   *Burris v Azadani* [1995] 4 All ER 802.
12   *F v West Berkshire Health Authority* [1989] 2 WLR 1025.
13   *Meade's Case* (1823) 1 Lew CC 184.

16.31 Trespass to land is any unlawful entry onto land, or the unlawful placing of something upon land which is in the exclusive possession of the plaintiff. This tort can be used by tenants, sub-tenants or owner-occupiers; the position relating to licensees is less clear.[14] It is actionable per se; damage need not be proved. The defendant, by definition, must not have any right to occupy the property.

16.32 Trespass to goods is the wrongful and direct interference with another person's belongings. An action may be brought under the Torts (Interference with Goods) Act 1977 to obtain an injunction for the return of the goods or their value, or damages.

16.33 Nuisance is interference with the reasonable use or enjoyment of land. It is available to tenants and owner-occupiers, who have a legal interest in land, and it has recently been extended to licensees. In *Khorasandjian v Bush*,[15] the Court of Appeal held that making harassing telephone calls which interfered with the reasonable enjoyment of property was actionable as private nuisance, even though the plaintiff did not have a interest in the property where she was staying (her parents' home). The same principle was applied in *Hunter v Canary Wharf Ltd*,[16] when the Court of Appeal held that occupation of property as a home confers upon the occupant a capacity to sue in private nuisance. It is necessary to prove damage, however, even if it is only loss of enjoyment.

Procedure

16.34 Applications for injunctions in tort and under the PFHA 1997 will be made in accordance with the general rules of civil procedure. It is possible to bring proceedings in the High Court, but the county court will be the normal venue. The limits for small claims will need to be borne in mind.

16.35 There are three types of claim, as follows:

– liquidated claim which does not include an application for an injunction; use a default summons (Form N1);
– unliquidated claim, or a liquidated claim which includes an injunction application; use a fixed date summons (Form N2 or N3);
– injunction application without a claim for damages (Form 16A).

14 See Carter and Dymond *Quiet Enjoyment* (Legal Action Group, 5th edn, 1998).
15 [1993] 3 All ER 669.
16 [1996] 1 All ER 482.

16.36 The cause(s) of action must be set out in the particulars of claim, and an application for an injunction must be supported by affidavit evidence. The defendant must be given at least two clear days' notice between service of proceedings and the hearing, although an application to abridge the notice period can be made. Ex parte applications can be made in cases of real emergencies on the plaintiff's undertaking to issue an application and affidavit within a given time. The order, whether obtained ex parte or on notice, must be personally served on the defendant.

CHAPTER 17

Procedure

17.1 The procedures in magistrates' and county courts are very similar, but they have some differences. For ease of use, procedure is set out separately for each jurisdiction. See Part V for copies of the relevant forms.

Magistrates' courts

Procedure in the magistrates' courts is governed by the Family Proceedings Courts (Matrimonial Proceedings etc) Rules 1991 SI No 1991 (hereafter referred to as FPC(MP)R 1991), as amended by the Family Proceedings Courts (Matrimonial Proceedings etc) (Amendment) Rules 1997 SI No 1894.

Applications (r3A)

17.2 Evidence will now normally be given by written statement which has been signed and declared to be true, but it can be given orally with the leave of the court.

17.3 Applications for non-molestation and occupation orders may be made in the course of other family proceedings or as discrete proceedings; in either case, applications are to be made on Form FL401 (supported by a written statement which is signed and declared to be true, unless evidence is being given orally with the leave of the court). Notices of hearings are to be made on Form FL402. Forms FL401 and FL402, together with a copy of the supporting statement, are to be served personally on the respondent. Where an applicant wishes to withhold her address from the application form, she may complete Form C8, which gives the court her actual address. No leave to do so is required from the court.

209

17.4 Applications to vary, extend or discharge an order must be made in form FL403.

17.5 In an urgent case applications can be made ex parte with the leave of the court or of the justices' clerk. The applicant's statement must give reasons why the application is made ex parte. Ex parte applications for non-molestation and occupation orders may be heard by a single justice. Form FL401 must be filed at the time of the ex parte application or at a time specified by the justices' clerk.

17.6 For hearings on notice, the respondent must be given two clear business days' notice, but time can be abridged by the court or by the justices' clerk.

Transfer of proceedings

17.7 The court *must*, either on application by one of the parties, or of its own motion, consider whether it should transfer the proceedings for non-molestation and/or occupation orders to another court.[1]

17.8 Under the Family Law Act 1996 (Part IV) (Allocation of Proceedings) Order 1997,[2] a family proceedings court shall, either of its own motion or on application, transfer proceedings under FLA 1996 Part IV to another family proceedings court where:

a) it considers it more appropriate that the Part IV proceedings be heard together with other family proceedings which are pending in the receiving court; and
b) the justices' clerk in the receiving court consents to the transfer.

17.9 A family proceedings court may also, either of its own motion or on application, transfer Part IV proceedings to a county court where it considers that:

a) it would be appropriate for the Part IV proceedings to be heard together with other family proceedings pending in the receiving county court; or
b) the proceedings involve:
   – conflict with the law of another jurisdiction;
   – some novel and difficult point of law;
   – some question of general public interest; or
c) the proceedings are exceptionally complex.

---

1   FPC(MP)R 1991 r3A(9).
2   SI No 1896.

17.10 Note, however, that the receiving county court can transfer the proceedings back to the family proceedings court if the other family proceedings in (a) above have already been determined, or it considers that the criteria in (b) or (c) above do not apply.

17.11 A family proceedings court *must* transfer Part IV proceedings to a county court where:

– a child under the age of 18 is the respondent or wishes to become a party to the proceedings; or
– a party to the proceedings is a person incapable of managing and administering his/her property and affairs because of a mental disorder within the meaning of the Mental Health Act 1983.

17.12 Magistrates' courts have no jurisdiction in cases involving a disputed question of property rights or rights to occupy,[3] unless determination of the question is unnecessary in order to deal with the application. So, where there is a dispute over whether one of the parties is 'entitled', and the issue is significant with regard to the determination of the application (which will not always be the case), the magistrates must transfer the proceedings to either the county court or the High Court. If the application before the court includes an application for a transfer of tenancy, it will similarly have to be moved to either the county court or the High Court.

17.13 A family proceedings court may, on its own motion or on application, transfer Part IV proceedings to the High Court where it considers that it would be appropriate for them to be heard together with other family proceedings which are pending in the receiving court.

17.14 Part IV proceedings can similarly be transferred from the High Court to a family proceedings court where the High Court considers it appropriate for them to be heard together with other family proceedings which are pending in the receiving court.

Service[4]

17.15 Applications for non-molestation orders and occupation orders (Form FL401) or variations, extensions and discharges of orders (Form FL403) made on notice must be served personally on the

---

3   FLA 1996 s29(1).
4   Service is generally covered by FPC(MP)R 1991 rr3A, 4 and 12A.

respondent not less than two business days before the hearing, together with the statements in support and the notice of hearing (Form FL402).[5]

17.16 Copies of applications for occupation orders under FLA 1996 ss33, 35 or 36 must be served by first class post on relevant mortgagees/landlords, with a notice in Form FL416 informing them of their rights to make representations in writing or at any hearing.[6]

17.17 The applicant must file a statement of service in Form FL415 after serving the application on the respondent and any relevant landlord/mortgagee.[7]

17.18 Orders, whether made on an application heard ex parte or inter partes, must be served personally on the respondent.[8] Following an ex parte hearing, copies of the application, statements and order must be served on the respondent personally.[9]

17.19 Unless otherwise specified, service of other documents is effected in the following manner:[10]

– if the respondent is not known to be acting by solicitor, by:
   a) delivering it to him personally; or
   b) delivering it at his residence or his last known residence; or
   c) sending it by first class post to his residence or last known residence;
– if the respondent is known to be acting by solicitor, by:
   a) delivering it to his solicitor's address for service; or
   b) sending it by first class post to his solicitor's address for service; or
   c) where his solicitor's address includes a numbered box at a document exchange, by leaving the document at the document exchange; or
   d) faxing a legible copy to his solicitor's office.

17.20 If documents are posted under FPC(MP)R 1991 r4 service, they will be deemed to be served on the second business day after first class posting. If a document exchange is used, they will be deemed to

---

5   Ibid, r3A(5).
6   Ibid, r3A(10). When a s33, s35 or s36 occupation order is made, a copy of the order must be similarly served (r12A(4)).
7   FPC(MP)R 1991 r3A(11).
8   Ibid, rr12(A)(2) and (5).
9   Ibid, r12(A)(2).
10 Ibid, r4.

be served on the second business day after being left at the document exchange. A statement of service of an application (Form FL415) must be filed at or before the first directions appointment or hearing.

17.21 Where an application has been sent to the respondent in accordance with the above rules for service, and an order is made, the court may later, of its own motion, set aside the order and give directions for hearing if it appears to the court that the application did not come to the knowledge of the respondent in due time.[11]

17.22 Where the applicant is acting in person, the justices' clerk may give leave for service of the application and/or an order heard inter partes to be effected in accordance with r4 above.[12] An applicant acting in person may request the justices' clerk to serve an order made in an ex parte hearing.[13]

Enforcement (rr20 and 21)

Arrests

17.23 *Powers of arrest (r20(1)).*   Where a power of arrest is attached to one or more provisions of an order (referred to as 'the relevant provisions'), note the following requirements:

- Form FL406 must be completed setting out the provisions to which the power of arrest has been attached;
- *only* the relevant provisions should be included in the form, and no other terms;
- a copy of the form must be delivered to the officer in charge of the applicant's local police station or any other police station specified by the court;
- the copy of the form delivered to the police station(s) must be accompanied by a statement showing that the respondent has been served with the order or informed of its terms, either during the hearing, or afterwards by telephone or otherwise.

17.24 Variations or discharges of powers of arrest shall be notified by the justices' clerk to the relevant police stations.[14]

---

11 Ibid, r24.
12 Ibid, r12A(6).
13 Ibid, r12A(3).
14 Ibid, r20(2).

17.25 Warrants for arrest (r20(3)). Applications for a warrant for the arrest of the respondent should be made on Form FL407.

17.26 When a warrant is issued, Form FL408 is used and is delivered to the police station by the justices' clerk.

17.27 Hearings following arrests (r20(4)). Following the respondent's arrest either under a power of arrest or warrant, the court has two options:

a) conduct a full hearing to determine whether the facts or circumstances leading to the arrest amounted to a breach of the order; or
b) adjourn the proceedings.

17.28 If the case is adjourned, the respondent may be released, in which case the proceedings should be listed for hearing within 14 days of the date of arrest. The respondent should be given at least two business days' notice of the adjourned hearing. If the case is not heard within the 14-day limit, it is possible to apply for committal, in which case a notice of committal proceedings (Form FL418) should be personally served on the respondent.

17.29 If the case is adjourned, the court may remand the respondent on bail, in which case the proceedings cannot be adjourned for longer than eight clear days, unless the respondent and applicant both consent to a longer adjournment. Conditions may be attached to the grant of bail. The court may also remand the respondent in custody for up to eight clear days at a time. If the period of remand is no longer than three clear days, the respondent may be remanded to the custody of the police. The court may order medical reports to be prepared and can remand the respondent in custody for that purpose.

17.30 The court also has the option of adjourning the proceedings without considering what penalty should be imposed, while imposing conditions with which the respondent must comply. If the respondent fails to comply with the conditions, the court can restore consideration of the penalty.

17.31 Applications for bail (r21). Applications for bail made by a person arrested either under a power of arrest or a warrant may be made orally or in writing.

17.32 Written applications must contain the following information:

a) the full name of the person making the application (the respondent);
b) the address where he is detained at the time of the application;
c) the address where he would reside if he were to be granted bail;
d) the amount of the recognisance in which he would agree to be bound;
e) the grounds on which the application is made; and
f) where a previous application was refused, full particulars of any change in circumstances which has occurred since that refusal.

17.33 A written application must be signed either by the person making the application (the respondent) or by someone authorised by him to do so. Where the person making the application is a minor or is incapable of acting, the application must be signed by a guardian ad litem. A copy of the bail application must be served on the other party (the applicant in the substantive proceedings).

17.34 Form FL410 is used for the recognisance of the person making the bail application, and Form FL411 is used for a surety. Form FL412 is a bail notice given to the respondent when he is remanded on bail.

Committals
a) Prior service/notification and penal notices

17.35 *Prerequisites in relation to enforcing orders (r20(6), (7) and (11)).* Before making a committal order, the court must be satisfied that:

– a copy of the order in Form FL404 has been served personally on the respondent; and
– where the order requires the respondent *to do an act*, a copy of the order was served prior to the deadline set out in the order or in any later order.

17.36 Service of a copy of the order may nevertheless be dispensed with if the court considers it just to do so.[15]

17.37 An order which requires the respondent *to refrain from doing an act* which has not been personally served on him can nevertheless be enforced by committal, provided that either:

15 Ibid, r20(12).

- he was present when the order was made; or
- he was notified of the terms of the order by telephone or by some other means.

17.38 All non-molestation orders must be endorsed with or contain a notice as to the consequences of disobedience. Similar notices must be included in occupation orders, if the court so directs.

17.39 *Prerequisites   in   relation   to   enforcing   undertakings (r20(14)).*   Before an order for committal can be made in respect of a breach of an undertaking, the court must be satisfied that a copy of the undertaking given in Form FL422 was delivered to the person giving the undertaking by one of the following means:

- the justices' clerk handing him a copy before he left the court building; or
- a copy was posted to his place of residence by the justices' clerk; or
- a copy was sent to him through his solicitor; or
- if none of the above is possible, personal service was effected on behalf of the applicant as soon as was practicable.

17.40 The court may dispense with the requirement for service of a copy of the undertaking prior to committal if it considers it just to do so.[16]

b) Applications for committal (r20(8) and (9))

17.41 Applications for committal hearings are treated as complaints and must meet the following requirements:

- specify which provisions of the order or undertaking have been disobeyed or broken;
- list the ways in which it is alleged that the order or undertaking has been disobeyed or broken;
- be supported by a statement signed and declared to be true by the applicant, which also states the ground on which the application has been made.

17.42 Applications are made to the clerk to the justices, who will then issue a notice in Form FL418 warning the respondent that an application will be made for him to be committed.

17.43 Form FL418 and a copy of the statement must be personally served on the respondent, unless the court considers that it is just to

16 Ibid.

dispense with service.[17] Where service of a notice in Form FL418 is dispensed with, the court may of its own motion fix a date and time when the respondent is to be bought before the court.[18]

17.44 Where a committal order is made (Form FL419), it must include provision for the issue of a warrant of committal (Form FL420) and be personally served on the respondent either before or at the time the warrant is executed, unless the court directs otherwise. Alternatively, the order for the issue of the warrant may be served on the respondent at any time within 36 hours after the execution of the warrant.

c) Suspended committal orders (r20(16), (17) and (18))

17.45 Courts have power to suspend the execution of committal orders for such period or on such terms or conditions as it thinks fit. Where a committal order is suspended, the applicant must serve a notice of the order and its terms on the respondent, unless the court directs otherwise.

17.46 Note that the court may adjourn a hearing without considering the penalty to be imposed, while at the same time imposing conditions on the respondent. If the respondent does not comply with the conditions, the adjourned hearing can then be restored for consideration of the appropriate penalty.

d) Orders under the Mental Health Act 1983[19]

17.47 When the court makes a hospital order (Form FL413) or a guardianship order (Form FL414) under the Mental Health Act (MHA) 1983, the justices' clerk should send any relevant information to the hospital and inform the applicant when the respondent is being transferred to hospital.

17.48 Where the respondent was remanded in custody and the Home Secretary directs transfer to a hospital under MHA 1983 s48, the justices' clerk must notify the governor of the prison to which the respondent was remanded and the hospital where he is detained of any committal hearing which the respondent is required to attend. The justices' clerk must also notify the hospital where the respondent is retained of any further remands.

---

17 Ibid, r20(12).
18 Ibid, r20(13).
19 Ibid, r20(19) and (20).

17.49 If the respondent is remanded for medical reports, the adjournment cannot be for more than four weeks if he is bailed, nor more than three weeks if he is remanded in custody.

e) Applications for discharge from custody[20]

17.50 An application for discharge from custody must be made in writing attested by the governor of the prison showing that the respondent has purged or is desirous of purging his contempt. It should be sent to the court which made the committal order. The justices' clerk should give the applicant at least one day's notice of the date that the respondent's application will be heard.

County courts

> Procedure in the county courts is governed by the Family Proceedings Rules 1991 SI No 1247 (hereafter referred to as FPR 1991), as amended by the Family Proceedings (Amendment No 3) Rules 1997 SI No 1893.

Applications (r3.8)

17.51 Applications for non-molestation and occupation orders must be made on Form FL401, even if made in other proceedings which are pending. An application made by a child under the age of 16 should be made on Form FL401, but it will be treated, in the first instance, as an application to the High Court for leave.[21]

17.52 Applications must be supported by the applicant's sworn statement. A sworn statement made in support of ex parte applications must state the reasons why notice was not given.[22]

17.53 Applications for occupation orders under FLA 1996 ss33, 35 or 36 and applications for transfer of a tenancy shall be dealt with under the ancillary relief rules regarding district judges' powers of investigation and powers to order discovery and production of documents and further affidavits.[23]

---

20 Ibid, r20(15).
21 FPR 1991, r3.8(1) to (3). Applications to vary, discharge or to amend an order are made on Form FL403 (r3.9(8)).
22 Ibid, r3.8(4) and (5).
23 Ibid, r3.8(13). The ancillary relief rules are contained in FPR 1991 rr2.62(4) to (6) and 2.63.

17.54 Applications for non-molestation and occupation orders are heard in chambers, unless otherwise directed.[24]

17.55 A minute of the draft order in Form FL404 should be prepared before hearings in the county court. The various terms available are included in the form. Note that penal notices are required for all non-molestation orders. If the order does not contain non-molestation terms, then a penal notice is discretionary. Form FL404 contains alternative notices to the respondent, depending on whether or not a penal notice is included.

Transfer of proceedings

17.56 Where an application for a non-molestation or occupation order is pending, the court must consider, either of its own motion or on application by one of the parties, whether to exercise its power to transfer the hearing of the application to another court.[25]

17.57 Under the Family Law Act 1996 (Part IV) (Allocation of Proceedings) Order 1997, a county court may transfer Part IV proceedings to a family proceedings court if it considers that it would be appropriate for them to be heard together with other family proceedings pending in the receiving court.

17.58 If proceedings have been transferred from a family proceedings court (court A) to the county court (court B) to be heard with proceedings which were pending in court B, court B may send them back to court A if the family proceedings have already been determined. A county court may also return proceedings to a family proceedings court if it considers that the reasons given for transfer (conflict of law, novel/difficult point of law, question of public interest, or exceptionally complex proceedings) do not apply.

17.59 A county court can transfer proceedings to another county court where:

a) it would be appropriate for them to be heard with other family proceedings pending in the receiving county court; or
b) the proceedings involve the determination of a question regarding a party's entitlement to occupy any property by virtue

---

24 Ibid, r3.9(1).
25 Ibid, r3.8(9).

of a beneficial estate or interest or contract or statutory right of occupation, and the property in question is located in the district of the receiving county court; or

c) it seems necessary or expedient to do so.

17.60 A county court can transfer Part IV proceedings to the High Court if it considers them to be more appropriate for determination by the High Court.

17.61 The High Court can transfer proceedings to the county court to be heard together with other family proceedings pending in the receiving court; or the proceedings are appropriate for determination in a county court; or it is appropriate for an application made by a child under the age of 18 to be heard in a county court.

Service (rr3.8 and 3.9)

17.62 Where applications are made on notice, Forms FL401 and FL402, together with a copy of the sworn statement in support, must be personally served on the respondent not less than two business days before the date of the hearing.[26] The court has power to abridge the period of notice, however, and can order substituted service.[27] If an applicant acting in person requests it, the court will effect service on her behalf or make an order for substituted service.[28]

17.63 Applications to vary, extend or discharge an order are made on Form FL403 and must be personally served on the other party not less than two business days before the date of the hearing. The court has the same powers to abridge the notice period and to order substituted service as above.[29]

17.64 A copy of an application for an occupation order made under FLA 1996 ss33, 35 or 36 must be served by first class post on the mortgagee/landlord of the dwelling in question, together with a notice in Form FL416 informing him of his right to be heard or to make representations in writing to the court.[30] Notice of an application for transfer of a tenancy must be served on the respondent

---

26 Ibid, r3.8(6).
27 Ibid, r3.8(7), (8).
28 Ibid, r3.8(8).
29 Ibid, r3.9(8).
30 Ibid, r3.8(11).

spouse/cohabitant and on the landlord, both of whom have the right to be heard at the hearing of the application.[31]

17.65 When an order is made at an ex parte hearing, the respondent must be personally served with a copy of the order, the application (Form FL401), and the sworn statement in support.[32] When an order is made at an inter partes hearing, it must also be served personally on the respondent.[33] If the applicant is acting in person, she can request that the court effects service of any orders made.[34] Form FL404 is used to record the orders made, and form FL405 is used to make a record of the hearing for the court file.[35]

17.66 Copies of occupation orders made under FLA 1996 ss33, 35 or 36 must be served by first class post on the mortgagee/landlord of the dwelling in question.[36] The court may direct that a further hearing be held in order to consider any representations made by a mortgagee or a landlord.[37]

Enforcement (r3.9A)

Arrests

17.67 *Powers of arrest (r3.9A(1) and (2)).*   Where a power of arrest is attached to one or more provisions of an order (referred to as 'the relevant provisions'), note the following requirements:

− Form FL406 must be completed setting out the provisions to which the power of arrest has been attached;
− *only* the relevant provisions should be included in the form, and no other terms;
− a copy of the form must be delivered to the officer in charge of the applicant's local police station or any other police station specified by the court;
− the copy of the form delivered to the police station(s) must be accompanied by a statement showing that the respondent has been

31 Ibid, r3.8(12).
32 Ibid, r3.9(2).
33 Ibid, r3.9(4).
34 Ibid, r3.9(5).
35 Ibid, r3.9(6).
36 Ibid, r3.9(3).
37 Ibid, r3.9(9).

served with the order or informed of its terms, either during the hearing, or afterwards by telephone or otherwise.[38]

17.68 Variations or discharges of powers of arrest shall be notified by the court to the relevant police stations.[39]

17.69 *Warrants for arrest (r3.9A (3)).* Applications for a warrant for the arrest of the respondent should be made on Form FL407 and must be substantiated on oath. When a warrant is issued, Form FL408 is used.[40]

17.70 *Hearings following arrests (r3.9A(4)).* Following the respondent's arrest either under a power of arrest or warrant, the court has two options:

a) conduct a full hearing to determine whether the facts or circumstances leading to the arrest amounted to a breach of the order; or
b) adjourn the proceedings.[41]

17.71 If the case is adjourned, the respondent may be released, in which case the proceedings should be listed for hearing within 14 days of the date of arrest. The respondent should be given at least two business days' notice of the adjourned hearing. If the case is not heard within the 14-day limit, it is possible for notice of committal proceedings to be served on the respondent, in accordance with CCR Ord 29 r1(4).[42]

17.72 If the case is adjourned, the court may remand the respondent on bail, in which case the proceedings cannot be adjourned for longer than eight clear days, unless the respondent and applicant both consent to a longer adjournment. Conditions may be attached to the grant of bail. The court may also remand the respondent in custody for up to eight clear days at a time. If the period of remand is no longer than three clear days, the respondent may be remanded to the custody of the police. The court may order medical reports to be prepared and can remand the respondent in custody for that purpose.[43]

17.73 The court also has the option of adjourning the proceedings

38 Ibid, r3.9A(1).
39 Ibid, r3.9A(2).
40 Ibid, r3.9A(3).
41 Ibid, r3.9A(4).
42 Ibid.
43 FLA 1996 Sch 5.

without considering what penalty should be imposed, while imposing conditions with which the respondent must comply. If the respondent fails to comply with the conditions, the court can restore consideration of the penalty.[44]

17.74 *Applications for bail (r3.10).* Applications for bail made by a person arrested either under a power of arrest or a warrant may be made orally or in writing.[45]

17.75 Written applications must contain the following information:

a) the full name of the person making the application (the respondent);
b) the address where he is detained at the time the application is made;
c) the address where he would reside if he were to be granted bail;
d) the amount of the recognisance in which he would agree to be bound;
e) the grounds on which the application is made; and
f) where a previous application was refused, full particulars of any change in circumstances which has occurred since that refusal.[46]

17.76 A written application must be signed either by the person making the application (the respondent) or by someone authorised by him to do so. Where the person making the application is a minor or is incapable of acting, the application must be signed by a guardian ad litem. A copy of the bail application must be served on the other party (the applicant in the substantive proceedings).[47]

17.77 The court has power to demand a recognisance with or without sureties.[48] Form FL410 is used for the recognisance of the person making the bail application, and Form FL411 is used for a surety. Form FL412 is a bail notice given to the respondent when he is remanded on bail.[49]

Committals[50]

a) Prior service/notification and penal notices

17.78 *Prerequisites in relation to enforcing orders.* Before making a committal order, the court must be satisfied that:

44 FPR 1991 r3.9A(6).
45 Ibid, r3.10(1).
46 Ibid, r3.10(2).
47 Ibid, r3.10(3).
48 FLA 1996 Sch 5.
49 FPR 1991 r3.10(6).
50 See generally CCR Ord 29.

- a copy of the order in Form FL404 has been served personally on the respondent; and
- where the order requires the respondent *to do an act*, a copy of the order was served prior to the deadline set out in the order or in any later order.

17.79 Service of a copy of the order may nevertheless be dispensed with if the court considers it just to do so.

17.80 An order which requires the respondent *to refrain from doing an act* which has not been personally served on him can nevertheless be enforced by committal, provided that either:

- he was present when the order was made; or
- he was notified of the terms of the order by telephone or by some other means.

17.81 It is mandatory for all non-molestation orders to be endorsed with or contain a notice as to the consequences of disobedience (Form N77). The court has a discretion to include similar notices in occupation orders. Where an order contains terms relating to non-molestation as well as occupation, a penal notice will therefore be required. Form FL404, which is used for non-molestation and occupation orders, contains alternative paragraphs which must be included in the order, depending on whether a penal notice has been attached.

17.82 *Prerequisites in relation to enforcing undertakings.* Before an order for committal can be made in respect of a breach of an undertaking, the court must be satisfied that a copy of the undertaking given in Form FL422 was delivered to the person giving the undertaking by one of the following means:

- the clerk handing him a copy before he left the court building; or
- where his place of residence is known, a copy was posted to his place of residence by the court; or
- a copy was sent to him through his solicitor; or
- if none of the above is possible, personal service was effected on behalf of the applicant as soon as was practicable.

17.83 The court may dispense with the requirement for service of a copy of the undertaking prior to committal if it considers it just to do so.

b) Applications for committal (CCR Ord 29, r1(4A))

17.84 Applications for committal hearings ('notice to show good reason' in Form N78) must meet the following requirements:

- specify which provisions of the order or undertaking have been disobeyed or broken;
- list the ways in which it is alleged that the order has been disobeyed or the undertaking has been broken;
- be supported by an affidavit by the applicant, which also states the ground on which the application has been made.

17.85 The notice and a copy of the affidavit must be personally served on the respondent, unless the court considers that it is just to dispense with service. Where service of a notice is dispensed with, the court may of its own motion fix a date and time when the respondent is to be bought before the court.

17.86 If a committal order (Form N79) is made, the order will be for the issue of a warrant of committal in form N80, and unless the judge otherwise orders:

- a copy of the order shall be served on the respondent either before or at the time of the execution of the warrant; or
- where the warrant has been signed by the judge, the order for issue of the warrant may be served on the respondent at any time within 36 hours after the execution of the warrant.

c) Suspended committal orders (RSC Ord 52, r7)

17.87 Courts have power to suspend the execution of committal orders for such period or on such terms or conditions as it thinks fit. Where a committal order is suspended, the applicant must serve a notice of the order and its terms on the respondent, unless the court directs otherwise.[51]

17.88 Note that the court may adjourn a hearing without considering the penalty to be imposed, while at the same time imposing conditions on the respondent. If the respondent does not comply with the conditions, the adjourned hearing can then be restored for consideration of the appropriate penalty.[52]

d) Orders under the Mental Health Act 1983 (r3.9A)

17.89 When the court makes a hospital order (Form FL413) or a

51 RSC Ord 52 r7.
52 FPR 1991 r3.9A(6).

guardianship order (Form FL414) under the Mental Health Act (MHA) 1983, the court should send any relevant information to the hospital and inform the applicant when the respondent is being transferred to hospital.[53]

17.90 Where the respondent was remanded in custody and the Home Secretary directs transfer to a hospital under MHA 1983 s48, the court must notify the governor of the prison to which the respondent was remanded and the hospital where he is detained of any committal hearing which the respondent is required to attend. The court must also notify the hospital where the respondent is retained of any further remands.[54]

17.91 If the respondent is remanded for medical reports, the adjournment cannot be for more than four weeks if he is bailed, or more than three weeks if he is remanded in custody.[55]

e) Applications for discharge from custody (CCR Ord 29 r3)

17.92 An application for discharge from custody must be made in writing attested by the governor of the prison (or any other officer of the prison not below the rank of principal officer) showing that he has purged or is desirous of purging his contempt. It should be sent to the court which made the committal order. If the committal order does not direct that any application for discharge shall be made to a judge, or if the order was made by a district judge, any application for discharge may be made to the district judge. The applicant should be given at least one day's notice of the date that the application will be heard.[56]

Appeals

17.93 *Appeals from magistrates.*   Appeals from magistrates lie to the High Court and are usually heard by a single judge.[57] The appeal must be made within 14 days from the date of the order which is the subject of appeal, or later with the leave of the High Court.[58] If an application is being made to extend the time limit for appealing, a certificate (and

53 Ibid, r3.9A(7).
54 Ibid, r3.9A(8).
55 FLA 1996 s48.
56 CCR Ord 29 r3.
57 FPR 1991 r4.22(8).
58 Ibid, r4.22(3).

a copy) by the appellant's solicitor (or the appellant if acting in person) must be filed, setting out the reasons for the delay and the relevant dates.[59]

17.94 Family Proceedings Rules 1991 r4.22 applies. The following documents must be served by the appellant on the other parties to the proceedings, on any guardian ad litem, and on the justices' clerk of the relevant magistrates' court:

- notice of the appeal in writing, setting out the grounds of the appeal;
- certified copy of the application and of the order appealed against, and of any order staying its execution;
- copy of any notes of the evidence;
- copy of any reasons given for the decision.[60]

17.95 The last three documents can be filed after the notice of appeal, but must be filed and served as soon as practicable after the notice has been filed.[61] They must be filed in the registry of the High Court which is nearest to the magistrates' court from which the appeal is brought.[62]

17.96 Where an appeal is brought against the making of a hospital order or a guardianship order under the MHA 1983, a copy of any written evidence considered by the magistrates' court under 1983 Act s37(1)(a) shall be sent by the justices' clerk to the relevant High Court registry.

17.97 The respondent in the appeal must file a notice in writing, setting out grounds, if s/he wishes to:

- contend on the appeal that the decision of the court below should be varied, either in any event or in the event of the appeal being allowed in whole or in part; or
- contend that the decision of the court below should be affirmed on grounds other than those relied on by that court; or
- contend by way of cross-appeal that the decision of the court below was wrong in whole or in part.[63]

17.98 The time limit for filing and serving the respondent's notice is 14 days after receipt of the appellant's notice of appeal.[64]

59 Ibid, r8.2(4)(e).
60 Ibid, r4.22(2).
61 Ibid, r4.22(4).
62 Ibid, r8.1A(3).
63 Ibid, r4.22(5).
64 Ibid.

17.99 The court is not bound to allow an appeal on the ground merely of misdirection or improper reception or rejection of evidence, unless the court takes the view that a substantial wrong or miscarriage of justice has occurred as a result.[65]

17.100 An application to withdraw an appeal, have an appeal dismissed with the consent of all the parties, or amend the grounds of appeal may be heard by a district judge.[66] A district judge may also dismiss any appeal for want of prosecution and deal with questions relating to costs which arise.[67]

17.101 *Appeals from district judges.*   An appeal against an order made by a district judge lies to the circuit judge in the same court.

17.102 The procedure and time limits are the same as for appeals from magistrates set out in paras **17.93** to **17.100**, with the necessary modifications.

17.103 Any order or decision granting or varying an order, or refusing to do so, in proceedings relating to an application for:

- an occupation order which declares that the applicant is 'entitled' or has matrimonial home rights; or
- an occupation order containing any of the terms set out in FLA 1996 s33(3), where the applicant or the respondent has matrimonial home rights; or
- a transfer of tenancy order;

will be treated as a final order under CCR Ord 37 r6. The circuit judge hearing an appeal from such an order may exercise his/her own discretion in substitution for that of the district judge.[68]

17.104 *Appeals from circuit judges.*   Appeals from the decisions of circuit judges are made to the Court of Appeal, and the same rules set out in paras **17.93** to **17.100** apply, with the necessary modifications.

---

65   Ibid, r8.2(6).
66   Ibid, r4.22(7).
67   Ibid, r8.1A(5).
68   Ibid, r8.1A(6).

CHECKLIST FOR INSTRUCTIONS

1 Non-molestation orders

- Complete formalities for legal aid.
- Arrange for personal service to be effected following issue.
- Prepare:
  - Form FL401 (application used for both non-molestation and occupation orders);
  - Form FL402 (draft notice of hearing);
  - sworn statement (county court) or statement (magistrates' court);
  - Form FL404 (draft order – county court only);
  - Form FL406 if power of arrest being sought;
  - fee (currently £30).
- Have Forms FL401, FL402 and statement in support personally served on respondent.
- Have Form FL415 (statement of service) completed by the person effecting service; file at court on or before date of hearing.
- Check order is correct before leaving building. Arrange for personal service of the order.
- Following service of the order, have Form FL415 completed and file it at court.

NB: Some courts may supply and complete forms FL404 and FL406.

2 Occupation orders

Follow same procedure as for non-molestation orders, but also do the following:

- Decide under which section the application is to be made.
- Obtain the name and address of any mortgagee or landlord.
- In addition to the forms listed above, prepare form FL416 (notice to mortgagees and landlords).
- Following issue, serve Form FL416 and a copy of the application (Form FL401) on the mortgagee/landlord by first class post.
- Following the making of an occupation order, prepare Form FL416 and serve it with a copy of the order by first class post on the mortgagee/landlord.

- Prepare Form FL415 (statement of service) in relation to personal service of the order on the respondent and postal service of the order on the mortgagee/landlord.

3 Ex parte applications

Follow the same procedure set out under 1 and 2 above, depending on what orders are being applied for. The statement in support of the application must state the reasons why an ex parte order is being sought. Telephone relevant court to arrange hearing in advance of attending court.

4 Enforcement – Breach of undertaking; breach of order with no power of arrest

- Get legal aid extended, as appropriate.
- Prepare:
    - application for warrant of arrest (Form FL407);
    - supporting affidavit (county court only; oral evidence given in magistrates' court); and/or
    - apply for committal (Form N78 in county court; Form FL418 in magistrates' court).

Note that the issue of a warrant of arrest is discretionary. It is advisable to have an application for committal ready if the warrant is refused. The affidavit in support could be worded to take account of either outcome.

5 Applications to vary, discharge or extend

- Get legal aid extended, as appropriate.
- Prepare:
    - Form FL403;
    - Form FL402.
- Arrange for personal service, giving not less than two business days' notice; alternatively apply for abridged period of notice or substituted service.
- Have Form FL415 prepared following service and file it at court.
- Arrange for personal service of order made and file Form FL415 at court.

Tables

In this section:

OCCUPATION ORDERS IN TABULAR FORM
s33 orders: A and R are AP; A is 'person entitled'; R is or is not entitled

	A = Applicant R = Respondent AP = Associated person(s) All statutory references are to the Family Law Act 1996

A is entitled to occupy because she has:

- sole/joint ownership;
- sole/joint tenancy;
- beneficial interest in the property;
- licence to occupy;
- right to occupy under any legal enactment;
- matrimonial home rights.

R is AP, either entitled to occupy or not.

NB: If R is AP because couple were engaged, no application may be brought after expiry of three years following termination of engagement.

Property is, has been or was intended to be common home of A and R.

Possible discretionary orders	*Criteria for making orders (a) to (g)*	*Ancillary discretionary orders (s40)*	*Criteria for making ancillary discretionary orders*
(a) Enforce A's right to remain in occupation (s33(3)(a)). (b) Require R to permit A to enter and remain in the dwelling-house or part of it (s33(3)(b)). (c) Regulate the occupation of the dwelling-house by A and/or R (s33(3)(c)). (d) Prohibit, suspend or restrict R's exercise of right to occupy as owner, tenant, licensee, holder of beneficial interest, or under any other legal enactment (s33(3)(d)).	Court must have regard to all of the circumstances including: • housing needs and housing resources of A, R and any relevant child (s33(6)(a)); • financial resources of A and R (s33(6)(b)); • likely effect of any order, or of any decision by the court not to exercise its powers, on the health, safety or well-being of A, R and any relevant child (s33(6)(c));	(a) Impose obligations on either A or R as to: (i) the repair and maintenance of the dwelling-house; or (ii) the discharge of rent, mortgage payments or other outgoings related to the dwelling-house (s40(1)(a)).	Court must have regard to all of the circumstances of the case including: • financial needs and financial resources of A and R; • financial obligations which A and R have, or are likely to have in the foreseeable future, including financial obligations to each other and to any relevant child (s40(2)).

(e) Restrict or terminate R's matrimonial home rights (s33(3)(e)). (f) Require R to leave dwelling-house or part of it (s33(3)(f)). (g) Exclude R from a defined area in which dwelling-house is included (s33(3)(g)). (h) Make a declaration that A is entitled to occupy as owner, tenant, licensee, beneficial owner, or under any other legal enactment, or has matrimonial home rights (s33(4)). (i) Provide that A's matrimonial rights will not be brought to an end by R's death or termination of marriage, where R is other spouse and application is made during currency of marriage (s33(5)).	• conduct of A and R in relation to each other and otherwise (s33(6)(d)); • balance of harm test (s33(7)) (see paras **10.48** to **10.58**). NB: If balance of harm test favours A, discretionary orders (a) to (g) become mandatory. *Criteria for making order (i)* Court must consider that in all the circumstances it is just and reasonable to do so (s33(8)).	(b) Where both A and R are entitled to occupy, order any party in occupation of all or part of the dwelling-house to make periodical payments to the other party in respect of the accommodation (s40(1)(b)). (c) Grant either A or R possession or use of furniture or other contents of the dwelling-house (s40(1)(c)). (d) Order either A or R to take reasonable care of any furniture or other contents of dwelling-house (s(40)(1)(d)). (e) Order either A or R to take reasonable steps to keep the dwelling-house and any furniture or other contents secure (s40(1)(e)).

Duration of orders

Orders may be made for a specified period, until the occurrence of a specified event, or until further order (s33(10)). The ancillary discretionary orders will cease when the substantive occupation order ceases (S40(3)).

Orders cannot be made after the death of either A or R, and orders cease to have effect after the death of A or R, unless the court has specified otherwise (see order (i)) (s33(9)).

OCCUPATION ORDERS IN TABULAR FORM
s35 orders: A and R are former spouses; A is not 'person entitled'; R is entitled

A is a former spouse with no legal right to occupy, eg, former matrimonial home was solely owned/rented by R and divorce has terminated matrimonial home rights (s35(1)(b)). *NB: If A is a former spouse who has a beneficial interest in former matrimonial home solely owned by R, A may either apply for orders under this section (s35(11)) or as a 'person entitled' using s33 (s35(12)). An application under s35 as a 'person not entitled' will not prejudice an application for a declaration of a constructive trust on behalf of A (s35(11)).* R is a former spouse who is entitled to occupy because he has: • sole ownership; • sole tenancy; • beneficial interest in the property; • licence to occupy; • right to occupy under any legal enactment (s35(1)(a)). Property was or was intended to be the matrimonial home (s35(1)(c)).	A = Applicant R = Respondent AP = Associated person(s) All statutory references are to the Family Law Act 1996

Mandatory orders if A is in occupation	*Criteria for making mandatory orders*	*Possible discretionary orders*	*Criteria for making discretionary orders (s35(7))*	*Ancillary discretionary orders (s40)*	*Criteria for making ancillary discretionary orders*
(a) A be given the right not to be evicted or excluded by R from the dwelling-house or any part of it for a specified period stated in the order (s35(3)(a)). (b) R be prohibited from evicting or excluding A during the specified period stated in the order (s35(3)(b)).	Court must have regard to all of the circumstances including: • housing needs and housing resources of A, R, and any relevant child (s35(6)(a)); • financial resources of A and R (s35(6)(b)); • likely effect of any order, or of any decision by the court not to exercise its powers, on the health, safety or well-being of A, R and any relevant child (s35(6)(c));	(a) Regulate the occupation of the dwelling-house by A and/or R (s35(5)(a)). (b) Prohibit, suspend or restrict the exercise by R of his right to occupy (s35(5)(b)). (c) Require R to leave the dwelling-house or part of the dwelling-house (s35(5)(c)). (d) Exclude R from a defined area in which dwelling-house is situated (s35(5)(d)).	• Housing needs and housing resources of A, R, and any relevant child (s35(6)(a)). • Financial resources of A and R (s35(6)(b)). • Likely effect of any order, or of any decision by the court not to exercise its powers, on the health, safety or well-being of A, R and any relevant child (s35(6)(c)).	(a) Impose obligations on either A or R as to: (i) the repair and maintenance of the dwelling-house; or (ii) the discharge of rent, mortgage payments or other outgoings related to the dwelling-house (s40(1)(a)).	Court must have regard to all of the circumstances of the case including: • financial needs and financial resources of A and R; • financial obligations which A and R have, or are likely to have in the foreseeable future, including financial obligations to each other and to any relevant child (s40(2)).

Mandatory orders if A is out of occupation

(a) A be given the right to enter into and occupy the dwelling-house for a specified period stated in the order (s35(4)(a)).

(b) R be required to permit A to exercise the right to enter into and occupy the dwelling-house during the specified period stated in the order (s35(4)(b)).

- conduct of A and R in relation to each other and otherwise (s35(6)(d));
- length of time that has elapsed since A and R ceased living together (s35(6)(e));
- length of time that has elapsed since the marriage was dissolved or annulled (s35(6)(f));
- whether there are pending proceedings between A and R for property adjustment orders under the Matrimonial Causes Act 1973, or orders for financial relief under the Children Act 1989, or relating to the legal or beneficial ownership of the dwelling-house (s35(6)(g)).

- Conduct of A and R in relation to each other and otherwise (s35(6)(d)).
- Length of time that has elapsed since A and R ceased living together (s35(6)(e)).
- 'Balance of harm' test (s35(8)) (see paras **10.48** to **10.58**).

NB: If the balance of harm test favours A, discretionary orders become mandatory.

(b) Where both A and R are entitled to occupy, order any party in occupation of all or part of the dwelling-house to make periodical payments to the other party in respect of the accommodation (s40(1)(b)).

(c) Grant either A or R possession or use of furniture or other contents of the dwelling-house (s40(1)(c)).

(d) Order either A or R to take reasonable care of any furniture or other contents of dwelling-house (s(40)(1)(d)).

(e) Order either A or R to take reasonable steps to keep the dwelling-house and any furniture or other contents secure (s40(1)(e)).

Duration of mandatory and discretionary orders

Orders must be limited initially to a period not exceeding six months, but can be extended one or more times for further periods of up to six months (s35(10)). The ancillary orders will cease when the substantive occupation order ceases.

Orders cannot be made after death of A or R and cease to have effect on death of A or R.

OCCUPATION ORDERS IN TABULAR FORM
s36 orders: A and R are cohabitants/former cohabitants; A is not 'person entitled'; R is entitled

A = Applicant
R = Respondent
AP = Associated person(s)
All statutory references are to the Family Law Act 1996

A is a person who is living or has lived with R as man and wife but who has no legal right to occupy dwelling-house.

NB: If A has a beneficial interest in former home solely owned by R, A may either apply for orders under this section (s36(11)) or as a 'person entitled' using s33 (s35(12)). An application under s36 as a 'person not entitled' will not prejudice an application for a declaration of a constructive trust on behalf of A (s36(11)).

R is a person entitled to occupy because he has:

- sole ownership;
- sole tenancy;
- beneficial interest in the property;
- licence to occupy;
- right to occupy under any legal enactment (s36(1)(a)).

Property is home in which A and R are currently living, or in which they previously lived together, or in which they intended to live together (s36(1)(c)).

Mandatory orders if A is in occupation	Criteria for making mandatory orders	Possible discretionary orders (s36(5))	Criteria for making discretionary orders (s36(7))	Ancillary discretionary orders (s40)	Criteria for making ancillary discretionary orders
(a) A be given the right not to be evicted or excluded by R from the dwelling-house or any part of it for a specified period stated in the order (s36(3)(a)). (b) R be prohibited from evicting or excluding A during that period (s36(3)(b)).	• Housing needs and housing resources of A, R, and any relevant child (s36(6)(a)). • Financial resources of A and R (s36(6)(b)). • Likely effect of any order, or of any decision by the court not to exercise its powers, on the health, safety or well-being of A, R and any relevant child (s36(6)(c)).	(a) Regulate the occupation of the dwelling-house by A and/or R (s36(5)(a)). (b) Prohibit, suspend or restrict the exercise by R of his right to occupy (s36(5)(b)). (c) Require R to leave the dwelling-house or part of the dwelling-house (s36(5)(c)).	• Housing needs and housing resources of A, R, and any relevant child (s36(6)(a)). • Financial resources of A and R (s36(6)(b)). • Likely effect of any order, or of any decision by the court not to exercise its powers, on the health, safety or well-being of A, R and any relevant child (s36(6)(c)).	(a) Impose obligations on either A or R as to: (i) the repair and maintenance of the dwelling-house; or (ii) the discharge of rent, mortgage payments or other outgoings related to the dwelling-house (s40(1)(a)).	Court must have regard to all of the circumstances of the case including: • financial needs and financial resources of A and R; • financial obligations which A and R have, or are likely to have in the foreseeable future, including financial obligations to each other and to any relevant child (s40(2)).

Mandatory orders if A is out of occupation

Mandatory orders	Discretionary factors		Test	Ancillary discretionary orders
(a) A be given the right to enter into and occupy the dwelling-house for a period specified in the order (s36(4)(a)). (b) R be required to permit A to enter into and occupy the dwelling-house for a period specified in the order (s36(4)(b)).	• Conduct of A and R in relation to each other and otherwise (s36(6)(d)). • The nature of the parties' relationship (s36(6)(e)) and the fact that they have not given each other the commitment involved in marriage (s41(2)). • The length of time during which A and R lived together as husband and wife (s36(6)(f)). • Whether there are or have been any children who are children of both A and R, or for whom A and R have had parental responsibility (s36(6)(g)). • The length of time that has elapsed since A and R ceased living together (s36(6)(h)). • The existence of any pending proceedings between A and R for financial relief under the Children Act 1989 or relating to the legal or beneficial ownership of the dwelling-house (s36(6)(i)).	(d) Exclude R from a defined area in which dwelling-house is situated (s36(5)(d)).	• Conduct of A and R in relation to each other and otherwise (s36(6)(d)). • 'Balance of harm' test (s36(8)) (see paras **10.48** to **10.58**). NB: The court is never under a duty to make discretionary orders, even if the balance of harm test favours A.	(b) Where both A and R are entitled to occupy, order any party in occupation of all or part of the dwelling-house to make periodical payments to the other party in respect of the accommodation (s40(1)(b)). (c) Grant either A or R possession or use of furniture or other contents of the dwelling-house (s40(1)(c)). (d) Order either A or R to take reasonable care of any furniture or other contents of dwelling-house (s40(1)(d)). (e) Order either A or R to take reasonable steps to keep the dwelling-house and any furniture or other contents secure (s40(1)(e)).

Duration of mandatory and discretionary orders

Orders must be limited to a period not exceeding six months initially. Can be extended one time only for a further period not exceeding six months. The ancillary discretionary orders will cease when the substantive occupation order ceases.

Orders may not be made after death of either A or R and cease to have effect on death of either A or R.

OCCUPATION ORDERS IN TABULAR FORM
s37 orders: A and R are spouses/former spouses; neither A nor R is 'person entitled to occupy'

	A = Applicant R = Respondent AP = Associated person(s)
A is a spouse or former spouse not entitled to occupy dwelling-house under beneficial interest or by virtue of ownership, tenancy or licence or under any other enactment giving rights of occupation, eg, couple were living with a relative in relative's home.	All statutory references are to the Family Law Act 1996

R is a spouse or former spouse not entitled as above.

NB: Both parties equally entitled to make application under this section.

Property is or was the matrimonial home.

Possible discretionary orders	*Criteria for making discretionary orders (s37(4))*
(a) R be required to permit A to enter and remain in the dwelling-house or part of the dwelling-house (s37(3)(a)). (b) Regulate the occupation of the dwelling-house by A and/or R (s37(3)(b)). (c) Require R to leave the dwelling-house or part of the dwelling-house (s37(3)(c)). (d) Exclude R from a defined area in which dwelling-house is situated (s37(3)(d)).	• Housing needs and housing resources of A, R and any relevant child (s33(6)(a)). • Financial resources of A and R (s33(6)(b)). • Likely effect of any order, or of any decision by the court not to exercise its powers, on the health, safety or well-being of A, R and any relevant child (s33(6)(c)). • Conduct of A and R in relation to each other and otherwise (s33(6)(d)). • 'Balance of harm' test (s33(7)) (see paras **10.48** to **10.58**).

Duration of orders

Orders must be limited initially to periods not exceeding six months, but may be extended on one or more occasions for periods of up to six months.

TABLES

OCCUPATION ORDERS IN TABULAR FORM
s38 orders: A and R are cohabitants/former cohabitants and neither is 'person entitled to occupy'

A is a person who is living or has lived with R as husband and wife and is not entitled to occupy dwelling-house under beneficial interest or by virtue of ownership, tenancy or licence or under any other enactment giving rights of occupation, eg, couple were living with a relative in relative's home.	A = Applicant R = Respondent AP = Associated person(s) All statutory references are to the Family Law Act 1996

R is a cohabitant/former cohabitant and not entitled, as above.

NB: Both parties equally entitled to make application under this section (s38(2)).

Property is or was the home in which A and R lived together as husband and wife.

Possible discretionary orders

(a) R be required to permit A to enter and remain in the dwelling-house or part of the dwelling-house (s38(3)(a)).
(b) Regulate the occupation of the dwelling-house by A and/or R (s38(3)(b)).
(c) Require R to leave the dwelling-house or part of the dwelling-house (s38(3)(c)).
(d) Exclude R from a defined area in which dwelling-house is situated (s38(3)(d)).

Criteria for making discretionary orders

- Housing needs and housing resources of A, R and any relevant child (s38(4)(a)).
- Financial resources of A and R (s38(4)(b)).
- Likely effect of any order, or of any decision by the court not to exercise its powers, on the health, safety or well-being of A, R and any relevant child (s38(4)(c)).
- Conduct of A and R in relation to each other and otherwise (s38(4)(d)).
- 'Balance of harm' test (s38(5)) (see paras **10.48** to **10.58**).

Duration of discretionary orders

Orders must be limited initially to a period not exceeding six months, and may only be extended one time for a period of up to six months.

NON-MOLESTATION ORDERS (s42) IN TABULAR FORM

	A = Applicant R = Respondent AP = Associated person(s) All statutory references are to the Family Law Act 1996
Definition A non-molestation order contains either or both of the following provisions: (a) that R be prohibited from molesting another person who is associated with R (s41(1)(a)) (see paras **10.3** to **10.31** for definition of 'associated persons'); (b) that R be prohibited from molesting a relevant child. *NB: The order may be expressed so as to refer to molestation in general and/or to particular acts of molestation (s42(6)).*	
Who may apply • Associated persons (see paras **10.3** to **10.31** for definition). • A child under the age of 16 with the leave of the court, who may only grant leave if satisfied that the child has sufficient understanding to make the application (s43).	*Criteria for making non-molestation orders (s24(5))* Court must have regard to all the circumstances, including the need to secure the health, safety and well-being of: • the applicant; • where court is making an order of its own volition on behalf of a party in any family proceedings, the person who will benefit from the making of the order; • any relevant child (s42(5)).	*Circumstances in which a non-molestation order may be made (s42(2))* • Where an AP has made an application for a non-molestation order in family proceedings or without the institution of family proceedings. • Where court makes an order of its own volition in family proceedings in which R is a party in order to protect another party to the family proceedings or a relevant child. • Where A and R were engaged and the engagement has been terminated, the application must be made within three years of the termination of the engagement.

Duration of non-molestation orders

Non-molestation orders may be made for a specified period of any length, or until further order (s42(7)). A non-molestation order made in other family proceedings will cease if those proceedings are withdrawn or dismissed (s42(8)).

Part V

Precedents

Application for an order   Form C1
Children Act 1989

The court	To be completed by the court
	Date issued
	Case number
The full name(s) of the child(ren)	Child(ren)'s number(s)

1 About you (the applicant)

State
- *your title, full name, address, telephone number, date of birth and relationship to each child above*
- *your solicitor's name, address, reference, telephone, FAX and DX numbers.*

2 The child(ren) and the order(s) you are applying for

For each child state
- *the full name, date of birth and sex*
- *the type of order(s) you are applying for (for example, residence order, contact order, supervision order).*

Notes

1   This is the general application form for any order under the Children Act 1989. Some applications also require a supplementary application form to be completed.

2   This application form can be used on its own for any s8 application (including contact with a child in local authority accommodation) and for an application to discharge or vary an emergency protection order.

243

3   Other cases which concern the child(ren)

If there have ever been, or there are pending, any court cases which concern
- *a child whose name you have put in paragraph 2*
- *a full, half or step brother or sister of a child whose name you have put in paragraph 2*
- *a person in this case who is or has been, involved in caring for a child whose name you have put in paragraph 2*

attach a copy of the relevant order and give
- *the name of the court*
- *the name and panel address (if known) of the guardian ad litem, if appointed*
- *the name and contact address (if known) of the court welfare officer, if appointed*
- *the name and contact address (if known) of the solicitor appointed for the child(ren).*

4   The respondent(s)

Appendix 3 Family Proceedings Rules 1991; Schedule 2 Family Proceedings Courts (Children Act 1989) Rules 1991
For each respondent state
- *the title, full name and address*
- *the date of birth (if known) or the age*
- *the relationship to each child.*

5 Others to whom notice is to be given

Appendix 3 Family Proceedings Rules 1991; Schedule 2 Family Proceedings Courts (Children Act 1989) Rules 1991

For each person state • *the title, full name and address*
• *the date of birth (if known) or age*
• *the relationship to each child*

6 The care of the child(ren)

For each child in paragraph 2 state
• *the child's current address and how long the child has lived there*
• *whether it is the child's usual address and who cares for the child there*
• *the child's relationship to the other children (if any).*

7 Social Services

For each child in paragraph 2 state
• *whether the child is known to the Social Services.*
If so, give the name of the social worker and the address of the Social Services department.
• *whether the child is, or has been, on the Child Protection Register. If so, give the date of registrati*

8 The education and health of the child(ren)

For each child state
- *the name of the school, college or place of training which the child attends*
- *whether the child is in good health. Give details of any serious disabilities or ill health.*
- *whether the child has any special needs.*

9 The parents of the child(ren)

For each child state
- *the full name of the child's mother and father*
- *whether the parents are, or have been, married to each other*
- *whether the parents live together. If so, where.*
- *whether, to your knowledge, either of the parents have been involved in a court case concerning a child. If so, give the date and the name of the court.*

10 The family of the child(ren) (other children)

For any other child not already mentioned in the family (for example, a brother or a half sister) state
- *the full name and address*
- *the date of birth (if known) or age*
- *the relationship of the child to you.*

11 Other adults

State • *the full name of any other adults (for example, lodgers) who live at the same address as any child named in paragraph 2*
• *whether they live there all the time*
• *whether, to your knowledge, the adult has been involved in a court case concerning a child. If so, give the date and the name of the court.*

12 Your reason(s) for applying and any plans for the child(ren)

State briefly your reasons for applying and what you want the court to order.
• *Do not give a full statement if you are applying for an order under Section 8 of Children Act 1989. You may be asked to provide a full statement later.*
• *Do not complete this section if this form is accompanied by a prescribed supplement.*

13 At the court

State • *whether you will need an interpreter at court (parties are responsible for providing their ov If so, specify the language.*
• *whether disabled facilities will be needed at court.*

Signed   Date
(Applicant)

2 Application for leave (Form C2)   SPECIMEN

Application   Form C2

- for leave to commence proceedings
  Family Proceedings Rules 1991 Rule 4.3
  Family Proceedings Courts (Children Act 1989) Rules 1991 Rule 3

- for an order or directions in existing family proceedings
  Children Act 1989

- to be joined as, or cease to be, a party in existing family proceedings
  Family Proceedings Rules 1991 Rule 4.7(2)
  Family Proceedings Courts (Children Act 1989) Rules 1991 Rule 7(2)

The court	To be completed by the court
	Date issued
	Case number
The full name(s) of the child(ren)	Child(ren)'s number(s)

1 About you (the person making this application)

State • *your title, full name, address, telephone number, date of birth and relationship to each child above*

  • *your solicitor's name, address, reference, telephone, FAX and DX numbers*

  • *if you are already a party to the case, give your description (for example, applicant, respondent or other).*

2 The order(s) or direction(s) you are applying for

State for each child
- *the full name, date of birth and sex*
- *the type of order(s) you are applying for (for example, residence order, contact order, supervision order).*

3 Persons to be served with this application

For each respondent to this application state the title, full name and address.

4 Your reason(s) for applying and any plans for the child(ren)

State briefly your reasons for applying.
Do not give a full statement if you are applying for an order under Section 8 Children Act 1989.
You may be asked to provide a full statement later.

Signed	Date
(Applicant)	

3 Supplement for an application for contact with a child in care
(Form C15)   SPECIMEN

This form is to be used in conjunction with Form C1 (see p 243)

Supplement for an Application for   Form C15
Contact with a Child in Care
(Section 34(2) and (3) Children Act 1989)

The Court	To be completed by the Court
	Date issued
The full name(s) of the child(ren)	Case number
	Child(ren)'s number(s)

---

1. **Your relationship to the child(ren).**

    State whether ● *you are a parent or guardian*

    ● *you hold a residence order which was in force immediately before the care order was made (section 34(1)(c) Children Act 1989)*

    ● *you had care of the child(ren) through an order which was in force immediately before the care order was made (section 34(1)(d) Children Act 1989).*

2. **The order applied for and your reason(s) for the application.**
    If you are relying on a report or other documentary evidence, state the date(s) and author(s) and enclose a copy.

Signed   Date
(Applicant)

4 Application for an order authorising search for, taking charge of, and delivery of, a child (Form C3) SPECIMEN

Application for an Order Authorising Search for, Taking Charge of, and Delivery of, a Child (Section 34 Family Law Act 1986)	Form C3
The Court	To be completed by the Court
	Date issued
The full name(s) of the Child(ren)	
	Case number
	Child(ren)'s number(s)

1. About you (the Applicant).

State ● *your title, full name, address, telephone number, date of birth and relationship to each child above*

● *your solicitor's name, address, reference, telephone, fax and DX numbers.*

2. The child(ren).

For each child state ● *the full name, date of birth and sex*

● *the title, full name, address, telephone number of the person believed to have actual control of the child*

● *details which identify the child. You may enclose a recent photograph of the child, which should be dated.*

3. The grounds for the application.

State • *whether the application is ex parte and if so, why*
• *particulars of the order being disobeyed*
• *the best information available as to the whereabouts of the child.*

Signed   Date
(Applicant)

5 Application for an order for disclosure of a child's whereabouts (Form C4) SPECIMEN

Application for an Order for Disclosure of a Child's Whereabouts

Form C4

(Section 33 Family Law Act 1986)

The Court	To be completed by the Court
	Date issued
The full name(s) of the child(ren)	
	Case number
	Child(ren)'s number(s)

---

1. About you (the Applicant).

State • *your title, full name, address, telephone number, date of birth and relationship to each child above*
• *your solicitor's name, address, reference, telephone, fax and DX numbers.*

2. The child(ren).

For each child state • *the full name, date of birth and sex*
• *the title, full name, address, telephone number of the person believed to have actual control of the child*
• *details which identify the child. You may enclose a recent photograph of the child, which should be dated.*

3. The order you are seeking.

State • the name(s) of the person(s) to be directed by the Court to disclose relevant information as to the whereabouts of the child

• specific directions you would like the Court to give as to when and how the information shall be disclosed to the Court.

4. The grounds for the application.

State why you believe that • the Court does not have adequate information as to where the child is

• the person(s) to whom the order is directed may have relevant information.

Signed   Date
(Applicant)

6 Lord Chancellor's Department Child Abduction and Custody Act 1985 questionnaire in respect of children abducted to convention countries SPECIMEN

I DETAILS OF THE APPLICANT

surname and forenames . . . .
date and place of birth . . . .
nationality(ies) . . . .
occupation . . . .
country of habitual residence . . . .
passport or identity card no . . . .
relationship to child(ren) . . . .
address at which the applicant . . . .
can be contacted . . . .
. . . .
telephone no: home . . . .
business. . . . .

name of solicitor (if any) . . . .
name of firm of solicitors . . . .
address of solicitors . . . .
. . . .
telephone no:. . . . .

II DETAILS OF THE REMEDY REQUIRED BY THE APPLICANT
(please tick appropriate box)

☐ enforcement of rights of custody and return of child(ren)

☐ enforcement of rights of access

III DETAILS OF CHILD(REN)
(if more than four children continue on separate page)

surname and forenames 1) . . . .
2) . . . .
3) . . . .
4) . . . .

date and place of birth 1) . . . .
2) . . . .
3) . . . .
4) . . . .

country of habitual residence   1) ....
(immediately before removal)   2) ....
                                3) ....
                                4) ....

nationality(ies)   1) ....
                                2) ....
                                3) ....
                                4) ....

passport or identity card no. if   1) ....
child holds a separate passport   2) ....
(if not indicate whether child is 3) ....
included on mother's or father's   4) ....
passport)

description   1) ....
                                2) ....
                                3) ....
                                4) ....

IV   DETAILS OF PARENTS
1. Mother
(if mother is also the applicant there is no need to repeat personal details)
name and first names   ....
date and place of birth   ....
nationality   ....
occupation   ....
habitual residence   ....
passport or identity card no.   ....
2. Father
(if father is also the applicant there is no need to repeat personal details)
name and first names   ....
date and place of birth   ....
nationality   ....
occupation   ....
habitual residence   ....
passport or identity card no.   ....
3. Date and place of marriage
....

V   DETAILS OF PERSON WHO HAS TAKEN OR RETAINED CHILD(REN)
(if this person is the mother or father only answer questions 6 to 8)
1. surname and forenames   ....
2. date and place of birth   ....
3. nationality   ....

4. occupation   . . . .
5. passport or identity card no.   . . . .
6. relationship to child(ren)   . . . .
7. description   . . . .
   (please enclose photo if
   available)
8. last known address(es)   . . . .
   (in the country in which this   . . . .
   person now resides)   . . . .

VI   PLACE WHERE THE CHILD(REN) IS(ARE) THOUGHT TO BE
1. Present address(es) of the   . . . .
   child(ren) if different to   . . . .
   those of the person who has   . . . .
   taken the child(ren)   . . . .
2. Details of other persons in the country to which the child(ren) has been
   taken who might be able to supply additional information as to the whereabouts of the child(ren) ie, names, address, telephone nos, relationship to
   the child(ren) or taker of the child(ren)
   . . . .
   . . . .

VII   BRIEF DETAILS OF THE TIME, DATE, PLACE AND CIRCUM-
      STANCES OF THE REMOVAL OF THE CHILD(REN) FROM THE
      UK OR THE RETENTION OF THE CHILD(REN) OVERSEAS
      . . . .
      . . . .
      . . . .

VIII   DETAILS OF COURT PROCEEDINGS THAT HAVE TAKEN
       PLACE OR ARE TAKING PLACE (EG DIVORCE, CUSTODY,
       ACCESS, WARDSHIP ETC)
       Provide details of names of parties, name of court, case no (if known)
       and the stage reached (eg, decree nisi/absolute, custody order made)
1. England and Wales . . . .
   . . . . : . . . .
2. Outside England and Wales . . . .
   . . . .

IX   EVIDENCE THAT THE APPLICANT (OTHER THAN COURT
     ORDERS) HAD RIGHTS OF CUSTODY/ACCESS OVER THE
     CHILD AND WAS EXERCISING THOSE RIGHTS AT THE TIME
     OF REMOVAL
     . . . .
     . . . .

X　OTHER RELEVANT MATTERS

. . . .
. . . .
. . . .

XI　ARRANGEMENTS FOR THE RETURN OF THE CHILD(REN)

1. Please indicate whether the applicant is prepared to travel to the country to which the children have been taken, both to attend the court hearing, if necessary, and to collect the child(ren) should the application be successful, or any other person who could do so on their behalf

. . . .
. . . .

2. Does the applicant wish an application to be made to the overseas court for an order to be made that the person who has taken the child(ren) meet any additional costs incurred by them eg, air fares (Hague Convention only)?

. . . .
. . . .

signature of applicant or their solicitor

. . . .

date　. . . . .

7 Originating summons under the Child Abduction and Custody Act 1985 in respect of child abducted to England and Wales

SPECIMEN

IN THE HIGH COURT OF JUSTICE	No of matter
FAMILY DIVISION	
PRINCIPAL REGISTRY	

In the matter of TS (a Minor)
and in the matter of the Child Abduction and Custody Act 1985
and in the matter of the Supreme Court Act 1981

Between	[GS]	Plaintiff
and	[JS]	Defendant

ORIGINATING SUMMONS

LET JS attend before the Judge in Chambers at the Royal Courts of Justice, Strand, London WC2A 2LL on the   day of   1989 at   o'clock on the hearing of an Application by the Plaintiff of [*address*] that:

1 A declaration that the removal of TS from the State of Ontario, Canada and his retention outside the State of Ontario, Canada is wrongful pursuant to Article 3 of the Hague Convention on the Civil Aspects of International Child Abduction.[1]

2 The Minor TS be returned to the jurisdiction of the Queen's Bench of Ontario.

3 The Minor be returned to the joint custody of GS and JS.

4 The Plaintiff may exercise her rights of reasonable access to the Minor.

5 The costs of this Application be provided for.

The Minor TS was born on [*date*].

The Plaintiff is the child's mother and the Defendant is the child's father.

The minor was removed from his habitual residence at the home of the Defendant at [*address*] by the Defendant on the 13th April 1992. It is believed that the Defendant took the child to London, United Kingdom, from Toronto International Airport on British Airways flight no BY999. This was done without the knowledge of the Plaintiff and in breach of an order granted by the Honourable Justice [*name*] of the Court of the Queen's

Bench of Ontario on the 25th March 1989 which stated, inter alia, that the Defendant was restrained from taking or removing from the Province of Ontario the infant child of his marriage to the Plaintiff, namely TS either on Flight no BY999 leaving Toronto Airport on the 13th day of April 1992 or howsoever, in any other fashion.

It is believed that the child is or will shortly be at one of two addresses in the United Kingdom, namely at the home of SS of [address] (tel:) or at the home of R and SJ of [address] (tel:).

The Plaintiff and Defendant have joint custody of the child pursuant to a divorce judgment granted on the 22nd November 1988 by the Honourable Justice [name] of the Court of the Queen's Bench of Ontario.

AND LET the Defendant within seven days after service of this Summons on him, counting the day of service, return the accompanying Acknowledgement of Service to the appropriate Court Office.

[signature]

Solicitors for the Plaintiff

To the Defendant or his Solicitors

This Summons was taken out by [name of solicitors] of [address of solicitors] whose telephone number is   Solicitors for the said Plaintiff who resides at [address] and whose address is care of her Solicitors.

NOTE: If the Defendant does not attend personally or by his Counsel or Solicitor at the time and place above mentioned, such Order will be made as the Court may think just and expedient.

Dated this   day of   1992.

Notes
1 For the European Convention, substitute: 'pursuant to Article 1 of the European Convention on Recognition and Enforcement of Decisions concerning Custody of Children'.
2 For the European Convention, insert also the decisions relating to custody or access sought to be registered or enforced.
3 See paras 9.26 to 9.36 for the other documents that should be filed.

8 Application for a non-molestation order/an occupation order (Form FL401)   SPECIMEN

Application for:
a non-molestation order
an occupation order
Family Law Act 1996 (Part IV)

The court

Please read the accompanying notes as you complete this form.

1 About you (the applicant)

State your title (Mr, Mrs etc), full name, address, telephone number and date of birth (if under 18):

State your solicitor's name, address, reference, telephone, FAX and DX numbers:

2 About the respondent

State the respondent's name, address and date of birth (if known):

3 The Order(s) for which you are applying

This application is for:

☐ a non-molestation order

☐ an occupation order

☐ Tick this box if you wish the court to hear your application without notice being given to the respondent. The reasons relied on for an application being heard without notice must be stated in the statement in support.

4 Your relationship to the respondent (the person to be served with this application)

Your relationship to the respondent is:
Please tick only one of the following

1 ☐ Married

2 ☐ Were married

3 ☐ Cohabiting

4 ☐ Were cohabiting

5 ☐ Both of you live or have lived in the same household

6 ☐ Relative
State how related:

7 ☐ Agreed to marry.
Give the date the agreement was made. If the agreement has ended, state when.

8 ☐ Both of you are parents of or have parental responsibility for a child

9 ☐ One of you is a parent of a child and the other has parental responsibility for that child

10 ☐ One of you is the natural parent or
    grandparent of a child adopted or
    freed for adoption, and the other is:
       (i)   the adoptive parent
    or (ii) a person who has applied for
              an adoption order for the child
    or (iii) a person with whom the child
              has been placed for adoption
    or (iv) the child who has been adopted
              or freed for adoption.
    State whether (i), (ii), (iii) or (iv):

11 ☐ Both of you are parties to the same family
    proceedings (see also Section 11 below).

5 Application for a non-molestation order

If you wish to apply for a non-molestation order,
state briefly in this section the order you want.

Give full details in support of your application in
your supporting evidence

6 Application for an occupation order

*If you do not wish to apply for an occupation
order, please go to section 9 of this form.*

(A) State the address of the dwelling house to which
    your application relates:

(B) State whether it is occupied by you or the
    respondent now or in the past, or whether it was
    intended to be occupied by you or the respondent:

(C) State whether you are entitled to occupy
the dwelling-house: ☐ Yes ☐No

If yes, explain why:

(D) State whether the respondent is entitled to
occupy the dwelling-house:☐ Yes ☐No

If yes, explain why:

**On the basis of your answer to (C) and (D)
above, tick one of the boxes 1 to 5 below to
show the category into which you fit**

1 ☐ a spouse who has matrimonial home rights in
the dwelling-house, or a person who is
entitled to occupy it by virtue of a beneficial
estate or interest or contract or by virtue of
any enactment giving him or her the right to
remain in occupation.

If you tick box 1, state whether there is a
dispute or pending proceedings between you
and the respondent about your right to occupy
the dwelling-house.

2 ☐ a former spouse with no existing right to
occupy, where the respondent spouse is
entitled.

3 ☐ a cohabitant or former cohabitant with no
existing right to occupy, where the respondent
cohabitant or former cohabitant is so entitled.

4 ☐ a spouse or former spouse who is not entitled
to occupy, where the respondent spouse or
former spouse is also not entitled.

5 ☐ a cohabitant or former cohabitant who is not
entitled to occupy, where the respondent
cohabitant or former cohabitant is also not
entitled.

Matrimonial Home Rights

If you do have matrimonial home rights please:
State whether the title to the land is registered or
unregistered (if known):

If registered, state the Land Registry title number
(if known):

**If you wish to apply for an occupation order,
state briefly here the order you want.** Give full
details in support of your application in your
supporting evidence.

7 Application for additional order(s) about the dwelling house

If you want to apply for any of the orders listed in the
notes to this section, state what order you would like
the court to make:

8 Mortgage and rent

Is the dwelling house subject to a mortgage?

☐ Yes   ☐ No

If yes, please provide the name and address of the
mortgagee:

Is the dwelling house rented?

☐ Yes   ☐ No

If yes, please provide the name and address of the
landlord:

9 At the court

Will you need an interpreter at court?

☐ Yes   ☐ No

If 'Yes', specify the language:

If you need an interpreter because you do not
speak English, you are responsible for providing
your own.

If you need an interpreter or other facilities
because of a disability, please contact the court
to ask what help is available.

10 Other information

State the name and date of birth of any child
living with or staying with, or likely to live with
or stay with, you or the respondent:

State the name of any other person living in the
same household as you and the respondent, and
say why they live there:

11 Other Proceedings and Orders

If there are any other current family proceedings
or orders in force involving you and the
respondent, state the type of proceedings or
orders, the court and the case number. This
includes any application for an occupation order
or non-molestation order against you by the
respondent.

This application is to be served upon the respondent

Signed   Date

Application for a non-molestation order or occupation order
Notes for Guidance

Section 1

If you do not wish your address to be made known to the respondent, leave the space on the form blank and complete Confidential Address Form C8. The court can give you this form.

If you are under 18, someone over 18 must help you make this application. That person, who might be one of your parents, is called a 'next friend'.

If you are under 16 you need permission to make this application. You must apply to the High Court for permission, using this form. If the High Court gives you permission to make this application, it will then either hear the application itself or transfer it to a county court.

Section 3

An urgent order made by the court before notice of the application is served on the respondent is called an ex-parte order. In deciding whether to make an ex-parte order the court will consider all the circumstances of the case, including:

- *any risk of significant harm to the applicant or a relevant child, attributable to conduct of the respondent, if the order is not made immediately*

- *whether it is likely that the applicant will be deterred or prevented from pursuing the application if an order is not made immediately*

- *whether there is reason to believe that the respondent is aware of the proceedings but is deliberately evading service and that the applicant or a relevant child will be seriously prejudiced by the delay involved.*

If the court makes an ex-parte order, it must give the respondent an opportunity to make representations about the order as soon as just and convenient at a full hearing.

'Harm' in relation to a person who has reached the age of 18 means ill-treatment or the impairment of health, and in relation to a child means ill-treatment or the impairment of health and development. 'Ill-treatment' includes forms of ill-treatment which are not physical and, in relation to a child, includes sexual abuse. The court will require evidence of any harm which you allege in support of your application. This evidence should be included in the statement accompanying this application.

Section 4

For you to be able to apply for an order you must be related to the respondent in one of the ways listed in this section of the form. If you are not related in one of these ways you should seek legal advice.

Cohabitants are a man and a woman who, although not married to each other, are living or have lived together as husband and wife. People who have cohabited, but have then married will not fall within this category, but will fall within the category of married people.

Those who live or have lived in the same household do not include people who share the same household because one of them is the other's employee, tenant, lodger or boarder.

You will only be able to apply as a relative of the respondent if you are:

(A) the father, mother, stepfather, stepmother, son, daughter, stepson, stepdaughter, grandmother, grandfather, grandson or granddaughter of the respondent or of the respondent's spouse or former spouse.

(B) the brother, sister, uncle, aunt, niece or nephew (whether of the full blood or of the half blood or by marriage) of the respondent or of the respondent's spouse or former spouse.

This includes, in relation to a person who is living or has lived with another person as husband and wife, any person who would fall within (A) or (B) if the parties were married to each other (for example, your cohabitee's father or brother).

Agreements to marry: You will fall within this category only if you make this application within three years of the termination of the agreement. The court will require the following evidence of the agreement:

  evidence in writing

or the gift of an engagement ring in contemplation of marriage

or evidence that a ceremony has been entered into in the presence of one or more other persons assembled for the purpose of witnessing it.

Parents and parental responsibility: You will fall within this category if both you and the respondent are either the parents of a child or have parental responsibility for that child

or if one of you is the parent and the other has parental responsibility.

Under the Children Act 1989, parental responsibility is held automatically by a child's mother, and by the child's father if the child's mother were married to each other at the time of the child's birth or have married subsequently. Where this is not the case, parental responsibility can be acquired by the father in accordance with the provisions of the Children Act 1989.

Section 5

A non-molestation order can forbid the respondent to molest you or a relevant child. Molestation can include, for example, violence, threats, pestering and other forms of harassment. The court can forbid particular acts of the respondent, molestation in general, or both.

Section 6

If you wish to apply for an occupation order but you are uncertain about your answer to any of the questions in this part of the application form, you should seek legal advice.

(A) A dwelling-house includes any building or part of a building which is occupied as a dwelling; any caravan, houseboat or structure which is occupied as a dwelling; and any yard, garden, garage or outhouse belonging to it and occupied with it.

Section 6 (continued)

(C) & (D) *The following questions give examples to help you to decide if you or the respondent, or both of you, are entitled to occupy the dwelling-house:*

(a)   Are you the sole legal owner of the dwelling-house?

(b)   Are you and the respondent joint legal owners of the dwelling-house?

(c)   Is the respondent the sole legal owner of the dwelling-house?

(d)   Do you rent the dwelling-house as sole tenant?

(e)   Do you and the respondent rent the dwelling-house as joint tenants?

(f)   Does the respondent rent the dwelling house as sole tenant?

If you answer   ■ **Yes** *to (a), (b), (d) or (e) you are likely to be entitled to occupy the dwelling-house*

■ **Yes** *to (c) or (f) you may not be entitled (unless, for example, you are a spouse and have matrimonial home rights - see the notes under 'Matrimonial Home Rights' below)*

■ **Yes** *to (b), (c), (e) or (f), the respondent is likely to be entitled to occupy the dwelling-house.*

■ **Yes** *to (a) or (d) the respondent may not be entitled (unless, for example, he is a spouse and has matrimonial home rights).*

Box 1 *For example, if you are sole owner, joint owner, or if you rent the property. If you are not a spouse, former spouse, cohabitant or former cohabitant of the respondent, you will only be able to apply for an occupation order if you fall within this category.*

If you answer **Yes** *to this question, it will not be possible for a magistrates' court to deal with the application, unless the court decides that it is unnecessary for it to decide this question in order to deal with the application or make an order. If the court decides that it cannot deal with the application, it will transfer the application to a county court.*

Box 2 *For example, if the respondent was married to you and is sole owner or rents the property.*

Box 3 *For example, if the respondent is or was cohabiting with you and is sole owner or rents the property.*

Matrimonial Home Rights

Where one spouse is entitled to occupy the dwelling-house by virtue of a beneficial estate or interest or contract or by virtue of any enactment giving him or her the right to remain in occupation, and the other spouse is not so entitled, the spouse who is not entitled has matrimonial home rights. These are a right, if the spouse is in occupation; not to be evicted or excluded from the dwelling house except with the leave of the court and, if the spouse is not in occupation, the right with the leave of the court to enter into and occupy the dwelling-house.

Matrimonial home rights do not exist if the dwelling-house has never been, and was never intended to be, the matrimonial home of the two spouses. If the marriage has come to an end, matrimonial home rights will also have ceased, unless a court order has been made during the marriage for the rights to continue after the end of the marriage:

Occupation Orders *The possible orders are:*

If you have ticked box 1 above, an order under section 33 of the Act may:

■ *enforce the applicant's entitlement to remain in occupation as against the respondent*

■ *require the respondent to permit the applicant to enter and remain in the dwelling-house or part of it*

■ *regulate the occupation of the dwelling-house by either or both parties*

■ *if the respondent is also entitled to occupy, the order may prohibit, suspend or restrict the exercise by him, of that right*

■ *restrict or terminate any matrimonial home rights of the respondent*

■ *require the respondent to leave the dwelling-house or part of it*

■ *exclude the respondent from a defined area around the dwelling-house*

■ *declare that the applicant is entitled to occupy the dwelling-house or has matrimonial home rights in it*

■ *provide that matrimonial home rights of the applicant are not brought to an end by the death of the other spouse or termination of the marriage.*

If you have ticked box 2 or box 3 above, an order under section 35 or 36 of the Act may:

■ *give the applicant the right not to be evicted or excluded from the dwelling-house or any part of it by the respondent for a specified period*

■ *prohibit the respondent from evicting or excluding the applicant during that period*

■ *give the applicant the right to enter and occupy the dwelling house for a specified period*

■ *require the respondent to permit the exercise of that right*

■ *regulate the occupation of the dwelling-house by either or both of the parties*

■ *prohibit, suspend or restrict the exercise by the respondent of his right to occupy*

■ *require the respondent to leave the dwelling-house or part of it*

■ *exclude the respondent from a defined area around the dwelling-house.*

If you have ticked box 4 or box 5 above, an order under section 37 or 38 of the Act may:

■ *require the respondent to permit the applicant to enter and remain in the dwelling-house or part of it*

■ *regulate the occupation of the dwelling-house by either or both of the parties*

■ *require the respondent to leave the dwelling-house or part of it*

■ *exclude the respondent from a defined area around the dwelling-house.*

Section 6 (continued)

You should provide any evidence which you have on the following matters in your evidence in support of this application. If necessary, further statements may be submitted after the application has been issued.

If you have ticked box 1, 4 or 5 above, the court will need any available evidence of the following:

- *the housing needs and resources of you, the respondent and any relevant child*
- *the financial resources of you and the respondent*
- *the likely effect of any order, or of any decision not to make an order, on the health, safety and well-being of you, the respondent and any relevant child*
- *the conduct of you and the respondent in relation to each other and otherwise.*

If you have ticked box 2 above, the court will need any available evidence of:

- *the housing needs and resources of you, the respondent and relevant child*
- *the financial resources of you and the respondent*
- *the likely effect of any order, or of any decision not to make an order on the health, safety and well-being of you, the respondent and any relevant child*
- *the conduct of you and the respondent in relation to each other and otherwise.*
- *the length of time that has elapsed since you and the respondent ceased to live together*
- *the length of time that has elapsed since the marriage was dissolved or annulled*
- *the existence of any pending proceedings between you and the respondent:*

  under section 23A of the Matrimonial Causes Act 1973 (property adjustment orders in connection with divorce proceedings etc.)

  or under Schedule 1 para 1(2)(d) or (e) of the Children Act 1989 (orders for financial relief against parents)

  or relating to the legal or beneficial ownership of the dwelling-house.

If you have ticked box 3 above, the court will need any available evidence of:

- *the housing needs and resources of you, the respondent and any relevant child*
- *the financial resources of you and the respondent*
- *the likely effect of any order, or of any decision not to make an order, on the health, safety and well-being of you, the respondent and any relevant child*
- *the conduct of you and the respondent in relation to each other and otherwise*
- *the nature of you and the respondent's relationship*

- *the length of time which you have lived together as husband and wife*
- *whether you and the respondent have had any children, or have both had parental responsibility for any children*
- *the length of time which has elapsed since you and the respondent ceased to live together*
- *the existence of any pending proceedings between you and the respondent under Schedule 1 para 1(2)(d) or (e) of the Children Act 1989 or relating to the legal or beneficial ownership of the dwelling-house.*

Section 7

Under section 40 of the Act the court may make the following additional orders when making an occupation order:

- *impose on either party obligations as to the repair and maintenance of the dwelling-house*
- *impose on either party obligations as to the payment of rent, mortgage or other outgoings affecting it*
- *order a party occupying the dwelling-house to make periodical payments to the other party in respect of the accommodation, if the other party would (but for the order) be entitled to occupy it*
- *grant either party possession or use of furniture or other contents*
- *order either party to take reasonable care of any furniture or other contents*
- *order either party to take reasonable steps to keep the dwelling-house and any furniture or other contents secure.*

Section 8

If the dwelling-house is rented or subject to a mortgage, the landlord or mortgagee must be served with notice of the proceedings in Form FL416. He or she will then be able to make representations to the court regarding the rent or mortgage.

Section 10

A person living in the same household may, for example, be a member of the family or a tenant or employee of you or the respondent.

9 Notice of proceedings (Form FL402)   SPECIMEN

In

Telephone Number

FAX Number

Case Number

Notice of Proceedings
[Hearing] [Directions Appointment]

has applied to the court for an order.

About the [Hearing][Directions Appointment]

You should attend when the Court hears the application at

on

at   [am]   [pm]

What to do next

There is a copy of the application with this Notice. You have been named as a party in the application.
Read the application now, and the notes overleaf.

When you go to court please take this Notice with you and show it to a court official.

About this Notice

Note 1   It is in your own interest to attend the court on the date shown on this form. You should be ready to give any evidence which you think will help you to put your side of the case.

Note 2   For legal advice   go to a solicitor or an advice agency.

You can obtain the address of a solicitor or an advice agency from the Yellow Pages or the Solicitors' Regional Directory.

You will find these books at
a Citizens' Advice Bureau
a Law Centre
a local library

A solicitor or an advice agency will be able to tell you whether you may be eligible for legal aid.

Note 3   If you require an interpreter   because you do not speak English, you must bring your own.

because of a disability, please contact the court to ask what help is available.

Note 4   To the respondent   the following information only applies if the applicant has applied for an occupation order

If the applicant has ticked box 1,4 or 5 on page 4 of the application form, the court will need any available evidence of the following:

•   the housing needs and resources of you, the applicant and any relevant child

•   the financial resources of you and the applicant

•   the likely effect of any order, or of any decision not to make an order, on the health, safety and well being of you, the applicant and any relevant child

•   the conduct of you and the applicant in relation to each other and otherwise.

If the applicant has ticked box 2, the court will need any available evidence of:

•   the housing needs and resources of you, the applicant and relevant child

•   the financial resources of you and the applicant

•   the likely effect of any order, or of any decision not to make an order, on the health, safety and well being of you, the applicant and any relevant child.

•   the conduct of you and the applicant in relation to each other and otherwise

•   the length of time that has elapsed since you and the applicant ceased to live together.

•   the length of time that has elapsed since the marriage was dissolved or annulled

- the existence of any pending proceedings between you and the applicant:

  under section 23A of the Matrimonial Causes Act 1973 (property adjustment orders in connection with divorce proceedings etc.)

  or

  under Schedule 1 para 1(2)(d) or (e) of the Children Act 1989 (orders for financial relief against parents)

  or

  relating to the legal or beneficial ownership of the dwelling-house

If the applicant has ticked box 3, the court will need any available evidence of:

- the housing needs and resources of you, the applicant and any relevant child
- the financial resources of you and the applicant
- the likely effect of any order, or of any decision not to make an order, on the health, safety and well being of you, the applicant and any relevant child
- the conduct of you and the applicant in relation to each other and otherwise.
- the nature of you and the applicant's relationship
- the length of time during which you have lived together as husband and wife
- whether you and the applicant have any children, or have both had parental responsibility for any children
- the length of time which has elapsed since you and the applicant ceased to live together
- the existence of any pending proceedings between you and the applicant under Schedule 1 para 1(2)(d) or (e) of the Children Act 1989, or relating to the legal or beneficial ownership of the dwelling-house.

10 Application to vary, extend or discharge an order in existing proceedings (Form FL403)   SPECIMEN

Application to vary, extend or discharge an order in existing proceedings

Family Law Act 1996 (Part IV)

The court to which you are applying:
Note: you must make this application to the court which made the original order.

To be completed by the court
Date issued
Case number

1 About you (the applicant)

State your title, full name, address, telephone number and date of birth (if under 18).

If you do not wish your address to be made known to the respondent, leave this space blank and complete Confidential Address Form C8 (if you have not already done so). The court can give you this form.

State your solicitor's name, address, reference, telephone, FAX and DX numbers.

If you are already a party to the case, give your description (for example, applicant, respondent or other).

2 The order(s) for which you are applying   *Please attach a copy of the order if possible.*

I am applying to vary ☐
extend ☐
discharge ☐

the order dated:

If you are applying for an order to be varied or extended please give details of the order which you would like the court to make:

3 Your reason(s) for applying

State briefly your reasons for applying.

4 Person(s) to be served with this application

For each respondent to this application state
the title, full name and address.

Signed   Date
(Applicant)

11 Order or direction (Form FL404)　　SPECIMEN

In the

Case Number

[Order]	[Direction] Family Law Act 1996	Sheet　of

Ordered by　[Mr] [Mrs] Justice
[His] [Her] Honour Judge
[Deputy] District Judge [of the Family Division]
Justice[s] of the Peace
[Assistant] Recorder
Clerk of the Court

on

Orders under Family Law Act 1996 Part IV

(General heading followed by Notice A or Notice B and numbered options as appropriate)

Notice A – order includes non-molestation order – penal notice mandatory

Important Notice to the Respondent [name]

This order gives you instructions which you must follow. You should read it all carefully. If you do not understand anything in this order you should go to a solicitor, Legal Advice Centre or Citizens Advice Bureau. You have a right to ask the court to change or cancel the order but you must obey it unless the court does change or cancel it.

You must obey the instructions contained in this order. If you do not, you will be guilty of contempt of court, and you may be sent to prison.

Notice B – order does not include non-molestation order – * penal notice discretionary

Important Notice to the Respondent [name]

This order gives you instructions which you must follow. You should read it all carefully. If you do not understand anything in this order you should go to a solicitor, Legal Advice Centre or Citizens Advice Bureau. You have a right to ask the court to change or cancel the order but you must obey it unless the court does change or cancel it.

You must obey the instructions contained in this order. *[If you do not, you will be guilty of contempt of court, and you may be sent to prison.]

Occupation orders under s33 of the Family Law Act 1996

1. The court declares that the applicant [name] is entitled to occupy [*address of home or intended home*] as [*his/her*] home. **OR**

2. The court declares that the applicant [name] has matrimonial home rights in [*address of home or intended home*]. **AND/OR**

3. The court declares that the applicant [name]'s matrimonial home rights shall not end when the respondent [name] dies or their marriage is dissolved and shall continue until . . . or further order.

It is ordered that:

4. The respondent [name] shall allow the applicant [name] to occupy [*address of home or intended home*] **OR**

5. The respondent [name] shall allow the applicant [name] to occupy part of [*address of home or intended home*] namely: [*specify part*]

6. The respondent [name] shall not obstruct, harass or interfere with the applicant [name]'s peaceful occupation of [*address of home or intended home*]

7. The respondent [name] shall not occupy [*address of home or intended home*] **OR**

8. The respondent [name] shall not occupy [*address of home or intended home*] from [*specify date*] until [*specify date*] **OR**

9. The respondent [name] shall not occupy [*specify part of address of home or intended home*] **AND/OR**

10. The respondent [name] shall not occupy [*address or part of address*] between [*specify dates or times*]

11. The respondent [name] shall leave [*address or part of address*] [forthwith] [within ____ [*hours/days*] of service on [*him/her*] of this order. **AND/OR**

12. Having left [*address or part of address*], the respondent [name] shall not return to, enter or attempt to enter [or go within [*specify distance*] of] it.

Occupation orders under ss35 & 36 of the Family Law Act 1996

It is ordered that

13. The applicant [name] has the right to occupy [*address of home or intended home*] and the respondent [name] shall allow the applicant [name] to do so. **OR**

14. The respondent [name] shall not evict or exclude the applicant [name] from [*address of home or intended home*] or any part of it namely [*specify part*]. **AND/OR**

15. The respondent [name] shall not occupy [*address of home or intended home*]. **OR**

16. The respondent [name] shall not occupy [*address of home or intended home*] from [*specify date*] until [*specify date*] **OR**

17. The respondent [name] shall not occupy [*specify part of address of home or intended home*] **OR**

18. The respondent [name] shall leave [*address or part of address*] [forthwith] [within ____ [*hours/days*] of service on [*him/her*] of this order.] **AND/OR**

19. Having left [*address or part of address*], the respondent [name] shall not return to, enter or attempt to enter [or go within [*specify distance*] of] it.

Occupation orders under ss37 & 38 Family Law Act 1996

It is ordered that

20. The respondent [name] shall allow the applicant [name] to occupy [*address of home or intended home*] or part of it namely: [*specify*]. **AND/OR**

21. [One or both of the provisions in paragraphs 6 & 10 above may be inserted] **AND/OR**

22. The respondent [name] shall leave [*address or part of address*] [forthwith] [within ____ [*hours/days*] of service on [*him/her*] of this order]. **AND/OR**

23. Having left [*address or part of address*], the respondent [name] may not return to, enter or attempt to enter [or go within [*specify distance*] of] it.

Additional provisions which may be included in occupation orders made under ss33, 35 or 36 of Family Law Act 1996

It is ordered that

24. The [*applicant [name]*] [*respondent [name]*] shall maintain and repair [*address of home or intended home*] **AND/OR**

25. The [*applicant [name]*] [*respondent [name]*] shall pay the rent for [*address of home or intended home*]. **OR**

26 The [*applicant [name]*] [*respondent [name]*] shall pay the mortgage payments on [*address of home or intended home*]. **OR**

27. The [*applicant [name]*] [*respondent [name]*] shall pay the following for [*address of home or intended home*]: [*specify outgoings as bullet points*].

28. The [*party in occupation*] shall pay to the [*other party*] £   each [*week, month, etc*] for [*address of home etc*].

29. The [*party in occupation*] shall keep and use the [*furniture*] [*contents*] [*specify if necessary*] of [*address of home or intended home*] and the [*applicant [name]*] [*respondent [name]*] shall return to the [*party in occupation*] the [*furniture*] [*contents*] [*specify if necessary*] [*no later than [date/time]*].

30. The [*party in occupation*] shall take reasonable care of the [*furniture*] [*contents*] [*specify if necessary*] of [*address of home or intended home*].

31. The [*party in occupation*] shall take all reasonable steps to keep secure [*address of home or intended home*] and the furniture or other contents [*specify if necessary*].

Duration

Occupation orders under s33 of the Family Law Act 1996

32. This order shall last until [*specify event or date*]. **OR**

33. This order shall last until a further order is made.

Occupation orders under ss35 & 37 of the Family Law Act 1996

34. This order shall last until [*state date which must not be more than 6 months from the date of this order*].

35. The occupation order made on [*state date*] is extended until [*state date which must not be more than 6 months from the date of this extension*].

Occupation orders under ss36 & 38 Family Law Act 1996

36. This order shall last until [*state date which must not be more than 6 months from the date of this order*].

37. The occupation order made on [*state date*] is extended until [*state date which must not be more than 6 months from the date of this extension*] and must end on that date.

Non-molestation orders

It is ordered that

38. The respondent [name] is forbidden to use or threaten violence against the applicant [name] [*and must not instruct, encourage or in any way suggest that any other person should do so*]. **AND/OR**

39. The respondent [name] is forbidden to intimidate, harass or pester [*or* [*specify*]] the applicant [name] [and must not instruct, encourage or in any way suggest that any other person should do so]. **AND/OR**

40. The respondent [name] is forbidden to use or threaten violence against the relevant child(ren) [name(s)and date(s) of birth] [and must not instruct, encourage or in any way suggest that any other person should do so]. **AND/ OR**

41. The respondent [name] is forbidden to intimidate, harass or pester [*or* [*specify*]] [the relevant child(ren) [name(s) and date(s) of birth] [and must not instruct, encourage or in any way suggest that any other person should do so].

12 Power of arrest (Form FL406)

In the

Case Number

Power of Arrest
Family Law Act 1996

Applicant
Ref.
Respondent
Ref

The Court orders that   a power of arrest applies to the following paragraph(s) of an order made under this Act on the

(here set out those provisions
of the order to which this power
of arrest is attached and no others)

Power of Arrest   The court is satisfied that the respondent has used or threatened violence against the [applicant] [[and] [or] the following child[ren]

                                                                                ]

[and that there is a risk of significant harm to the applicant [[and] [or] the above child[ren]] attributable to the conduct of the respondent if the power of arrest is not attached immediately].

A power of arrest is attached to the order whereby any constable may (under the power given by section 47(6) of the Family Law Act 1996) arrest without warrant the respondent if the constable has any reasonable cause for suspecting that the respondent may be in breach of any provision to which the power of arrest is attached.

This Power of
Arrest expires on

Note to the
Arresting Officer   Where the respondent is arrested under the power given by section 47 of the Family Law Act 1996, that section requires that:

        the respondent must be brought before the court within 24 hours of the time of his arrest

and   if the matter is not then disposed of forthwith, the court may remand the respondent.

Nothing in section 47 authorises the detention of the respondent after the expiry of the period of 24 hours beginning at the time of his arrest, unless remanded by the court.
The period of 24 hours shall not include Christmas Day, Good Friday or a Sunday.

Ordered by   [Mr] [Mrs] Justice

[His] [Her] Honour Judge

[Deputy]District Judge [of the Family Division]

Justice[s] of the Peace

[Assistant] Recorder

on

13 Application for a warrant of arrest (Form FL407)

SPECIMEN

In the

Case Number

Application for a Warrant of Arrest

Applicant
Ref.
Respondent
Ref.

---

(1) Set out the precise parts of the order or undertaking relevant to this application

On the   day of   19   , the Court made an order

[or the respondent gave an undertaking] as follows:(1)

(2) Insert name of applicant

I, (2)   apply for an order that a warrant should be issued for the arrest of the

(3) Insert name of person against whom the warrant of arrest is sought

respondent(3)

(4) List the ways in which it is alleged that the respondent has disobeyed the order or broken the undertaking. If necessary continue on a separate sheet

The respondent has disobeyed the order [or broken the undertaking] by (4)

Signed   Date

---

14 Warrant of arrest (Form FL408)

In the

Case Number

Warrant of Arrest
Family Law Act 1996

	Applicant
	Ref.
	Respondent
	Ref

The Court directs	all police constables, [the district judge and bailiffs] [and the Tipstaff of the High Court] to arrest the respondent whose address is [believed to be]:

and to bring the respondent before this court immediately.

The Court heard	an application, supported by [sworn written statement] [evidence on oath], that the respondent had disobeyed the order made

on

at the   [Magistrates'] [County] [High] Court

by

[Notice of bail]	On arrest, the respondent shall be released on bail:

 ■ on entering into a recognisance in the sum of [£   ]

 ■ [and on providing [   ] suret[y] [ies] in the sum of [£   ] and [£   ]]

 ■ [and subject to the following conditions:

                                                   ]

The Next Hearing is	[on at [am] [pm]]
	[on a day and at a time to be specified]]

Ordered by	[Mr] [Mrs] Justice
	[His] [Her] Honour Judge
	District Judge [of the Family Division]
	Justice[s] of the Peace
	[Assistant] Recorder

on

15 Order for remand (Form FL409)   SPECIMEN

In the

Case Number

Remand Order
Family Law Act 1996

Applicant

Ref.

Respondent

Ref.

The Court orders that

the respondent be [remanded in custody to
until the next hearing] [released on bail] [remanded to enable a medical examination and report to be made under section 35 of the Mental Health Act 1983.]

the respondent[be produced before][attend][the court at the next hearing]

[the respondent be admitted to, and detained in,

[The Court further orders that]

* state by whom respondent is to be conveyed

Hospital

and conveyed there by*   ]

[and pending admission to that Hospital within 7 days, the respondent is to be detained at a place of safety, namely

and conveyed there by*   ]

The Court heard that

an order had been made on

at the   [Magistrates'] [County] [High] Court

and that the respondent had disobeyed the order by

[The Court [heard] [considered]]

[the [written] evidence of a medical practitioner, namely

as required by the provisions of section 35 of the Mental Health Act 1983 that the respondent is suffering from [mental illness] [severe mental impairment] within the meaning of that Act.]

[Notice of bail]   [The respondent shall be released on bail:

■ on entering into a recognisance in the sum of [£

■ [and on providing [   ] suret[y][ies]] in the sum of [£   ] [and] [£   ]]

■ [and subject to the following condition[s]]:
    [that a medical examination and report be made on the respondent under section 35
    of the Mental Health Act 1983.]

The next hearing is   on   at   [am] [pm]

Ordered by   [Mr] [Mrs] Justice
              [His] [Her] Honour Judge
              District Judge [of the Family Division]
              Justice[s] of the Peace
              [Assistant] Recorder

on

16 Taking of recognisances (Form FL410)   SPECIMEN

In the

Case Number

Recognisance of respondent
Family Law Act 1996

Applicant
Ref.
Respondent
Ref

About you

Your name   Please put your surname or
              family name in CAPITAL LETTERS.

Your address

Your undertaking   I promise to pay to the court the sum of £
                        if I do not comply with the following condition.

The condition is

that   I appear before the court
        at:

on

at   [am] [pm]
or at any other place and time which may be ordered.

Signed   Date
(Respondent)

For official use
Taken before me
(name and title)   Signed

on   at   [am] [pm]

17 Taking of sureties (Form FL411)   SPECIMEN

In the

Case Number

Recognisance of respondent's surety
Family Law Act 1996

Applicant
Ref.
Respondent
Ref

About the respondent

Name

Address

About you (the surety)

Your name

Please put your surname or family name in CAPITAL LETTERS.

Your address

Your undertaking

About your undertaking

When you sign the undertaking below you agree to pay a sum of money if the respondent does not comply with the condition which follows.

The undertaking

I promise to pay to the court the sum of £

if the respondent does not comply with the following condition.

The condition is that

the respondent must appear before the court at:

on

at   [am] [pm]

or at any other place and time which may be ordered.

Signed   Date
(Surety)

For official use

Taken before me
(name and title)

Signed

on   at   [am] [pm]

18 Bail notice (Form FL412)   SPECIMEN

In the

Case Number

Bail Notice
Family Law Act 1996

Applicant
Ref.
Respondent
Ref.

Notice to   *(Name of respondent)*

Date of birth:

of *(Address)*

Warning   The order dated   continues in force. You must attend the
hearing below. The court has the power to send you to prison if it finds that any of the
allegations made against you are true.

**The Court is
satisfied that**
you disobeyed the order made on

at the   [Magistrates'] [County] [High] Court

by *(specify breaches proven)*

About your bail   You have been remanded on bail which has been granted on condition that:
■ [you provide a recognisance in the sum of [£   ]]
■ [you provide [   ] suret[y][ies]] of [£   ] [and] [£   ]]
■ [

]

The next hearing is   at

[on   at   [am] [pm]]

[on a date and at a time to be fixed by the court. The court will tell you when to attend].
On surrendering to the custody of the court, you may not leave the building without the
consent of a court officer.

Signed
(name and title)

Date

19 Hospital order (Form FL413)   SPECIMEN

In the

Case Number

[Interim] Hospital Order
Family Law Act 1996

	Applicant
	Ref.
	Respondent
	Ref.

The Court orders that the respondent whose address is

be admitted to and detained in the following hospital

[*(name and address)*

                                                                                                                    ]

[and that the respondent be conveyed there by   ]

[The Court directs that] [pending admission to that hospital within the period of 28 days the respondent shall be detained at a place of safety, namely:

                                                                                                                    ]

[and shall be conveyed there by   ]

The Court found that the respondent had breached one or more of the following:

- an occupation order
- a non-molestation order
- an exclusion requirement included by virtue of section 38A of the Children Act 1989 in an interim care order made under section 38 of that Act
- an exclusion requirement included by virtue of section 44A of the Children Act 1989 in an emergency protection order under section 44 of that Act.

The Court [heard] [considered] the [written] evidence of two medical practitioners, namely

as required by the provisions of section 37 of the Mental Health Act 1983 that the respondent is suffering from [mental illness] [severe mental impairment] within the meaning of that Act.

The Court was satisfied that

- all other conditions, which under section [37] [38] of the Mental Health Act 1983 are required to be satisfied for the making of [a] [an interim] hospital order, are satisfied in respect of the respondent
- arrangements have been made for the respondent's admission to the hospital named above within 28 days of the date of this order.

Ordered by [Mr] [Mrs] Justice

[His] [Her] Honour Judge

District Judge [of the Family Division]

Justice[s] of the Peace

[Assistant] Recorder

on

20   Guardianship order (Form FL414)   SPECIMEN

In the

Case Number

Guardianship Order
Family Law Act 1996

	Applicant
	Ref.
	Respondent
	Ref.

The Court orders that   the respondent

whose address is

be placed under the guardianship of

[social services authority]

[being a person approved by
                                         social services authority]

The Court found that   the respondent had breached one or more of the following:

- an occupation order
- a non-molestation order
- an exclusion requirement included by virtue of section 38A of the Children Act 1989 in an interim care order made under section 38 of that Act
- an exclusion requirement included by virtue of section 44A of the Children Act 1989 in an emergency protection order under section 44 of that Act.

The Court [heard]
[considered]   the [written] evidence of two medical practitioners, namely

as required by the provisions of section 37 of the Mental Health Act 1983 that the respondent is suffering from [mental illness] [severe mental impairment] within the meaning of that Act.

The Court was
satisfied that   - all other conditions, which under section 37 of the Mental Health Act 1983 are required to be satisfied for the making of a guardianship order, are satisfied in respect of the respondent
                          - the [authority] [person] specified above is willing to receive the respondent into guardianship.

Ordered by   [Mr] [Mrs] Justice

[His] [Her] Honour Judge

District Judge [of the Family Division]

Justice[s] of the Peace

[Assistant] Recorder

on

21 Statement of service (Form FL415)   SPECIMEN

Statement of Service *Family Law Act 1996*	Case number
	Applicant *Ref.*
The court at which your case is being heard	Respondant *Ref.*

You must
- give details of service of the application on each of the other parties
- give details of service on the mortgagee or landlord of the dwelling-house (if appropriate)
- file this form with the court on or before the first Directions Appointment or Hearing of the Proceedings

You should   if the person's solicitor was served, give his or her name and address

You must indicate   the manner, date, time and place of service
or where service was effected by post, the date, time and place of posting

Name and address of person served	Means of identification of person, and how, when and where served	Prescribed forms served

I have served the [application] [Notice of Proceedings] as stated above.
I am the [applicant] [solicitor for the applicant] [other] *(state)*

Signed: Date:

22 Notice to mortgagees/landlords (Form FL416) SPECIMEN

In the

Case Number

Notice to Mortgagees and Landlords
Family Law Act 1996

Applicant
Ref.
Respondent
Ref

Notice to

concerning the
dwelling-house at

Take Notice that an [application] [order] has been made in proceedings under the Family Law Act 1996 which affects the occupation of the above dwelling-house and the payment of the [mortgage] [rent] thereon.
[A copy of the order is attached.]

[The next hearing is at

on   at   [am] [pm]]

What you may
do next   **If either the applicant or respondent has matrimonial home rights:**
you may apply to be made a party to these proceedings if you wish to do so.

If neither the applicant nor the respondent has matrimonial home rights, or you do not wish to be made a party:
you may make representations to the court about these proceedings.
This should be done in writing to the court where the proceedings are taking place.
If you write to a county court or the High Court, your letter should be addressed to The Court Manager. If you write to a magistrates' court your letter should be addressed to the Clerk to the Justices.

Signed

Date

23 Transfer of proceedings (Form FL417)   SPECIMEN

In the

Case Number

Transfer of Proceedings to [the High Court] [a county court] [a family proceedings court]

Family Law Act 1996

	Applicant
	Ref.
	Respondent
	Ref.

The Court orders that   these proceedings be transferred to the

_____

[High Court] [County Court] [Family Proceedings Court]

because

The next [hearing]   at
[directions
appointment] is

on   at   [am] [pm]

**Please address all future
correspondence to**

Ordered by   [Mr] [Mrs] Justice

[His] [Her] Honour Judge

[Deputy] District Judge [of the Family Division]

Justice[s] of the Peace

[Assistant] Recorder

Clerk of the Court

on

24 Notice of an application to commit (Form FL418)

SPECIMEN

Magistrates' Court

Case Number

Notice To Show Good Reason why an Order for Your Committal to Prison should not be made

Applicant
Ref
Respondent
Ref

(1) Insert name of person against whom the committal order is sought

To [1]

(2) Insert full address

of [2]

On the   day of   19   , the Court made an order

(3) Set out the precise parts of the order or undertaking relevant to this committal application

[*or* you gave an undertaking] as follows:[1]

(4) Insert name of applicant

[4]   has applied for an order that you should be committed to prison.

(5) List the ways in which it is alleged that the respondent has disobeyed the order or broken the undertaking If necessary continue on a separate sheet

It is alleged that you have disobeyed the order [or broken the undertaking] by [5]

You must attend Court

on the _____ at _____ [am] [pm]

at _____

to show good reason why you should not be sent to prison

- If the Court is satisfied that any of the allegations are true, it may order that you be imprisoned for your contempt of this Court.
- Important instructions about what you should do are set out overleaf

Ordered by   Justice[s] of the Peace

Clerk of the Court

on

Case No:	

Important notes

- The Court has the power to send you to prison if it finds that any of the allegations made against you are true. Full details of the allegations are contained in the applicant's statement.

- You must attend court on the date shown on the front of this form. It is in your own interest to do so. You should bring any witnesses and documents with you which you think will help you put your side of the case.

- If you can show good reason why you should not be sent to prison you must tell the Court.

- If you need advice you should show this document at once to your Solicitor or go to a Citizens' Advice Bureau.

25 Committal or other order upon proof of disobedience of a court order or breach of an undertaking (Form FL419)

SPECIMEN

Magistrates' Court

Case Number

Order   Committal or Other Order upon Proof of Disobedience of a Court Order or
Breach of an Undertaking

Applicant
Ref
Respondent
Ref

---

1 **An application having been made by**   for committal of   to
prison for disobeying the order [breach of the undertaking] dated   The relevant terms of the order
(undertaking) and the allegations made by the applicant are recited on the attached notice to show good reason

   or

2 **Whereas**   has been suspected of a breach of the attached order
   dated   and has been arrested by a constable and brought before the
   Court under Section 47 of the Family Law Act 1996.

─────────────────────IMMEDIATE CUSTODIAL ORDER────────────────────

It is ordered that   be committed for contempt to Her Majesty's Prison
(be detained under section 9(1) of the Criminal Justice Act 1982) at   for a
(total) period of   or until lawfully discharged if sooner, and that a warrant of arrest
and committal be issued forthwith.

And the contemnor can apply to the (court) to purge his contempt and ask for release.

[**And**, as the court by order dated   dispensed with service of the notice of application for a committal
order,
It is ordered that the contemnor be brought before this court as soon as practicable.]

─────────────────────────ALTERNATIVE DISPOSAL─────────────────────

It is ordered that   be committed for contempt to prison for a
(total) period of

The order is suspended until   **19**   and will not be put in force if during that time the contemnor
complies with the following terms:

And it is further ordered that in the event of non compliance any application for issue of the warrant shall be made
to the court (on notice to the contemnor)

It is ordered that   be fined the sum of £
Such sum to be paid into the office of the court within 14 days of the date of this order.

It is ordered that consideration of the penalty for the contempts found proved be adjourned until   **19**
and may be restored for decision during that time

─────────────────────────PROVISION FOR COSTS─────────────────────

And it is ordered that

Dated
For record of service, hearing and contempts found proved, see overleaf

RECORD OF SERVICE, HEARING AND CONTEMPTS FOUND PROVED

At the hearing

[appeared personally] [was represented by solicitor / counsel] [did not attend]
[appeared personally] [was represented by solicitor / counsel] [did not attend]

The court read the evidence of (Names)	Date statement(s) made

And the court heard oral evidence given by
Name(s)

And the court is satisfied having considered the facts disclosed by the evidence and/or admitted in court by him/her
that   has been guilty of contempt of this court by
disobeying the order (breaking the undertaking) dated   by (and as set out in the attached schedule)

And for the particular contempt the court
imposed the penalty of:

1.   1.

2.   2.

RECORD OF SERVICE

Service of Order with Penal Notice incorporated or indorsed

(Order dated   19
(for substituted) (dispensing with) service
Service proved by
☐ statement of
    made on   19
☐ oral evidence of

Service of Notice to show good reason in form FL418

(Order dated   19
(for substituted) (dispensing with) service)
Service proved by
☐ statement of
    made on   19
☐ oral evidence of

Service of Immediate Custodial Order

I *(name of Officer)*   certify that I served the contemnor with a copy of this order by:

☐ delivery by hand to the contemnor before he was taken from the court building or other place of arrest to the place of detention
☐ delivery by hand to the contemnor at *(time)*   on *(date)*   19   at *(place)*

Where a suspended committal order is made, the applicant is responsible for service.
Where there is suspended committal order or penalty is adjourned on terms, personal service is advisable.

26 Warrant of committal to prison (Form FL420) SPECIMEN

Magistrates' Court

Case Number

Notice   Warrant of Committal to prison

Applicant
Ref
Respondent
Ref

To
[1] name of prison

- every constable within his jurisdiction
- the Governor (of Her Majesty's Prison at)[1]

On the   day of   19   ,

it was ordered that[2]

(2)(3) name and address of committed

of[3]

[4]Where the person to be committed is aged less than 21 years and at least 18 delete all references to prison otherwise delete reference to Section 9(1)CJA

should be committed to Prison[4] (detained under Section 9(1) Criminal Justice Act 1982) for

a period of[5]   for contempt of this court

You the Constables are therefore required forthwith to arrest

(2)(3)

You the [Constable][authorised person(s)]are required to deliver

(2)(3)

to Her Majesty's Prison at[1]

And you, the Governor, are required to receive and keep[2]

[5] state term of imprisonment

safely (in prison) from the arrest under this warrant for a period of[5]   or until

lawfully discharged, if sooner.

[6] Add if so ordered otherwise delete

[[6] And, as the court by order dated   dispensed with service of the notice of

application for committal order,

it is ordered that you, the Governor, bring[2]

before this court at such time and place as the court shall specify and afterwards,

return him to the prison unless the court orders his discharge.]

Please address all future
correspondence to

Ordered by   Justice[s] of the Peace

on

27 Order for discharge from custody under warrant of committal (Form FL421)
SPECIMEN

Magistrates' Court

Case Number

Notice   Discharge from Custody under Warrant of Committal

Applicant
Ref
Respondent
Ref

Upon application made this   day of   19

by

who was committed to prison for contempt by an order of this court dated the   day of   19   ,

and upon reading the application of

attested on the   day of   19   , showing that he is desirous of purging

his contempt,

and upon hearing

⁽¹⁾ or, if no one appears for him   ⁽¹⁾(and upon being satisfied that the notice of this application has been duly served upon the

)

The Court ordered that

⁽²⁾insert name of prison   be discharged out of the custody of the Governor of Her Majesty's Prison at⁽²⁾

⁽³⁾add if so ordered   ⁽³⁾**And the Court further ordered** that

⁽⁴⁾insert name of person to whom payment is to be made   do pay the sum £   , the costs of this application, such costs to be taxed and paid

to⁽⁴⁾

by   (or within 14 days of taxation)

Please address all future
correspondence to

Ordered by   Justice[s] of the Peace

on

28 General form of undertaking (Form FL422) SPECIMEN

Magistrates' Court

Case Number

This form is to be used only for an undertaking, not for an order.

General Form of Undertaking
Family Law Act 1996

Applicant
Ref.
Respondent
Ref.

On the   day of

(1)   Name of the person giving undertaking   (1)

[appeared in person] [was represented by [Solicitor] [Counsel]]

(2)   Set out the terms of the undertaking   and gave an undertaking to the Court promising (2)

(3)   Give the date and time or event when the undertaking will expire   **And to be bound by these promises until** (3)

The Court explained to (1)

the meaning of his undertaking and the consequences of failing to keep his promises,

(4)   The court may direct that the party who gives the undertaking shall personally sign the statement overleaf   **And the Court accepted his undertaking** (4) [and *if so ordered* directed that

(1)   should sign the statement overleaf].

(5)   Set out any other directions given by the court   **And the Court ordered that** (5)

Ordered by   Justice[s] of the Peace

on

Important Notice

To (1)

(6) Address of the person giving the undertaking   of (6)

- You may be sent to prison for contempt of court if you break the promises that you have given to the Court.

- If you do not understand anything in this document you should go to a solicitor, Legal Advice Centre or a Citizens' Advice Bureau.

General Form of Undertaking (Statement)

The Court may direct that the party who gives the undertaking shall personally sign the statement opposite.

Statement

I understand the undertaking that I have given, and that if I break any of my promises to the Court I may be sent to prison for contempt of court.

Signed

Date

To be completed by the Court

Delivered:

☐ By posting on:

☐ By hand on:

☐ Through a solicitor on:

Signed:
(Officer)

Date:

29 Extradition Treaties

The Extradition Act 1989 (which consolidated the Extradition Acts 1870–1935) applies as between the UK and the following countries (see s37 of the Extradition Act 1989, which also continues in force Orders made under the Extradition Act 1870, s2):

Albania	Liberia
Argentine Republic	Luxembourg
Austria	Mexico
Belgium	Monaco
Bolivia	Netherlands
Chile	Nicaragua
Colombia	Norway
Cuba	Panama
Czechoslovakia	Paraguay
Denmark	Peru
Ecuador	Poland
Finland	Portugal
France	Roumania
Germany (Federal Republic)	Salvador
Greece	San Marino
Guatemala	Spain
Haiti	Sweden
Hungary	Switzerland
Iceland	Thailand
Iraq	USA
Israel	Uruguay
Italy	Yugoslavia

Part VI

Materials

Family Law Act 1996 Part IV

FAMILY HOMES AND DOMESTIC VIOLENCE

Rights to occupy matrimonial home

Rights concerning matrimonial home where one spouse has no estate, etc.

30.–(1) This section applies if–

(a) one spouse is entitled to occupy a dwelling-house by virtue of
  (i) a beneficial estate or interest or contract; or
  (ii) any enactment giving that spouse the right to remain in occupation; and

(b) the other spouse is not so entitled.

(2) Subject to the provisions of this Part, the spouse not so entitled has the following rights ("matrimonial home rights")–

(a) if in occupation, a right not to be evicted or excluded from the dwelling-house or any part of it by the other spouse except with the leave of the court given by an order under section 33;

(b) if not in occupation, a right with the leave of the court so given to enter into and occupy the dwelling-house.

(3) If a spouse is entitled under this section to occupy a dwelling-house or any part of a dwelling-house, any payment or tender made or other thing done by that spouse in or towards satisfaction of any liability of the other spouse in respect of rent, mortgage payments or other outgoings affecting the dwelling-house is, whether or not it is made or done in pursuance of an order under section 40, as good as if made or done by the other spouse.

(4) A spouse's occupation by virtue of this section–

(a) is to be treated, for the purposes of the Rent (Agriculture) Act 1976 and the Rent Act 1977 (other than Part V and sections 103 to 106 of that Act), as occupation by the other spouse as the other spouse's residence, and

(b) if the spouse occupies the dwelling-house as that spouse's only or principal home, is to be treated, for the purposes of the Housing Act 1985 and

305

Part I of the Housing Act 1988, as occupation by the other spouse as the other spouse's only or principal home.

(5) If a spouse ("the first spouse")–

(a) is entitled under this section to occupy a dwelling-house or any part of a dwelling-house, and

(b) makes any payment in or towards satisfaction of any liability of the other spouse ("the second spouse") in respect of mortgage payments affecting the dwelling-house,

the person to whom the payment is made may treat it as having been made by the second spouse, but the fact that that person has treated any such payment as having been so made does not affect any claim of the first spouse against the second spouse to an interest in the dwelling-house by virtue of the payment.

(6) If a spouse is entitled under this section to occupy a dwelling-house or part of a dwelling-house by reason of an interest of the other spouse under a trust, all the provisions of subsections (3) to (5) apply in relation to the trustees as they apply in relation to the other spouse.

(7) This section does not apply to a dwelling-house which has at no time been, and which was at no time intended by the spouses to be, a matrimonial home of theirs.

(8) A spouse's matrimonial home rights continue–

(a) only so long as the marriage subsists, except to the extent that an order under section 33(5) otherwise provides; and

(b) only so long as the other spouse is entitled as mentioned in subsection (1) to occupy the dwelling-house, except where provision is made by section 31 for those rights to be a charge on an estate or interest in the dwelling-house.

(9) It is hereby declared that a spouse–

(a) who has an equitable interest in a dwelling-house or in its proceeds of sale, but

(b) is not a spouse in whom there is vested (whether solely or as joint tenant) a legal estate in fee simple or a legal term of years absolute in the dwelling-house,

is to be treated, only for the purpose of determining whether he has matrimonial home rights, as not being entitled to occupy the dwelling-house by virtue of that interest.

Effect of matrimonial home rights as charge on dwelling-house

31.–(1) Subsections (2) and (3) apply if, at any time during a marriage, one spouse is entitled to occupy a dwelling-house by virtue of a beneficial estate or interest.

(2) The other spouse's matrimonial home rights are a charge on the estate or interest.

(3) The charge created by subsection (2) has the same priority as if it were an equitable interest created at whichever is the latest of the following dates–

(a) the date on which the spouse so entitled acquires the estate or interest;

(b) the date of the marriage; and

(c) 1st January 1968 (the commencement date of the Matrimonial Homes Act 1967).

(4) Subsections (5) and (6) apply if, at any time when a spouse's matrimonial home rights are a charge on an interest of the other spouse under a trust, there are, apart from either of the spouses, no persons, living or unborn, who are or could become beneficiaries under the trust.

(5) The rights are a charge also on the estate or interest of the trustees for the other spouse.

(6) The charge created by subsection (5) has the same priority as if it were an equitable interest created (under powers overriding the trusts) on the date when it arises.

(7) In determining for the purposes of subsection (4) whether there are any persons who are not, but could become, beneficiaries under the trust, there is to be disregarded any potential exercise of a general power of appointment exercisable by either or both of the spouses alone (whether or not the exercise of it requires the consent of another person).

(8) Even though a spouse's matrimonial home rights are a charge on an estate or interest in the dwelling-house, those rights are brought to an end by—

(a) the death of the other spouse, or

(b) the termination (otherwise than by death) of the marriage,

unless the court directs otherwise by an order made under section 33(5).

(9) If—

(a) a spouse's matrimonial home rights are a charge on an estate or interest in the dwelling-house, and

(b) that estate or interest is surrendered to merge in some other estate or interest expectant on it in such circumstances that, but for the merger, the person taking the estate or interest would be bound by the charge,

the surrender has effect subject to the charge and the persons thereafter entitled to the other estate or interest are, for so long as the estate or interest surrendered would have endured if not so surrendered, to be treated for all purposes of this Part as deriving title to the other estate or interest under the other spouse or, as the case may be, under the trustees for the other spouse, by virtue of the surrender.

(10) If the title to the legal estate by virtue of which a spouse is entitled to occupy a dwelling-house (including any legal estate held by trustees for that spouse) is registered under the Land Registration Act 1925 or any enactment replaced by that Act—

(a) registration of a land charge affecting the dwelling-house by virtue of this Part is to be effected by registering a notice under that Act; and

(b) a spouse's matrimonial home rights are not an overriding interest within the meaning of that Act affecting the dwelling-house even though the spouse is in actual occupation of the dwelling-house.

(11) A spouse's matrimonial home rights (whether or not constituting a charge) do not entitle that spouse to lodge a caution under section 54 of the Land Registration Act 1925.

(12) If–

(a) a spouse's matrimonial home rights are a charge on the estate of the other spouse or of trustees of the other spouse, and

(b) that estate is the subject of a mortgage,

then if, after the date of the creation of the mortgage ("the first mortgage"), the charge is registered under section 2 of the Land Charges Act 1972, the charge is, for the purposes of section 94 of the Law of Property Act 1925 (which regulates the rights of mortgagees to make further advances ranking in priority to subsequent mortgages), to be deemed to be a mortgage subsequent in date to the first mortgage.

(13) It is hereby declared that a charge under subsection (2) or (5) is not registrable under subsection (10) or under section 2 of the Land Charges Act 1972 unless it is a charge on a legal estate.

Further provisions relating to matrimonial home rights

32.–[*Not reproduced.*]

Occupation orders

Occupation orders where applicant has estate or interest etc. or has matrimonial home rights

33.–(1) If–

(a) a person ("the person entitled")

   (i) is entitled to occupy a dwelling-house by virtue of a beneficial estate or interest or contract or by virtue of any enactment giving him the right to remain in occupation, or

   (ii) has matrimonial home rights in relation to a dwelling-house, and

(b) the dwelling-house–

   (i) is or at any time has been the home of the person entitled and of another person with whom he is associated, or

   (ii) was at any time intended by the person entitled and any such other person to be their home,

the person entitled may apply to the court for an order containing any of the provisions specified in subsections (3), (4) and (5).

(2) If an agreement to marry is terminated, no application under this section may be made by virtue of section 62(3)(e) by reference to that agreement after the end of the period of three years beginning with the day on which it is terminated.

(3) An order under this section may–

(a) enforce the applicant's entitlement to remain in occupation as against the other person ("the respondent");

(b) require the respondent to permit the applicant to enter and remain in the dwelling-house or part of the dwelling-house;

(c) regulate the occupation of the dwelling-house by either or both parties;

(d) if the respondent is entitled as mentioned in subsection (l)(a)(i), prohibit, suspend or restrict the exercise by him of his right to occupy the dwelling-house;

(e) if the respondent has matrimonial home rights in relation to the dwelling-house and the applicant is the other spouse, restrict or terminate those rights;

(f) require the respondent to leave the dwelling-house or part of the dwelling-house; or

(g) exclude the respondent from a defined area in which the dwelling-house is included.

(4) An order under this section may declare that the applicant is entitled as mentioned in subsection (1)(a)(i) or has matrimonial home rights.

(5) If the applicant has matrimonial home rights and the respondent is the other spouse, an order under this section made during the marriage may provide that those rights are not brought to an end by–

(a) the death of the other spouse; or

(b) the termination (otherwise than by death) of the marriage.

(6) In deciding whether to exercise its powers under subsection (3) and (if so) in what manner, the court shall have regard to all the circumstances including–

(a) the housing needs and housing resources of each of the parties and of any relevant child;

(b) the financial resources of each of the parties;

(c) the likely effect of any order, or of any decision by the court not to exercise its powers under subsection (3), on the health, safety or well-being of the parties and of any relevant child; and

(d) the conduct of the parties in relation to each other and otherwise.

(7) If it appears to the court that the applicant or any relevant child is likely to suffer significant harm attributable to conduct of the respondent if an order under this section containing one or more of the provisions mentioned in subsection (3) is not made, the court shall make the order unless it appears to it that–

(a) the respondent or any relevant child is likely to suffer significant harm if the order is made; and

(b) the harm likely to be suffered by the respondent or child in that event is as great as, or greater than, the harm attributable to conduct of the respondent which is likely to be suffered by the applicant or child if the order is not made.

(8) The court may exercise its powers under subsection (5) in any case where it considers that in all the circumstances it is just and reasonable to do so.

(9) An order under this section–

(a) may not be made after the death of either of the parties mentioned in subsection (1); and

(b) except in the case of an order made by virtue of subsection (5)(a), ceases to have effect on the death of either party.

(10) An order under this section may, in so far as it has continuing effect, be made for a specified period, until the occurrence of a specified event or until further order.

Effect of order under s33 where rights are charge on dwelling-house

34.–(1) If a spouse's matrimonial home rights are a charge on the estate or interest of the other spouse or of trustees for the other spouse–

(a) an order under section 33 against the other spouse has, except so far as a contrary intention appears, the same effect against persons deriving title under the other spouse or under the trustees and affected by the charge, and

(b) sections 33(1), (3), (4) and (10) and 30(3) to (6) apply in relation to any person deriving title under the other spouse or under the trustees and affected by the charge as they apply in relation to the other spouse.

(2) The court may make an order under section 33 by virtue of subsection (l)(b) if it considers that in all the circumstances it is just and reasonable to do so.

One former spouse with no existing right to occupy

35.–(1) This section applies if–

(a) one former spouse is entitled to occupy a dwelling-house by virtue of a beneficial estate or interest or contract, or by virtue of any enactment giving him the right to remain in occupation;

(b) the other former spouse is not so entitled; and

(c) the dwelling-house was at any time their matrimonial home or was at any time intended by them to be their matrimonial home.

(2) The former spouse not so entitled may apply to the court for an order under this section against the other former spouse ("the respondent").

(3) If the applicant is in occupation, an order under this section must contain provision–

(a) giving the applicant the right not to be evicted or excluded from the dwelling-house or any part of it by the respondent for the period specified in the order; and

(b) prohibiting the respondent from evicting or excluding the applicant during that period.

(4) If the applicant is not in occupation, an order under this section must contain provision–

(a) giving the applicant the right to enter into and occupy the dwelling-house for the period specified in the order; and

(b) requiring the respondent to permit the exercise of that right.

(5) An order under this section may also–

(a) regulate the occupation of the dwelling-house by either or both of the parties;

(b) prohibit, suspend or restrict the exercise by the respondent of his right to occupy the dwelling-house;

(c) require the respondent to leave the dwelling-house or part of the dwelling-house; or

(d) exclude the respondent from a defined area in which the dwelling-house is included.

(6) In deciding whether to make an order under this section containing provision of the kind mentioned in subsection (3) or (4) and (if so) in what manner, the court shall have regard to all the circumstances including–

(a) the housing needs and housing resources of each of the parties and of any relevant child;

(b) the financial resources of each of the parties;

(c) the likely effect of any order, or of any decision by the court not to exercise its powers under subsection (3) or (4), on the health, safety or well-being of the parties and of any relevant child;

(d) the conduct of the parties in relation to each other and otherwise;

(e) the length of time that has elapsed since the parties ceased to live together;

(f) the length of time that has elapsed since the marriage was dissolved or annulled; and

(g) the existence of any pending proceedings between the parties–

    (i) for an order under section 23A or 24 of the Matrimonial Causes Act 1973 (property adjustment orders in connection with divorce proceedings etc.);

    (ii) for an order under paragraph 1(2)(d) or (e) of Schedule 1 to the Children Act 1989 (orders for financial relief against parents); or

    (iii) relating to the legal or beneficial ownership of the dwelling-house.

(7) In deciding whether to exercise its power to include one or more of the provisions referred to in subsection (5) ("a subsection (5) provision") and (if so) in what manner, the court shall have regard to all the circumstances including the matters mentioned in subsection (6)(a) to (e).

(8) If the court decides to make an order under this section and it appears to it that, if the order does not include a subsection (5) provision, the applicant or any relevant child is likely to suffer significant harm attributable to conduct of the respondent, the court shall include the subsection (5) provision in the order unless it appears to the court that–

(a) the respondent or any relevant child is likely to suffer significant harm if the provision is included in the order; and

(b) the harm likely to be suffered by the respondent or child in that event is as great as or greater than the harm attributable to conduct of the respondent which is likely to be suffered by the applicant or child if the provision is not included.

(9) An order under this section–

(a) may not be made after the death of either of the former spouses; and

(b) ceases to have effect on the death of either of them.

(10) An order under this section must be limited so as to have effect for a specified period not exceeding six months, but may be extended on one or more occasions for a further specified period not exceeding six months.

(11) A former spouse who has an equitable interest in the dwelling-house or in the proceeds of sale of the dwelling-house but in whom there is not vested (whether solely or as joint tenant) a legal estate in fee simple or a legal term of years absolute in the dwelling-house is to be treated (but only for the purpose of determining whether he is eligible to apply under this section) as not being entitled to occupy the dwelling-house by virtue of that interest.

(12) Subsection (11) does not prejudice any right of such a former spouse to apply for an order under section 33.

(13) So long as an order under this section remains in force, subsections (3) to (6) of section 30 apply in relation to the applicant–
(a) as if he were the spouse entitled to occupy the dwelling-house by virtue of that section; and
(b) as if the respondent were the other spouse.

One cohabitant or former cohabitant with no existing right to occupy

36.–(1) This section applies if–
(a) one cohabitant or former cohabitant is entitled to occupy a dwelling-house by virtue of a beneficial estate or interest or contract or by virtue of any enactment giving him the right to remain in occupation;
(b) the other cohabitant or former cohabitant is not so entitled; and
(c) that dwelling-house is the home in which they live together as husband and wife or a home in which they at any time so lived together or intended so to live together.

(2) The cohabitant or former cohabitant not so entitled may apply to the court for an order under this section against the other cohabitant or former cohabitant ("the respondent").

(3) If the applicant is in occupation, an order under this section must contain provision–
(a) giving the applicant the right not to be evicted or excluded from the dwelling-house or any part of it by the respondent for the period specified in the order; and
(b) prohibiting the respondent from evicting or excluding the applicant during that period.

(4) If the applicant is not in occupation, an order under this section must contain provision–
(a) giving the applicant the right to enter into and occupy the dwelling-house for the period specified in the order; and
(b) requiring the respondent to permit the exercise of that right.

(5) An order under this section may also–
(a) regulate the occupation of the dwelling-house by either or both of the parties

(b) prohibit, suspend or restrict the exercise by the respondent of his right to occupy the dwelling-house;

(c) require the respondent to leave the dwelling-house or part of the dwelling-house; or

(d) exclude the respondent from a defined area in which the dwelling-house is included.

(6) In deciding whether to make an order under this section containing provision of the kind mentioned in subsection (3) or (4) and (if so) in what manner, the court shall have regard to all the circumstances including–

(a) the housing needs and housing resources of each of the parties and of any relevant child;

(b) the financial resources of each of the parties;

(c) the likely effect of any order, or of any decision by the court not to exercise its powers under subsection (3) or (4), on the health, safety or well-being of the parties and of any relevant child;

(d) the conduct of the parties in relation to each other and otherwise;

(e) the nature of the parties' relationship;

(f) the length of time during which they have lived together as husband and wife;

(g) whether there are or have been any children who are children of both parties or for whom both parties have or have had parental responsibility;

(h) the length of time that has elapsed since the parties ceased to live together; and

(i) the existence of any pending proceedings between the parties–

    (i) for an order under paragraph 1(2)(d) or (e) of Schedule 1 to the Children Act 1989 (orders for financial relief against parents); or

    (ii) relating to the legal or beneficial ownership of the dwelling-house.

(7) In deciding whether to exercise its powers to include one or more of the provisions referred to in subsection (5) ("a subsection (5) provision") and (if so) in what manner, the court shall have regard to all the circumstances including–

(a) the matters mentioned in subsection (6)(a) to (d); and

(b) the questions mentioned in subsection (8).

(8) The questions are–

(a) whether the applicant or any relevant child is likely to suffer significant harm attributable to conduct of the respondent if the subsection (5) provision is not included in the order; and

(b) whether the harm likely to be suffered by the respondent or child if the provision is included is as great as or greater than the harm attributable to conduct of the respondent which is likely to be suffered by the applicant or child if the provision is not included.

(9) An order under this section–

(a) may not be made after the death of either of the parties; and

(b) ceases to have effect on the death of either of them.

(10) An order under this section must be limited so as to have effect for a specified period not exceeding six months, but may be extended on one occasion for a further specified period not exceeding six months.

(11) A person who has an equitable interest in the dwelling-house or in the proceeds of sale of the dwelling-house but in whom there is not vested (whether solely or as joint tenant) a legal estate in fee simple or a legal term of years absolute in the dwelling-house is to be treated (but only for the purpose of determining whether he is eligible to apply under this section) as not being entitled to occupy the dwelling-house by virtue of that interest.

(12) Subsection (11) does not prejudice any right of such a person to apply for an order under section 33.

(13) So long as the order remains in force, subsections (3) to (6) of section 30 apply in relation to the applicant—

(a) as if he were a spouse entitled to occupy the dwelling-house by virtue of that section; and

(b) as if the respondent were the other spouse.

Neither spouse entitled to occupy

37.–(1) This section applies if—

(a) one spouse or former spouse and the other spouse or former spouse occupy a dwelling-house which is or was the matrimonial home; but

(b) neither of them is entitled to remain in occupation—

    (i) by virtue of a beneficial estate or interest or contract; or

    (ii) by virtue of any enactment giving him the right to remain in occupation.

(2) Either of the parties may apply to the court for an order against the other under this section.

(3) An order under this section may—

(a) require the respondent to permit the applicant to enter and remain in the dwelling-house or part of the dwelling-house;

(b) regulate the occupation of the dwelling-house by either or both of the spouses;

(c) require the respondent to leave the dwelling-house or part of the dwelling-house; or

(d) exclude the respondent from a defined area in which the dwelling house is included.

(4) Subsections (6) and (7) of section 33 apply to the exercise by the court of its powers under this section as they apply to the exercise by the court of its powers under subsection (3) of that section.

(5) An order under this section must be limited so as to have effect for a specified period not exceeding six months, but may be extended on one or more occasions for a further specified period not exceeding six months.

Neither cohabitant nor former cohabitant entitled to occupy

38.–(1) This section applies if—

(a) one cohabitant or former cohabitant and the other cohabitant or former cohabitant occupy a dwelling-house which is the home in which they live or lived together as husband and wife; but

(b) neither of them is entitled to remain in occupation–
  (i) by virtue of a beneficial estate or interest or contract; or
  (ii) by virtue of any enactment giving him the right to remain in occupation.

(2) Either of the parties may apply to the court for an order against the other under this section.

(3) An order under this section may–

(a) require the respondent to permit the applicant to enter and remain in the dwelling-house or part of the dwelling-house;

(b) regulate the occupation of the dwelling-house by either or both of the parties;

(c) require the respondent to leave the dwelling-house or part of the dwelling-house; or

(d) exclude the respondent from a defined area in which the dwelling-house is included.

(4) In deciding whether to exercise its powers to include one or more of the provisions referred to in subsection (3) ("a subsection (3) provision") and (if so) in what manner, the court shall have regard to all the circumstances including–

(a) the housing needs and housing resources of each of the parties and of any relevant child;

(b) the financial resources of each of the parties;

(c) the likely effect of any order, or of any decision by the court not to exercise its powers under subsection (3), on the health, safety or well-being of the parties and of any relevant child;

(d) the conduct of the parties in relation to each other and otherwise; and

(e) the questions mentioned in subsection (5).

(5) The questions are–

(a) whether the applicant or any relevant child is likely to suffer significant harm attributable to conduct of the respondent if the subsection (3) provision is not included in the order; and

(b) whether the harm likely to be suffered by the respondent or child if the provision is included is as great as or greater than the harm attributable to conduct of the respondent which is likely to be suffered by the applicant or child if the provision is not included.

(6) An order under this section shall be limited so as to have effect for a specified period not exceeding six months, but may be extended on one occasion or a further specified period not exceeding six months.

Supplementary provisions

39.–(1) In this Part an "occupation order" means an order under section 33, 35, 36, 37 or 38.

(2) An application for an occupation order may be made in other family proceedings or without any other family proceedings being instituted.

(3) If–

(a) an application for an occupation order is made under section 33, 35, 36, 37 or 38, and

(b) the court considers that it has no power to make the order under the section concerned, but that it has power to make an order under one of the other sections,

the court may make an order under that other section.

(4) The fact that a person has applied for an occupation order under sections 35 to 38, or that an occupation order has been made, does not affect the right of any person to claim a legal or equitable interest in any property in any subsequent proceedings (including subsequent proceedings under this Part).

Additional provisions that may be included in certain occupation orders

40.–(1) The court may on, or at any time after, making an occupation order under section 33, 35 or 36–

(a) impose on either party obligations as to–

  (i) the repair and maintenance of the dwelling-house; or

  (ii) the discharge of rent, mortgage payments or other outgoings affecting the dwelling-house;

(b) order a party occupying the dwelling-house or any part of it (including a party who is entitled to do so by virtue of a beneficial estate or interest or contract or by virtue of any enactment giving him the right to remain in occupation) to make periodical payments to the other party in respect of the accommodation, if the other party would (but for the order) be entitled to occupy the dwelling-house by virtue of a beneficial estate or interest or contract or by virtue of any such enactment;

(c) grant either party possession or use of furniture or other contents of the dwelling-house;

(d) order either party to take reasonable care of any furniture or other contents of the dwelling-house;

(e) order either party to take reasonable steps to keep the dwelling-house and any furniture or other contents secure.

(2) In deciding whether and, if so, how to exercise its powers under this section, the court shall have regard to all the circumstances of the case including–

(a) the financial needs and financial resources of the parties; and

(b) the financial obligations which they have, or are likely to have in the foreseeable future, including financial obligations to each other and to any relevant child.

(3) An order under this section ceases to have effect when the occupation order to which it relates ceases to have effect.

Additional considerations if parties are cohabitants or former cohabitants

41.–(1) This section applies if the parties are cohabitants or former cohabitants.

(2) Where the court is required to consider the nature of the parties' relationship, it is to have regard to the fact that they have not given each other the commitment involved in marriage.

Non-molestation orders

Non-molestation orders

42.–(1) In this Part a "non-molestation order" means an order containing either or both of the following provisions–

(a) provision prohibiting a person ("the respondent") from molesting another person who is associated with the respondent;

(b) provision prohibiting the respondent from molesting a relevant child.

(2) The court may make a non-molestation order–

(a) if an application for the order has been made (whether in other family proceedings or without any other family proceedings being instituted) by a person who is associated with the respondent; or

(b) if in any family proceedings to which the respondent is a party the court considers that the order should be made for the benefit of any other party to the proceedings or any relevant child even though no such application has been made.

(3) In subsection (2) "family proceedings" includes proceedings in which the court has made an emergency protection order under section 44 of the Children Act 1989 which includes an exclusion requirement (as defined in section 44A(3) of that Act).

(4) Where an agreement to marry is terminated, no application under subsection (2)(a) may be made by virtue of section 62(3)(e) by reference to that agreement after the end of the period of three years beginning with the day on which it is terminated.

(5) In deciding whether to exercise its powers under this section and, if so, in what manner, the court shall have regard to all the circumstances including the need to secure the health, safety and well-being–

(a) of the applicant or, in a case falling within subsection (2)(b), the person for whose benefit the order would be made; and

(b) of any relevant child.

(6) A non-molestation order may be expressed so as to refer to molestation in general, to particular acts of molestation, or to both.

(7) A non-molestation order may be made for a specified period or until further order.

(8) A non-molestation order which is made in other family proceedings ceases to have effect if those proceedings are withdrawn or dismissed.

Further provisions relating to occupation and non-molestation orders

Leave of court required for applications by children under sixteen

43.–(1) A child under the age of sixteen may not apply for an occupation order or a non-molestation order except with the leave of the court.

(2) The court may grant leave for the purposes of subsection (1) only if it is satisfied that the child has sufficient understanding to make the proposed application for the occupation order or non-molestation order.

Evidence of agreement to marry

44.–(1) Subject to subsection (2), the court shall not make an order under section 33 or 42 by virtue of section 62(3)(e) unless there is produced to it evidence in writing of the existence of the agreement to marry.

(2) Subsection (1) does not apply if the court is satisfied that the agreement to marry was evidenced by–

(a) the gift of an engagement ring by one party to the agreement to the other in contemplation of their marriage, or

(b) a ceremony entered into by the parties in the presence of one or more other persons assembled for the purpose of witnessing the ceremony.

Ex parte orders

45.–(1) The court may, in any case where it considers that it is just and convenient to do so, make an occupation order or a non-molestation order even though the respondent has not been given such notice of the proceedings as would otherwise be required by rules of court.

(2) In determining whether to exercise its powers under subsection (1), the court shall have regard to all the circumstances including–

(a) any risk of significant harm to the applicant or a relevant child, attributable to conduct of the respondent, if the order is not made immediately;

(b) whether it is likely that the applicant will be deterred or prevented from pursuing the application if an order is not made immediately; and

(c) whether there is reason to believe that the respondent is aware of the proceedings but is deliberately evading service and that the applicant or a relevant child will be seriously prejudiced by the delay involved–

    (i) where the court is a magistrates' court, in effecting service of proceedings; or

    (ii) in any other case, in effecting substituted service.

(3) If the court makes an order by virtue of subsection (1) it must afford the respondent an opportunity to make representations relating to the order as soon as just and convenient at a full hearing.

(4) If, at a full hearing, the court makes an occupation order ("the full order"), then–

(a) for the purposes of calculating the maximum period for which the full order may be made to have effect, the relevant section is to apply as if the period for which the full order will have effect began on the date on which the initial order first had effect; and

(b) the provisions of section 36(10) or 38(6) as to the extension of orders are to apply as if the full order and the initial order were a single order.

(5) In this section—

"full hearing" means a hearing of which notice has been given to all the parties in accordance with rules of court;

"initial order" means an occupation order made by virtue of subsection (1); and

"relevant section" means section 33(10), 35(10), 36(10), 37(5) or 38(6).

Undertakings

46.–(1) In any case where the court has power to make an occupation order or non-molestation order, the court may accept an undertaking from any party to the proceedings.

(2) No power of arrest may be attached to any undertaking given under subsection (1).

(3) The court shall not accept an undertaking under subsection (1) in any case where apart from this section a power of arrest would be attached to the order.

(4) An undertaking given to a court under subsection (1) is enforceable as if it were an order of the court.

(5) This section has effect without prejudice to the powers of the High Court and the county court apart from this section.

Arrest for breach of order

47.–(1) In this section "a relevant order" means an occupation order or a non-molestation order.

(2) If—

(a) the court makes a relevant order; and

(b) it appears to the court that the respondent has used or threatened violence against the applicant or a relevant child,

it shall attach a power of arrest to one or more provisions of the order unless satisfied that in all the circumstances of the case the applicant or child will be adequately protected without such a power of arrest.

(3) Subsection (2) does not apply in any case where the relevant order is made by virtue of section 45(1), but in such a case the court may attach a power of arrest to one or more provisions of the order if it appears to it—

(a) that the respondent has used or threatened violence against the applicant or a relevant child; and

(b) that there is a risk of significant harm to the applicant or child, attributable to conduct of the respondent, if the power of arrest is not attached to those provisions immediately.

(4) If, by virtue of subsection (3), the court attaches a power of arrest to any provisions of a relevant order, it may provide that the power of arrest is to have effect for a shorter period than the other provisions of the order.

(5) Any period specified for the purposes of subsection (4) may be extended by the court (on one or more occasions) on an application to vary or discharge the relevant order.

(6) If, by virtue of subsection (2) or (3), a power of arrest is attached to certain provisions of an order, a constable may arrest without warrant a person whom he has reasonable cause for suspecting to be in breach of any such provision.

(7) If a power of arrest is attached under subsection (2) or (3) to certain provisions of the order and the respondent is arrested under subsection (6)—

(a) he must be brought before the relevant judicial authority within the period of 24 hours beginning at the time of his arrest; and

(b) if the matter is not then disposed of forthwith, the relevant judicial authority before whom he is brought may remand him.

In reckoning for the purposes of this subsection any period of 24 hours, no account is to be taken of Christmas Day, Good Friday or any Sunday.

(8) If the court has made a relevant order but—

(a) has not attached a power of arrest under subsection (2) or (3) to any provisions of the order, or

(b) has attached that power only to certain provisions of the order,

then, if at any time the applicant considers that the respondent has failed to comply with the order, he may apply to the relevant judicial authority for the issue of a warrant for the arrest of the respondent.

(9) The relevant judicial authority shall not issue a warrant on an application under subsection (8) unless—

(a) the application is substantiated on oath; and

(b) the relevant judicial authority has reasonable grounds for believing that the respondent has failed to comply with the order.

(10) If a person is brought before a court by virtue of a warrant issued under subsection (9) and the court does not dispose of the matter forthwith, the court may remand him.

(11) Schedule 5 (which makes provision corresponding to that applying in magistrates' courts in civil cases under sections 128 or 129 of the Magistrates' Courts Act 1980) has effect in relation to the powers of the High Court and a county court to remand a person by virtue of this section.

(12) If a person remanded under this section is granted bail (whether in the High Court or a county court under Schedule 5 or in a magistrates' court under section 128 or 129 of the Magistrates' Courts Act 1980), he may he required by the relevant judicial authority to comply, before release on bail or later, with such requirements as appear to that authority to be necessary to secure that he does not interfere with witnesses or otherwise obstruct the course of justice.

Remand for medical examination and report

48.–(1) If the relevant judicial authority has reason to consider that a medical report will be required, any power to remand a person under section

47(7)(b) or (10) may be exercised for the purpose of enabling a medical examination and report to be made.

(2) If such a power is so exercised, the adjournment must not be for more than 4 weeks at a time unless the relevant judicial authority remands the accused in custody.

(3) If the relevant judicial authority so remands the accused, the adjournment must not be for more than 3 weeks at a time.

(4) If there is reason to suspect that a person who has been arrested–

(a) under section 47(6), or

(b) under a warrant issued on an application made under section 47(8), is suffering from mental illness or severe mental impairment, the relevant judicial authority has the same power to make an order under section 35 of the Mental Health Act 1983 (remand for report on accused's mental condition) as the Crown Court has under section 35 of the Act of 1983 in the case of an accused person within the meaning of that section.

Variation and discharge of orders

49.–(1) An occupation order or non-molestation order may be varied or discharged by the court on an application by–

(a) the respondent, or

(b) the person on whose application the order was made.

(2) In the case of a non-molestation order made by virtue of section 42(2)(b), the order may be varied or discharged by the court even though no such application has been made.

(3) If a spouse's matrimonial home rights are a charge on the estate or interest of the other spouse or of trustees for the other spouse, an order under section 33 against the other spouse may be varied or discharged by the court on an application by any person deriving title under the other spouse or under the trustees and affected by the charge.

(4) If, by virtue of section 47(3), a power of arrest has been attached to certain provisions of an occupation order or non-molestation order, the court may vary or discharge the order under subsection (1) in so far as it confers a power of arrest (whether or not any application has been made to vary or discharge any other provision of the order).

Enforcement powers of magistrates' courts

Power of magistrates' court to suspend execution of committal order

50.–(1) If, under section 63(3) of the Magistrates' Courts Act 1980, a magistrates' court has power to commit a person to custody for breach of a relevant requirement, the court may by order direct that the execution of the order of committal is to be suspended for such period or on such terms and conditions as it may specify.

(2) In subsection (1) "a relevant requirement" means–

(a) an occupation order or non-molestation order;

(b) an exclusion requirement included by virtue of section 38A of the Children Act 1989 in an interim care order made under section 38 of that Act; or

(c) an exclusion requirement included by virtue of section 44A of the Children Act 1989 in an emergency protection order under section 44 of that Act.

Power of magistrates' court to order hospital admission or guardianship

51.–(1) A magistrates' court has the same power to make a hospital order or guardianship order under section 37 of the Mental Health Act 1983 or an interim hospital order under section 38 of that Act in the case of a person suffering from mental illness or severe mental impairment who could otherwise be committed to custody for breach of a relevant requirement as a magistrates' court has under those sections in the case of a person convicted of an offence punishable on summary conviction with imprisonment.

(2) In subsection (1) "a relevant requirement" has the meaning given by section 50(2).

Amendments of Children Act 1989

52. [*Not reproduced.*]

Transfer of certain tenancies

53. [*Not reproduced.*]

Dwelling-house subject to mortgage

Dwelling-house subject to mortgage

54.–(1) In determining for the purposes of this Part whether a person is entitled to occupy a dwelling-house by virtue of an estate or interest, any right to possession of the dwelling-house conferred on a mortgagee of the dwelling-house under or by virtue of his mortgage is to be disregarded.

(2) Subsection (1) applies whether or not the mortgagee is in possession.

(3) Where a person ("A") is entitled to occupy a dwelling-house by virtue of an estate or interest, a connected person does not by virtue of–

(a) any matrimonial home rights conferred by section 30, or

(b) any rights conferred by an order under section 35 or 36,

have any larger right against the mortgagee to occupy the dwelling-house than A has by virtue of his estate or interest and of any contract with the mortgagee.

(4) Subsection (3) does not apply, in the case of matrimonial home rights, if under section 31 those rights are a charge, affecting the mortgagee, on the estate or interest mortgaged.

(5) In this section "connected person", in relation to any person, means that person's spouse, former spouse, cohabitant or former cohabitant.

Actions by mortgagees: joining connected persons as parties

55.–(1) This section applies if a mortgagee of land which consists of or includes a dwelling-house brings an action in any court for the enforcement of his security.

(2) A connected person who is not already a party to the action is entitled to be made a party in the circumstances mentioned in subsection (3).

(3) The circumstances are that–

(a) the connected person is enabled by section 30(3) or (6) (or by section 30(3) or (6) as applied by section 35(13) or 36(13)), to meet the mortgagor's liabilities under the mortgage;

(b) he has applied to the court before the action is finally disposed of in that court; and

(c) the court sees no special reason against his being made a party to the action and is satisfied–

  (i) that he may be expected to make such payments or do such other things in or towards satisfaction of the mortgagor's liabilities or obligations as might affect the outcome of the proceedings; or

  (ii) that the expectation of it should be considered under section 36 of the Administration of Justice Act 1970.

(4) In this section "connected person" has the same meaning as in section 54.

Actions by mortgagees: service of notice on certain persons

56.–(1) This section applies if a mortgagee of land which consists, or substantially consists, of a dwelling-house brings an action for the enforcement of his security, and at the relevant time there is–

(a) in the case of unregistered land, a land charge of Class F registered against the person who is the estate owner at the relevant time or any person who, where the estate owner is a trustee, preceded him as trustee during the subsistence of the mortgage; or

(b) in the case of registered land, a subsisting registration of–

  (i) a notice under section 31(10);

  (ii) a notice under section 2(8) of the Matrimonial Homes Act 1983; or

  (iii) a notice or caution under section 2(7) of the Matrimonial Homes Act 1967.

(2) If the person on whose behalf–

(a) the land charge is registered, or

(b) the notice or caution is entered,

is not a party to the action, the mortgagee must serve notice of the action on him.

(3) If–

(a) an official search has been made on behalf of the mortgagee which would disclose any land charge of Class F, notice or caution within subsection (1)(a) or (b),

(b) a certificate of the result of the search has been issued, and the action is commenced within the priority period,

the relevant time is the date of the certificate.

(4) In any other case the relevant time is the time when the action is commenced.

(5) The priority period is, for both registered and unregistered land, the period for which, in accordance with section 11(5) and (6) of the Land Charges Act 1972, a certificate on an official search operates in favour of a purchaser.

Jurisdiction and procedure etc.

Jurisdiction of courts

57.–(1) For the purposes of this Part "the court" means the High Court, a county court or a magistrates' court.

(2) Subsection (1) is subject to the provision made by or under the following provisions of this section, to section 59 and to any express provision as to the jurisdiction of any court made by any other provision of this Part.

(3) The Lord Chancellor may by order specify proceedings under this Part which may only be commenced in–

(a) a specified level of court;

(b) a court which falls within a specified class of court; or

(c) a particular court determined in accordance with, or specified in, the order.

(4) The Lord Chancellor may by order specify circumstances in which specified proceedings under this Part may only be commenced in–

(a) a specified level of court;

(b) a court which falls within a specified class of court; or

(c) a particular court determined in accordance with, or specified in, the order.

(5) The Lord Chancellor may by order provide that in specified circumstances the whole, or any specified part of any specified proceedings under this Part is to be transferred to–

(a) a specified level of court;

(b) a court which falls within a specified class of court; or

(c) a particular court determined in accordance with, or specified in, the order.

(6) An order under subsection (5) may provide for the transfer to be made at any stage, or specified stage, of the proceedings and whether or not the proceedings, or any part of them, have already been transferred.

(7) An order under subsection (5) may make such provision as the Lord Chancellor thinks appropriate for excluding specified proceedings from the operation of section 38 or 39 of the Matrimonial and Family Proceedings

Act 1984 (transfer of family proceedings) or any other enactment which would otherwise govern the transfer of those proceedings, or any part of them.

(8) For the purposes of subsections (3),(4) and (5), there are three levels of court—

(a) the High Court;

(b) any county court; and

(c) any magistrates' court.

(9) The Lord Chancellor may by order make provision for the principal registry of the Family Division of the High Court to be treated as if it were a county court for specified purposes of this Part, or of any provision made under this Part.

(10) Any order under subsection (9) may make such provision as the Lord Chancellor thinks expedient for the purpose of applying (with or without modifications) provisions which apply in relation to the procedure in county courts to the principal registry when it acts as if it were a county court.

(11) In this section "specified" means specified by an order under this section.

Contempt proceedings

58.–The powers of the court in relation to contempt of court arising out of a person's failure to comply with an order under this Part may be exercised by the relevant judicial authority.

Magistrates' courts

59.–(1) A magistrates' court shall not be competent to entertain any application, or make any order, involving any disputed question as to a party's entitlement to occupy any property by virtue of a beneficial estate or interest or contract or by virtue of any enactment giving him the right to remain in occupation, unless it is unnecessary to determine the question in order to deal with the application or make the order.

(2) A magistrates' court may decline jurisdiction in any proceedings under this Part if it considers that the case can more conveniently be dealt with by another court.

(3) The powers of a magistrates' court under section 63(2) of the Magistrates' Courts Act 1980 to suspend or rescind orders shall not apply in relation to any order made under this Part.

Provision for third parties to act on behalf of victims of domestic violence

60.–(1) Rules of court may provide for a prescribed person, or any person in a prescribed category, ("a representative") to act on behalf of another in relation to proceedings to which this Part applies.

(2) Rules made under this section may, in particular, authorise a representative to apply for an occupation order or for a non-molestation order for

which the person on whose behalf the representative is acting could have applied.

(3) Rules made under this section may prescribe—

(a) conditions to be satisfied before a representative may make an application to the court on behalf of another; and

(b) considerations to be taken into account by the court in determining whether, and if so how, to exercise any of its powers under this Part when a representative is acting on behalf of another.

(4) Any rules made under this section may be made so as to have effect for a specified period and may make consequential or transitional provision with respect to the expiry of the specified period.

(5) Any such rules may be replaced by further rules made under this section.

Appeals

61.–(1) An appeal shall lie to the High Court against—

(a) the making by a magistrates' court of any order under this Part, or

(b) any refusal by a magistrates' court to make such an order,

but no appeal shall lie against any exercise by a magistrates' court of the power conferred by section 59(2).

(2) On an appeal under this section, the High Court may make such orders as may be necessary to give effect to its determination of the appeal.

(3) Where an order is made under subsection (2), the High Court may also make such incidental or consequential orders as appear to it to be just.

(4) Any order of the High Court made on an appeal under this section (other than one directing that an application be re-heard by a magistrates' court) shall, for the purposes—

(a) of the enforcement of the order, and

(b) of any power to vary, revive or discharge orders,

be treated as if it were an order of the magistrates' court from which the appeal was brought and not an order of the High Court.

(5) The Lord Chancellor may by order make provision as to the circumstances in which appeals may be made against decisions taken by courts on questions arising in connection with the transfer, or proposed transfer, of proceedings by virtue of any order under section 57(5).

(6) Except to the extent provided for in any order made under subsection (5), no appeal may be made against any decision of a kind mentioned in that subsection.

General

Meaning of "cohabitants", "relevant child" and "associated persons"

62.–(1) For the purposes of this Part—

(a) "cohabitants" are a man and a woman who, although not married to each other, are living together as husband and wife; and

(b) "former cohabitants" is to be read accordingly, but does not include cohabitants who have subsequently married each other.

(2) In this Part, "relevant child", in relation to any proceedings under this Part, means–

(a) any child who is living with or might reasonably be expected to live with either party to the proceedings;

(b) any child in relation to whom an order under the Adoption Act 1976 or the Children Act 1989 is in question in the proceedings; and

(c) any other child whose interests the court considers relevant.

(3) For the purposes of this Part, a person is associated with another person if–

(a) they are or have been married to each other;

(b) they are cohabitants or former cohabitants;

(c) they live or have lived in the same household, otherwise than merely by reason of one of them being the other's employee, tenant, lodger or boarder;

(d) they are relatives;

(e) they have agreed to marry one another (whether or not that agreement has been terminated);

(f) in relation to any child, they are both persons falling within subsection (4); or

(g) they are parties to the same family proceedings (other than proceedings under this Part).

(4) A person falls within this subsection in relation to a child if–

(a) he is a parent of the child; or

(b) he has or has had parental responsibility for the child

(5) If a child has been adopted or has been freed for adoption by virtue of any of the enactments mentioned in section 16(1) of the Adoption Act 1976, two persons are also associated with each other for the purposes of this Part if–

(a) one is a natural parent of the child or a parent of such a natural parent; and

(b) the other is the child or any person–

(i) who has become a parent of the child by virtue of an adoption order or has applied for an adoption order, or

(ii) with whom the child has at any time been placed for adoption.

(6) A body corporate and another person are not, by virtue of subsection (3)(f) or (g), to be regarded for the purposes of this Part as associated with each other.

Interpretation of Part IV

63.–(1) In this Part–

"adoption order" has the meaning given by section 72(1) of the Adoption Act 1976;

"associated", in relation to a person, is to be read with section 62(3) to (6);

"child" means a person under the age of eighteen years;

"cohabitant" and "former cohabitant" have the meaning given by section 62(1);

"the court" is to be read with section 57;

"development" means physical, intellectual, emotional, social or behavioural development;

"dwelling-house" includes (subject to subsection (4))–

(a) any building or part of a building which is occupied as a dwelling,

(b) any caravan, house-boat or structure which is occupied as a dwelling,

and any yard, garden, garage or outhouse belonging to it and occupied with it;

"family proceedings" means any proceedings–

(a) under the inherent jurisdiction of the High Court in relation to children; or

(b) under the enactments mentioned in subsection (2);

"harm"–

(a) in relation to a person who has reached the age of eighteen years, means ill-treatment or the impairment of health; and

(b) in relation to a child, means ill-treatment or the impairment of health or development;

"health" includes physical or mental health;

"ill-treatment" includes forms of ill-treatment which are not physical and, in relation to a child, includes sexual abuse;

"matrimonial home rights" has the meaning given by section 30;

"mortgage", "mortgagor" and "mortgagee" have the same meaning as in the Law of Property Act 1925;

"mortgage payments" includes any payments which, under the terms of the mortgage, the mortgagor is required to make to any person;

"non-molestation order" has the meaning given by section 42(1);

"occupation order" has the meaning given by section 39;

"parental responsibility" has the same meaning as in the Children Act 1989;

"relative", in relation to a person, means–

(a) the father, mother, stepfather, stepmother, son, daughter, stepson, step-daughter, grandmother, grandfather, grandson or granddaughter of that person or of that person's spouse or former spouse, or

(b) the brother, sister, uncle, aunt, niece or nephew (whether of the full blood or of the half blood or by affinity) of that person or of that person's spouse or former spouse,

and includes, in relation to a person who is living or has lived with another person as husband and wife, any person who would fall within paragraph (a) or (b) if the parties were married to each other;

"relevant child", in relation to any proceedings under this Part, has the meaning given by section 62(2);

"the relevant judicial authority", in relation to any order under this Part, means–

(a) where the order was made by the High Court, a judge of that court;

(b) where the order was made by a county court, a judge or district judge of that or any other county court; or

(c) where the order was made by a magistrates' court, any magistrates' court.

(2) The enactments referred to in the definition of "family proceedings" are–

(a) Part II;

(b) this Part;

(c) the Matrimonial Causes Act 1973;

(d) the Adoption Act 1976;

(e) the Domestic Proceedings and Magistrates' Courts Act 1978;

(f) Part III of the Matrimonial and Family Proceedings Act 1984;

(g) Parts I, II and IV of the Children Act 1989;

(h) section 30 of the Human Fertilisation and Embryology Act 1990.

(3) Where the question of whether harm suffered by a child is significant turns on the child's health or development, his health or development shall be compared with that which could reasonably be expected of a similar child.

(4) For the purposes of sections 31, 32, 53 and 54 and such other provisions of this Part (if any) as may be prescribed, this Part is to have effect as if paragraph (b) of the definition of "dwelling-house" were omitted.

(5) It is hereby declared that this Part applies as between the parties to a marriage even though either of them is, or has at any time during the marriage been, married to more than one person.

Extracts from the Family Proceedings Rules 1991 SI No 1247

The following rules are reproduced in this section.

PART III – OTHER MATRIMONIAL ETC PROCEEDINGS

Applications under Part IV of the Family Law Act 1996 (Family Homes and Domestic Violence)

3.8–(1) An application for an occupation order or a non-molestation order under Part IV of the Family Law Act 1996 shall be made in Form FL401.

(2) An application for an occupation order or a non-molestation order made by a child under the age of sixteen shall be made in Form FLA401 but shall be treated, in the first instance, as an application to the High Court for leave.

(3) An application for an occupation order or a non-molestation order which is made in other proceedings which are pending shall be made in Form FL401.

(4) An application in Form FL401 shall be supported by a statement which is signed by the applicant and is sworn to be true.

(5) Where an application is made without giving notice, the sworn statement shall state the reasons why notice was not given.

(6) An application made on notice (together with the sworn statement and a notice in Form FL402) shall be served by the applicant on the respondent personally not less than 2 days before the date on which the application will be heard.

(7) The court may abridge the period specified in paragraph (6).

(8) Where the applicant is acting in person, service of the application shall be effected by the court if the applicant so requests.

This does not affect the court's power to order substituted service.

(9) Where an application for an occupation order or a non-molestation order is pending, the court shall consider (on the application of either party or of its own motion) whether to exercise its powers to transfer the hearing of that application to another court and shall make an order for transfer in Form FL417 if it seems necessary or expedient to do so.

(10) Rule 9.2A shall not apply to an application for an occupation order or a non-molestation order under Part IV of the Family Law Act 1996.

(11) A copy of an application for an occupation order under section 33, 35 or 36 of the Family Law Act 1996 shall be served by the applicant by first-class post on the mortgagee or, as the case may be, the landlord of the dwelling-house in question, with a notice in Form FL416 informing him of his rights to make representations in writing or at any hearing.

(12) Where an application is for the transfer of a tenancy, notice of the

application shall be served by the applicant on the other cohabitant or spouse and on the landlord (as those terms are defined by paragraph 1 of Schedule 7 to the Family Law Act 1996) and any person so served shall be entitled to be heard on the application.

(13) Rules 2.6(4) to (6) and 2.63 (investigation, requests for further information) shall apply, with the necessary modifications, to—

(a) an application for an occupation order under section 33, 35 or 36 of the Family Law Act 1996, and

(b) an application for the transfer of a tenancy, as they apply to an application for ancillary relief.

(14) Rule 3.6(7) to (9) (Married Women's Property Act 1882) shall apply, with the necessary modifications, to an application for the transfer of a tenancy, as they apply to an application under rule 3.6.

(15) The applicant shall file a statement in Form FL415 after he has served the application.

Hearing of applications under Part IV of the Family Law Act 1996

3.9–(1) An application for an occupation order or a non-molestation order under Part IV of the Family Law Act 1996 shall be dealt with in chambers unless the court otherwise directs.

(2) Where an order is made on an application made ex parte, a copy of the order together with a copy of the application and of the sworn statement in support shall be served by the applicant on the respondent personally.

(3) Where the application is for an occupation order under section 33, 35 or 36 of the Family Law Act 1996, a copy of any order made on the application shall be served by the applicant by first-class post on the mortgagee or, as the case may be, the landlord of the dwelling-house in question.

(4) A copy of an order made on an application heard inter partes shall be served by the applicant on the respondent personally.

(5) Where the applicant is acting in person, service of a copy of any order made on the hearing of the application shall be effected by the court if the applicant so requests.

(6) The following forms shall be used in connection with hearings of applications under Part IV of the Family Law Act 1996–

(a) a record of the hearing shall be made on Form FL405, and

(b) any order made on the hearing shall be issued in Form FL404.

(7) The court may direct that a further hearing be held in order to consider any representations made by a mortgagee or a landlord.

(8) An application to vary, extend or discharge an order made under Part IV of the Family Law Act 1996 shall be made in Form FL403 and this rule shall apply to the hearing of such an application.

Enforcement of orders made on applications under Part IV of the Family Law Act 1996

3.9A–(1) Where a power of arrest is attached to one or more of the provisions ('the relevant provisions') of an order made under Part IV of the Family Act 1996–

(a) the relevant provisions shall be set out in Form FL406 and the form shall not include any provisions of the order to which the power of arrest was not attached; and

(b) a copy of the form shall be delivered to the officer for the time being in charge of any police station for the applicant's address or of such other police station as the court may specify.

The copy of the form delivered under sub-paragraph (b) shall be accompanied by a statement showing that the respondent has been served with the order or informed of its terms (whether by being present when the order was made or by telephone or otherwise).

(2) Where an order is made varying or discharging the relevant provisions, the proper officer shall–

(a) immediately inform the officer who received a copy of the form under paragraph (1) and, if the applicant's address has changed, the officer for the time being in charge of the police station for the new address; and

(b) deliver a copy of the order to any officer so informed.

(3) An application for the issue of a warrant for the arrest of the respondent shall be made in Form FL407 and the warrant shall be issued in Form FL408.

(4) The court before whom a person is brought following his arrest may–

(a) determine whether the facts, and the circumstances which led to the arrest, amounted to disobedience of the order, or

(b) adjourn the proceedings and, where such an order is made, the arrested person may be released and–

(i) be dealt with within 14 days of the day on which he was arrested; and

(ii) be given not less than 2 days' notice of the adjourned hearing.

Nothing in this paragraph shall prevent the issue of a notice under CCR Order 29, rule 1(4) if the arrested person is not dealt with within the period mentioned in sub-paragraph (b) (i) above.

(5) The following provisions shall apply, with the necessary modifications, to the enforcement of orders made on applications under Part IV of the Family Law Act 1996–

(a) RSC Order 52, rule 7 (power to suspend execution of committal order);

(b) (in a case where an application for an order of committal is made to the High Court) RSC Order 52, rule 2 (application for leave);

(c) CCR Order 29, rule 1 (committal for breach or order);

(d) CCR Order 29, rule 1A (undertakings);

(e) CCR Order 29, rule 3 (discharge of person in custody);

and CCR Order 29, rule 1 shall have effect, as if for paragraph (3), there were substituted the following–

'(3) At the time when the order is drawn up, the proper officer shall–

(a) where the order made is (or includes) a non-molestation order and

(b) where the order made is an occupation order and the court so directs, issue a copy of the order, indorsed with or incorporating a notice as to the consequences of disobedience, for service in accordance with paragraph (2).'

(6) The court may adjourn consideration of the penalty to be imposed for contempts found proved and such consideration may be restored if the respondent does not comply with any conditions specified by the court.

(7) Where the court makes a hospital order in Form FL413 or a guardianship order in Form FL414 under the Mental Health Act 1983, the proper officer shall—

(a) send to the liospital any information which will be of assistance in dealing with the patient;

(b) inform the applicant when the respondent is being transferred to hospital.

(8) Where a transfer direction given by the Sectretary of State under section 48 of the Mental Health Act 1983 is in force in respect of a person remanded in custody by the court under Schedule 5 to the Family Law Act 1996, the proper officer shall notify—

(a) the governor of the prison to which the person was remanded; and

(b) the hospital where he is detained,

of any committal hearing which that person is required to attend and the proper officer shall give notice in writing to the hospital where that person is detained of any further remand under paragraph 3 of Schedule 5 to the Family Law Act 1996.

(9) An order for the remand of the respondent shall be in Form FL409.

(10) In paragraph (4) 'arrest' means arrest under a power of arrest attached to an order or under a warrant of arrest.

Applications under Part IV of the Family Law Act 1996: bail

3.10–(1) An application for bail made by a person arrested under a power of arrest or a warrant of arrest may be made either orally or in writing.

(2) Where an application is made in writing, it shall contain the following particulars—

(a) the full name of the person making the application;

(b) the address of the place where the person making the application is detained at the time when the application is made;

(c) the address where the person making the application would reside if he were to be granted bail;

(d) the amount of the recognizance in which he would agree to be bound; and

(e) the grounds on which the application is made and, where a previous application has been refused, full particulars of any change in circumstances which has occurred since that refusal.

(3) An application made in writing shall be signed by the person making the application or by a person duly authorised by him in that behalf or,

where the person making the application is a minor or is for any reason incapable of acting, by a guardian ad litem acting on his behalf and a copy shall be served by the person making the application on the applicant for the Part IV order.

(4) The persons prescribed for the purposes of paragraph 4 of Schedule 5 to the Family Law Act 1996 (postponement of taking of recognizance) are—

(a) a district judge,
(b) a justice of the peace,
(c) a justices' clerk,
(d) a police officer of the rank of inspector or above or in charge of a police station, and
(e) (where the person making the application is in his custody) the governor or keeper of a prison.

(5) The person having custody of the person making the application shall—

(a) on receipt of a certificate signed by or on behalf of the district judge stating that the recognizance of any sureties required have been taken, or on being otherwise satisfied that all such recognizances have been taken; and
(b) on being satisfied that the person making the application has entered into his recognizance,

release the person making the application.

(6) The following forms shall be used—

(a) the recognizance of the person making the application shall be in Form FL410 and that of a surety in Form FL411;
(b) a bail notice in Form FL412 shall be given to the respondent where he is remanded on bail.

PART IV – PROCEEDINGS UNDER THE CHILDREN ACT 1989

Interpretation and application

4.1–(1) In this Part of these rules, unless a contrary intention appears—

a section or schedule referred to means the section or schedule so numbered in the Act of 1989;

'a section 8 order' has the meaning assigned to it by section 8(2);

'application' means an application made under or by virtue of the Act of 1989 or under these rules, and 'applicant' shall be construed accordingly;

'child', in relation to proceedings to which this Part applies—

(a) means, subject to sub-paragraph (b), a person under the age of 18 with respect to whom the proceedings are brought, and
(b) where the proceedings are under Schedule 1, also includes a person who has reached the age of 18;

'directions appointment' means a hearing for directions under rule 4.14(2);

'emergency protection order' means an order under section 44;

'guardian ad litem' means a guardian ad litem, appointed under section 41, of the child with respect to whom the proceedings are brought;

'leave' includes permission and approval;

'note' includes a record made by mechanical means;

'parental responsibility' has the meaning assigned to it by section 3;

'recovery order' means an order under section 50;

'specified proceedings' has the meaning assigned to it by section 41(6) and rule 4.2(2); and

'welfare officer' means a person who has been asked to prepare a welfare report under section 7.

(2) Except where the contrary intention appears, the provisions of this Part apply to proceedings in the High Court and the county courts—

(a) on an application for a section 8 order;

(b) on an application for a care order or a supervision order;

(c) on an application under section 4(1)(a), 4(3), 5(1), 6(7), 13(1), 16(6), 33(7), 34(2), 34(3), 34(4), 34(9), 36(1), 38(8)(b), 39(1), 39(2), 39(3), 39(4), 43(1), 43(12), 44, 45, 46(7), 48(9), 50(1) or 102(1);

(d) under Schedule 1, except where financial relief is also sought by or on behalf of an adult,

(e) on an application under paragraph 19(1) of Schedule 2;

(f) on an application under paragraph 6(3), 15(2) or 17(1) of Schedule 3;

(g) on an application under paragraph 11(3) or 16(5) of Schedule 14; or

(h) under section 25.

Matters prescribed for the purposes of the Children Act 1989

4.2–(1) The parties to proceedings in which directions are given under section 38(6), and any person named in such a direction, form the prescribed class for the purposes of section 38(8) (application to vary directions made with interim care or interim supervision order).

(2) The following proceedings are specified for the purposes of section 41 in accordance with subsection (6)(i)thereof—

(a) proceedings under section 25;

(b) applications under section 33(7);

(c) proceedings under paragraph 19(1) of Schedule 2;

(d) applications under paragraph 6(3) of Schedule 3.

(e) appeals against the determination of proceedings of a kind set out in sub-paragraphs (a) to (d).

(3) The applicant for an order that has been made under section 43(1) and the persons referred to in section 43(11) may, in any circumstances, apply under section 43(12) for a child assessment order to be varied or discharged.

(4) The following persons form the prescribed class for the purposes of section 44(9) (application to vary directions)—

(a) the parties to the application for the order in respect of which it is sought to vary the directions;

(b) the guardian ad litem;

(c) the local authority in whose area the child concerned is ordinarily resident;

(d) any person who is named in the directions.

Application for leave to commence proceedings

4.3–(1) Where the leave of the court is required to bring any proceedings to which this Part applies, the person seeking leave shall file–

(a) a written request for leave in Form C2 setting out the reasons for the application; and

(b) a draft of the application (being the documents referred to in rule 4.4(1A)) for the making of which leave is sought together with sufficient copies for one to be served on each respondent.

(2) On considering a request for leave filed under paragraph (1), the court shall–

(a) grant the request, whereupon the proper officer shall inform the person making the request of the decision, or

(b) direct that a date be fixed for the hearing of the request, whereupon the proper officer shall fix such a date and give such notice as the court directs to the person making the request and to such other persons as the court requires to be notified, of the date so fixed.

(3) Where leave is granted to bring proceedings to which this Part applies the application shall proceed in accordance with rule 4.4; but paragraph (1)(a) of that rule shall not apply.

(4) In the case of a request for leave to bring proceedings under Schedule 1, the draft application under paragraph (1) shall be accompanied by a statement setting out the financial details which the person seeking leave believes to be relevant to the request and containing a declaration that it is true to the maker's best knowledge and belief, together with sufficient copies for one to be served on each respondent.

Application

4.4–(1) Subject to paragraph (4), an applicant shall–

(a) file the documents referred to in paragraph (1A) below (which documents shall together be called the 'application') together with sufficient copies for one to be served on each respondent, and

(b) serve a copy of the application together with Form C6 and such (if any) of Forms C7 and C10A as are given to him by the proper officer under paragraph (2)(b), on each respondent such number of days prior to the date fixed under paragraph (2)(a) as is specified for that application in column (ii) of Appendix 3 to these rules.

(1A) the documents to be filed under paragraph (1)(a) above are–

(a) (i) whichever is appropriate of Forms C1 to C4 or C51, and

   (ii) such of the supplemental Forms C10 or C11 to C20 as may be appropriate, or

(b) where there is no appropriate form a statement in writing of the order sought, and where the application is made in respect of more than one child, all the children shall be included in one application.

(2) On receipt of the documents filed under paragraph (1)(a) the proper officer shall–

(a) fix the date for a hearing or a directions appointment, allowing sufficient time for the applicant to comply with paragraph (1)(b),

(b) endorse the date so fixed upon Form C6 and, where appropriate, Form C6A, and

(c) return forthwith to the applicant the copies to the application and Form C10A if filed with it, together with Form C6 and such of Forms C6A and C7 as are appropriate.

(3) The applicant shall, at the same time as complying with paragraph (1)(b), serve Form C6A on the persons set out for the relevant class of proceedings in column (iv)of Appendix 3 to these rules.

(4) An application for–

(a) a section 8 order,

(b) an emergency protection order,

(c) a warrant under section 48(9),

(d) a recovery order, or

(e) a warrant under section 102(1),

may be made ex parte in which case the applicant shall–

(i) file the application in the appropriate form in Appendix 1 to these rules–

(a) where the application is made by telephone, within 24 hours after the making of the application, or

(b) in any other case, at the time when the application is made, and

(ii) in the case of an application for a section 8 order or an emergency protection order, serve a copy of the application on each respondent within 48 hours after the making of the order.

(5) Where the court refuses to make an order on an ex parte application it may direct that the application be made inter partes.

(6) In the case of proceedings under Schedule 1, the application under paragraph (1) shall be accompanied by a statement in Form C10A setting out the financial details which the applicant believes to be relevant to the application together with sufficient copies for one to be served on each respondent.

Withdrawal of application

4.5–(1) An application may be withdrawn only with leave of the court.

(2) Subject to paragraph (3), a person seeking leave to withdraw an application shall file and serve on the parties a written request for leave setting out the reasons for the request.

(3) The request under paragraph (2) may be made orally to the court if the parties and either the guardian ad litem or the welfare officer are present.

(4) Upon receipt of a written request under paragraph (2) the court shall–

(a) if–

(i) the parties consent in writing,

(ii) the guardian ad litem has had an opportunity to make representations, and

(iii) the court thinks fit,

grant the request, in which case the proper officer shall notify the parties, the guardian ad litem and the welfare officer of the granting of the request, or

(b) direct that a date be fixed for the hearing of the request in which case the proper officer shall give at least 7 days' notice to the parties, the guardian ad litem and the welfare officer, of the date fixed.

Transfer

4.6–(1) Where an application is made, in accordance with the provisions of the Allocation Order, to a county court for an order transferring proceedings from a magistrates' court following the refusal of the magistrates' court to order such a transfer, the applicant shall–

(a) file the application in Form C2, together with a copy of the certificate issued by the magistrates' court, and

(b) serve a copy of the documents mentioned in sub-paragraph (a) personally on all parties to the proceedings which it is sought to have transferred, within 2 days after receipt by the applicant of the certificate.

(2) Within 2 days after receipt of the documents served under paragraph (1)(b), any party other than the applicant may file written representations.

(3) The court shall, not before the fourth day after the filing of the application under paragraph (1), unless the parties consent to earlier consideration, consider the application and either–

(a) grant the application, whereupon the proper officer shall inform the parties of that decision, or

(b) direct that a date be fixed for the hearing of the application, whereupon the proper officer shall fix such a date and give not less than 1 day's notice to the parties of the date so fixed.

(4) Where proceedings are transferred from a magistrates' court to a county court in accordance with the provisions of the Allocation Order, the county court shall consider whether to transfer those proceedings to the High Court in accordance with that Order and either–

(a) determine that such an order need not be made,

(b) make such an order,

(c) order that a date be fixed for the hearing of the question whether such an order should be made, whereupon the proper officer shall give such notice to the parties as the court directs of the date so fixed, or

(d) invite the parties to make written representations, within a specified period, as to whether such an order should be made; and upon receipt of the representations the court shall act in accordance with sub-paragraph (a), (b) or (c).

(5) The proper officer shall notify the parties of an order transferring the proceedings from a county court or from the High Court made in accordance with the provisions of the Allocation Order.

(6) Before ordering the transfer of proceedings from a county court to a magistrates' court in accordance with the Allocation Order, the county court shall notify the magistrates' court of its intention to make such an order and invite the views of the clerk of the justices on whether such an order should be made.

(7) An order transferring proceedings from a county court to a magistrates' court in accordance with the Allocation Order shall–

(a) be in form C49, and

(b) be served by the court on the parties.

(8) In this rule 'the Allocation Order' means the Children (Allocation of Proceedings) Order 1991 or any Order replacing that Order.

Parties

4.7–(1) The respondents to proceedings to which this Part applies shall be those persons set out in the relevant entry in column (iii) of Appendix 3 to these rules.

(2) In proceedings to which this Part applies, a person may file a request in Form C2 that he or another person–

(a) be joined as a party, or

(b) cease to be a party.

(3) On considering a request under paragraph (2) the court shall, subject to paragraph (4)–

(a) grant it without a hearing or representations, save that this shall be done only in the case of a request under paragraph (2)(a), whereupon the proper officer shall inform the parties and the person making the request of that decision, or

(b) order that a date be fixed for the consideration of the request, whereupon the proper officer shall give notice of the date so fixed, together with a copy of the request–

  (i) in the case of a request under paragraph (2)(a), to the applicant, and–

  (ii) in the case of a request under paragraph (2)(b), to the parties, or

(c) invite the parties or any of them to make written representations, within a specified period, as to whether the request should be granted; and upon the expiry of the period the court shall act in accordance with sub-paragraph (a) or (b).

(4) Where a person with parental responsibility requests that he be joined under paragraph (2)(a), the court shall grant his request.

(5) In proceedings to which this Part applies the court may direct–

(a) that a person who would not otherwise be a respondent under these rules be joined as a party to the proceedings, or

(b) that a party to the proceedings cease to be a party.

Service

4.8–(1) Subject to the requirement in rule 4.6(1)(b) of personal service, where service of a document is required under this Part (and not by a provision to which section 105(8) (Service of notice or other document under the Act) applies) it may be effected–

(a) if the person to be served is not known by the person serving to be acting by solicitor–
   (i) by delivering it to him personally, or
   (ii) by delivering it at, or by sending it by first-class post to, his residence or his last known residence, or

(b) if the person to be served is known by the person serving to be acting by solicitor–
   (i) by delivering the document at, or sending it by first-class post to, the solicitor's address for service,
   (ii) where the solicitor's address for service includes a numbered box at a document exchange, by leaving the document at that document exchange or at a document exchange which transmits documents on every business day to that document exchange, or
   (iii) by sending a legible copy of the document by facsimile transmission to the solicitor's office.

(2) In this rule 'first-class post' means first-class post which has been pre-paid or in respect of which pre-payment is not required.

(3) Where a child who is a party to proceedings to which this Part applies is not prosecuting or defending them without a next friend or guardian ad litem under rule 9.2A and is required by these rules or other rules of court to serve a document, service shall be effected by–

(a) the solicitor acting for the child, or
(b) where there is no such solicitor, the guardian ad litem, or
(c) where there is neither such a solicitor nor a guardian ad litem, the court.

(4) Service of any document on a child who is not prosecuting or defending the proceedings concerned without a next friend or guardian ad litem under rule 9.2A shall, subject to any direction of the court, be effected by service on–

(a) the solicitor acting for the child, or
(b) where there is no such solicitor, the guardian ad litem, or
(c) where there is neither such a solicitor nor a guardian ad litem, with leave of the court, the child.

(5) Where the court refuses leave under paragraph (4)(c) it shall give a direction under paragraph (8).

(6) A document shall, unless the contrary is proved, be deemed to have been served–

(a) in the case of service by first-class post, on the second business day after posting, and
(b) in the case of service in accordance with paragraph (1)(b)(ii), on the second business day after the day on which it is left at the document exchange.

(7) At or before the first directions appointment in, or hearing of, pro-

ceedings to which this Part applies the applicant shall file a statement in Form C9 that service of–
(a) a copy of the application and other documents referred to in rule 4.4(1)
    (b) has been effected on each respondent, and
(b) notice of the proceedings has been effected under rule 4.4(3);
and the statement shall indicate–
    (i) the manner, date, time and place of service, or
    (ii) where service was effected by post, the date, time and place of posting.

(8) In proceedings to which this Part applies, where these rules or other rules of court require a document to be served, the court may, without prejudice to any power under rule 4.14, direct that–
(a) the requirement shall not apply;
(b) the time specified by the rules for complying with the requirement shall be abridged to such extent as may be specified in the direction;
(c) service shall be effected in such manner as may be specified in the direction.

Acknowledgement of application

4.9–(1) Within 14 days of service of an application for a section 8 order or an application under Schedule 1, each respondent shall file, and serve on the parties, an acknowledgement of the application in Form C7.

(2) [*Repealed.*]

(3) Following service of an application to which this Part applies, other than an application under rule 4.3 or for a section 8 order, a respondent may, subject to paragraph (4), file a written answer, which shall be served on the other parties.

(4) An answer under paragraph (3) shall, except in the case of an application under section 25, 31, 34, 38, 43, 44, 45, 46, 48 or 50, be filed, and served, not less than 2 days before the date fixed for the hearing of the application.

Appointment of guardian ad litem

4.10–(1) As soon as practicable after the commencement of specified proceedings, or the transfer of such proceedings to the court, the court shall appoint a guardian ad litem, unless–
(a) such an appointment has already been made by the court which made the transfer and is subsisting, or
(b) the court considers that such an appointment is not necessary to safeguard the interests of the child.

(2) At any stage in specified proceedings a party may apply, without notice to the other parties unless the court directs otherwise, for the appointment of a guardian ad litem.

(3) The court shall grant an application under paragraph (2) unless it considers such an appointment not to be necessary to safeguard the interests of the child, in which case it shall give its reasons; and a note of such reasons shall be taken by the proper officer.

(4) At any stage in specified proceedings the court may, of its own motion, appoint a guardian ad litem.

(5) The proper officer shall, as soon as practicable, notify the parties and any welfare officer of an appointment under this rule or, as the case may be, of a decision not to make such an appointment.

(6) Upon the appointment of a guardian ad litem the proper officer shall, as soon as practicable, notify him of the appointment and serve on him copies of the application and of documents filed under rule 4.17(1).

(7) A guardian ad litem appointed from a panel established by regulations made under section 41(7) shall not–

(a) be a member, officer or servant of a local authority which, or an authorised person (within the meaning of section 31(9)) who, is a party to the proceedings, unless he is employed by such an authority solely as a member of a panel of guardians ad litem and reporting officers;

(b) be, or have been, a member, officer or servant of a local authority or voluntary organisation (within the meaning of section 105(1)) who has been directly concerned in that capacity in arrangements relating to the care, accommodation or welfare of the child during the five years prior to the commencement of the proceedings;

(c) be a serving probation officer (except that a probation officer who has not in that capacity been previously concerned with the child or his family and who is employed part-time may, when not engaged in his duties as a probation officer, act as a guardian ad litem).

(8) When appointing a guardian ad litem the court shall consider the appointment of anyone who has previously acted as guardian ad litem of the same child.

(9) The appointment of a guardian ad litem under this rule shall continue for such time as is specified in the appointment or until terminated by the court.

(10) When terminating an appointment in accordance with paragraph (9), the court shall give its reasons in writing for so doing.

(11) Where the court appoints a guardian ad litem in accordance with this rule or refuses to make such an appointment, the court or the proper officer shall record the appointment or refusal in Form C47.

Powers and duties of guardian ad litem

4.11–(1) In carrying out his duty under section 41(2), the guardian ad litem shall have regard to the principle set out in section 1(2) and the matters set out in section 1(3)(a) to (f) as if for the word 'court' in that section there were substituted the words 'guardian ad litem'.

(2) The guardian ad litem shall–

(a) appoint a solicitor to represent the child unless such a solicitor has already been appointed, and

(b) give such advice to the child as is appropriate having regard to his understanding and, subject to rule 4.12(1)(a), instruct the solicitor representing the child on all matters relevant to the interests of the child, including possibilities for appeal, arising in the course of the proceedings.

(2A) Where the guardian ad litem is the Official Solicitor, paragraph 2(a) shall not require him to appoint a solicitor for the child if he intends to act as the child's solicitor in the proceedings, unless—

(a) the child wishes to instruct a solicitor direct; and

(b) the Official Solicitor or the court considers that he is of sufficient understanding to do so.

(3) Where it appears to the guardian ad litem that the child—

(a) is instructing his solicitor direct, or

(b) intends to, and is capable of conducting the proceedings on his own behalf,

he shall so inform the court and thereafter—

(i) shall perform all of his duties set out in this rule, other than duties under paragraph (2)(a) and such other duties as the court may direct,

(ii) shall take such part in the proceedings as the court may direct, and

(iii) may, with leave of the court, have legal representation in his conduct of those duties.

(4) The guardian ad litem shall, unless excused by the court, attend all directions appointments in and hearings of the proceedings and shall advise the court on the following matters—

(a) whether the child is of sufficient understanding for any purpose including the child's refusal to submit to a medical or psychiatric examination or other assessment that the court has power to require, direct or order;

(b) the wishes of the child in respect of any matter relevant to the proceedings, including his attendance at court;

(c) the appropriate forum for the proceedings;

(d) the appropriate timing of the proceedings or any part of them;

(e) the options available to it in respect of the child and the suitability of each such option including what order should be made in determining the application;

(f) any other matter concerning which the court seeks his advice or concerning which he considers that the court should be informed.

(5) The advice given under paragraph (4) may, subject to any order of the court, be given orally or in writing; and if the advice be given orally, a note of it shall be taken by the court or the proper officer.

(6) The guardian ad litem shall, where practicable, notify any person whose joinder as a party to those proceedings would be likely, in the guardian ad litem's opinion, to safeguard the interests of the child, of that person's right to apply to be joined under rule 4.7(2) and shall inform the court—

(a) of any such notification given,

(b) of anyone whom he attempted to notify under this paragraph but was unable to contact, and

(c) of anyone whom he believes may wish to be joined to the proceedings.

(7) The guardian ad litem shall, unless the court otherwise directs, not less than seven days before the date fixed for the final hearing of the proceedings, file a written report advising on the interests of the child; and the proper officer shall, as soon as practicable, serve a copy of the report on the parties.

(8) The guardian ad litem shall serve and accept service of documents on behalf of the child in accordance with rule 4.8(3)(b) and (4)(b) and, where the child has not himself been served, and has sufficient understanding, advise the child of the contents of any document so served.

(9) The guardian ad litem shall make such investigations as may be necessary for him to carry out his duties and shall, in particular–

(a) contact or seek to interview such persons as he thinks appropriate or as the court directs,

(b) if he inspects records of the kinds referred to in section 42, bring to the attention of the court and such other persons as the court may direct all such records and documents which may, in his opinion, assist in the proper determination of the proceedings, and

(c) obtain such professional assistance as is available to him which he thinks appropriate or which the court directs him to obtain.

(10) In addition to his duties under other paragraphs of this rule, the guardian ad litem shall provide to the court such other assistance as it may require.

(11) A party may question the guardian ad litem about oral or written advice tendered by him to the court under this rule.

Solicitor for child

4.12–(1) A solicitor appointed under section 41(3) or in accordance with rule 4.11(2)(a) shall represent the child–

(a) in accordance with instructions received from the guardian ad litem (unless the solicitor considers, having taken into account the views of the guardian ad litem and any direction of the court under rule 4.11(3), that the child wishes to give instructions which conflict with those of the guardian ad litem and that he is able, having regard to his understanding, to give such instructions on his own behalf in which case he shall conduct the proceedings in accordance with instructions received from the child), or

(b) where no guardian ad litem has been appointed for the child and the condition in section 41(4)(b) is satisfied, in accordance with instructions received from the child, or

(c) in default of instructions under (a) or (b), in furtherance of the best interests of the child.

(2) A solicitor appointed under section 41(3) or in accordance with rule 4.11(2)(a) shall serve and accept service of documents on behalf of the child in accordance with rule 4.8(3)(a) and (4)(a) and, where the child has not

himself been served and has sufficient understanding, advise the child of the contents of any document so served.

(3) Where the child wishes an appointment of a solicitor under section 41(3) or in accordance with rule 4.11(2)(a) to be terminated, he may apply to the court for an order terminating the appointment; and the solicitor and the guardian ad litem shall be given an opportunity to make representations.

(4) Where the guardian ad litem wishes an appointment of a solicitor under section 41(3) to be terminated, he may apply to the court for an order terminating the appointment; and the solicitor and, if he is of sufficient understanding, the child, shall be given an opportunity to make representations.

(5) When terminating an appointment in accordance with paragraph (3) or (4), the court shall give its reasons for so doing, a note of which shall be taken by the court or the proper officer.

(6) Where the court appoints a solicitor under section 41(3) or refuses to make such an appointment, the court or the proper officer shall record the appointment or refusal in Form C48.

Welfare officer

4.13–(1) Where the court has directed that a written report be made by a welfare officer, the report shall be filed at or by such time as the court directs or, in the absence of such a direction, at least 14 days before a relevant hearing; and the proper officer shall, as soon as practicable, serve a copy of the report on the parties and any guardian ad litem.

(2) In paragraph (1), a hearing is relevant if the proper officer has given the welfare officer notice that his report is to be considered at it.

(3) After the filing of a report by a welfare officer, the court may direct that the welfare officer attend any hearing at which the report is to be considered; and

(a) except where such a direction is given at a hearing attended by the welfare officer, the proper officer shall inform the welfare officer of the direction; and

(b) at the hearing at which the report is considered any party may question the welfare officer about his report.

(4) This rule is without prejudice to any power to give directions under rule 4.14.

Directions

4.14–(1) In this rule, 'party' includes the guardian ad litem and, where a request or a direction concerns a report under section 7, the welfare officer.

(2) In proceedings to which this Part applies the court may, subject to paragraph (3), give, vary or revoke directions for the conduct of the proceedings, including–

(a) the timetable for the proceedings;

(b) varying the time within which or by which an act is required, by these rules or by other rules or court, to be done;

(c) the attendance of the child;

(d) the appointment of a guardian ad litem, whether under section 41 or otherwise, or of a solicitor under section 41(3);

(e) the service of documents;

(f) the submission of evidence including experts' reports;

(g) the preparation of welfare reports under section 7;

(h) the transfer of the proceedings to another court;

(i) consolidation with other proceedings.

(3) Directions under paragraph (2) may be given, varied or revoked either–

(a) of the court's own motion having given the parties notice of its intention to do so, and an opportunity to attend and be heard or to make written representations,

(b) on the written request in Form C2 of a party specifying the direction which is sought, filed and served on the other parties, or

(c) on the written request in Form C2 of a party specifying the direction which is sought, to which the other parties consent and which they or their representatives have signed .

(4) In an urgent case the request under paragraph (3)(b) may, with the leave of the court, be made–

(a) orally, or

(b) without notice to the parties, or

(c) both as in sub-paragraph (a) and as in sub-paragraph (b).

(5) On receipt of a written request under paragraph (3)(b) the proper officer shall fix a date for the hearing of the request and give not less than 2 days' notice in Form C6 to the parties of the date so fixed.

(6) On considering a request under paragraph (3)(c) the court shall either–

(a) grant the request, whereupon the proper officer shall inform the parties of the decision, or

(b) direct that a date be fixed for the hearing of the request, whereupon the proper officer shall fix such a date and give not less than 2 days' notice to the parties of the date so fixed.

(7) A party may apply for an order to be made under section 11(3) or, if he is entitled to apply for such an order, under section 38(1) in accordance with paragraph (3)(b) or (c).

(8) Where a court is considering making, of its own motion, a section 8 order, or an order under section 31, 34 or 38, the power to give directions under paragraph (2) shall apply

(9) Directions of a court which are still in force immediately prior to the transfer of proceedings to which this Part applies to another court shall continue to apply following the transfer, subject to any changes of terminology which are required to apply those directions to the court to which the proceedings are transferred, unless varied or discharged by directions under paragraph (2).

(10) The court or the proper officer shall take a note of the giving, variation or revocation of a direction under this rule and serve, as soon as practicable, a copy of the note on any party who was not present at the giving, variation or revocation.

Timing of proceedings

4.15–(1) Where these rules or other rules of court provide a period of time within which or by which a certain act is to be performed in the course of proceedings to which this Part applies, that period may not be extended otherwise than by direction of the court under rule 4.14.

(2) At the–

(a) transfer to a court of proceedings to which this Part applies,

(b) postponement or adjournment of any hearing or directions appointment in the course of proceedings to which this Part applies, or

(c) conclusion of any such hearing or directions appointment other than one at which the proceedings are determined, or so soon thereafter as is practicable,

the court or the proper officer shall–

    (i) fix a date upon which the proceedings shall come before the court again for such purposes as the court directs, which date shall, where paragraph (a) applies, be as soon as possible after the transfer, and

    (ii) give notice to the parties, the guardian ad litem or the welfare officer of the date so fixed.

Attendance at directions appointment and hearing

4.16–(1) Subject to paragraph (2), a party shall attend a directions appointment of which he has been given notice in accordance with rule 4.14(5) unless the court otherwise directs.

(2) Proceedings or any part of them shall take place in the absence of any party, including the child, if–

(a) the court considers it in the interests of the child, having regard to the matters to be discussed or the evidence likely to be given, and

(b) the party is represented by a guardian ad litem or solicitor;

and when considering the interests of the child under sub-paragraph (a) the court shall give the guardian ad litem, the solicitor for the child and, if he is of sufficient understanding, the child an opportunity to make representations.

(3) Subject to paragraph (4), where at the time and place appointed for a hearing or directions appointment the applicant appears but one or more of the respondents do not, the court may proceed with the hearing or appointment.

(4) The court shall not begin to hear an application in the absence of a respondent unless–

(a) it is proved to the satisfaction of the court that he received reasonable notice of the date of the hearing; or

(b) the court is satisfied that the circumstances of the case justify proceeding with the hearing.

(5) Where, at the time and place appointed for a hearing or directions appointment one or more of the respondents appear but the applicant does not, the court may refuse the application or, if sufficient evidence has previously been received, proceed in the absence of the applicant.

(6) Where at the time and place appointed for a hearing or directions appointment neither the applicant nor any respondent appears, the court may refuse the application.

(7) Unless the court otherwise directs, a hearing of, or directions appointment in, proceedings to which this Part applies shall be in chambers.

Documentary evidence

4.17–(1) Subject to paragraphs (4) and (5), in proceedings to which this Part applies a party shall file and serve on the parties, any welfare officer and any guardian ad litem of whose appointment he has been given notice under rule 4.10(5)–

(a) written statements of the substance of the oral evidence which the party intends to adduce at a hearing of, or a directions appointment in, those proceedings, which shall–
   (i) be dated,
   (ii) be signed by the person making the statement,
   (iii) contain a declaration that the maker of the statement believes it to be true and understands that it may be placed before the court; and
   (iv) show in the top right hand corner of the first page–
      (a) the initials and surname of the person making the statement,
      (b) the number of the statement in relation to the maker,
      (c) the date on which the statement was made, and
      (d) the party on whose behalf it is filed; and
(b) copies of any documents, including experts' reports, upon which the party intends to rely at a hearing of, or a directions appointment in, those proceedings,
at or by such time as the court directs or, in the absence of a direction, before the hearing or appointment.

(2) A party may, subject to any direction of the court about the timing of statements under this rule, file and serve on the parties a statement which is supplementary to a statement served under paragraph (1).

(3) At a hearing or a directions appointment a party may not, without the leave of the court–
(a) adduce evidence, or
(b) seek to rely on a document,
in respect of which he has failed to comply with the requirements of paragraph (1).

(4) In proceedings for a section 8 order a party shall–

(a) neither file nor serve any document other than as required or authorised by these rules, and

(b) in completing a form prescribed by these rules, neither give information, nor make a statement, which is not required or authorised by that form, without the leave of the court.

(5) In proceedings for a section 8 order no statement or copy may be filed under paragraph (1) until such time as the court directs.

Expert evidence – examination of child

4.18–(1) No person may, without the leave of the court, cause the child to be medically or psychiatrically examined, or otherwise assessed, for the purpose of the preparation of expert evidence for use in the proceedings.

(2) An application for leave under paragraph (1) shall, unless the court otherwise directs, be served on all parties to the proceedings and on the guardian ad litem.

(3) Where the leave of the court has not been given under paragraph (1), no evidence arising out of an examination or assessment to which that paragraph applies may be adduced without the leave of the court.

Amendment

4.19–(1) Subject to rule 4.17(2), a document which has been filed or served in proceedings to which this Part applies, may not be amended without the leave of the court which shall, unless the court otherwise directs, be requested in writing.

(2) On considering a request for leave to amend a document the court shall either–

(a) grant the request, whereupon the proper officer shall inform the person making the request of that decision, or

(b) invite the parties or any of them to make representations, within a specified period, as to whether such an order should be made.

(3) A person amending a document shall file it and serve it on those persons on whom it was served prior to amendment; and the amendments shall be identified.

Oral evidence

4.20–The court or the proper officer shall keep a note of the substance of the oral evidence given at a hearing of, or directions appointment in, proceedings to which this Part applies.

Hearing

4.21–(1) The court may give directions as to the order of speeches and evidence at a hearing, or directions appointment, in the course of proceedings to which this Part applies.

(2) Subject to directions under paragraph (1), at a hearing of, or directions appointment in, proceedings to which this Part applies, the parties and

the guardian ad litem shall adduce their evidence in the following order–
(a) the applicant,
(b) any party with parental responsibility for the child,
(c) other respondents,
(d) the guardian ad litem,
(e) the child, if he is a party to the proceedings and there is no guardian ad litem.

(3) After the final hearing of proceedings to which this Part applies, the court shall deliver its judgment as soon as is practicable.

(4) When making an order or when refusing an application, the court shall–
(a) where it makes a finding of fact state such finding and complete Form C22; and
(b) state the reason's for the court's decision.

(5) An order made in proceedings to which this Part applies shall be recorded, by the court or the proper officer, either in the appropriate form in Appendix 1 to these rules or, where there is no such form, in writing.

(6) Subject to paragraph (7), a copy of an order made in accordance with paragraph (5) shall, as soon as practicable after it has been made, be served by the proper officer on the parties to the proceedings in which it was made and on any person with whom the child is living.

(7) Within 48 hours after the making ex parte of–
(a) a section 8 order, or
(b) an order under section 44, 48(4), 48(9) or 50,
the applicant shall serve a copy of the order in the appropriate form in Appendix 1 to these Rules on–
   (i) each party,
   (ii) any person who has actual care of the child or who had such care immediately prior to the making of the order, and
   (iii) in the case of an order referred to in sub-paragraph (b), the local authority in whose area the child lives or is found.

(8) At a hearing of or directions appointment in, an application which takes place outside the hours during which the court office is normally open, the court or the proper officer shall take a note of the substance of the proceedings.

Attachment of penal notice to section 8 order

4.21A CCR Order 29, rule 1 (committal for breach of order or undertaking) shall apply to section 8 orders as if for paragraph (3) of that rule there were substituted the following:–

'(3) In the case of a section 8 order (within the meaning of section 8(2) of the Children Act 1989) enforceable by committal order under paragraph (1), the judge or the district judge may, on the application of the person entitled to enforce the order, direct that the proper officer issue a copy of the order, indorsed with or incorporating a notice as to the consequences of disobedience, for service in accordance with paragraph (2); and no copy of the order shall be issued with any such notice indorsed or incorporated save in accordance with such a direction.'

Appeals

4.22–(1) Where an appeal lies–
(a) to the High Court under section 94, or
(b) from any decision of a district judge to the judge of the court in which the decision was made,

it shall be made in accordance with the following provisions; and references to 'the court below' are references to the court from which, or person from whom, the appeal lies.

(2) The appellant shall file and serve on the parties to the proceedings in the court below, and on any guardian ad litem,
(a) notice of the appeal in writing, setting out the grounds upon which he relies;
(b) a certified copy of the summons or application and of the order appealed against, and of any order staying its execution;
(c) a copy of any notes of the evidence;
(d) a copy of any reasons given for the decision.

(2A) In relation to an appeal to the High Court under section 94, the documents required to be filed by paragraph (2) shall,–
(a) where the care centre listed in column (ii) of Schedule 2 to the Children (Allocation of Proceedings) Order 1991 against the entry in column (i) relating to the petty sessions area or London commission area in which the court below is situated–
 (i) is the principal registry, or
 (ii) has a district registry in the same place,
be filed in that registry,
(b) in any other case, be filed in the district registry, being in the same place as a care centre within the meaning of article 2(c) of the said Order, which is nearest to the court below.

(3) The notice of appeal shall be filed and served in accordance with paragraph (2)(a)
(a) within 14 days after the determination against which the appeal is brought, or
(b) in the case of an appeal against an order under section 38(1), within 7 days after the making of the order, or
(c) with the leave of the court to which, or judge to whom, the appeal is to be brought, within such other time as that court or judge may direct.

(4) The documents mentioned in paragraph (2)(b) to (d) shall, subject to any direction of the court to which, or judge to whom, the appeal is to be brought, be filed and served as soon as practicable after the filing and service of the notice of appeal under paragraph (2)(a).

(5) Subject to paragraph (6), a respondent who wishes–

(a) to contend on the appeal that the decision of the court below should be varied, either in any event or in the event of the appeal being allowed in whole or in part, or

(b) to contend that the decision of the court below should be affirmed on grounds other than those relied upon by that court, or

(c) to contend by way of cross-appeal that the decision of the court below was wrong in whole or in part,

shall, within 14 days of receipt of notice of the appeal, file and serve on all other parties to the appeal a notice in writing, setting out the grounds upon which he relies.

(6) No notice under paragraph (5) may be filed or served in an appeal against an order under section 38.

(7) In the case of an appeal mentioned in paragraph (1)(a), an application to—

(a) withdraw the appeal,

(b) have the appeal dismissed with the consent of all the parties, or

(c) amend the grounds of appeal,

may be heard by a district judge.

(8) An appeal of the kind mentioned in paragraph (1)(a) shall, unless the President otherwise directs, be heard and determined by a single judge.

Confidentiality of documents

4.23–(1) Notwithstanding any rule of court to the contrary, no document, other than a record of an order, held by the court and relating to proceedings to which this Part applies shall be disclosed, other than to—

(a) a party,

(b) the legal representative of a party,

(c) the guardian ad litem,

(d) the Legal Aid Board, or

(e) a welfare officer,

without leave of the judge or district judge.

(2) Nothing in this rule shall prevent the notification by the court or the proper officer of a direction under section 37(1) to) the authority concerned.

(3) Nothing in this rule shall prevent the disclosure of a document prepared by a guardian ad litem for the purpose of—

(a) enabling a person to perform functions required by regulations made under section 41(7);

(b) assisting a guardian ad litem or a reporting officer (within the meaning of section 65(1)(b) of the Adoption Act 1976) who is appointed under any enactment to perform his functions.

Notification of consent

4.24 Consent for the purposes of—

(a) section 16(3), or

(b) [*Repealed.*]

(c) paragraph 19(3)(c) or (d) of Schedule 2,

shall be given either
  (i) orally in court, or
  (ii) in writing to the court signed by the person giving his consent.

Secure accommodation – evidence

4.25 In proceedings under section 25, the court shall, if practicable, arrange for copies of all written reports before it to be made available before the hearing to–
(a) the applicant;
(b) the parent or guardian of the child;
(c) any legal representative of the child;
(d) the guardian ad litem; and
(e) the child, unless the court otherwise directs;
and copies of such reports may, if the court considers it desirable, be shown to any person who is entitled to notice of the proceedings in accordance with these Rules.

Investigation under section 37

4.26–(1) This rule applies where a direction is given to an appropriate authority by the High Court or a county court under section 37(1).

(2) On giving a direction the court shall adjourn the proceedings and the court or the proper officer shall record the direction in Form C40.

(3) A copy of the direction recorded under paragraph (2) shall, as soon as practicable after the direction is given, be served by the proper officer on the parties to the proceedings in which the direction is given and, where the appropriate authority is not a party, on that authority.

(4) When serving the copy of the direction on the appropriate authority the proper officer shall also serve copies of such of the documentary evidence which has been, or is to be, adduced in the proceedings as the court may direct.

(5) Where a local authority informs the Court of any of the matters set out in section 37(3)(a) to (c) it shall do so in writing.

Direction to local education authority to apply for education supervision order

4.27–(1) For the purposes of section 40(3) and (4) of the Education Act 1944 a direction by the High Court or a county court to a local education authority to apply for an education supervision order shall be given in Form C37.

(2) Where, following such a direction, a local education authority informs the court that they have decided not to apply for an education supervision order, they shall do so in writing.

Transitional provision

4.28 Nothing in any provision of this Part of these rules shall affect any proceedings which are pending (within the meaning of paragraph 1 of

Schedule 14 to the Act of 1989) immediately before these rules come into force.

PART VI – CHILD ABDUCTION AND CUSTODY

Interpretation
6.1   In this Part, unless the context otherwise requires–
(a) 'the Act' means the Child Abduction and Custody Act 1985 and words or expressions bear the same meaning as in that Act;
(b) 'the Hague Convention' means the convention defined in section 1(1) of the Act and 'the European Convention' means the convention defined in section 12(1) of the Act.

Mode of application
6.2–(1) Except as otherwise provided by this Part, every application under the Hague Convention and the European Convention shall be made by originating summons, which shall be in Form No. 10 in Appendix A to the Rules of the Supreme Court 1965 and issued out of the principal registry.

(2)   An application in custody proceedings for a declaration under section 23(2) of the Act shall be made by summons in those proceedings.

Contents of originating summons: general provisions
6.3–(1) The originating summons under which any application is made under the Hague Convention or the European Convention shall state–
(a) the name and date of birth of the child in respect of whom the application is made;
(b) the names of the child's parents or guardians;
(c) the whereabouts or suspected whereabouts of the child;
(d) the interest of the plaintiff in the matter and the grounds of the application; and
(e) particulars of any proceedings (including proceedings out of the jurisdiction and concluded proceedings) relating to the child, and shall be accompanied by all relevant documents including but not limited to the documents specified in Article 8 of the Hague Convention or, as the case may be, Article 13 of the European Convention.

Contents of originating summons: particular provisions
6.4–(1) In applications under the Hague Convention, in addition to the matters specified in rule 6.3–
(a) the originating summons under which an application is made for the purposes of Article 8 for the return of a child shall state the identity of the person alleged to have removed or retained the child and, if different, the identity of the person with whom the child is presumed to be;
(b) the originating summons under which an application is made for the purposes of Article 15 for a declaration shall identify the proceedings in which the request that such a declaration be obtained was made.

(2) In applications under the European Convention, in addition to the matters specified in rule 6.3 the originating summons shall identify the decision relating to custody or rights of access which is sought to be registered or enforced or in relation to which a declaration that it is not to be recognised is sought.

Defendants

6.5 The defendants to an application under the Act shall be–
(a) the person alleged to have brought into the United Kingdom the child in respect of whom an application under the Hague Convention is made;
(b) the person with whom the child is alleged to be;
(c) any parent or guardian of the child who is within the United Kingdom and is not otherwise a party;
(d) the person in whose favour a decision relating to custody has been made if he is not otherwise a party; and
(e) any other person who appears to the court to have a sufficient interest in the welfare of the child.

Acknowledgement of service

6.6 The time limited for acknowledging service of an originating summons by which an application is made under the Hague Convention or the European Convention shall be seven days after service of the originating summons (including the day of service) or, in the case of a defendant referred to in rule 6.5(d) or (e), such further time as the Court may direct.

Evidence

6.7–(1) The plaintiff, on issuing an originating summons under the Hague Convention or the European Convention, may lodge affidavit evidence in the principal registry in support of his application and serve a copy of the same on the defendant with the originating summons.

(2) A defendant to an application under the Hague Convention or the European Convention may lodge affidavit evidence in the principal registry and serve a copy of the same on the plaintiff within seven days after service of the originating summons on him.

(3) The plaintiff in an application under the Hague Convention or the European Convention may within seven days thereafter lodge in the principal registry a statement in reply and serve a copy thereof on the defendant.

Hearing

6.8 Any application under the Act (other than an application (a) to join a defendant, (b) to dispense with service or extend the time for acknowledging service, or (c) for the transfer of proceedings) shall be heard and determined by a judge and shall be dealt with in chambers unless the court otherwise directs.

Dispensing with service

6.9 The court may dispense with service of any summons (whether originating or ordinary) in any proceedings under the Act.

Adjournment of summons

6.10 The hearing of the originating summons under which an application under the Hague Convention or the European Convention is made may be adjourned for a period not exceeding 21 days at any one time.

Stay of proceedings

6.11–(1) A party to proceedings under the Hague Convention shall, where he knows that an application relating to the merits of rights of custody is pending in or before a relevant authority, file in the principal registry a concise statement of the nature of the application which is pending, including the authority before which it is pending.

(2) A party–

(a) to pending proceedings under section 16 of the Act, or

(b) to proceedings as a result of which a decision relating to custody has been registered under section 16 of the Act,

shall, where he knows that such an application as is specified in section 20(2) of the Act or section 42(2) of the Child Custody Act 1987 (an Act of Tynwald) is pending in or before a relevant authority, file a concise statement of the nature of the application which is pending.

(3) The proper officer shall on receipt of such a statement as is mentioned in paragraph (1) or (2) notify the relevant authority in which or before whom the application is pending and shall subsequently notify it or him of the result of the proceedings.

(4) On the court receiving notification under paragraph (3) above or equivalent notification from the Court of Session, the High Court in Northern Ireland or the High Court of Justice of the Isle of Man–

(a) where the application relates to the merits of rights of custody, all further proceedings in the action shall be stayed unless and until the proceedings under the Hague Convention in the High Court, Court of Session, High Court in Northern Ireland or the High Court of Justice of the Isle of Man as the case may, are dismissed, and the parties to the action shall be notified by the proper officer of the stay and of any such dismissal accordingly, and

(b) where the application is such a one as is specified in section 20(2) of the Act, the proper officer shall notify the parties to the action.

(5) In this rule 'relevant authority' includes the High Court, a county court, a magistrates' court, the Court of Session, a sheriff court, a children's hearing within the meaning of Part III of the Social Work (Scotland) Act 1968, the High Court in Northern Ireland, a county court in Northern Ireland, a court of summary jurisdiction in Northern Ireland, the High Court of Justice of the Isle of Man, a court of summary jurisdiction in the Isle of Man or the Secretary of State.

Transfer of proceedings

6.12–(1) At any stage in the proceedings under the Act the court may, of its own motion or on the application by summons of any party to the proceedings issued on two days' notice, order that the proceedings be transferred to the Court of Session, the High Court in Northern Ireland or the High Court of Justice of the Isle of Man.

(2) Where an order is made under paragraph (1) the proper officer shall send a copy of the order, which shall state the grounds therefor, together with the originating summons, the documents accompanying it and any evidence, to the Court of Session, the High Court in Northern Ireland or the High Court of Justice of the Isle of Man as the case may be.

(3) Where proceedings are transferred to the Court of Session, the High Court in Northern Ireland or the High Court of Justice of the Isle of Man the costs of the whole proceedings both before and after the transfer shall be at the discretion of the Court to which the proceedings are transferred.

(4) Where proceedings are transferred to the High Court from the Court of Session, the High Court in Northern Ireland or the High Court of Justice of the Isle of Man the proper officer shall notify the parties of the transfer and the proceedings shall continue as if they had begun by originating summons under rule 6.2.

Interim directions

6.13 An application for interim directions under section 5 or section 19 of the Act may where the case is one of urgency be made ex parte on affidavit but shall otherwise be made by summons.

6.14 [*Not reproduced*]

Revocation and variation of registered decisions

6.15–(1) This rule applies to decisions which have been registered under section 16 of the Act and are subsequently varied or revoked by an authority in the Contracting State in which they were made.

(2) The court shall, on cancelling the registration of a decision which has been revoked, notify–

(a) the person appearing to the court to have care of the child;

(b) the person on whose behalf the application for registration of the decision was made; and

(c) and other party to that application,

of the cancellation.

(3) The court shall, on being notified of the variation of a decision, notify–

(a) the person appearing to the court to have care of the child; and

(b) any party to the application for registration of the decision,

of the variation and any such person may apply by summons in the proceedings for the registration of the decision, for the purpose of making representations to the court before the registration is varied.

(4) Any person appearing to the court to have an interest in the matter may apply by summons in the proceedings for the registration of a decision for the cancellation or variation of the registration.

Orders for disclosure of information

6.16 At any stage in proceedings under the European Convention the court may, if it has reason to believe that any person may have relevant information about the child who is the subject of those proceedings, order that person to disclose such information and may for that purpose order that the person attend before it or file affidavit evidence.

Applications and Orders under sections 33 and 34 of the Family Law Act 1986

6.17–(1) In this rule 'the 1986 Act' means the Family Law Act 1986.

(2) An application under section 33 of the 1986 Act shall be in Form C4 and an order made under that section shall be in Form C30.

(3) An application under section 34 of the 1986 Act shall be in Form C3 and an order made under that section shall be in Form C31.

(4) An application under section 33 or section 34 of the 1986 Act may be made ex parte in which case the applicant shall file the application–
(a) where the application is made by telephone, within 24 hours after the making of the application, or
(b) in any other case at the time when the application is made,
and shall serve a copy of the application on each respondent 48 hours after the making of the order.

(5) Where the court refuses to make an order on an ex parte application it may direct that the application be made inter partes.

PART VII – ENFORCEMENT OF ORDERS

Chapter 3   Registration and enforcement of custody orders

Registration under the Family Law Act 1986

7.7–(1) In this Chapter, unless context otherwise requires–
'the appropriate court', means in relation to Scotland, the Court of Session and, in relation to Northern Ireland, the High Court in Northern Ireland and, in relation to a specified dependent territory, the corresponding Court in that territory;
'the appropriate officer' means, in relation to the Court of Session, the Deputy Principal Clerk of Session, in relation to the High Court in Northern Ireland, the Master (Care and Protection) of that court and, in relation to the appropriate court in a specified dependent territory, the corresponding officer of that court;
'Part I order' means an order under Part I of the Act of 1986;

'the Master' means the Master (Care and Protection) of the High Court in Northern Ireland;

'registration' means registration under Part I of the Act of 1986, and 'register' and 'registered' shall be construed accordingly;

'specified dependent territory' means a dependent territory specified in column 1 of Schedule 1 to the Family Law Act 1986 (Specified Dependent Territories) Order 1991.

(2) The prescribed officer for the purposes of sections 27(4) and 28(1) of the Act shall be the family proceedings department manager of the principal registry and the functions of the court under sections 27(3) and 28(1) of the Act of 1986 shall be performed by the proper officer.

Application to register English Part I order

7.8–(1) An application under section 27 of the Act of 1986 for the registration of a Part I order made by the High Court shall be made by lodging in the principal registry or the district registry, as the case may be, a certified copy of the order, together with a copy of any order which has varied any of the terms of the original order and an affidavit by the applicant in support of his application, with a copy thereof.

(2) An application under section 27 of the Act of 1986 for the registration of a Part I order made by a county court shall be made by filing in that court a certified copy of the order, together with a certified copy of any order which has varied any of the terms of the original order and an affidavit in support of the application, with a copy thereof.

(3) The affidavit in support under paragraphs (1) and (2) above shall state—

(a) the name and address of the applicant and his interest under the order;

(b) the name and date of birth of the child in respect of whom the order was made, his whereabouts or suspected whereabouts and the name of any person with whom he is alleged to be;

(c) the name and address of any other person who has an interest under the order and whether it has been served on him;

(d) in which of the jurisdictions of Scotland, Northern Ireland or a specified dependent territory the order is to be registered;

(e) that, to the best of the applicant's information and belief, the order is in force;

(f) whether, and if so where, the order is already registered; and

(g) details of any order known to the applicant which affects the child and is in force in the jurisdiction in which the Part I order is to be registered;

and there shall be exhibited to the affidavit any document relevant to the application.

(4) Where the documents referred to in paragraphs (1) and (3), or (2) and (3), as the case may be are to be sent to the appropriate court, the proper officer shall—

(a) retain the original affidavit and send the other documents to the appropriate officer;

(b) record the fact of transmission in the records of the court; and

(c) file a copy of the documents.

(5) On receipt of notice of the registration of a Part I order in the appropriate court the proper officer shall record the fact of registration in the records of the court.

(6) If it appears to the proper officer that the Part I order is no longer in force or that the child has attained the age of 16, he shall refuse to send the documents to the appropriate court and shall within 14 days of such refusal give notice of it, and the reason for it, to the applicant.

(7) If the proper officer refuses to send the documents to the appropriate court, the applicant may apply to the judge in chambers for an order that the documents (or any of them) be sent to the appropriate court.

Registration of orders made in Scotland, Northern Ireland or a specified dependent territory

7.9 On receipt of a certified copy of an order made in Scotland, Northern Ireland or a specified dependent territory for registration, the prescribed officer shall—

(a) record the order in the register by entering particulars of—

    (i) the name and address of the applicant and his interest under the order;

    (ii) the name and whereabouts or suspected whereabouts of the child, his date of birth, and the date on which he will attain the age of 16; and

    (iii) the terms of the order, its date and the court which made it;

(b) file the certified copy and accompanying documents; and

(c) give notice to the court which sent the certified copy and to the applicant for registration that the order has been registered.

Revocation and variation of English order

7.10–(1) Where a Part I order which is registered in the appropriate court is revoked or varied, the proper officer of the court making the subsequent order shall—

(a) send a certified copy of that order to the appropriate officer, and to the court which made the Part I order, if that court is different from the court making the subsequent order, for filing by that court;

(b) record the fact of transmission in the records of the court; and

(c) file a copy of the order.

(2) On receipt of notice from the appropriate court of the amendment of its register, the proper officers of the court which made the Part I order and of the court which made the subsequent order shall each record the fact of amendment.

Registration of revoked, recalled or varied orders made in Scotland, Northern Ireland or a specified dependent territory

7.11–(1) On receipt of a certified copy of an order made in Scotland, Northern Ireland or specified dependent territory which revokes, recalls or varies a registered Part I order, the proper officer shall enter particulars of the revocation, recall or variation, as the case may be, in the register, and give notice of the entry to–

(a) the court which sent the certified copy;

(b) if different, the court which made the Part I order;

(c) the applicant for registration; and

(d) if different, the applicant for the revocation, recall or variation of the order.

(2) An application under section 28(2) of the Act of 1986 shall be made by summons and may be heard and determined by a district judge.

(3) If the applicant for the Part I order is not the applicant under section 28(2) of the Act of 1986 he shall be made a defendant to the application.

(4) Where the court cancels a registration of its own motion or on an application under paragraph (2), the proper officer shall amend the register accordingly and shall give notice of the amendment to the court which made the Part I order.

Interim directions

7.12–(1) An application for interim directions under section 29 of the Act of 1986 may be heard and determined by a district judge.

(2) The parties to the proceedings for enforcement and, if he is not a party thereto, the applicant for the Part I order, shall be made parties to the application.

Staying and dismissal of enforcement proceedings

7.13–(1) An application under section 30(1) or 31(1) of the Act of 1986 may be heard and determined by a district judge.

(2) The parties to the proceedings for enforcement which are sought to be stayed and, if he is not a party thereto, the applicant for the Part I order shall be made parties to an application under either of the said sections.

(3) Where the court makes an order under section 30(2) or (3) or section 31(3) of the Act of 1986, the proper officer shall amend the register accordingly and shall give notice of the amendment to the court which made the Part I order and to the applicants for registration, for enforcement and for the stay or dismissal of the proceedings for enforcement.

Particulars of other proceedings

7.14 A party to proceedings for or relating to a Part I order who knows of other proceedings (including proceedings out of the jurisdiction and concluded proceedings) which relate to the child concerned shall file an affidavit stating–

(a) in which jurisdiction and court the other proceedings were instituted;

(b) the nature and current state of such proceedings and the relief claimed or granted;

(c) the names of the parties to such proceedings and their relationship to the child; and

(d) if applicable, and if known, the reasons why the relief claimed in the proceedings for or relating to the Part I order was not claimed in the other proceedings.

Inspection of register

7.15 The following persons, namely—

(a) the applicant for registration of a registered Part I order;

(b) any person who satisfies a district judge that he has an interest under the Part I order; and

(c) any person who obtains the leave of a district judge,

may inspect any entry in the register relating to the order and may bespeak copies of the order and of any document relating thereto.

PART VIII – APPEALS

Appeals from district judges

8.1–(1) Except where paragraph (2) applies, any party may appeal from an order or decision made or given by the district judge in family proceedings in a county court to a judge on notice; and in such a case—

(a) CCR Order 13, rule 1(10) (which enables the judge to vary or rescind an order made by the district judge in the course of proceedings), and

(b) CCR Order 37, rule 6 (which gives a right of appeal to the judge from a judgment or final decision of the district judge),

shall not apply to the order or decision.

(2) Any order or decision granting or varying an order (or refusing to do so)—

(a) on an application for ancillary relief, or

(b) in proceedings to which rules 3.1, 3.2, 3.3, 3.6 or 3.8 apply,

shall be treated as a final order for the purposes of CCR Order 37, rule 6.

(3) On hearing an appeal to which paragraph (2) above applies, the judge may exercise his own discretion in substitution for that of the district judge.

(4) Unless the court otherwise orders, any notice under this rule must be issued within 14 days of the order or decision appealed against and served not less than 14 days before the day fixed for the hearing of the appeal.

(5) Appeals under this rule shall be heard in chambers unless the judge otherwise directs.

(6) Unless the court otherwise orders, an appeal under this rule shall not operate as a stay of proceedings on the order or decision appealed against.

Appeals from orders made under Part IV of the Family Law Act 1996

8.1A–(1) This rule applies to all appeals from orders made under Part IV of

the Family Law Act 1996 and on such an appeal–
(a) paragraphs (2), (3), (4), (5), (7) and (8) of rule 4.22,
(b) paragraphs (5) and (6) of rule 8.1, and
(c) paragraphs (4)(e) and (6) of rule 8.2
shall apply subject to the following provisions of this rule and with the necessary modifications.

(2) The justices' clerk of the magistrates' court from which an appeal is brought shall be served with the documents mentioned in rule 4.22(2).

(3) Where an appeal lies to the High Court, the documents required to be filed by rule 4.22(2) shall be filed in the registry of the High Court which is nearest to the magistrates' court from which the appeal is brought.

(4) Where the appeal is brought against the making of a hospital order or a guardianship order under the Mental Health Act 1983, a copy of any written evidence considered by the magistrates' court under section 37(1)(a) of the 1983 Act shall be sent by the justices' clerk to the registry of the High Court in which the documents relating to the appeal are filed in accordance with paragraph (3).

(5) A district judge may dismiss an appeal to which this rule applies for want of prosecution and may deal with any question of costs arising out of the dismissal or withdrawal of an appeal.

(6) Any order or decision granting or varying an order (or refusing to do so) in proceedings in which in application is made in accordance with rule 3.8 for–
(a) an occupation order as described in section 33(4) of the Family Law Act 1996,
(b) an occupation order containing any of the provisions specified in section 33(3) where the applicant or the respondent has matrimonial home rights, or
(c) a transfer of tenancy,
shall be treated as a final order for the purposes of CCR Order 37, rule 6 and, on an appeal from such an order, the judge may exercise his own discretion in substitution for that of the district judge and the provisions of CCR Order 37, rule 6 shall apply.

PART IX – DISABILITY

Person under disability must sue by next friend etc
9.2–(1) Except where rule 9.2A or any other rule otherwise provides, a person under disability may begin and prosecute any family proceedings only by his next friend and may defend any such proceedings only by his guardian ad litem and, except as otherwise provided by this rule, it shall not be necessary for a guardian ad litem to be appointed by the court.

(2) No person's name shall be used in any proceedings as next friend of a per son under disability unless he is the Official Solicitor or the documents mentioned in paragraph (7) have been filed.

(3) Where a person is authorised under Part VII to conduct legal proceedings in the name of a patient or on his behalf, that person shall, subject to paragraph (2), be entitled to be next friend or guardian ad litem of the patient in any family proceedings to which his authority extends.

(4) Where a person entitled to defend any family proceedings is a patient and there is no person authorised under Part VII to defend the proceedings in his name or on his behalf, then–

(a) the Official Solicitor shall, if he consents, be the patient's guardian ad litem, but at any stage of the proceedings an application may be made on not less than four days' notice to the Official Solicitor, for the appointment of some other person as guardian;

(b) in any other case, an application may be made on behalf of the patient for the appointment of a guardian ad litem;

and there shall be filed in support of any application under this paragraph the documents mentioned in paragraph (7).

(5) Where a petition, answer, originating application or originating summons has been served on a person whom there is reasonable ground for believing to be a person under disability and no notice of intention to defend has been given, or answer or affidavit in answer filed, on his behalf, the party at whose instance the document was served shall, before taking any further steps in the proceedings, apply to a district judge for directions as to whether a guardian ad litem should be appointed to act for that person in the cause, and on any such application the district judge may, if he considers it necessary in order to protect the interests of the person served, order that some proper person be appointed his guardian ad litem.

(6) Except where a minor is prosecuting or defending proceedings under rule 9.2A, no notice of intention to defend shall be given, or answer or affidavit in answer filed, by or on behalf of a person under disability unless the person giving the notice or filing the answer or affidavit–

(a) is the Official Solicitor or, in a case to which paragraph (4) applies, is the Official Solicitor or has been appointed by the court to be guardian ad litem; or

(b) in any other case, has filed the documents mentioned in paragraph (7).

(7) The documents referred to in paragraphs (2), (4) and (6) are–

(a) a written consent to act by the proposed next friend or guardian ad litem;

(b) where the person under disability is a patient and the proposed next friend or guardian ad litem is authorised under Part VII to conduct the proceedings in his name or on his behalf, an office copy, sealed with the seal of the Court of Protection, of the order or other authorisation made or given under Part VII; and

(c) except where the proposed next friend or guardian ad litem is authorised as mentioned in sub-paragraph (b), a certificate by the solicitor acting for the person under disability–

(i) that he knows or believes that the person to whom the certificate relates is a minor or patient, stating (in the case of a patient) the grounds of his knowledge or belief and, where the person under disability is a patient, that there is no person authorised as aforesaid, and

(ii) that the person named in the certificate as next friend or guardian ad litem has no interest in the cause or matter in question adverse to that of the person under disability and that he is a proper person to be next friend or guardian.

Certain minors may sue without next friend etc

9.2A–(1) Where a person entitled to begin, prosecute or defend any proceedings to which this rule applies, is a minor to whom this Part applies, he may, subject to paragraph (4), begin, prosecute or defend, as the case may be, such proceedings without a next friend or guardian ad litem—

(a) where he has obtained the leave of the court for that purpose; or

(b) where a solicitor—

(i) considers that the minor is able, having regard to his understanding, to give instructions in relation to the proceedings; and

(ii) has accepted instructions from the minor to act for him in the proceedings and, where the proceedings have begun, is so acting.

(2) A minor shall be entitled to apply for the leave of the court under paragraph (1)(a) without a next friend or guardian ad litem either—

(a) by filing a written request for leave setting out the reasons for the application, or

(b) by making an oral request for leave at any hearing in the proceedings.

(3) On considering a request for leave filed under paragraph (2)(a), the court shall either—

(a) grant the request, whereupon the proper officer shall communicate the decision to the minor and, where the leave relates to the prosecution or defence of existing proceedings, to the other parties to those proceedings, or

(b) direct that the request be heard ex parte, whereupon the proper officer shall fix a date for such a hearing and give to the minor making the request such notice of the date so fixed as the court may direct.

(4) Where a minor has a next friend or guardian ad litem in proceedings and the minor wishes to prosecute or defend the remaining stages of the proceedings without a next friend or guardian ad litem, the minor may apply to the court for leave for that purpose and for the removal of the next friend or guardian ad litem; and paragraph (2) shall apply to the application as if it were an application under paragraph (1)(a).

(5) On considering a request filed under paragraph (2) by virtue of paragraph (4), the court shall either—

(a) grant the request, whereupon the proper officer shall communicate the decision to the minor and next friend or guardian ad litem concerned and to all other parties to the proceedings, or

(b) direct that the request be heard, whereupon the proper officer shall fix a date for such a hearing and give to the minor and next friend or guardian ad litem concerned such notice of the date so fixed as the court may direct;

provided that the court may act under sub-paragraph (a) only if it is satisfied that the next friend or guardian ad litem does not oppose the request.

(6) Where the court is considering whether to—

(a) grant leave under paragraph (1)(a), or

(b) grant leave under paragraph (4) and remove a next friend or guardian ad litem,

it shall grant the leave sought and, as the case may be, remove the next friend or guardian ad litem if it considers that the minor concerned has sufficient understanding to participate as a party in the proceedings concerned or proposed without a next friend or guardian ad litem.

(7) Where a request for leave is granted at a hearing fixed under paragraph (3)(b) (in relation to the prosecution or defence of proceedings already begun) or (5)(b), the proper officer shall forthwith communicate the decision to the other parties to the proceedings.

(8) The court may revoke any leave granted under paragraph (1)(a) where it considers that the child does not have sufficient understanding to participate as a party in the proceedings concerned without a next friend or guardian ad litem.

(9) Without prejudice to any requirement of CCR Order 50, rule 5 or RSC Order 67, where a solicitor is acting for a minor in proceedings which the minor is prosecuting or defending without a next friend or guardian ad litem by virtue of paragraph (1)(6) and either of the conditions specified in paragraph (1)(b)(i)and (ii)cease to be fulfilled, he shall forthwith so inform the court.

(10) Where—

(a) the court revokes any leave under paragraph (8), or

(b) either of the conditions specified in paragraph (1)(b)(i) and (ii) is no longer fulfilled,

the court may, if it considers it necessary in order to protect the interests of the minor concerned, order that some proper person be appointed his next friend or guardian ad litem.

(11) Where a minor is of sufficient understanding to begin, prosecute or defend proceedings without a next friend or guardian ad litem—

(a) he may nevertheless begin, prosecute or defend them by his next friend or guardian ad litem; and

(b) where he is prosecuting or defending proceedings by his next friend or guardian ad litem, the respective powers and duties of the minor and next friend or guardian ad litem, except those conferred or imposed by this rule, shall not be affected by the minor's ability to dispense with a next friend or guardian ad litem under the provisions of this rule.

Service on person under disability

9.3–(1) Where a document to which rule 2.9 applies is required to be served on a person under disability, it shall be served–
(a) in the case of a minor who is not also a patient, on his father or guardian or, if he has no father or guardian, on the person with whom he resides or in whose care he is;
(b) in the case of a patient–
  (i) on the person (if any) who is authorised under Part VII to conduct in the name of the patient or on his behalf the proceedings in connection with which the document is to be served, or
  (ii) if there is no person so authorised, on the Official Solicitor if he has consented under rule 9.2(4) to be the guardian ad litem of the patient, or
  (iii) in any other case, on the person with whom the patient resides or in whose care he is–
  Provided that the court may order that a document which has been, or is to be, served on the person under disability or on a person other than one mentioned in sub-paragraph (a) or (b) shall be deemed to be duly served on the person under disability.

(2) Where a document is served in accordance with paragraph (1) it shall be indorsed with a notice in Form M24; and after service has been effected the person at whose instance the document was served shall, unless the Official Solicitor is the guardian ad litem of the person under disability or the court otherwise directs, file an affidavit by the person on whom the document was served stating whether the contents of the document were, or its purport was, communicated to the person under disability and, if not, the reasons for not doing so.

Separate representation of children

9.5–(1) Without prejudice to rules 2.57 and 9.2A, if in any family proceedings it appears to the court that any child ought to be separately represented, the court may appoint–
(a) the Official Solicitor, or
(b) some other proper person,
(provided, in either case, that he consents) to be the guardian ad litem of the child, with authority to take part in the proceedings on the child's behalf.

(2) An order under paragraph (1) may be made by the court of its own motion or on the application of a party to the proceedings or of the proposed guardian ad litem.

(3) The court may at any time direct that an application be made by a party for an order under paragraph (1) and may stay the proceedings until the application has been made.

(4) Unless otherwise directed, on making an application for an order under paragraph (1) the applicant shall–

(a) unless he is the proposed guardian ad litem, file a written consent by the proposed guardian to act as such;

(b) unless the proposed guardian ad litem is the Official Solicitor, file a certificate by a solicitor that the proposed guardian has no interest in the proceedings adverse to that of the child and that he is a proper person to be a guardian.

(5) Unless otherwise directed, a person appointed under this rule or rule 2.57 to be the guardian ad litem of a child in any family proceedings shall be treated as a party for the purpose of any provision of these rules requiring a document to be served on or notice to be given to a party to the proceedings.

Extracts from the Family Proceedings Courts (Children Act 1989) Rules 1991 SI No 1395

The following rules are reproduced in this section.

PART II – GENERAL

Application for leave to commence proceedings

3–(1) Where the leave of the court is required to bring any relevant proceedings, the person seeking leave shall file–

(a) a written request for leave in Form C2 setting out the reasons for the application; and

(b) a draft of the application (being the documents referred to in rule 4(1A)) for the making of which leave is sought together with sufficient copies for one to be served on each respondent.

(2) On considering a request for leave filed under paragraph (1), the court shall—

(a) grant the request, whereupon the justices' clerk shall inform the person making the request of the decision, or

(b) direct that a date be fixed for a hearing of the request, whereupon the justices' clerk shall fix such a date and give such notice as the court directs to the person making the request and to such other persons as the court requires to be notified, of the date so fixed.

(3) Where leave is granted to bring any relevant proceedings, the application shall proceed in accordance with rule 4; but paragraph (1)(a) of that rule shall not apply.

Application

4–(1) Subject to paragraph (4), an applicant shall—

(a) file the documents referred to in paragraph (1A) below (which docu- -ments shall together be called the 'application') together with sufficient copies for one to be served on each respondent, and

(b) serve a copy of the application together with Form C6 and such (if any) of Forms C7 and C10A as are given to him by the justices' clerks under paragraph (2)(b), on each respondent such minimum number of days prior to the date fixed under paragraph (2)(a) as is specified in relation to that application in column (ii) of Schedule 2 to these Rules.

(1A) The documents to be filed under paragraph (1)(a) above are—

(a) (i)   whichever is appropriate of Forms C1 to C5 or C51, and

(ii)   such of the supplemental Forms C10 or C11 to C20 as may be appropriate, or

(b) where there is no appropriate form a statement in writing of the order sought,

and where the application is made in respect of more than one child, all the children shall be included in one application.

(2) On receipt of the documents filed under paragraph (1)(a), the justices' clerk shall—

(a) fix the date, time and place for a hearing or a directions appointment allowing sufficient time for the applicant to comply with paragraph (1) (b),

(b) endorse the date, time and place so fixed upon Form C6, and where appropriate, Form C6A, and

(c) return forthwith to the applicant the copies of the application and Form C10A if filed with it, together with Form C6 and such of Forms C6A and C7 as are appropriate.

(3) The applicant shall, at the same time as complying with paragraph (1) (b), serve Form C6A on the persons set out in relation to the relevant class of proceedings in column (iv) of Schedule 2 to these Rules.

(4) An application for—
(a) section 8 order,
(b) an emergency protection order,
(c) a warrant under section 48(9),
(d) a recovery order, or
(e) a warrant under section 102(1),
may, with leave of the justices' clerk, be made ex parte in which case the applicant shall—
(i) file with the justices' clerk or the court the application in the appropriate form in Schedule 1 to these Rules at the time when the application is made or as directed by the justices' clerk, and
(ii) in the case of an application under section 8 or an emergency protection order, and also in the case of an application for an order under section 75(1) where the application is ex parte, serve a copy of the application on each respondent within 48 hours after the making of the order.

(5) Where the court refuses to make an order on an ex parte application it may direct that the application be made inter partes.

(6) In the case of proceedings under Schedule 1, the application under paragraph (1) shall be accompanied by a statement in Form C10A setting out the financial details which the applicant believes to be relevant to the application together with sufficient copies for one to be served on each respondent.

Withdrawal of application

5–(1) An application may be withdrawn only with leave of the court.

(2) Subject to paragraph (3), a person seeking leave to withdraw an application shall file and serve on the parties a written request for leave setting out the reasons for the request.

(3) The request under paragraph (2) may be made orally to the court if the parties and, if appointed, the guardian ad litem or the welfare officer are present.

(4) Upon receipt of a written request under paragraph (2), the court shall
(a) if—
    (i) the parties consent in writing,
    (ii) any guardian ad litem has had an opportunity to make representations, and
    (iii) the court thinks fit,
    grant the request; in which case the justices' clerk shall notify the parties, the guardian ad litem and the welfare officer of the granting of the request; or
(b) the justices' clerk shall fix a date for the hearing of the request and give at least 7 days' notice to the parties, the guardian ad litem and the welfare officer of the date fixed.

Transfer of proceedings

6–(1) Where, in any relevant proceedings, the justices' clerk or the court receives a request in writing from a party that the proceedings be transferred to another family proceedings court or to a county court, the justices' clerk or court shall issue an order or certificate in the appropriate form in Schedule 1 to these Rules, granting or refusing the request in accordance with any Order made by the Lord Chancellor under Part I of Schedule 11.

(2) Where a request is granted under paragraph (1), the justices' clerk shall send a copy of the order–

(a) to the parties,

(b) to any guardian ad litem, and

(c) to the family proceedings court or to the county court to which the proceedings are to be transferred.

(3) Any consent given or refused by a justices' clerk in accordance with any Order made by the Lord Chancellor under Part I of Schedule 11 shall be recorded in writing by the justices' clerk at the time it is given or refused or as soon as practicable thereafter.

(4) Where a request to transfer proceedings to a county court is refused under paragraph (1), the person who made the request may apply in accordance with rule 4.6 of the Family Proceedings Rules 1991 for an order under any Order made by the Lord Chancellor under Part I of Schedule 11.

Parties

7–(1) The respondents to relevant proceedings shall be those persons set out in the relevant entry in column (iii) of Schedule 2 to these Rules.

(2) In any relevant proceedings a person may file a request in Form C2 that he or another person–

(a) be joined as a party, or

(b) cease to be a party.

(3) On considering a request under paragraph (2) the court shall, subject to paragraph (4)–

(a) grant it without a hearing or representations, save that this shall be done only in the case of a request under paragraph (2)(a), whereupon the justices' clerk shall inform the parties and the person making the request of that decision, or

(b) order that a date be fixed for the consideration of the request, whereupon the justices' clerk shall give notice of the date so fixed, together with a copy of the request–

   (i) in the case of a request under paragraph (2)(a), to the applicant, and

   (ii) in the case of a request under paragraph (2)(b), to the parties, or

(c) invite the parties or any of them to make written representations, within a specified period, as to whether the request should be granted; and upon the expiry of the period the court shall act in accordance with sub-paragraph (a) or (b).

(4) Where a person with parental responsibility requests that he be joined under paragraph (2)(a), the court shall grant his request.

(5) In any relevant proceedings the court may direct–

(a) that a person who would not otherwise be a respondent under these Rules be joined as a party to the proceedings, or
(b) that a party to the proceedings cease to be a party.

Service

8–(1) Where service of a document is required by these Rules (and not by a provision to which section 105(8) (service of notice or other document under the Act) applies) it may be effected–
(a) if the person to be served is not known by the person serving to be acting by solicitor–
  (i) by delivering it to him personally, or
  (ii) by delivering it at, or by sending it by first-class post to, his residence or his last known residence, or
(b) if the person to be served is known by the person serving to be acting by solicitor–
  (i) by delivering the document at, or sending it by first-class post to, the solicitor's address for service,
  (ii) where the solicitor's address for service includes a numbered box at a document exchange, by leaving the document at that document exchange or at a document exchange which transmits documents on every business day to that document exchange, or
  (iii) by sending a legible copy of the document by facsimile transmission to the solicitor's office.

(2) In this rule, 'first-class post' means first-class post which has been pre-paid or in respect of which pre-payment is not required.

(3) Where a child who is a party to any relevant proceedings is required by these Rules to serve a document, service shall be effected by–
(a) the solicitor acting for the child,
(b) where there is no such solicitor, the guardian ad litem, or
(c) where there is neither such a solicitor nor a guardian ad litem, the justices' clerk.

(4) Service of any document on a child shall, subject to any direction of the justices' clerk or the court, be effected by service on–
(a) the solicitor acting for the child,
(b) where there is no such solicitor, the guardian ad litem, or
(c) where there is neither such a solicitor nor a guardian ad litem, with leave of the justices' clerk or the court, the child.

(5) Where the justices' clerk or the court refuses leave under paragraph (4)(c), a direction shall be given under paragraph (8).

(6) A document shall, unless the contrary is proved, be deemed to have been served–
(a) in the case of service by first-class post, on the second business day after posting, and
(b) in the case of service in accordance with paragraph (1)(b)(ii), on the second business day after the day on which it is left at the document exchange.

(7) At or before the first directions appointment in, or hearing of, relevant proceedings, whichever occurs first, the applicant shall file a statement in Form C9 that service of–

(a) a copy of the application and other documents referred to in rule 4(1)(b) has been effected on each respondent, and

(b) notice of the proceedings has been effected under rule 4(3);

and the statement shall indicate–

    (i) the manner, date, time and place of service, or

    (ii) where service was effected by post, the date, time and place of posting.

(8) In any relevant proceedings, where these rules require a document to be served, the court or the justices' clerk may, without prejudice to any power under rule 14, direct that–

(a) the requirement shall not apply;

(b) the time specified by the rules for complying with the requirement shall be abridged to such extent as may be specified in the direction;

(c) service shall be effected in such manner as may be specified in the direction.

Acknowledgement of application

9 Within 14 days of service of an application for a section 8 order or an application under Schedule 1, each respondent shall file and serve on the parties an acknowledgement of the application in Form C7.

Appointment of guardian ad litem

10–(1) As soon as practicable after the commencement of specified proceedings or the transfer of such proceedings to the court, the justices' clerk or the court shall appoint a guardian ad litem unless–

(a) such an appointment has already been made by the court which made the transfer and is subsisting, or

(b) the justices' clerk or the court considers that such an appointment is not necessary to safeguard the interests of the child.

(2) At any stage in specified proceedings a party may apply, without notice to the other parties unless the justices' clerk or the court otherwise directs, for the appointment of a guardian ad litem.

(3) The justices' clerk or the court shall grant an application under paragraph (2) unless it is considered that such an appointment is not necessary to safeguard the interests of the child, in which case reasons shall be given; and a note of such reasons shall be taken by the justices' clerk.

(4) At any stage in specified proceedings the justices' clerk or the court may appoint a guardian ad litem even though no application is made for such an appointment.

(5) The justices' clerk shall, as soon as practicable, notify the parties and any welfare officer of an appointment under this rule or, as the case may be, of a decision not to make such an appointment.

(6) Upon the appointment of a guardian ad litem the justices' clerk shall, as soon as practicable, notify him of the appointment and serve on him copies of the application and of documents filed under rule 17(1).

(7) A guardian ad litem appointed from a panel established by regulations made under section 41(7) shall not–

(a) be a member, officer or servant of a local authority which, or an authorised person (within the meaning of section 31(9)) who, is a party to the proceedings unless he is employed by such an authority solely as a member of a panel of guardians ad litem and reporting officers;

(b) be, or have been, a member, officer or servant of a local authority or voluntary organisation (within the meaning of section 105(1)) who has been directly concerned in that capacity in arrangements relating to the care, accommodation or welfare of the child during the five years prior to the commencement of the proceedings;

(c) be a serving probation officer (except that a probation officer who has not in that capacity been previously concerned with the child or his family and who is employed part-time may, when not engaged in his duties as a probation officer, act as a guardian ad litem).

(8) When appointing a guardian ad litem, the justices' clerk or the court shall consider the appointment of anyone who has previously acted as guardian ad litem of the same child.

(9) The appointment of a guardian ad litem under this rule shall continue for such time as is specified in the appointment or until terminated by the court.

(10) When terminating an appointment in accordance with paragraph (9), the court shall give reasons in writing for so doing, a note of which shall be taken by the justices' clerk.

(11) Where the justices' clerk or the court appoints a guardian ad litem in accordance with this rule or refuses to make such an appointment, the justices' clerk shall record the appointment or refusal in the appropriate form in Schedule 1 to these Rules.

Powers and duties of guardian ad litem

11–(1) In carrying out his duty under section 41(2), the guardian ad litem shall have regard to the principle set out in section 1(2) and the matters set out in section 1(3)(a) to (f) as if for the word 'court' in that section there were substituted the words 'guardian ad litem'.

(2) The guardian ad litem shall–

(a) appoint a solicitor to represent the child, unless such a solicitor has already been appointed, and

(b) give such advice to the child as is appropriate having regard to his understanding and, subject to rule 12(1)(a), instruct the solicitor representing the child on all matters relevant to the interests of the child, including possibilities for appeal, arising in the course of the proceedings.

(3) Where it appears to the guardian ad litem that the child–

(a) is instructing his solicitor direct, or

(b) intends to, and is capable of, conducting the proceedings on his own behalf, he shall so inform the court through the justices' clerk and thereafter–

  (i) shall perform all of his duties set out in this rule, other than duties under paragraph (2)(a) and such other duties as the justices' clerk or the court may direct,

  (ii) shall take such part in the proceedings as the justices' clerk or the court may direct, and

  (iii) may, with leave of the justices' clerk or the court, have legal representation in his conduct of those duties.

(4) The guardian ad litem shall, unless excused by the justices' clerk or the court, attend all directions appointments in, and hearings of, the proceedings and shall advise the justices' clerk or the court on the following matters–

(a) whether the child is of sufficient understanding for any purpose including the child's refusal to submit to a medical or psychiatric examination or other assessment that the court has power to require, direct or order;

(b) the wishes of the child in respect of any matter relevant to the proceedings, including his attendance at court;

(c) the appropriate forum for the proceedings;

(d) the appropriate timing of the proceedings or any part of them;

(e) the options available to it in respect of the child and the suitability of each such option including what order should be made in determining the application;

(f) any other matter concerning which the justices' clerk or the court seeks his advice or concerning which he considers that the justices' clerk or the court should be informed.

(5) The advice given under paragraph (4) may, subject to any order of the court, be given orally or in writing; and if the advice be given orally, a note of it shall be taken by the justices' clerk or the court.

(6) The guardian ad litem shall, where practicable, notify any person whose joinder as a party to those proceedings would be likely, in the guardian ad litem's opinion, to safeguard the interests of the child, of that person's right to apply to be joined under rule 7(2) and shall inform the justices' clerk or the court–

(a) of any such notification given,

(b) of anyone whom he attempted to notify under this paragraph but was unable to contact, and

(c) of anyone whom he believes may wish to bejoined to the proceedings.

(7) The guardian ad litem shall, unless the justices' clerk or the court otherwise directs, not less than 7 days before the date fixed for the final hearing of the proceedings, file a written report advising on the interests of the child; and the justices' clerk shall, as soon as practicable, serve a copy of the report on the parties.

(8) The guardian ad litem shall serve and accept service of documents on behalf of the child in accordance with rule 8(3)(b) and (4)(b) and, where the child has not himself been served, and has sufficient understanding, advise the child of the contents of any documents so served.

(9) The guardian ad litem shall make such investigations as may be necessary for him to carry out his duties and shall, in particular–

(a) contact or seek to interview such persons as he thinks appropriate or as the court directs,

(b) if he inspects records of the kinds referred to in section 42, bring to the attention of the court, through the justices' clerk, and such other persons as the justices' clerk or the court may direct, all such records and documents which may, in his opinion, assist in the proper determination of the proceedings, and

(c) obtain such professional assistance as is available to him which he thinks appropriate or which the justices' clerk or the court directs him to obtain.

(10) In addition to his duties under other paragraphs of this rule, the guardian ad litem shall provide to the justices' clerk and the court such other assistance as may be required.

(11) A party may question the guardian ad litem about oral or written advice tendered by him to the justices' clerk or the court under this rule.

Solicitor for child

12–(1) A solicitor appointed under section 41(3) or in accordance with rule 11(2)(a) shall represent the child–

(a) in accordance with instructions received from the guardian ad litem (unless the solicitor considers, having taken into account the views of the guardian ad litem and any direction of the court under rule 11(3), that the child wishes to give instructions which conflict with those of the guardian ad litem and that he is able, having regard to his understanding, to give such instructions on his own behalf in which case he shall conduct the proceedings in accordance with instructions received from the child), or

(b) where no guardian ad litem has been appointed for the child and the condition in section 41(4)(b) is satisfied, in accordance with instructions received from the child, or

(c) in default of instructions under (a) or (b), in furtherance of the best interests of the child.

(2) A solicitor appointed under section 41(3) or in accordance with rule 11(2)(a) shall serve and accept service of documents on behalf of the child in accordance with rule 8(3)(a) and (4)(a) and, where the child has not himself been served and has sufficient understanding, advise the child of the contents of any document so served.

(3) Where the child wishes an appointment of a solicitor under section 41(3) or in accordance with rule 11(2)(a) to be terminated, he may apply to the court for an order terminating the appointment; and the solicitor and the

guardian ad litem shall be given an opportunity to make representations.

(4) Where the guardian ad litem wishes an appointment of a solicitor under section 41(3) to be terminated, he may apply to the court for an order terminating the appointment; and the solicitor and, if he is of sufficient understanding, the child, shall be given an opportunity to make representations.

(5) When terminating an appointment in accordance with paragraph (3) or (4), the court shall give reasons for so doing, a note of which shall be taken by the justices' clerk.

(6) Where the justices' clerk or the court appoints a solicitor under section 41(3) or refuses to make such an appointment, the justices' clerk shall record the appointment or refusal in the appropriate form in Schedule 1 to these Rules and serve a copy on the parties and, where he is appointed, on the solicitor.

Welfare officer

13–(1) Where the court or a justices' clerk has directed that a written report be made by a welfare officer, the report shall be filed at or by such time as the court or justices' clerk directs or, in the absence of such a direction, at least 14 days before a relevant hearing; and the justices' clerk shall, as soon as practicable, serve a copy of the report on the parties and any guardian ad litem.

(2) In paragraph (1), a hearing is relevant if the justices' clerk has given the welfare officer notice that his report is to be considered at it.

(3) After the filing of a written report by a welfare officer, the court or the justices' clerk may direct that the welfare officer attend any hearing at which the report is to be considered; and

(a) except where such a direction is given at a hearing attended by the welfare officer, the justices' clerk shall inform the welfare officer of the direction; and

(b) at the hearing at which the report is considered any party may question the welfare officer about his report.

(4) This rule is without prejudice to the court's power to give directions under rule 14.

Directions

14–(1) In this rule, 'party' includes the guardian ad litem and, where a request or direction concerns a report under section 7, the welfare officer.

(2) In any relevant proceedings the justices' clerk or the court may, subject to paragraph (5), give, vary or revoke directions for the conduct of the proceedings, including–

(a) the timetable for the proceedings;

(b) varying the time within which or by which an act is required, by these Rules, to be done;

(c) the attendance of the child;

(d) the appointment of a guardian ad litem whether under section 41 or otherwise, or of a solicitor under section 41(3);

(e) the service of documents;

(f) the submission of evidence including experts' reports;

(g) the preparation of welfare reports under section 7;

(h) the transfer of the proceedings to another court in accordance with any Order made by the Lord Chancellor under Part I of Schedule 11;

(i) consolidation with other proceedings;

and the justices' clerk shall, on receipt of an application, or where proceedings have been transferred to his court, consider whether such directions need to be given.

(3) Where the justices' clerk or a single justice who is holding a directions appointment considers, for whatever reason, that it is inappropriate to give a direction on a particular matter, he shall refer the matter to the court which may give any appropriate direction.

(4) Where a direction is given under paragraph (2)(h), an order shall be issued in the appropriate form in Schedule 1 to these Rules and the justices' clerk shall follow the procedure set out in rule 6(2).

(5) Directions under paragraph (2) may be given, varied or revoked either—

(a) of the justices' clerk or the court's own motion having given the parties notice of the intention to do so and an opportunity to attend and be heard or to make written representations,

(b) on the written request in Form C2 of a party specifying the direction which is sought, filed and served on the other parties, or

(c) on the written request in Form C2 of a party specifying the direction which is sought, to which the other parties consent and which they or their representatives have signed.

(6) In an urgent case, the request under paragraph (5)(b) may, with the leave of the justices' clerk or the court, be made—

(a) orally,

(b) without notice to the parties, or

(c) both as in sub-paragraph (a) and as in sub-paragraph (b).

(7) On receipt of a request under paragraph (5)(b) the justices' clerk shall fix a date for the hearing of the request and give not less than 2 days' notice in Form C6 to the parties of the date so fixed.

(8) On considering a request under paragraph (5)(c) the justices' clerk or the court shall either—

(a) grant the request, whereupon the justices' clerk shall inform the parties of the decision, or

(b) direct that a date be fixed for the hearing of the request, whereupon the justices' clerk shall fix such a date and give not less than 2 days' notice to the parties of the date so fixed.

(9) Subject to rule 28, a party may request, in accordance with paragraph 5(b) or (c), that an order be made under section 11(3) or, if he is entitled to

apply for such an order, under section 38(1), and paragraphs (6), (7) and (8) shall apply accordingly.

(10) Where, in any relevant proceedings, the court has power to make an order of its own motion, the power to give directions under paragraph *(2)* shall apply.

(11) Directions of the justices' clerk or a court which are still in force immediately prior to the transfer of relevant proceedings to another court shall continue to apply following the transfer, subject to any changes of terminology which are required to apply those directions to the court to which the proceedings are transferred, unless varied or discharged by directions under paragraph (2).

(12) The justices' clerk or the court shall record the giving, variation or revocation of a direction under this rule in the appropriate form in Schedule 1 to these Rules and serve, as soon as practicable, a copy of the form on any party who was not present at the giving, variation or revocation.

Timing of proceedings

15–(1) Any period of time fixed by these Rules, or by any order or direction, for doing any act shall be reckoned in accordance with this rule.

(2) Where the period, being a period of 7 days or less, would include a day which is not a business day, that day shall be excluded.

(3) Where the time fixed for filing a document with the justices' clerk expires on a day on which the justices' clerk's office is closed, and for that reason the document cannot be filed on that day, the document shall be filed in time if it is filed on the next day on which the justices' clerk's office is open.

(4) Where these Rules provide a period of time within which or by which a certain act is to be performed in the course of relevant proceedings, that period may not be extended otherwise than by a direction of the justices' clerk or the court under rule 14.

(5) At the—

(a) transfer to a court of relevant proceedings,

(b) postponement or adjournment of any hearing or directions appointment in the course of relevant proceedings, or

(c) conclusion of any such hearing or directions appointment other than one at which the proceedings are determined, or so soon thereafter as is practicable,

the justices' clerk or the court shall—

(i) fix a date upon which the proceedings shall come before the justices' clerk or the court again for such purposes as the justices' clerk or the court directs, which date shall, where paragraph (a) applies, be as soon as possible after the transfer, and

(ii) give notice to the parties and to the guardian ad litem or the welfare officer of the date so fixed.

Attendance at directions appointment and hearing

16–(1) Subject to paragraph (2), a party shall attend a directions appointment of which he has been given notice in accordance with rule 14(5) unless the justices' clerk or the court otherwise directs.

(2) Relevant proceedings shall take place in the absence of any party including the child if–

(a) the court considers it in the interests of the child, having regard to the matters to be discussed or the evidence likely to be given, and

(b) the party is represented by a guardian ad litem or solicitor;

and when considering the interests of the child under sub-paragraph (a) the court shall give the guardian ad litem, solicitor for the child and, if he is of sufficient understanding, the child, an opportunity to make representations.

(3) Subject to paragraph (4) below, where at the time and place appointed for a hearing or directions appointment the applicant appears but one or more of the respondents do not, the justices' clerk or the court may proceed with the hearing or appointment.

(4) The court shall not begin to hear an application in the absence of a respondent unless–

(a) it is proved to the satisfaction of the court that he received reasonable notice of the date of the hearing; or

(b) the court is satisfied that the circumstances of the case justify proceeding with the hearing.

(5) Where, at the time and place appointed for a hearing or directions appointment, one or more respondents appear but the applicant does not, the court may refuse the application or, if sufficient evidence has previously been received, proceed in the absence of the applicant.

(6) Where at the time and place appointed for a hearing or directions appointment neither the applicant nor any respondent appears, the court may refuse the application.

(7) If the court considers it expedient in the interests of the child, it shall hear any relevant proceedings in private when only the officers of the court, the parties, their legal representatives and such other persons as specified by the court may attend.

Documentary evidence

17–(1) Subject to paragraphs (4) and (5), in any relevant proceedings a party shall file and serve on the parties, any welfare officer and any guardian ad litem of whose appointment he has been given notice under rule 10(5)–

(a) written statements of the substance of the oral evidence which the party intends to adduce at a hearing of, or a directions appointment in, those proceedings, which shall–

(i) be dated,

(ii) be signed by the person making the statement,

(iii) contain a declaration that the maker of the statement believes it to be true and understands that it may be placed before the court, and

(iv) show in the top right hand corner of the first page–
  (a) the initials and surname of the person making the statement,
  (b) the number of the statement in relation to the maker,
  (c) the date on which the statement was made, and
  (d) the party on whose behalf it is filed; and
(b) copies of any documents, including, subject to rule 18(3), experts
  reports, upon which the party intends to rely, at a hearing of, or a directions appointment in, those proceedings,
at or by such time as the justices' clerk or the court directs or, in the absence
of a direction, before the hearing or appointment.

(2) A party may, subject to any direction of the justices' clerk or the court
about the timing of statements under this rule, file and serve on the parties
a statement which is supplementary to a statement served under paragraph (1).

(3) At a hearing or directions appointment a party may not, without the
leave of the justices' clerk, in the case of a directions appointment, or the
court–
(a) adduce evidence, or
(b) seek to rely on a document,
in respect of which he has failed to comply with the requirements of paragraph (1).

(4) In proceedings for a section 8 order a party shall–
(a) neither file nor serve any document other than as required or authorised
  by these Rules, and
(b) in completing a form prescribed by these Rules, neither give information,
  nor make a statement, which is not required or authorised by that form,
without the leave of the justices' clerk or the court.

(5) In proceedings for a section 8 order, no statement or copy may be filed
under paragraph (1) until such time as the justices' clerk or the court directs.

Expert evidence – examination of child

18–(1) No person may, without the leave of the justices' clerk or the court,
cause the child to be medically or psychiatrically examined, or otherwise
assessed for the purpose of the preparation of expert evidence for use in the
proceedings.

(2) An application for leave under paragraph (1) shall, unless the justices'
clerk or the court otherwise directs, be served on all the parties to the proceedings and on the guardian ad litem.

(3) Where the leave of the justices' clerk or the court has not been given
under paragraph (1), no evidence arising out of an examination or assessment to which that paragraph applies may be adduced without the leave of
the court.

Amendment

19–(1) Subject to rule 17(2), a document which has been filed or served in
any relevant proceedings may not be amended without the leave of the

justices' clerk or the court which shall, unless the justices' clerk or the court otherwise directs, be requested in writing.

(2) On considering a request for leave to amend a document the justices' clerk or the court shall either–

(a) grant the request, whereupon the justices' clerk shall inform the person making the request of that decision, or

(b) invite the parties or any of them to make representations, within a specified period, as to whether such an order should be made.

(3) A person amending a document shall file it with the justices' clerk and serve it on those persons on whom it was served prior to amendment; and the amendments shall be identified.

Oral evidence

20 The justices' clerk or the court shall keep a note of the substance of the oral evidence given at a hearing of, or directions appointment in, relevant proceedings.

Hearing

21–(1) Before the hearing, the justice or justices who will be dealing with the case shall read any documents which have been filed under rule 17 in respect of the hearing.

(2) The justices' clerk at a directions appointment, or the court at a hearing or directions appointment, may give directions as to the order of speeches and evidence.

(3) Subject to directions under paragraph (2), at a hearing of, or directions appointment in, relevant proceedings, the parties and the guardian ad litem shall adduce their evidence in the following order–

(a) the applicant,

(b) any party with parental responsibility for the child,

(c) other respondents,

(d) the guardian ad litem,

(e) the child if he is a party to the proceedings and there is no guardian ad litem.

(4) After the final hearing of relevant proceedings, the court shall make its decision as soon as is practicable.

(5) Before the court makes an order or refuses an application or request, the justices' clerk shall record in writing–

(a) the names of the justice or justices constituting the court by which the decision is made, and

(b) in consultation with the justice or justices, the reasons for the court's decision and any findings of fact.

(6) When making an order or when refusing an application, the court, or one of the justices constituting the court by which the decision is made, shall–

(a) where it makes a finding of fact state such finding and complete Form C22; and

(b) state the reasons for the court's decision.

(7) After the court announces its decision, the justices' clerk shall as soon as practicable–

(a) make a record of any order made in the appropriate form in Schedule 1 to these Rules or, where there is no such form, in writing; and

(b) subject to paragraph (8), serve a copy of any order made on the parties to the proceedings and on any person with whom the child is living.

(8) Within 48 hours after the making of an order under section 48(4) or the making, ex parte, of–

(a) a section 8 order or

(b) an order under section 44, 48(9), 50, or 75(1),

the applicant shall serve a copy of the order in the appropriate form in Schedule 1 to these Rules on–

(i) each party,

(ii) any person who has actual care of the child, or who had such care immediately prior to the making of the order, and

(iii) in the case of an order referred to in sub-paragraph (b), the local authority in whose area the child lives or is found.

Extracts from the Family Proceedings Courts (Matrimonial Proceedings etc) Rules 1991 SI No 1991

The following rules are reproduced in this section.

PART II – MATRIMONIAL PROCEEDINGS UNDER THE DOMESTIC
PROCEEDINGS AND MAGISTRATES' COURTS ACT 1978 AND PROCEEDINGS
UNDER PART IV OF THE FAMILY LAW ACT 1996

Interpretation, application and savings

2–(1) In this Part of these Rules, unless a contrary intention appears–
any reference to a rule shall be construed as a reference to a rule contained in
these Rules; and any reference in a rule to a paragraph shall be construed as a
reference to a paragraph of that rule,
'application' means an application for an order made under or by virtue of
the Act or, as the case may be, the Family Law Act 1996 and 'applicant' shall
be construed accordingly,
'business day' means any day other than–
(a) a Saturday, Sunday, Christmas Day or Good Friday; or
(b) a bank holiday, that is to say, a day which is, or is to be observed as, a
    bank holiday or a holiday under the Banking and Financial Dealings Act
    1971, in England and Wales,
court' means a family proceedings court constituted in accordance with
sections 66 and 67 of the Magistrates' Courts Act 1980 or, in respect of those
proceedings prescribed in rule 25, a single justice who is a member of a
family panel,
'directions appointment' means a hearing for directions under rule 6(1),
'file' means deposit with the justices' clerk,
'form' means a form in Schedule I to these Rules and, where a form is
referred to by number, means the form so numbered in that Schedule, with
such variation as the circumstances of the particular case may require,
'note' includes a record made by mechanical means,
respondent' includes, as the case may be, more than one respondent,
'the Act' means the Domestic Proceedings and Magistrates' Courts Act 1978.

(2) Expressions used in this Part of these Rules have the meaning which
they bear in the Act or, as the case may be, the Family Law Act 1996.

(3) This Part of these Rules shall not apply in relation to any such application or order as is referred to in paragraph 1 or 2 of Schedule 1 to the
Domestic Proceedings and Magistrates' Courts Act 1978 (transitional provisions); and, accordingly, the Magistrates' Courts (Matrimonial Proceedings)
Rules 1960 shall continue to apply in relation to any such application or
order but with the following modification, that is to say, on any complaint
made by virtue of paragraph 2(d) of the said Schedule 1 for the variation or
revocation of a provision requiring access to a child to be given to a grandparent, rule 7 of the said Rules of 1960 shall be construed as applying to the
complaint as it applies to a complaint made by virtue of section 8 of the
Matrimonial Proceedings (Magistrates' Courts) Act 1960 and as if paragraph (5) of that rule included a reference to that grandparent.

(4) Subject to rule 1(2), the provisions of the Magistrates' Courts Rules
1981 shall have effect subject to this Part of these Rules.

Applications

3–(1) Subject to paragraph (3) and Rule 3A, an applicant shall–

(a) file the application in the appropriate form in Schedule 1 to these Rules or, where there is no such form, in writing, together with sufficient copies for one to be served on the respondent, and

(b) serve a copy of the application, endorsed in accordance with paragraph (2)(b), together with any notice attached under paragraph (2)(c), on the respondent at least 21 days prior to the date fixed under paragraph (2)(a).

(2) On receipt of the documents filed under paragraph (1)(a), the justices' clerk shall–

(a) fix the date, time and place for a hearing or a directions appointment, allowing sufficient time for the applicant to comply with paragraph (1)(b),

(b) endorse the date, time and place so fixed upon the copies of the application filed by the applicant,

(c) [*Repealed.*]

(d) return the copies to the applicant forthwith.

(3) A court may proceed on an application made orally where it is made by virtue of section 6(4) of the Act and where an application is so made paragraph (1) shall not apply.

(4) [*Repealed.*]

Applications under Part IV of the Family Law Act 1996

3A–(1) An application for an occupation order or a non-molestation order under Part IV of the Family Law Act 1996 (Family Homes and Domestic Violence) shall be made in Form FL401.

(2) An application for an occupation order or a non-molestation order which is made in other proceedings which are pending shall be made in Form FL401.

(3) An application in Form FL401 shall be supported–

(a) by a statement which is signed and is declared to be true; or

(b) with the leave of the court, by oral evidence.

(4) An application in Form FL401 may, with the leave of the justices' clerk or of the court, be made ex parte, in which case–

(a) the applicant shall file with the justices' clerk or the court the application at the time when the application is made or as directed by the justices' clerk; and

(b) the evidence in support of the application shall state the reasons why the application is made ex parte.

(5) An application made on notice (together with any statement supporting it and a notice in Form FL402) shall be served by the applicant on the respondent personally not less than 2 business days prior to the date on which the application will be heard.

(6) The court or the justices' clerk may abridge the period specified in paragraph (5).

(7) Where the applicant is acting in person, service of the application may, with the leave of thejustices' clerk, be effected in accordance with rule 4.

(8) Where an application for an occupation order or a non-molestation order is pending, the court shall consider (on the application of either party or of its own motion) whether to exercise its powers to transfer the hearing of that application to another court and the justices' clerk or the court shall make an order for transfer in Form FL417 if it seems necessary or expedient to do so.

(9) Where an order for transfer is made, the justices' clerk shall send a copy of the order–

(a) to the parties, and

(b) to the family proceedings court or to the county court to which the proceedings are to be transferred.

(10) A copy of an application for an occupation order under section 33, 35 or 36 of the Family Law Act 1996 shall be served by the applicant by first-class post on the mortgagee or, as the case may be, the landlord of the dwelling-house in question, with a notice in Form FL416 informing him of his right to make representations in writing or at any hearing.

(11) The applicant shall file a statement in Form FL415 after he has served the application.

(12) Rule 33A of the Family Proceedings Courts (Children Act 1989) Rules 1991 (disclosure of addresses) shall apply for the purpose of preventing the disclosure of addresses where an application is made in Form FL401 as it applies for that purpose in proceedings under the Children Act 1989.

Service

4–(1) Where service of a document is required by these Rules it may be effected, unless the contrary is indicated–

(a) if the person to be served is not known by the person serving to be acting by solicitor

   (i) by delivering it to him personally, or

   (ii) by delivering at, or by sending it by first-class post to, his residence or his last known residence, or

(b) if the person to be served is known by the person serving to be acting by solicitor

   (i) by delivering the document at, or sending it by first-class post to, the solicitor's address for service,

   (ii) where the solicitor's address for service includes a numbered box at a document exchange, by leaving the document at that document exchange or at a document exchange which transmits documents on every business day to that document exchange, or

   (iii) by sending a legible copy of the document by facsimile transmission to the solicitor's office.

(2) In this rule, 'first-class post' means first-class post which has been pre-paid or in respect of which pre-payment is not required.

(3) A document shall, unless the contrary is proved, be deemed to have been served–

(a) in the case of service by first-class post, on the second business day after posting, and

(b) in the case of service in accordance with paragraph (1)(b)(ii), on the second business day after the day on which it is left at the document exchange.

(4) At or before the first directions appointment in, or hearing of, the proceedings, whichever occurs first, the applicant shall file a statement that service of a copy of the application has been effected on the respondent and the statement shall indicate–

(a) the manner, date, time and place of service, or

(b) where service was effected by post, the date, time and place of posting.

(5) In any proceedings, the justices' clerk or the court may direct that a requirement in this Part of these Rules to serve a document shall not apply or shall be effected in such manner as the justices' clerk or the court directs.

Answer to application

5 Within 14 days of service of an application for an order under section 2, 6, 7 or 20 of the Act, the respondent shall file and serve on the parties an answer to the application in the appropriate form in Schedule 1 to these Rules.

Directions

6–(1) In any proceedings under the Act, the justices' clerk or the court may, subject to paragraph (3), give, vary or revoke directions for the conduct of the proceedings, including–

(a) the timetable for the proceedings;

(b) varying the time within which or by which an act is required, by this Part of these Rules, to be done;

(c) the service of documents; and

(d) the submission of evidence;

and the justices' clerk shall, on receipt of an application, consider whether such directions need to be given.

(2) Where the justices' clerk or a single justice who is holding a directions appointment considers, for whatever reason, that it is inappropriate to give a direction on a particular matter, he shall refer the matter to the court which may give any appropriate direction.

(3) Directions under paragraph (1) may be given, varied or revoked either–

(a) of the justices' clerk's or the court's own motion having given the parties notice of the intention to do so and an opportunity to attend and be heard or to make written representations,

(b) on the written request of a party specifying the direction which is sought, which request has been filed and served on the other parties, or

(c) on the written request of a party specifying the direction which is sought, to which the other parties consent and which they or their representatives have signed.

(4) In an urgent case, the request under paragraph (3)(b) may, with the leave of the justices' clerk or the court, be made–

(a) orally,

(b) without notice to the other parties, or

(c) both as in sub-paragraph (a) and as in sub-paragraph (b).

(5) On receipt of a request under paragraph (3)(b) the justices' clerk shall fix a date for the hearing of the request and give not less than 2 days' notice to the parties of the date so fixed.

(6) On considering a request under paragraph (3)(c) the justices' clerk or the court shall either–

(a) grant the request, whereupon the justices' clerk shall inform the parties of the decision, or

(b) direct that a date be fixed for the hearing of the request, whereupon the justices' clerk shall fix such a date and give not less than 2 days' notice to the parties of the date so fixed.

(7) The justices' clerk or the court shall take a note of the giving, variation or revocation of a direction under this rule and serve, as soon as practicable, a copy of the note on any party who was not present at the giving, variation or revocation.

Timing of proceedings

7–(1) Any period of time fixed by this Part of these Rules, or by any order or direction, for the doing of any act shall be reckoned in accordance with this rule.

(2) Where the period, being a period of 7 days or less, would include a day which is not a business day, that day shall be excluded.

(3) Where the time fixed for filing a document with the justices' clerk expires on a day on which the justices' clerk's office is closed, and for that reason the document cannot be filed on that day, the document shall be filed in time if it is filed on the next day on which the justices' clerk's office is open.

(4) Where. these Rules provide a period of time within which or by which a certain act is to be performed in the course of proceedings under the Act, that period may not be extended otherwise than by a direction of the justices' clerk or the court under rule 6(1).

(5) At the–

(a) postponement or adjournment of any hearing or directions appointment in the course of proceedings under the Act, or

(b) conclusion of any such hearing or directions appointment other than one at which the proceedings are determined, or as soon thereafter as is practicable,

the justices' clerk or the court shall–

(i) fix a date upon which the proceedings shall come before the justices' clerk or the court again for such purposes as the justices' clerk or the court directs, and

(ii) give notice to the parties of the date so fixed.

Attendance at directions appointment and hearing

8–(1) Subject to paragraph (2), a party shall attend a directions appointment of which he has been given notice in accordance with rule 6(3) unless the justices' clerk or the court otherwise directs.

(2) Subject to rules 18(2) and 22(2), the court shall not begin to hear an application in the absence of the respondent unless—

(a) it is proved to the satisfaction of the court that he received reasonable notice of the date of the hearing; or

(b) the court is satisfied that the circumstances of the case justify proceeding with the hearing.

(3) Where, at the time and place appointed for a hearing, the respondent appears but the applicant does not, the court may refuse the application or, if sufficient evidence has previously been received, proceed in the absence of the applicant.

(4) Where at the time and place appointed for a hearing neither the applicant nor the respondent appears, the court may refuse the application.

Documentary evidence

9–(1) In any proceedings the parties shall file and serve on the other parties—

(a) written statements of the substance of the oral evidence which the party intends to adduce at a hearing of, or a directions appointment in, those proceedings, which shall—

(i) be dated,

(ii) be signed by the person making the statement, and

(iii) contain a declaration that the maker of the statement believes it to be true and understands that it may be placed before the court, and

(b) copies of any documents upon which the party intends to rely at a hearing of, or a directions appointment in, those proceedings,

at or by such time as the justices' clerk or the court directs or, in the absence of a direction, before the hearing or appointment.

(2) A party may, subject to any direction of the justices' clerk or the court about the timing of statements under this rule, file and serve on the parties a statement which is supplementary to a statement served under paragraph (1).

(3) At a hearing or directions appointment a party may not, without the leave of the justices' clerk in the case of a directions appointment, or the court—

(a) adduce evidence, or

(b) seek to rely on a document,

in respect of which he has failed to comply with the requirements of paragraph (1).

Amendment

10–(1) Subject to rule 9(2), a copy of a document which has been filed or served in any proceedings may not be amended without the leave of the justices' clerk or the court which shall, unless the justices' clerk or the court otherwise directs, be requested in writing.

(2) On considering a request for leave to amend a document the justices' clerk or the court shall either–

(a) grant the request, whereupon the justices' clerk shall inform the person making the request of that decision, or

(b) invite the parties or any of them to make representations, within a specified period, as to whether such an order should be made.

(3) A person amending a document shall file it with the justices' clerk and serve it on those persons on whom it was served prior to amendment; and the amendments shall be identified.

Oral evidence

11 The justices' clerk or the court shall keep a note of the substance of the oral evidence given at a hearing of, or directions appointment in, proceedings under the Act.

Hearing

12–(1) Before the hearing, the justice or justices who will be dealing with the case shall read any documents which have been filed under rule 9 in respect of the hearing.

(2) The justices' clerk at a directions appointment or the court at a hearing or directions appointment, may give directions as to the order of speeches and evidence.

(3) Subject to directions under paragraph (2), at a hearing of, or directions appointment in, proceedings, the parties shall adduce their evidence in the following order–

(a) the applicant,

(b) the respondent other than the child, and

(c) the child if he is a respondent.

(4) After the final hearing of proceedings, the court shall make its decision as soon as is practicable.

(5) Before the court makes an order or refuses an application, the justices' clerk shall record in writing–

(a) the names of the justice or justices constituting the court by which the decision is made, and

(b) in consultation with the justice or justices, the reasons for the court's decision and any findings of fact.

(6) When making an order or when refusing an application, the court, or

one of the justices constituting the court by which the decision is made, shall state any findings of fact and the reasons for the court's decision.

(7) After the court announces its decision, the justices' clerk shall as soon as practicable–
(a) make a record of any order made in the appropriate form in Schedule 1 to these Rules, or, where there is no such form, in writing; and
(b) serve, in accordance with these Rules, a copy of any order made on the parties to the proceedings.

(8) The justices' clerk shall supply a copy of the record of the reasons for a decision made in pursuance of paragraph (5)(b) to any person on request, if satisfied that it is required in connection with an appeal or possible appeal.

Hearing of applications under Part IV of the Family Law Act 1996

12A–(1) This rule applies to the hearing of applications under Part IV of the Family Law Act 1996 and the following forms shall be used in connection with such hearings:
(a) a record of the hearing shall be made on Form FL405, and
(b) any order made on the hearing shall be issued in Form FL404.

(2) Where an order is made on an application made ex parte, a copy of the order together with a copy of the application and of any statement supporting it shall be served by the applicant on the respondent personally.

(3) Where the applicant is acting in person, service of a copy of an order made on an application made ex parte shall be effected by the justices' clerk if the applicant so requests.

(4) Where the application is for an occupation order under section 33, 35 or 36 of the Family Law Act 1996, a copy of any order made on the application shall be served by the applicant by first-class post on the mortgagee or, as the case may be, the landlord of the dwelling-house in question.

(5) A copy of an order made on an application heard inter parties shall be served by the applicant on the respondent personally.

(6) Where the applicant is acting in person, service of a copy of the order made on an application heard inter partes may, with the leave of the justices' clerk, be effected in accordance with rule 4.

(7) The court may direct that a further hearing be held in order to consider any representations made by a mortgage or a landlord.

Applications to vary etc orders made under Part IV of the Family Law Act 1996

12B An application to vary, extend or discharge an order made under Part IV of the Family Law Act 1996 shall be made in Form FL403 and rules 12 and 12A shall apply to the hearing of such an application.

Costs

13–(1) In any proceedings the court may, at any time during the proceedings, make an order that a party pay the whole or any part of the costs of any other party.

(2) A party against whom the court is considering making a costs order shall have an opportunity to make representations as to why the order should not be made.

Confidentiality of documents

14 No document, other than a record of an order, held by the court and relating to proceedings shall be disclosed other than to—
(a) a party,
(b) the legal representative of a party, or
(c) the Legal Aid Board,
without leave of the justices' clerk or the court.

Delegation by justices' clerk

15—(1) In this rule, 'employed as a clerk in court' has the same meaning as in rule 2(1) of the Justices' Clerks (Qualifications of Assistants) Rules 1979.

(2) Anything authorised to be done by, to or before a justices' clerk under this Part of these Rules, or under paragraph 15 or 15D of the Schedule to the Justices' Clerks Rules 1970 as amended by Schedule 2 to these Rules, may be done instead by, to or before a person employed as a clerk in court where that person is appointed by the Magistrates' Courts Committee to assist him and where that person has been specifically authorised by the justices' clerk for that purpose.

(3) Any authorisation by the justices' clerk under paragraph (2) shall be recorded in writing at the time the authority is given or as soon as practicable thereafter.

Application of enactments governing procedure in proceedings brought on complaint

16—(1) Section 53(3) of the Magistrates' Courts Act 1980 (orders with the consent of the defendant without hearing evidence) shall apply to applications under section 20 of the Act for the variation of orders for periodical payments, as it applies to complaints for the variation of the rate of any periodical payments ordered by a magistrates' court to be made.

(2) Section 97 of the Magistrates' Courts Act 1980 (issue of a witness summons) shall apply to proceedings as it applies to a hearing of a complaint under that section.

Enforcement of orders made on application under Part IV of the Family Law Act 1996

20—(1) Where a power of arrest is attached to one or more of the provisions ('the relevant provisions') of an order made under Part IV of the Family Law Act 1996—

(a) the relevant provisions shall be set out in Form FL406 and the form shall not include any provisions of the order to which the power of arrest was not attached; and

(b) a copy of the form shall be delivered to the officer for the time being in charge of any police station for the applicant's address or of such other police station as the court may specify.

The copy of the form delivered under sub-paragraph (b) shall be accompanied by a statement showing that the respondent has been served with the order or informed of its terms (whether by being present when the order was made or by telephone or otherwise).

(2) Where an order is made varying or discharging the relevant provisions, the justices' clerk shall—

(a) immediately inform the officer who received a copy of the form under paragraph (1) and, if the applicant's address has changed, the officer for the time being in charge of the police station for the new address; and

(b) deliver a copy of the order to any officer so informed.

(3) An application for the issue of a warrant for the arrest of the respondent shall be made in Form FL407 and the warrant shall be issued in Form FL408 and delivered by the justices' clerk to the officer for the time being in charge of any police station for the respondent's address or of such other police station as the court may specify.

(4) The court before whom a person is brought following his arrest may—

(a) determine whether the facts, and the circumstances which led to the arrest, amounted to disobedience of the order, or

(b) adjourn the proceedings and, where such an order is made, the arrested person may be released and

  (i) be dealt with within 14 days of the day on which he was arrested; and

  (ii) be given not less than 2 business days' notice of the adjourned hearing.

Nothing in this paragraph shall prevent the issue of a notice under paragraph (8) if the arrested person is not dealt with within the period mentioned in subparagraph (b)(i) above.

(5) Paragraphs (6) to (13) shall apply for the enforcement of orders made on applications under Part IV of the Family Law Act 1996 by committal order.

(6) Subject to paragraphs (11) and (12), an order shall not be enforced by committal order unless—

(a) a copy of the order in Form FL404 has been served personally on the respondent; and

(b) where the order requires the respondent to do an act, the copy has been so served before the expiration of the time within which he was required to do the act and was accompanied by a copy of any order, made between the date of the order and the date of service, fixing that time.

(7) At the time when the order is drawn up, the justices' clerk shall—

(a) where the order made is (or includes) a non-molestation order, and

(b) where the order made is an occupation order and the court so directs,
   issue a copy of the order, indorsed with or incorporating a notice as to
   the consequences of disobedience, for service in accordance with paragraph (6).

(8) If the respondent fails to obey the order, the justices' clerk shall, at the
request of the applicant, issue a notice in Form FL418 warning the respondent that an application will be made for him to be committed and, subject to
paragraph (12), the notice shall be served on him personally.

(9) The request for issue of the notice under paragraph (8) shall be treated
as a complaint and shall—

(a) identify the provisions of the order or undertaking which it is alleged
   have been disobeyed or broken;

(b) list the ways in which it is alleged that the order or undertaking has been
   disobeyed or broken;

(c) be supported by a statement which is signed and is declared to be true
   and which states the grounds on which the application is made,

and, unless service is dispensed with under paragraph (12), a copy of the
statement shall be served with the notice.

(10) If an order in Form FL419 (a committal order) is made, it shall
include provision for the issue of a warrant of committal in Form FL420 and,
unless the court otherwise orders—

(a) a copy of the order shall be served personally on the person to be
   committed either before or at the time of the execution of the warrant; or

(b) the order for the issue of the warrant may be served on the person to be
   committed at any time within 36 hours after the execution of the
   warrant.

(11) An order requiring a person to abstain from doing an act may be
enforced by committal order notwithstanding that a copy of the order has
not been served personally if the court is satisfied that, pending such service,
the respondent had notice thereof either—

(a) by being present when the order was made;

(b) by being notified of the terms of the order whether by telephone or
   otherwise.

(12) The court may dispense with service of a copy of the order under
paragraph (6) or a notice under paragraph (8) if the court thinks it just to do
so.

(13) Where service of a notice to show cause is dispensed with under
paragraph (12) and a committal order is made, the court may of its own
motion fix a date and time when the person to be committed is to be brought
before the court.

(14) Paragraphs (6) to (10), (12) and (13) shall apply to the enforcement of
undertakings with the necessary modifications and as if—

(a) for paragraph (6) there were substituted the following—

   '(6) A copy of Form FL422 recording the undertaking shall be delivered
   by the justices' clerk to the party giving the undertaking

(a) by handing a copy of the document to him before he leaves the court building; or
(b) where his place of residence is known, by posting a copy to him at his place of residence; or
(c) through his solicitor,
and, where delivery cannot be effected in this way, the justices' clerk shall deliver a copy of the document to the party for whose benefit the undertaking is given and that party shall cause it to be served personally as soon as is practicable.';
(b) in paragraph (12), the words from 'a copy' to 'paragraph (6) or' were omitted.

(15) Where a person in custody under a warrant or order, desires to apply to the court for his discharge, he shall make his application in writing attested by the governor of the prison showing that he has purged or is desirous of purging his contempt and the justices' clerk shall, not less than one day before the application is heard, serve notice of it on the party (if any) at whose instance the warrant or order was issued.

(16) The Court by whom an order of committal is made may by order direct that the execution of the order of committal shall be suspended for such period or on such terms or conditions as it may specify.

(17) Where execution of an order of committal is suspended by an order under paragraph (16), the applicant for the order of committal must, unless the court otherwise directs, serve on the person against whom it was made a notice informing him of the making and terms of the order under that paragraph.

(18) The court may adjourn consideration of the penalty to be imposed for contempts found proved and such consideration may be restored if the respondent does not comply with any conditions specified by the court.

(19) Where the court makes a hospital order in Form FL413 or a guardianship order in Form FL414 under the Mental Health Act 1983, the justices' clerk shall—
(a) send to the hospital any information which will be of assistance in dealing with the patient;
(b) inform the applicant when the respondent is being transferred to hospital.

(20) Where a transfer direction given by the Secretary of State under section 48 of the Mental Health Act 1983 is in force in respect of a person remanded in custody by the court, the justices' clerk shall notify—
(a) the governor of the prison to which that person was remanded; and
(b) the hospital where he is detained,
of any committal hearing which that person is required to attend and the justices' clerk shall give notice in writing to the hospital where that person is detained of any further remand.

(21) An order for the remand of the respondent shall be in Form FL409 and an order discharging the respondent from custody shall be in Form FL421.

(22) In paragraph (4) 'arrest' means arrest under a power of arrest attached to an order or under a warrant of arrest.

Applications under Part IV of the Family Law Act 1996: bail

21–(1) An application for bail made by a person arrested under a power of arrest or a warrant of arrest may be made either orally or in writing.

(2) Where an application is made in writing, it shall contain the following particulars–
(a) the full name of the person making the application;
(b) the address of the place where the person making the application is detained at the time when the application is made;
(c) the address where the person making the application would reside if he were to be granted bail;
(d) the amount of the recognizance in which he would agree to be bound; and
(e) the grounds on which the application is made and, where a previous application has been refused, full particulars of any change in circumstances which has occurred since that refusal.

(3) An application made in writing shall be signed by the person making the application or by a person duly authorised by him in that behalf or, where the person making the application is a minor or is for any reason incapable of acting, by a guardian ad litem acting on his behalf and a copy shall be served by the person making the application on the applicant for the Part IV order.

(4) The following forms shall be used:
(a) the recognizance of the person making the application shall be in Form FL410 and that of a surety in Form FL411;
(b) a bail notice in Form FL412 shall be given to the respondent where he is remanded on bail.

Setting aside on failure of service

24 Where an application has been sent to a respondent in accordance with rule 4(1) and, after an order has been made on the application, it appears to the court that the application did not come to the knowledge of the respondent in due time, the court may of its own motion set aside the order and may give such directions as it thinks fit for the rehearing of the application.

Proceedings with respect to which a single justice may discharge the functions of a court

25 The following proceedings are prescribed as proceedings with respect to which a single justice may discharge the functions of a court, that is to say, proceedings–

(a) in which an application is made ex parte for an occupation order or a non-molestation order under Part IV of the Family Law Act 1996;
(b) in accordance with rules 3, 3A(2), (6) and (8), 4, 6 (except paragraph (2)), 7 to 14 and 20(4).

Index